*The Phenomenon of Torture*

PENNSYLVANIA STUDIES IN HUMAN RIGHTS
Bert B. Lockwood, Jr., Series Editor

A complete list of books in the series is available from the publisher.

# The Phenomenon of Torture

## Readings and Commentary

EDITED AND WITH AN INTRODUCTION
BY WILLIAM F. SCHULZ

Foreword by Juan E. Méndez,
President, International Center for Transitional Justice,
Special Advisor to the United Nations Secretary-General
on the Prevention of Genocide

**PENN**

University of Pennsylvania Press

Philadelphia

Published by
University of Pennsylvania Press
Philadelphia, Pennsylvania 19104-4112

Printed in the United States of America on acid-free paper

10  9  8  7  6  5  4  3  2  1

Library of Congress Cataloging-in-Publication Data

The phenomenon of torture : readings and commentary / edited and with an
    introduction by William F. Schulz ; foreword by Juan E. Méndez.
        p.   cm. — (Pennsylvania studies in human rights.)
    Includes bibliographical references.
    ISBN-13: 978-0-8122-1982-1 (alk. paper)
    ISBN-10: 0-8122-1982-1 (alk. paper)
    1. Torture. 2. Human rights I. Schulz, William F.
HV8593.P52   2007
323.4'9—dc22

                                                              2006053093

*To all those who have experienced torture*
*And to all those—especially*
*my revered colleagues at Amnesty International—*
*who have tried to stop it*

# Contents

## CHAPTER III. WHO ARE THE TORTURERS?

x  Contents

CHAPTER VII. HEALING THE VICTIMS, STOPPING THE TORTURE

# Foreword

JUAN E. MÉNDEZ

Of all human rights violations, torture is the most universally condemned and repudiated. The prohibition on torture is so widely shared across cultures and ideologies that there is little room for disagreement about the fact that physical and psychological abuse, when committed in a widespread or systematic manner, constitutes a crime against humanity, akin to genocide and war crimes in that the world community has pledged to prevent its occurrence and prosecute and punish those who perpetrate it.

And yet despite this unanimity of thought around torture, it is practiced routinely and systematically in more than half of the countries that form the United Nations, and individual instances of torture or cruel, inhuman, or degrading treatment can be found in virtually all countries, no matter how decent and democratic their institutions. This seeming inability to abolish torture in practice (and not just in law) is the most important challenge faced by the international human rights movement. It is also an occasion for deep frustration for its members who have otherwise made such impressive gains in the last few decades.

There are varied reasons for the pervasiveness of torture and there is no unanimity as to which is the most important. In many countries, an important factor lies in the weakness of institutions set up to protect the human person from abuse. The lack of accountability of members of armed and security forces also contributes. Poor education of law enforcement agents no doubt plays a role. In almost every case, however, responsibility lies at the top: with public officials and leaders who use torture to gain and retain power and to repress any challenge to their authority.

These conditions that provide a fertile ground for torture are notoriously difficult to remove. It has been only through the demands of a highly organized civil society, moved by the moral superiority of its human rights posture, that important breakthroughs have been achieved in many countries. Unfortunately, after September 11, 2001, the struggle against torture has been made more complicated. In the discourse of a worldwide "war" against terrorism, the temptation to cut corners and achieve quick results has resulted in a "gloves off" attitude that in turn creates a permissive attitude towards torture. It almost goes without saying that a permissive attitude by the most powerful nation on earth should be considered a devastating blow to the struggle to abolish torture.

The permissiveness is well documented: refusal to apply the Geneva Conventions to persons arrested in the "war on terror"; memoranda approved at the highest levels of the Justice and Defense Departments approving certain methods of interrogation and pretending that they don't amount to torture; rewarding the authors of those memos with federal judgeships or nominations to courts. In a way, the perversion of language that redefines torture to be so severe as to result in death or organ failure is a tribute to the moral condemnation that torture elicits. But it is definitely immoral to continue to hold that we do not condone torture after we have redefined it so that what every sensible person knows to be torture is no longer labeled that way.

The problem of redefinition would be less harmful if it were not part of a larger framework of public discourse in which well-known intellectuals have contributed to the permissive atmosphere by urging us to accept the lesser evil of torture for the greater good of defeating terrorism. Among other faulty arguments, we are asked to accept the "ticking bomb scenario" as one in which torture is justified. The criminal law of every country already contemplates mitigating circumstances for the perpetrator of a crime if he or she believes in good faith to be acting to avoid a larger harm. So the argument is unnecessary and worse: it opens up the floodgates to torture under all kinds of false analogies to the ticking bomb scenario. It bears remembering that, before 9/11, this precise argument was made by the military dictators and their sycophants and cheerleaders who wanted to offer lame excuses for barbaric human rights violations. They always started with the "ticking bomb" exception.

More important, the argument of the lesser evil would be relevant if their proponents were willing to test whether in fact torture is effective in fighting crime (any crime, let alone the terrorism unleashed by a committed, fanatical group bent on their own destruction together with that of everything they hate). Every serious law enforcement specialist agrees that torture elicits highly doubtful information, if any at all. And even if some short-term gain could be made, proponents of torture should demonstrate that those gains can actually offset the risks in using torture: the fact that our own soldiers will be subject to it by our enemies, the demoralizing impact on our troops that comes from recognizing that we have now stooped to the levels of the enemy we are fighting, the distrust and fear on the part of communities we are trying to protect. In fact, historical experience shows that the use of torture has undermined the credibility and moral standing of nations, precisely at the time when they need it the most to overcome conflict.

The present state of the public debate about torture should not obscure the fact that humankind has devised several means of dealing effectively with the practice. In recent years there have been many encouraging attempts at making torturers accountable through criminal prosecution and effective punishment. This applies not only to the men (they are almost always men) who inflict terrifying suffering on detainees, but also to those who give the orders, cover the crime up, or surround it with impunity. Of course, prosecution is never simple. Even where there is political will, or domestic unwillingness or inability is overcome through international courts, there will always be evidentiary problems and difficulty in establishing guilt through the chain of command. In fact, the risk of making scapegoats of low-level perpetrators can never be discounted. No one has a right to plead obedience to orders as an excuse when the order is so manifestly illegal. But the prosecutorial effort needs to avoid frustration and discredit by ensuring that those bearing the greatest responsibility do not go unpunished.

Another effective tool against torture is the normative scheme by which all evidence gathered under torture is deprived of legal effect, through a rule that excludes that evidence from being used at trial. This is a key provision of the UN Convention against Torture and therefore a legal obligation of all states that have signed and ratified it. A further development of this notion, that may eventually become an international norm as well, is the legal doctrine of the "fruit of the poisonous tree." It was first developed by U.S. courts, and it excludes from trial not only the evidence directly obtained through torture, but also all evidence obtained in violation of procedural norms designed to prevent mistreatment, and all evidence indirectly obtained through an initial breach of those norms. In this fashion, the interrogator knows that if he violates the prohibition, not only will he be unable to use the proofs thus gathered, but that he actually jeopardizes the case even when there is solid evidence against the defendant. When this doctrine first appeared in American jurisprudence it was met with doomsday predictions about the police's inability to fight crime with their hands tied. In fact, decades afterward, law enforcement bodies have praised it, not only because it has forced them to be more professional in interrogating suspects, but because it has gone a long way in building trust in the police among the community.

Unfortunately, there is always the risk of erosion of this doctrine, by its slow adoption in some countries, by the practice of reversing the burden of proof so that it will be triggered only if the application of torture is proven beyond a reasonable doubt, and simply by refusing to investigate torture charges seriously. In some countries, nominal adoption of the Convention's prohibition is erased by the judicial practice of admitting confessions into evidence, even if properly recanted, as indicia to be used in conjunction with other evidence.

There is also great potential for the prevention of torture in the Optional Protocol to the UN Convention that has recently entered into force, after the twentieth ratification. This protocol institutes a system of domestic and international visits to detention centers, to be organized periodically but also as surprise visits, so that prison authorities know that they can incur criminal liability if they allow their inmates to be mistreated. In addition, there are many good practices of human rights education directed to military and law enforcement personnel, and some even to judges, prosecutors, and court officials that result in better training and greater awareness of the need to maintain high standards and retain the moral high ground in the fight against crime. Needless to say, not all of these are "good practices": there is a lot of teaching with a wink and a nod. Even if taken seriously and in good faith, like all other educational activities these initiatives make slow progress and require constant attention and nurturing.

While all of the above measures are useful—and should be pursued with zeal—torture will be abolished only through a major cultural shift that moves all of us from moral condemnation to decisive intolerance in practice. Human culture will abolish torture as it did, not more than a century ago, with slavery. In order to do that, culture will need to continue to address the retentionist arguments and expose them for what they are, and to rebut them effectively with the lessons learned through history. At the same time, we need cultural artifacts that demonstrate the horrendous nature of torture without sensationalizing it and avoiding the pornography of horror. We need to confront those who are willing to contemplate torture (as long as it is done by others and to others) with what precisely they are condoning. We need to show the irrationality of torture by reference to the high moral values that we hold dear and consider fundamental to our own societies. And we need to show torture is irrational by pointing out its consequences, not so much for the victim of torture, but to ourselves, to our children and to our communities. We can show that there are better ways, more effective and more morally rewarding ways, to combat crime and terrorism.

That is why this book is so valuable. It is meant to build a culture of moral rejection of the horrors of torture, and also to show the dangers of "exceptionalism." Sooner or later, all societies are confronted with challenges that seem poised to achieve their destruction. At those points, there is always the temptation to think that norms are well and good, and that they do apply across the board, but that they don't apply to us because we are in an emergency. In those circumstances, a great society is one that applies the highest moral and legal standards first and foremost to itself. It is not only a matter of leading by example, but also of reinforcing the values that make us great, by drawing from them the strength to confront the deadly challenge. But it is not only a matter of public policy and social discourse. Torture will be abolished when all of us make ourselves responsible for it; for abolishing it and for enforcing its prohibition. Especially if cruelty is inflicted on others in our name and for our sake, we are guilty of it unless we take responsibility for rejecting it and for campaigning to abolish it.

# Introduction

By definition torturers are cruel. But the corpses proved that they could also be clever. The Mujahadeen in Afghanistan, reported Amnesty International in 1994, were strapping live prisoners to newly dead corpses and leaving them, eye to eye, to rot together in the sun.

What a simple, economical form of torture, I thought to myself as I read the report shortly after becoming executive director of Amnesty International U.S.A. Low-tech but terrifying.

As my tenure at Amnesty lengthened, as I began to learn more, to meet survivors of torture and to hear their stories, and then to go into prisons and police stations where torture took place, I accumulated a longer and longer list of ways people inflict suffering on others. Beatings of one kind or another were the simplest and most commonplace while electroshock gained in popularity over the past decade or so with the manufacture of ever more sophisticated equipment. But these techniques are prized only by those of limited vision. If you ever doubt the human capacity for ingenuity, you have but to consider the many other ways the human mind has fancied to torment the body and crush the spirit.

In King Leopold's Congo a whip was made of raw, sun-dried hippopotamus hide cut into long, sharp-edged corkscrew strips. Twenty-five lashes brought unconsciousness. One hundred brought death.[1] In Pinochet's Chile women were raped by men with "visible open syphlitic sores," sexually abused by dogs trained in that practice, and forced to eat the human remains of their fellow captives.[2] In Brazil prisoners were stripped naked and locked in small, bare concrete cells with only one other occupant—a boa constrictor.[3] The Americans have always been fond of water torture. During our occupation of the Philippines at the turn of the twentieth century, our soldiers inserted bamboo tubes into victims' throats and poured in gallons of water, the filthier the better. The Filipinos got their revenge, however. They buried captured American soldiers up to their heads in manure, poured molasses over their heads, and dropped hundreds of fire ants into the molasses.[4] Today we use the technique called waterboarding in which victims are forced underwater until they are convinced they will drown; then drawn back out for a moment; and immediately forced back in.

Most of us pay very little attention to torture; it is, after all, such an unpleasant subject. I have lived with it, albeit at secondhand, for twelve years now. On one level I understand it today as little as I did when I started. But on another I understand it all too well.

Jean Paul Sartre said that Nothingness lies curled deep inside Being like a worm in an apple.[5] In similar fashion, the capacity to harm another lies buried inside most of us.

Fortunately the vast majority of us are taught to control the impulse. (Suppression of feelings has gotten a bad rap over the years but, as Sartre also once observed somewhere, if it were not for the petty rules of polite society, human beings would destroy one another.) But a few of us are taught the opposite. Chapter I ("Torture in Western History") reveals that in historical terms those "few" have a good bit of company.

When people learned that I worked for Amnesty International, two reactions were not uncommon. One was an expression of wonderment that I could hear so regularly of all the horrors in the world and not undergo a crisis of faith in humanity that rendered me depressed or paralyzed. The other was to make a joke about torture. Because it is so frightening, we joke about it to keep it at a distance. David Letterman delivered this line in one of his monologues on *The Late Show*:

The guy who was the former chef at the White House has written a tell-all book. He says Dick Cheney's favorite recipe is Chicken Gitmo [Guantanamo Bay]. It's chicken bound and gagged on a bed of rice.

The problem is that torture truly is, quite literally, *unimaginable* to those of us who have never undergone it. Unless you have been physically or psychologically abused yourself, it cannot be fully conjured up. When I am speaking about the subject, I sometimes invite the audience to swallow their saliva repeatedly to see how long they can do it before beginning to become uncomfortable and then imagine being forced to do that for two or three hours without stopping—which is a form of torture even simpler than the Mujahadeen's. Or I ask them to bring back to memory the most acute physical pain they ever had—for me, it was kidney stones—and pretend that that pain lasted steadily for eight hours, twelve hours, or twenty-four hours *at another's behest.*

But these exercises, I am the first to admit, are utterly inadequate to convey the real physical or emotional impact of torture. Torture yields up her acquaintance only grudgingly. Virtually every one of us can have some idea of why due process rights deserve protection because there is hardly anyone who has never wanted to proclaim to a parent or a sibling or a teacher or a police officer or the IRS, "But that's not fair!" Almost every one of us has the *capacity* to understand how dire a decision it is to send soldiers into war because most of us value our own lives and most adults at least have some familiarity with the pain of grieving because we have experienced the death of a loved one or a friend or even a pet. But, again, with the exception of those who have been abused (which is, I grant, a considerable number), how many of us have experienced torture? How many of us have known victims of *political* torture? And how many of us have met face to face with those who have inflicted it?

The kind of empathy that emerges with either firsthand knowledge or prolonged exposure to those who've suffered; the kind that makes not just for wincing when we learn of another's pain but for believing deep in our hearts that it is *unacceptable* and then doing something about it— that kind of empathy is too often missing for too many of us when it comes to torture because, despite Abu Ghraib, for most Americans torture is so alien. Is it easier to imagine your home destroyed in a fire or a storm or an earthquake than to imagine yourself being held in a six by eight foot cell and tortured day and night? It is indeed and that is one reason disaster relief receives so many more dollars than human rights.

So since we *don't* want to increase the number of people who experience torture personally but we *do* want to motivate people to do what they can to stop it, the best thing we can do is to let the survivors of torture tell their stories. You'll find those stories spread throughout the book but especially in Chapter II ("Being Tortured").

But the stories tell only part of the tale.[6] Having heard them, we immediately want to know why we humans are capable of bestowing so much pain on others and sometimes with such relish.

David Buss, a professor of psychology at the University of Texas, posted the following comment on a Website in response to an invitation to describe one's "most dangerous idea":

The unfortunate fact is that killing has proved to be an effective solution to an array of adaptive problems in the ruthless evolutionary games of survival and reproductive competition: preventing injury, rape, or death; protecting one's children; eliminating a crucial antagonist; acquiring a rival's resources; securing sexual access to a competitor's mate; preventing an interloper from appropriating one's own mate; and protecting vital resources needed for reproduction. . . .

[W]e view as evil people who inflict massive evolutionary fitness costs on us, our families, or our allies. No one summarized these fitness costs better than the feared conqueror, Genghis Khan (1167–1227): "The greatest pleasure is to vanquish your enemies, to chase them before you, to rob them of their wealth, to see their near and dear bathed in tears, to ride their horses and sleep on the bellies of their wives and daughters."[7]

Competition, territorial aggression, killing in the service of evolutionary adaptation or a cause we can convince ourselves is noble—all these may well be written into our gene pools. Some instances of torture may arguably serve those pools as well: interrogatory torture designed to procure information to protect our community or even intimidatory torture designed to frighten off our adversaries. But so much of torture is gratuitous and even that which begins as limited soon slips off the slope. The guards at Abu Ghraib were told merely to "soften up" the detainees for questioning (see Chapter II, Reading 3 for the result); they ended up humiliating and abusing them and smiling all the way. The Israeli Landau Commission permitted "moderate physical pressure," which soon took the form of shaking that spiraled into death (Chapter VI, Readings 9 and 10).

Why do we take such pleasure in another's suffering? What is the source of such widespread *Schadenfreund*?

When I was seven or eight years old, I lived across the street from a little dog named Amy. Every afternoon after my school let out, Amy and I would play together for an hour. One of Amy's favorite games was a dancing game in which I held her two forepaws in my hands and we would dance around the yard. Sometimes Amy even put her paws in my lap to signal that she wanted to dance. But I noticed that after a few minutes Amy's hind legs would get sore and she would pull her paws away. The first few times we played our dancing game, I dropped her paws the moment I sensed her discomfort and we went on to something else.

But one day I decided to hold on. The more Amy tugged, the tighter I held until finally, when she yelped in agony, I let her go. But the next day I repeated my demonic variation on our dance. It was fascinating to feel this little creature, so much less powerful than I was, entirely at my mercy.

I was lucky that Amy was such a gentle dog for she had every right to have bitten me and when, after two or three days, I saw that my friend, who had previously scrambled eagerly toward me on first site, now cowered at my approach, I realized with a start what I had done and was suddenly frightened of myself and much ashamed. Whatever had come over me that I would treat someone I had loved that way?

What had come over me, I now know in retrospect, was the displacement of anger onto one who held no threat to me. Bullies at school might pick on me. My two parents might tell their only child what he could and could not do. My piano teacher might try to slam the keyboard cover on my fingers when I played off key. But in that yard I ruled supreme. Not only did I hold the power but the one who was powerless for a change was Not-Me.

Is anyone capable of being a torturer? I don't think so. I believe there are some people in the world who would rather die than harm another, but I also believe that we underestimate the extent to which feelings of powerlessness and lack of control over our lives may lead to violence— not just in individuals but societies as well. It is no coincidence that the torture scandals most recently associated with the United States come at a time when this nation feels itself most vulnerable to threats beyond its control nor that at just such a time 63 percent say that torture is at least occasionally justified.[8] During the Cold War the enemy was known; his location coordinates were clear; his weapons were evident; and we had similar weapons equally, if not more effective, with which to counter his. None of that is true of terrorists.

And when that sense of powerlessness is coupled with sanction of torture, denigration of its victims, and assurances of impunity, the deed is as good as done. One need not visit a traditional torture chamber to see what I mean. At the all-male prep school that I attended in the 1960s, a quadrangle in front of the main academic building was designated the Senior Campus. If any underclassman set foot on it and was caught, a well-established ritual would ensue. At the close of classes for the day, the entire community—students, faculty, administrators, visitors—would gather around the Senior Campus while a group of senior class students, including some who in other contexts were among the sweetest and mildest of the bunch, would strip the offender of his clothes, hold him down, and pour a noxious blend of paint, vinegar, lye, urine, and feces all over him before hoisting his pants to the top of the flagpole where they would remain while the victim ignominiously made his way home. Until a new headmaster came to town in 1966 and stopped the practice, not only did no one, including teachers, parents, or alumni, object to the "tea parties," as they ironically were called; such institutionalized brutality was in fact encouraged as good for "school spirit," its victims universally labeled "weenies," its perpetrators heroes.

Now I do not for an instant seek to equate this typical and, by some male prep school standards, relatively tame venture with torture. I want only to illustrate that whatever the sources of our impulses to brutality, they can be exploited and exacerbated by social contexts that provide them approbation. If such mayhem can be incited in a group of high school students over the "crime" of trespassing on a certain piece of real estate, imagine how much easier it would be to convince members of the police or military, taught from the start to obey their superiors, to do vicious damage to those outsiders whom they are told are intent on destroying their homes, their families, and their very way of life.

Not everyone can be made a torturer, but every torturer must be made.

If this is true of those who actually supply the shock or wield the truncheon, however, is it also true of those who order them to do it? Do the Saddam Husseins of the world, the Augusto Pinochets and their military minions act out of a sense of powerlessness or megalomania? Certainly it is easy to believe that dictators, so inflated by their power of command and so insulated from the lives of those who suffer its consequences, need little more than opportunity and acquiescence to indulge their penchants for brutality. But even in these cases they often feel the need to supply themselves and their followers with a larger purpose on whose behalf they toil: restoring the glory of Mesopotamia; saving Chile from the Communists. How refreshing it would be to find an autocrat who admitted that he tortured his enemies simply because he didn't like the bastards!

The need to rationalize mistreatment of the adversary is even greater in those who regard themselves as democrats and provide cover for misdeeds through what we might call "explicit indirection." When President Bush in 2002, for example, opened the floodgates to abuse of detainees by ordering that, though they should be treated "humanely," that treatment needed to be "in a manner consistent with [the] Geneva [Convention]" only "*to the extent appropriate and consistent with military necessity*" (emphasis added), he did so in recognition, he said, of the fact that "the war against terrorism ushers in a new paradigm, one in which groups with broad, international reach commit horrific acts against innocent civilians" and that "this new paradigm—ushered in not by us, but by terrorists—requires new thinking in the law of war."[9] One can only hope Vice President Cheney had that argument in mind (which at least had the virtue of being a rational, if misguided, calculation) when five days after September 11, 2001, he kicked off the campaign to deprive those accused of terrorism of any semblance of humanity—and hence as ripe for torture—by likening them to "barbarians."[10]

Not everyone can be led into torture but every torturer requires a leader. Chapters III ("Who Are the Torturers?"), IV ("The Dynamics of Torture"), and V ("The Social Context of Torture") elucidate the circumstances in which torture flourishes.

Virtually all those leaders contend of course that they do not sanction torture. Most of them are just lying. But some are relying upon the ambiguities inherent in the definition of torture.

The Convention against Torture (CAT) (see Appendix) defines torture in Article I as

any act by which severe pain or suffering, whether physical or mental, is intentionally inflicted on a person for such purposes as obtaining from him or a third person information or a confession, punishing him for an act he or a third person has committed or is suspected of having committed, or intimidating or coercing him or a third person, or for any reason based on discrimination of any kind, when such pain or suffering is inflicted by or at the instigation of or with the consent or acquiescence of a public official or other person acting in an official capacity. It does not include pain or suffering arising only from, inherent in or incidental to lawful sanctions.

But what is the definition of "severe"? We know that the infamous Bybee memo restricted torture to

Pain . . . equivalent in intensity to the pain accompanying serious physical injury, such as organ failure, impairment of bodily function, or even death. For purely mental pain or suffering to amount to torture . . . , it must result in significant psychological harm of significant duration, e.g., lasting for months or even years.[11]

Under such a definition, being subjected to an hour of nonlethal electric shock or being tied to a rotting corpse for a day or two is something less than torture. And if you recover your mental faculties (from, say, sharing a small prison cell with a boa constrictor), in less than a period of months or years, you may make no torture claims. Yet even if we discount the Bybee memo as extreme, the perception of what is "severe" pain or suffering contains a subjective element and certainly differs from person to person.

And then there is the question of motivation. For cruelty to constitute torture under CAT, it must be designed to (1) elicit information or a confession; (2) serve as punishment; (3) inflict intimidation or coercion; or (4) be based on discrimination. That covers a great deal of what we want to call torture but perhaps not all. When mistreatment exceeds all rationalized bounds and becomes the province, in Jean Améry's eloquent words, of "absolute . . . sovereignty revealed . . . as the power to inflict suffering and to destroy" (Chapter III, Reading 8), does it cease to become torture? Of course not.

Nor need the suffering be inflicted "by or at the instigation of or with the consent or acquiescence of a public official or other person acting in an official capacity" to be considered torture. Neither the terrorist nor the spouse batterer acts in an "official capacity," but the harm they do deserves no less a label than that of "torture" (Chapter IV, Reading 6).

So the definition is not perfect.[12] (God knows that "lawful sanctions" may be cruel beyond belief.) But on one level it doesn't matter, because the CAT isn't just about torture. Its official title is the Convention against Torture *and Other Cruel, Inhuman or Degrading Treatment or Punishment* (emphasis added)—the latter phrase is popularly known as "CID"—and it mandates that governments "prevent . . . other acts of cruel, inhuman or degrading treatment or punishment which do not amount to torture as defined in article I" with just as much fervor as they must seek to prevent torture. There is no advantage, therefore, for states that are party to the Convention to make casuistical distinctions between torture and CID. It's *all* illegal.[13]

But is it all *morally* indefensible? I used to find it curious that those who defended the death penalty would take umbrage when I pointed out that, if they really believed in an eye for an eye, they would support raping a rapist or torturing a torturer in return for the crime rather than sentencing such people to long prison terms, and yet no respectable death penalty supporter would ever think of endorsing such punishments. Why a bout of conscience when torture was involved but not death? Surely killing someone is as bad as or worse than maiming them.

But no. Somehow inflicting pain on a creature is less acceptable, less "civilized" than doing away with them altogether. That is why we go to great lengths to make sure that the process of capital execution is as sterile and painless as possible. If we actually appeared to be enjoying another's suffering, if we indulged too openly that part of us that revels in revenge on those who do us wrong, we would see something about ourselves mighty important to keep hidden. The State is meant to be a projection of our values, a mirror of our best selves, and hence, though the State may do away with criminals, it may not gloat in their demise.

When it comes to torture, the stakes, then, are even higher. The State may not publicly acknowledge its use of torture, for to do so would mean that its people were the kind who might approve of things like forcing human beings into cannibalism. So torture, unlike state executions, must be hidden. (Whatever we may think of the Landau Commission's conclusions, its candor was remarkable—Chapter VI, Reading 9). It does not even lend itself, as some claim capital punishment does, to defense on the grounds of justifiable retribution. It is *always* beyond the pale. Except perhaps . . . when it is required for self-defense.

Here the ethical argument is joined. For do we have to leave ourselves vulnerable to destruction if a carefully calibrated use of torture might save us? That is the perennial debate taken up in Chapter VI ("The Ethics of Torture").

Is the use of torture and cruel, inhumane, and degrading treatment (CID) increasing or declining? The truth is that nobody knows. What we do know is that every year Amnesty International documents more than a hundred countries that utilize one or the other or both.

At the end of ACT III, Scene 1 of Ariel Dorfman's classic play about torture, *Death and the Maiden*, Paulina is threatening to kill Roberto, the man she believes has tortured her. As she counts to ten, Roberto pleads with her: "So someone did terrible things to you and now you're doing something terrible to me and tomorrow somebody else is going to— on and on and on. I have children, two boys, a girl. Are they supposed to spend the next fifteen years looking for you until they find you? And then—"

Paulina keeps counting: "Nine." "Oh, Paulina," Roberto begs, "—isn't it time we stopped?" And Paulina replies, "And why does it always have to be people like me who have to sacrifice, why are we always the ones who have to make concessions when something has to be conceded, why always me who has to bite her tongue, why? Well, not this time. This time I am going to think about myself, about what I need. If only to do justice in one case, just one. What do we lose? What do we lose by killing one of them? What do we lose? What do we lose?"

Fortunately, the alternatives to "killing them" have increased markedly since Paulina/Dorfman posed that question in 1990. For while the use of torture is still widespread, efforts to curtail its use are markedly on the rise. Some 141 countries have ratified the Convention Against Torture. Legal remedies are beginning to proliferate. Government officials who order or countenance brutality are being stripped of their immunity; their henchmen named; the truth exposed. It is a slow process but an inexorable one, as described in Chapter VII ("Healing the Victims, Stopping the Torture").

I can only hope that this book makes its own small contribution to those developments. What you will read about here is humanity at its worst. That you are reading it is cause for celebration.

I have always loved this little story from the Russian poet, Anna Akhmatova. "I spent seventeen months waiting in line outside the prison in Leningrad," she recalled in 1957. "One day somebody in the crowd identified me. Standing behind me was a woman, with lips blue from the cold. . . . 'Can you describe this?' [she asked]. And I said, 'I can.' Then something like a smile passed fleetingly over what once had been her face."[14]

*Chapter I*
# Torture in Western History

Torture has been around for a long time. The readings in this chapter are not meant to constitute a definitive taxonomy of the practice by any means. (For one thing, our focus is limited to Western history, though torture has been employed in virtually all cultures.) But they do suggest some of the ways torture has changed over the centuries—it is no longer codified in legal writ as it once was, for example—and some of the ways it remains the same—for instance it is often associated with discrimination against one class or set of victims. Does history reflect a progressive improvement in human behavior? There is no question that the boundaries of the acceptable are far more tightly drawn today than in centuries past. But that may mean that we moderns are just more skillful at hiding our less felicitous selves from public view.

# "The Slave's Truth"

The ancient Greeks were quite discriminating when it came to who could be tortured. Free citizens were spared the ordeal while slaves (and sometimes foreigners) were ready candidates. That in and of itself is not surprising. Torture has often been reserved for the least powerful and the Other. But why did the ancient Greeks torture slaves? Because, as the following excerpt from Page DuBois's *Torture and Truth* points out, by not possessing reason a slave is incapable of dissembling. In the search for truth, a slave is the best possible source. For argument's sake, as one of the passages from the writings of Aristotle (384–322 B.C.E.) illustrates, one can speculate that information obtained under torture is unreliable. But in fact a slave is merely an extension of that part of a master that knows the truth and, under force, no slave can help but tell it.

Torture performs at least two functions in the Athenian state. As an instrument of demarcation, it delineates the boundary between slave and free, between the untouchable bodies of free citizens and the torturable bodies of slaves. The ambiguity of slave status, the difficulty of sustaining an absolute sense of differences, is addressed through this practice of the state, which carves the line between slave and free on the bodies of the unfree. In the work of the wheel, the rack, and the whip, the torturer carries out the work of the *polis*[1]; citizen is made distinct from noncitizen, Greek from barbarian, slave from free. [. . .]

But the desire to clarify the respective status of slave and free is not the motive, never the explicit motive, of torture. Rather, again and again, even in the face of arguments discounting evidence derived from torture, speakers in the courts describe the *basanos*[2] as a search for truth. How is this possible? And how are the two desires related? The claim is made that truth resides in the slave body.

Isaios[3] uses language almost identical to that of Demosthenes[4] to claim that torture provides truth:

You Athenians hold the opinion that both in public and in private matters examination under torture is the most searching test; and so, when you have slaves and free men before you, and it is necessary that some contested point should be cleared up, you do not employ the evidence of free men but seek to establish the truth . . . by putting the slaves to torture. This is a perfectly reasonable course, for you are well aware that before now witnesses have appeared not to be giving true evidence, whereas no one who has been examined under torture . . . has ever been convicted of giving false evidence as the result of being tortured. . . .

The evidence derived from the slave's body and reported to the court, evidence from the past, is considered superior to that given freely in the court, before the jury, in the presence of the litigants.

Aristotle says, in distinguishing among master, slave, and animal:

> He is by nature a slave who is capable of belonging to another (and that is why he does so belong), and who participates in reason so far as to apprehend it but not to possess it; for the animals other than man are subservient not to reason, by apprehending it, but to feelings. (*Politics* 1254b)

That is, the master possesses reason, *logos*. When giving evidence in court, he knows the difference between truth and falsehood, he can reason and produce true speech, *logos*, and he can reason about the consequences of falsehood. [. . .] The slave, on the other hand, possessing not reason, but rather a body strong for service, must be forced to utter the truth, which he can apprehend, although not possessing reason as such. Unlike an animal, a being that possesses only feelings, and therefore can neither apprehend reason, nor speak, the slave can testify when his body is tortured because he recognizes reason without possessing it himself.

What kind of truth is the slave's truth? Aristotle says of the relationship between slave and master:

> The slave is a part of the master—he is, as it were, a part of the body, alive but yet separated from it. (*Politics* 1255b)

Thus, according to Aristotle's logic, representative or not, the slave's truth is the master's truth; it is in the body of the slave that the master's truth lies, and it is in torture that his truth is revealed. The torturer reaches through the master to the slave's body, and extracts the truth from it. The master can conceal the truth, since he possesses reason and can choose between truth and lie, can choose the penalty associated with false testimony. His own point of vulnerability is the body of his slave, which can be compelled not to lie, can be forced to produce the truth. If he decides to deny the body of his slave to the torturer, assumptions will be made that condemn him.

In his *Rhetoric*, addressed to an audience requiring instruction in techniques of persuasion, Aristotle discusses the value of torture as evidence in forensic rhetoric. [. . .]

> Torture is a kind of evidence, which appears trustworthy, because a sort of compulsion is attached to it. Nor is it difficult to see what may be said concerning it, and by what arguments, if it is in our favour, we can exaggerate its importance by asserting that it is the only true kind of evidence; but if it is against us and in favour of our opponent, we can destroy its value by telling the truth about all kinds of torture generally; for those under compulsion are as likely to give false evidence as true, some being ready to endure everything rather than tell the truth,

while others are equally ready to make false charges against others, in the hope of being sooner released from torture. It is also necessary to be able to quote actual examples of the kind with which the judges are acquainted. It may also be said that evidence given under torture is not true [. . .]; for many thick-witted and thick-skinned persons, and those who are stout-hearted heroically hold out under sufferings, while the cowardly and cautious, before they see the sufferings before them, are bold enough; wherefore evidence from torture may be considered utterly untrustworthy. (*Rhetoric* 1376b–1377a)

Aristotle advocates the pragmatic approach; one can argue either side concerning the truth of torture. The weight of Aristotle's exposition lies on the falsity of evidence produced under torture, either because he believes it to be more likely false, or because speakers in the court are more likely to claim its truth, and therefore those he is instructing, if faced with evidence from torture, need assistance in refuting its claims. If we heed Demosthenes' and Isaios' claim that no evidence from torture was ever proven false, we see the difficulty of the litigant faced with slave torture. It appears that common wisdom attributed a superior value to the evidence of a tortured slave, a value weighted above that of the free man, and that Aristotle must labor on behalf of his readers to counter the weight of evidence from this privileged source. [. . .]

The very ambiguity of evidence derived from torture, an ambiguity that Aristotle recognizes and accounts for, replicates the ambiguity of social status on which it depends. Slave is only circumstantially differentiable from free; truth in the lawcourt can only provisionally and polemically be distinguished from falsehood. The two issues are linked in the body of the tortured, who on the rack, on the wheel, under the whip assumes a relationship to truth. Truth is constituted as residing in the body of the slave; because he can apprehend reason, without possessing reason, under coercion he is assumed to speak the truth. The free man, the citizen, because he possesses reason, can lie freely, recognizing that he may lose his rights, but choosing to gamble that his authority will authorize his speech. The slave, incapable of reasoning, [. . .] can produce only truth under coercion. The court assumes that he will lie unless compelled by physical force to speak truly and that when compelled he will speak truly. [. . .] Proof, and therefore truth, are constituted by the Greeks as best found in the evidence derived from torture.

# The Torture of Jesus

Few acts of torture have had as far-ranging an effect on human history as those committed against Jesus of Nazareth. For traditional Christians, of course, it is Jesus' crucifixion and resurrection that are the most important features of the story. But the pain and indignity he suffered on the way to Golgotha, as well as the agony he endured on the cross before he died, contributed to the subsequent understanding of him as a suffering servant. After all, the Roman soldiers were not interested in obtaining information from him; only in humiliating him and, not incidentally, weakening him in order to hasten his death. The biblical passage is from Mark: 15–24, the New English Bible version; the annotations are from an article in the *Journal of the American Medical Association* that describes from a medical point of view the physical abuse Jesus endured.

15 So Pilate [. . .] had Jesus flogged[a] and handed him over to be crucified.

16 Then the soldiers took him inside the courtyard (the Governor's head-quarters) and called together the whole company.

17 They dressed him in purple, and plaiting a crown of thorns, placed it on his head.

18 Then they began to salute him with "Hail, King of the Jews!"

19 They beat him about the head with a cane and spat upon him, and then knelt and paid mock homage to him.

20 When they had finished their mockery, they stripped him of the purple and dressed him in his own clothes.[b]

21 Then they took him out to crucify him. A man called Simon [. . .] was passing by on his way in from the country. And they pressed him into service to carry his cross.

22 They brought him to the place called Golgotha, which means "Place of a skull."

23 He was offered drugged wine, but he would not take it.

24 Then they fastened him to the cross.[c]

## Annotations

a. Flogging was a legal preliminary to every Roman execution. [. . .] The usual instrument was a short whip [. . .] with several single or braided leather thongs of variable lengths, in which small iron balls or sharp pieces of sheep bones were tied at intervals. Occasionally, staves also were used. For scourging, the man was stripped of his clothing, and his hands were tied to an upright post. The back, buttocks, and legs were flogged either by two soldiers (lictors) or by one who alternated positions. The severity of the scourging depended on the disposition of the lictors and was intended to weaken the victim to a state just short of collapse or death. After the scourging, the soldiers often taunted their victim. As the Roman soldiers repeatedly struck the victim's back with full force, the iron balls would cause deep contusions, and the leather thongs and sheep bones would cut into the skin and subcutaneous tissues. Then, as the flogging continued, the lacerations would tear into the underlying skeletal muscles and produce quivering ribbons of bleeding flesh. Pain and blood loss generally set the stage for circulatory shock. The extent of blood loss may well have determined how long the victim would survive on the cross.

b. The Roman soldiers, amused that this weakened man had claimed to be a king, began to mock him by placing a robe on his shoulders, a crown of thorns on his head, and a wooden staff as a scepter in his right hand. Next, they spat on Jesus and struck him on the head with the wooden staff. Moreover, when the soldiers tore the robe from Jesus' back, they probably reopened the scourging wounds. The severe scourging, with its intense pain and appreciable blood loss, most probably left Jesus in a pre-shock state. [. . .] The physical and mental abuse meted out by the Jews and the Romans, as well as the lack of food, water, and sleep, also contributed to his generally weakened state. Therefore, even before the actual crucifixion, Jesus' physical condition was at least serious and possibly critical.

c. At the site of execution, by law, the victim was given a bitter drink of wine mixed with myrrh (gall) as a mild analgesic. The criminal was then thrown to the ground on his back, with his arms outstretched along the [crossbar]. The hands could be nailed or tied to the crossbar, but nailing apparently was preferred by the Romans. The archaeological remains of a crucified body, found in an ossuary near Jerusalem and dating from the time of Christ, indicate that the nails were tapered iron spikes approximately 5 to 7 in (13 to 18 cm) long with a square shaft 3/8 in (1 cm) across. Furthermore, ossuary findings and the Shroud of Turin have documented that the nails commonly were driven through the wrists rather than the palms.

After both arms were fixed to the crossbar, the [crossbar] and the victim, together, were lifted onto the stipes [the vertical bar of the cross]. On

[a] low cross, four soldiers could accomplish this relatively easily. However, on [a] tall cross, the soldiers used either wooden forks or ladders.

Next, the feet were fixed to the cross, either by nails or ropes. Ossuary findings and the Shroud of Turin suggest that nailing was the preferred Roman practice. Although the feet could be fixed to the sides of the stipes or to a wooden footrest, they usually were nailed directly to the front of the stipes. To accomplish this, flexion of the knees may have been quite prominent, and the bent legs may have been rotated laterally. [. . .]

The soldiers and the civilian crowd often taunted and jeered the condemned man, and the soldiers customarily divided up his clothes among themselves. The length of survival generally ranged from three or four hours to three or four days and appears to have been inversely related to the severity of the scourging. However, even if the scourging had been relatively mild, the Roman soldiers could hasten death by breaking the legs below the knees.

Not uncommonly, insects would light upon or burrow into the open wounds or the eyes, ears, and nose of the dying and helpless victim, and birds of prey would tear at these sites. [. . .]

The major pathophysiologic effect of crucifixion, beyond the excruciating pain, was a marked interference with normal respiration, particularly exhalation. The weight of the body, pulling down on the outstretched arms and shoulders, would tend to fix the [. . .] muscles in an inhalation state and thereby hinder passive exhalation. Accordingly, exhalation was primarily diaphragmatic, and breathing was shallow. [. . .]

Adequate exhalation required lifting the body by pushing up on the feet and by flexing the elbows and adducting the shoulders [drawing them toward the axis of the body]. However, this maneuver would place the entire weight of the body on the tarsals and would produce searing pain. Furthermore, flexion of the elbows would cause rotation of the wrists about the iron nails and cause fiery pain along the damaged median nerves. Lifting of the body would also painfully scrape the scourged back against the rough wooden stipes. [. . .] As a result, each respiratory effort would become agonizing and tiring and lead eventually to asphyxia.

The actual cause of death by crucifixion was multifactorial and varied somewhat with each case, but the two most prominent causes probably were hypovolemic shock and exhaustion asphyxia. Other possible contributing factors included dehydration, stress-induced arrhythmias, and congestive heart failure. [. . .] Crucifracture (breaking the legs below the knees), if performed, led to an asphyxic death within minutes. Death by crucifixion was, in every sense of the word, excruciating (Latin, *excruciatus*, or "out of the cross").

# Torture and the Law of Proof

An enormous change took place in Europe during the twelfth century with regard to how offenses—what today we would call "crimes"—were resolved. No longer was it sufficient to decide fault in a conflict based upon the reputation and honor of the parties involved or the credibility of oaths they might swear. Ordeals in which the accused was subjected to a physical test (such as whether she or he floated or sank in water) were deemed an unreliable means to determine God's judgment. Justice officials now required *evidence* that they themselves had gathered in order to render verdicts. And what more certain evidence might there be than a confession? So certain in fact that it came to be known as "the queen of proofs." And what more efficient way was there to elicit a confession than torture? The very verb "to question" (in Latin, *quaestio*) came to be synonymous with torture. In this essay from his book *Torture and the Law of Proof*, the legal historian John H. Langbein traces the development of torture as an instrument of jurisprudence.

From the late Middle Ages and throughout the ancien régime, torture was an incident of the legal systems of all the great states of continental Europe. Torture was part of the ordinary criminal procedure, regularly employed to investigate and prosecute routine crime before the ordinary courts. The system was one of *judicial torture*.

There was in fact a jurisprudence of torture, with its own rules, treatises, and learned doctors of law. This law of torture developed in northern Italy in the thirteenth century within the Roman-canon[5] inquisitorial tradition, and it spread through Europe in the movement that is called the reception of Roman law. By the sixteenth century a substantially similar law of torture was in force from the Kingdom of Sicily north to Scandinavia, from Iberia across France and the German Empire to the Slavic East. Well into the eighteenth century the law of torture was still current everywhere, and it survived into the nineteenth century in some corners of central Europe. [. . .]

When we speak of "judicial torture," we are referring to the use of physical coercion by officers of the state in order to gather evidence for judicial proceedings. The law of torture regulated this form of judicial investigation. In matters of state, torture was also used to extract information in circumstances not directly related to judicial proceedings. Torture has to be kept separate from the various painful modes of punishment used as sanctions against persons already convicted and condemned. No punishment, no matter how gruesome, should be called torture.[6]

It is universally acknowledged that judicial torture as it existed in the national legal systems of Western Europe in early modern times was the creature of the so-called statutory system of proofs—the Roman-canon law of evidence. But historians have generally pointed to factors other than the law of proof as having brought about the abolition of torture. They have especially emphasized the forceful writing of publicists like Beccaria and Voltaire and the political wisdom of Enlightenment rulers like Frederick the Great and the emperor Joseph II. [. . .]

[But] the conventional account of the abolition of torture in the eighteenth century is wrong. [. . .] [T]he explanation for the disappearance of judicial torture is neither publicistic nor political, but juristic. In the two centuries preceding the abolition of torture, there occurred a revolution in the law of proof in Europe. The Roman-canon law remained formally in force, but with its power eroded away. The true explanation for the abolition of torture is that by the age of abolition torture was no longer needed. The system of proof which had required the use of torture was dead.

## The Jurisprudence of Torture

The Roman-canon law of proof governed judicial procedure in cases of serious crime, cases where blood sanctions (death or severe physical maiming) could be imposed. In brief, there were three fundamental rules.

First, the court could convict and condemn an accused upon the testimony of two eyewitnesses to the gravamen[7] of the crime.

Second, if there were not two eyewitnesses, the court could convict and condemn the accused only upon the basis of his own confession.

Third, circumstantial evidence, so-called *indicia*, was not an adequate basis for conviction and condemnation, no matter how compelling. It does not matter, for example, that the suspect is seen running away from the murdered man's house and that the bloody dagger and the stolen loot are found in his possession. The court cannot convict him of the crime.

At least, the court cannot convict him without his confession, and that is where torture fitted into the system. In certain cases where there was neither the voluntary confession nor the testimony of the two eyewitnesses, the court could order that the suspect be examined about the crime under torture in order to secure his confession.

However, examination under torture was permitted only when there was a so-called half proof against the suspect. That meant either (1) one eyewitness, or (2) circumstantial evidence of sufficient gravity, according to a fairly elaborate tariff of gravity worked out by the later jurists. So, in the example where the suspect is caught with the dagger and the loot, each of those indicia would be a quarter proof. Together they cumulate to a half proof, and he could therefore be dispatched to a session in the local torture chamber.

Now what was the logic of creating a system of safeguards, followed by a system of coercion to overcome the safeguards? Manifestly, under sufficient coercion nearly anyone can be made to confess to anything. To the extent that the explanation is to be found in logic, it is that the system did not allow indiscriminate coercion. The coercion was carefully limited by rule in two important respects.

First, there was the threshold requirement of half proof. It amounted to what Anglo-American lawyers would call a rule of probable cause. It was designed to assure that only those persons highly likely to be guilty would be examined under torture.

Second, the use of torture was surrounded by various rules designed to enhance the reliability of the confession. Torture was not supposed to be used to secure what Anglo-American lawyers call a guilty plea, that is, an abject confession of guilt. Rather, torture was supposed to be employed in such a way that the accused would also confess to details of the crime— information which, in the words of the German *Constitutio Criminalis Carolina* of 1532, "no innocent person can know."

To this end the Carolina forbids so-called suggestive questioning, in which the examiner supplies the accused with the details he wishes to hear from him. Further, the Carolina directs that the information admitted under torture be investigated and verified to the extent feasible. If the accused confesses to the slaying, he is supposed to be asked where he put the dagger. If he says he buried it under the old oak tree, the examining magistrate is supposed to send someone out to dig it up. [. . .]

## The Origins of Judicial Torture

This curious system of proof developed in the thirteenth century, although it has some roots in the twelfth century. The Roman-canon law of proof was the successor to the ordeals, the nonrational proofs of Germanic antiquity. When the Fourth Lateran Council of 1215[8] abolished the ordeals, it destroyed an entire system of proof: The ordeals were means of provoking the judgment of God. God revealed the innocence of an accused whose hand withstood infection from the hot iron; God pronounced the guilt of one who floated when subjected to the water ordeal.

The abolition of this system meant not only a fundamental change in the rules of proof, but a profound change in thinking about the nature of government and law. The attempt to make God the fact finder for human disputes was being abandoned. Henceforth, humans were going to replace God in deciding guilt or innocence, humans called judges. It is almost impossible for us to imagine how difficult it must have been for the ordinary people of that age to accept that substitution. The question that springs to the lips is "You who are merely another mortal like me, who are you to sit in judgment upon me?"

Over many later centuries Western political theory developed its answer to that question. "I, the judge, sit in judgment upon you because I have the power to do so. I derive my power from the state, which selects, employs, and controls me." And the state now claims to legitimate its power by purporting to derive it not from God but from the consent of the governed. In the thirteenth century, however, the modern theoretical solution lay very far in the future. The problem that confronted the legal systems of the church and of the secular governments (initially in the North Italian city-states) was to make this fundamental change acceptable in the tradition-conscious and religiously devout societies of that day. How could men be persuaded to accept the judgment of professional judges today, when only yesterday the decision was being remitted to God?

The system of statutory proofs was the answer. Its overwhelming emphasis is upon the elimination of judicial discretion, and that is why it forbids the judge the power to convict upon circumstantial evidence. Circumstantial evidence depends for its efficacy upon the subjective persuasion of the trier, the judge. He has to draw an inference of guilt from indirect evidence. By contrast, the system of statutory proofs insists upon objective criteria of proof. The judge who administers it is an automaton. He condemns a criminal upon the testimony of two eyewitnesses, evidence which is in the famous phrase "as clear as the light of day." There should be no doubt about guilt in such a case. Likewise, when the accused himself admits his guilt, there ought to be no doubt. (Even under the former system of proof, confession constituted waiver. If the culprit admitted his guilt, the authorities were not going to waste their time and God's by asking for a confirmation under ordeal.)

The Roman-canon law of proof solved the problem of how to make the judgment of men palatable. That judgment was to rest on certainty. It was to rest upon standards of proof so high that no one would be concerned that God was no longer being asked to resolve the doubts. There could be no doubts. The difficulty with this system is to our eyes quite obvious. The jurists who devised it had solved one problem by creating another. They had constructed a system of proof that could handle the easy cases but not the hard ones. Their system could deal with most cases of overt crime but seldom with cases of covert crime—cases where there were no eyewitnesses. If that sounds completely absurd, do bear in mind that even today many cases are easy—crimes committed in anger or in haste, and either witnessed or voluntarily confessed in remorse.

Nevertheless, the Roman-canon law of proof was unworkable standing alone. No society will long tolerate a legal system in which there is no prospect of convicting unrepentant persons who commit clandestine crimes. Something had to be done to extend the system to those cases. The two-eyewitness rule was hard to compromise or evade, but the confession rule invited "subterfuge." To go from accepting a voluntary confession to coercing a confession from someone against whom there was already strong suspicion was a relatively small step, indeed, one which was probably taken almost from the inception of the system. There is considerable evidence of the use of torture in northern Italy already in the first half of the thirteenth century. Pope Innocent IV issued a decretal in 1252 confirming the use of torture in canon procedure. [. . .] Actually, judicial torture may not have seemed to contemporaries to be very far from the ordeals. Both were physically discomforting modes of procedure ordered by the court upon a preliminary showing of cogent incriminating evidence, usually circumstantial evidence. In this sense, the ordeals may have helped suggest and legitimate the system of judicial torture that displaced them.

The law of torture found a place for circumstantial evidence in the law of proof, but a subsidiary place. Circumstantial evidence was not consulted directly on the ultimate question—guilt or innocence. It was technically relevant only to an issue of interlocutory procedure—whether or not to examine the accused under torture. Even there the *ius commune*[9] attempted to limit judicial discretion by promulgating predetermined, supposedly objective standards for evaluating the indicia and assigning them numerical values (quarter proofs, half proofs, and the like).

The practice of coercing evidence from suspects did not need to be invented by medieval lawyers. "Dreadful or not, compelling a person through violence to admit or disclose something against his will is a method of procedure so humanly obvious that it proves difficult to imagine an age in which it could not have been known." [. . .] Eberhard Schmidt has convincingly shown that torture was in use in medieval Germany in advance of the German reception of the Roman-canon law of proof. The crux of the relationship between torture and the Roman-canon system of statutory proofs was this: there could be torture without the Roman-canon system, but the reverse was not true. The two-eyewitness rule left the Roman-canon system dependent upon the use of torture.

## The Classical Critique of Judicial Torture

What was wrong with the law of torture, after all? Superficially, it looks like a surprisingly good system, both efficient and just. The accused will not be tortured unless there is cogent incriminating evidence against him. When he is tortured, he will be asked for information, not just for a guilty plea, and the information he confesses will be examined and verified.

From a purely practical standpoint, laying aside moral objections to the use of coercion, there were a number of things wrong with the system. Inquisitorial procedure had a prosecutorial bias that torture magnified. "Only a judge equipped with superhuman capabilities could keep himself in his decisional function free from the . . . influences of his own instigating and investigating activity." Because torture tests an accused's capacity to endure pain, not his veracity, innocent persons might yield to "the pain and torment and confess things they never did."

Further, the safeguards that were designed to prevent the condemnation of an innocent man on the basis of a false confession extracted from him were quite imperfect. If the judge did engage in suggestive questioning, even accidentally, that could seldom be detected or prevented. If the accused knew something about the crime, but was still innocent of it, what he did know might be enough to give his confession verisimilitude. For certain crimes, especially heresy and witchcraft, there was seldom any objective evidence that might be used to verify the confession, and condemnation was allowed on the basis of an unverified confession. In many jurisdictions the requirement of verification was not enforced, or was indifferently enforced.

These defects were well known. Today we associate their denunciation with Thomasius,[10] Beccaria, and especially Voltaire.[11] But those writers were in fact latecomers to a tradition as ancient as the system itself. The warnings from imperial Roman law were never forgotten. The jurists of the *ius commune* report failings. The English jurist Fortescue, writing about 1470, recounts many of the dangers of the system. The treatise writers who elaborate the law of torture in northern Europe in the sixteenth, seventeenth, and eighteenth centuries admit the dangers. Long before Voltaire, French writers of the sixteenth and seventeenth centuries are pointing to cases in which an innocent person confesses and is executed, after which the real culprit is discovered.

The law of torture survived into the eighteenth century, not because its defects had been concealed, but rather in spite of their having been long revealed. European criminal procedure had no alternative; the law of proof was absolutely dependent upon coerced confessions.

By contrast, the British Isles and some peripheral parts of the Continent remained free from judicial torture throughout the later Middle Ages because the jury system rather than the Roman-canon law of proof replaced the ordeals. And, to this day, an English jury can convict an accused criminal on mere circumstantial evidence. It can convict on less evidence than the Glossators[12] and their successors stipulated as a bare prerequisite for further investigation under torture.

Another point which emphasizes the connection between torture and the Roman-canon law of proof is that in Europe itself, torture was not allowed in cases of petty crime, *delicta levia.* The statutory proofs pertained only to cases of capital crime. *Delicta levia* were governed by what would today be called *freie Beweiswürdigung* or *l'intime conviction*, that is, the subjective persuasion of the judge. Because conviction on less than full proof (meaning in practice conviction on circumstantial evidence) was unobjectionable, judicial torture had no sphere.

## Abolition and the Fairy Tale

In the middle of the eighteenth century the leading states of Europe abolished judicial torture within the space of a generation. Prussia all but terminated judicial torture in 1740; it was used for the last time in 1752 and authoritatively abolished in 1754. In 1770 Saxony abolished torture; in 1776 Poland and Austria-Bohemia; in 1780 France; in 1786 Tuscany; in 1787 the Austrian Netherlands (hereafter called Belgium); in 1789 Sicily. By the next generation, abolition was complete throughout Europe.

How did this abolition movement happen, how was it possible? In all the literature that discusses and celebrates the abolition of judicial torture, one meets the same account. We call it the fairy tale, and it goes like this: (1) The system of judicial torture persisted into the eighteenth century unabated. (2) There then arose a series of able publicists, most notably Beccaria and Voltaire, who revealed the incurable deficiencies of the jurisprudence of torture. (3) These writers shocked the conscience of Europe, and inspired the great monarchs of the Enlightenment to abolish torture. (4) Having abolished torture, the Europeans found themselves in a bit of a mess. There were lots of manifestly guilty criminals who could no longer be convicted, suspects whom it had previously been necessary to torture. (5) Various stopgap remedies were tried. Physical coercion is not the only form of coercion. Psychological duress could still be used (for example, isolating a suspect and talking him into a confession). The courts even went so far as to impose punishments for failure to cooperate with the investigating authorities, called variously in the German sources *Lügenstrafen, Ungehorsamstrafen, Verdachtsstrafen* (punishments for lying, for insubordination, for suspicion). (6) Ultimately, however, the Europeans realized that the Roman-canon law of proof without torture was unworkable, and it would be necessary to introduce a system of free judicial evaluation of the evidence. Therefore, the system of statutory proofs had to be abolished—in the various German states in the middle of the nineteenth century, in France somewhat earlier (during the 1790s).

Now there are two major reasons why, without any further historical evidence, this conventional account of the abolition of torture should be doubted. First, it posits as the decisive causative element the moral outrage awakened by the likes of Beccaria and Voltaire. The difficulty with that is plain. The eighteenth-century writers were advancing arguments against torture that had been known for centuries. It seems unpersuasive to say that the abolitionist critique became decisive in the eighteenth century when it had been brushed aside in the seventeenth century and before, even allowing for the changed worldview that we customarily call the Enlightenment. To say that abolition was an idea whose time had come is to beg the question, why had it come?

Second, the fairy tale would have it that the abolition of torture *preceded* the abolition of the Roman-canon system of proof, in some states by nearly a century. In view of the function of torture, this must appear highly unlikely. The Roman-canon system, we have seen, was simply unworkable without torture. How could the European states abolish torture and still continue to operate under the Roman-canon law of proof?

That is the mystery that has inspired the fairy tale. For if we look at the sources, this sequence of events seems to be confirmed: the eighteenth century abolished torture, the nineteenth century abolished the Roman-canon law of proof. Consequently, it has been assumed that the abolition of torture was not to be explained in terms of the law of proof, and the fairy tale took on its plausibility. [. . .]

[But] the Roman-canon law of proof lost its force not in the nineteenth century but in the seventeenth. A new system of proof, which was in fact free judicial evaluation of the evidence although not described as such, was developed in the legal science and the legal practice of the sixteenth and seventeenth centuries, and confirmed in the legislation of the seventeenth and eighteenth centuries.

This new system of proof developed alongside the Roman-canon system. The Roman-canon law of proof survived in form, but in the seventeenth century it lost its monopoly. Thereafter the standards of the Roman-canon law continued to be complied with for easy cases, cases where there was a voluntary confession or where there were two eyewitnesses. But for cases where there was neither, the Roman-canon standards no longer had to be complied with. That is to say, in just those cases where it had previously been necessary to use torture, it now became possible to punish the accused without meeting the evidentiary standards that had led to torture.

What happened was no less than a revolution in the law of proof. Concealed under various misleading labels, a system of free judicial evaluation of the evidence achieved subsidiary validity. This development liberated the law of Europe from its dependence on torture. Torture could be abolished in the eighteenth century because the law of proof no longer required it.

# Heresy and Torture

The use of torture was not limited of course to investigation of civil crimes. As Edward Peters explains in this brief passage from his definitive history of torture, *quaestio* was a popular means to uncover heretical religious views as well. Inquisition courts deriving their authority from the pope operated in Europe from the twelfth through the fifteenth centuries. A later tribunal, the Spanish Inquisition, established in 1480 at the behest of the Spanish monarch, was not formally abolished until 1834.

The twelfth century [. . .] witnessed new (or apparently new) forms of religious dissent. In some specific areas, notably the schools and universities, an enormous leeway in discussion and disputation was entirely permissible, but among those who were thought to have no professional qualifications for dispute, and indeed those who opposed the universally understood teaching *magisterium*[13] of the bishops and pastors, the appearance of religious dissent, whether aimed at the structure and powers of the Church or at actual dogma, was perceived by orthodox laity and clergy alike as far more dangerous than any ordinary crime, no matter how despicable. The apparent magnitude of dissent in society, the newly articulated authority of the Church and clergy, and the unique problems involved with the discovery of intellectual crime generated considerable ecclesiastical and lay concern, and for several reasons the new inquisitorial procedure (particularly in cases where accusers were hard to find, or unwilling to testify) offered an appealing approach to the problem. [. . .]

By the second quarter of the century the crime of heresy had been aligned with the crimes of treason and contumacy[14] in secular society, the heretic had been declared "infamous," and therefore the category of heresy had come to be considered identical to those crimes which in secular law led to serious criminal penalties, required the application of the full hierarchy of proofs, and demanded confession for full conviction. The ecclesiastical inquisition did not create the inquisitorial process, with torture to secure confession, but adapted it well on in the process of discovering heresy and developing a number of different means to combat it. [. . .]

Since the Christianization of the Roman Empire in the fourteenth century, a number of crimes later considered purely ecclesiastical were made public offences. Among these were certain acts committed against churches and the clergy, most forms of religious backsliding and, most important, heresy. Thus, heresy was a crime "on the books" of Roman law, and the emperor and his judges were obliged to act against it. Since secular courts had one power which church courts were for a long time denied, the power to shed blood, the Church consistently turned to lay defenders and rulers and courts in cases where clerical personnel were canonically prohibited from acting. When the crisis of religious dissent in the twelfth century became acute, many popes insisted that lay courts undertake the investigation of heresy. [. . .]

Yet, by the beginning of the thirteenth century, it seemed to popes and other churchmen that both routine Episcopal courts and lay courts were failing in their duty. With the charge to the Dominican convent at Regensburg by Gregory IX [1227–41] in 1231, the popes created a new kind of official, an investigator deriving his authority from the pope alone, from whose decision no appeal lay, and who operated according to the traditional ecclesiastical mode of inquisitorial procedure. In addition [. . .] popes from Lucius III [1181–85] to Innocent III [1198–1216] aligned heresy with other kinds of crimes: contumacy, treason and even theft, and they declared heretics infamous and prescribed other punishments common to the secular sphere, such as confiscation of goods and property, penitential exile and fines.

In addition, the most spectacular kinds of heresy, Waldensianism[15] and Catharism,[16] were discovered in those lands in which the influence of Roman law was particularly strong and in which magistrates had already spread widely the use of the inquisitorial process—in the cities of northern and central Italy and in the centre and south of France. The analogies between heretics and other types of criminals were pursued by a series of legally trained popes until the pontificate of the most able of the lawyer-popes, Innocent IV [1243–54], drew the two even closer together. In his famous decretal, *Ad extirpanda*[17] of 1252, Innocent stated that heretics were thieves and murderers of souls, and they ought to be treated no better than were literal thieves and murderers. [. . .] Although Innocent's decretal permitted the introduction of torture into the process of investigating heretics, it still did not permit clerics themselves to inflict torture. But during the next pontificate, that of Alexander IV [1254–61], the decretal *Ut negotium*[18] in 1256 permitted inquisitors to absolve each other if they had incurred any canonical irregularities in their important work. After the mid-thirteenth century, torture had a secure place in ecclesiastical inquisitorial procedure.

Yet the crime of heresy, in spite of papal analogies, did not resemble ordinary grave crimes in a way that permitted the routine application even of extraordinary procedure. It was a difficult crime to prove; although heretics were said to behave in certain ways, it was essentially an intellectual and voluntary crime; it was rooted in places in which neighbours and families knew each other and people might be reluctant to testify, or might testify for other reasons than disinterested respect for truth; witnesses to heresy might come from social ranks or have reputations which could have excluded their testimony in an ordinary criminal case; finally, heresy was a shared offence: heretics did not exist individually, and besides the salvation of the heretic's soul, inquisitors needed the names of fellow heretics. [. . .]

These circumstances, added to the fact that the early inquisitors seem not to have been particularly expert in legal procedure, [. . .] appear to have led the new judges of heresy to apply the most drastic aspects of inquisitorial procedure, often without understanding or appreciating its conventional safeguards for the defendant—indeed, perhaps, out of fear that those accused of heresy were far more dangerous to Christian society than ordinary thieves, murderers or traitors.

The early personnel of the inquisitions, then, mark one difference in ecclesiastical inquisitorial procedure. A second is their readiness to withhold the names and substantial testimony of witnesses. A third is their customary restriction of the aid of counsel for the defendant. Fourth was the admission of testimony of otherwise incompetent witnesses: interested parties, those declared infamous, those already convicted of perjury and so forth. A fifth was the relaxation of the rules of evidence and the greater weight given to some *indicia*, particularly in the area of facial expressions, behaviour, apparent nervousness, and so on. A sixth consisted of the policy of deceiving the accused by introducing spies into their cells, making promises of leniency, and developing a system of carefully designed forms of interrogation that were much broader than those prescribed in the ordinary inquisitorial procedure. A seventh was the category of degree of suspicion in which accused heretics were held; these determined the intensity of the procedure used against them. In short, the ecclesiastical inquisitors had greatly altered the character of the inquisitorial process as they had found it in the mid-thirteenth century.

# Torture of the Truth

If confession extracted by torture is the principal means of resolving guilt or innocence, two questions present themselves. What if the person being tortured is innocent? And what if a guilty person is made of stern enough stuff to resist the torment? Michel Foucault explored these questions in this passage from his *Discipline and Punish.*

One may see the functioning of judicial torture, or interrogation torture, as a torture of the truth. To begin with, judicial torture was not a way of obtaining the truth at all costs; it was not the unrestrained torture of modern interrogations; it was certainly cruel, but it was not savage. It was a regulated practice, obeying a well-defined procedure; the various stages, their duration, the instruments used, the length of ropes and the heaviness of the weights used, the number of interventions made by the interrogating magistrate, all this was, according to the different local practices, carefully codified. [. . .] Torture was a strict judicial game. And, as such, it was linked to the old tests or trials—ordeals, judicial duels, judgments of God—that were practised in accusatory procedures long before the techniques of the Inquisition. Something of the joust survived, between the judge who ordered the judicial torture and the suspect who was tortured; the "patient"—this is the term used to designate the victim—was subjected to a series of trials, graduated in severity, in which he succeeded if he "held out," or failed if he confessed. (The first degree of torture was the sight of the instruments. In the case of children or of persons over the age of seventy, one did not go beyond this stage.) But the examining magistrate did not employ torture without himself taking certain risks (apart, that is, from the danger of causing the suspect's death); he had a stake in the game, namely, the evidence that he had already collected; for the rule was that if the accused "held out" and did not confess, the magistrate was forced to drop the charges. The tortured man had then won. Hence the custom, which had been introduced for the most serious cases, of imposing judicial torture "pending proof": in this case the magistrate could continue with his investigation after the torture had failed; the suspect was not declared innocent by his resistance; but at least his victory saved him from being condemned to death. The judge kept all his cards, except the principal one. *Omnia citra mortem.*[19] Hence the recommendation often made to magistrates, in the case of the most serious crimes, not to subject to judicial torture a suspect against whom the evidence was sufficiently convincing for, if he managed to resist the torture, the magistrate would no longer have the right to pass the death sentence, which he nevertheless deserved; in such a joust, justice would be the loser: if the evidence was sufficient "to condemn such a guilty person to death," one should not "leave the conviction to chance and to the outcome of a provisional interrogation that often leads to nothing; for it is in the interest of public safety to make examples of grave, horrible and capital crimes."

Beneath an apparently determined, impatient search for truth, one finds in classical torture the regulated mechanism of an ordeal: a physical challenge that must define the truth; if the patient is guilty, the pains that it imposes are not unjust; but it is also a mark of exculpation if he is innocent. In the practice of torture, pain, confrontation and truth were bound together: they worked together on the patient's body. The search for truth through judicial torture was certainly a way of obtaining evidence—the most serious of all the confession of the guilty person; but it was also the battle, and this victory of one adversary over the other, that "produced" truth according to a ritual. In torture employed to extract a confession, there was an element of the investigation; there also was an element of the duel.

It is as if investigation and punishment had become mixed. And this is not the least paradoxical thing about it. Judicial torture was indeed defined as a way of complementing the demonstration when "there are not sufficient penalties in the trial." For it was included among the penalties; it was a penalty so grave that, in the hierarchy of punishments, the ordinance of 1760 placed it immediately after death. How can a penalty be used as a means? one was later to ask. How can one treat as a punishment what ought to be a method of demonstration? The reason is to be found in the way in which criminal justice, in the classical period, operated the production of truth. The different pieces of evidence did not constitute so many neutral elements, until such time as they could be gathered together into a single body of evidence that would bring the final certainty of guilt. Each piece of evidence aroused a particular degree of abomination. Guilt did not begin when all the evidence was gathered together; piece by piece, it was constituted by each of the elements that made it possible to recognize a guilty person. Thus a semi-proof did not leave the suspect innocent until such time as it was completed; it made him semi-guilty; slight evidence of a serious crime marked someone as slightly criminal. In short, penal demonstration did not obey a dualistic system: true or false; but a principle of continuous gradation; a degree reached in the demonstration already formed a degree of guilt and consequently involved a degree of punishment. The suspect, as such, always deserved a certain punishment; one could not be the object of suspicion and be completely innocent. Suspicion implied an element of demonstration as regards the judge, the mark of a certain degree of guilt as regards the suspect and a limited form of penalty as regards punishment. A suspect, who remained a suspect, was not for all that declared innocent, but was partially punished. When one reached a certain degree of presumption, one could then legitimately bring into play a practice that had a dual role: to begin the punishment in pursuance of the information already collected and to make use of this first stage of punishment in order to extort the truth that was still missing. In the eighteenth century, judicial torture functioned in that strange economy in which the ritual that produced the truth went side by side with the ritual that imposed the punishment. The body interrogated in torture constituted the point of application of the punishment and the locus of extortion of the truth. And just as presumption was inseparably an element in the investigation and a fragment of guilt, the regulated pain involved in judicial torture was a means both of punishment and of investigation.

# Abolition

In 1734 Sweden became the first country in Europe to abolish most forms of torture. Just a few years later Prussia became the first to do away with all of them. Criticism of the torture of alleged witches and heretics had begun to emerge as early as the sixteenth century and a gradual shift away from judicial torture occurred in the seventeenth century as alternative forms of punishment, short of death or torment, such as the workhouse or banishment (transportation) to distant lands, developed. Judges acquired options other than torture with which to punish those they suspected of being guilty but from whom they had no confession. These new forms of punishment made judicial torture something of a moot point.[20]

The most influential arguments against the use of torture arose out of the thought of the Enlightenment. The eighteenth century saw a wholesale attack upon orthodoxy and "superstition" and the cruelty that had been carried out in their name. Michel Foucault has noted in particular the growing repulsion at public displays of brutality. "Punishment had gradually ceased to be a spectacle," he wrote. "It was as if the punishment was thought to equal, if not exceed, in savagery the crime itself . . . [and] to reverse roles at the last moment, to make the tortured criminal an object of pity and admiration."[21]

Two of the most eloquent and influential opponents of torture were Voltaire and the Italian economist Cesare Beccaria, whose 1764 "An Essay on Crimes and Punishments" was translated immediately into French and English. Voltaire called it a plea "in behalf of reason and humanity"—high praise considering that Voltaire, not one to tolerate rivals readily, himself published that same year his own commentary, "On Torture and Capital Punishment," in his *Philosophical Dictionary*. Both are excerpted below.

# Crimes and Punishments

A cruelty consecrated among most nations by custom is the torture of the accused during his trial, on the pretext of compelling him to confess his crime, of clearing up contradictions in his statements, of discovering his accomplices, of purging him in some metaphysical and incomprehensible way from infamy, or finally of finding out other crimes of which he may possibly be guilty, but of which he is not accused.

A man cannot be called *guilty* before sentence has been passed on him by a judge, nor can society deprive him of its protection till it has been decided that he has broken the condition on which it was granted. What, then, is that right but one of mere might by which a judge is empowered to inflict a punishment on a citizen whilst his guilt or innocence are still undetermined? The following dilemma is no new one: either the crime is certain or uncertain; if certain, no *other* punishment is suitable for it than that affixed to it by law; and torture is useless, for the same reason that the criminal's confession is useless. If it is uncertain it is wrong to torture an innocent person, such as the law adjudges him to be, whose crimes are not yet proved.

What is the political object of punishments? The intimidation of other men. But what shall we say of the secret and private tortures which the tyranny of custom exercises alike upon the guilty and the innocent? It is important, indeed, that no open crime shall pass unpunished; but the public exposure of a criminal whose crime was hidden in darkness is utterly useless. An evil that has been done and cannot be undone can only be punished by civil society insofar as it may affect others with the hope of impunity. If it be true that there are a greater number of men who either from fear or virtue respect the laws than of those who transgress them, the risk of torturing an innocent man should be estimated according to the probability that any man will have been more likely, other things being equal, to have respected than to have despised the laws.

But I say in addition: it is to seek to confound all the relations of things to require a man to be at the same time accuser and accused, to make pain the crucible of truth, as if the test of it lay in the muscles and sinews of an unfortunate wretch. The law which ordains the use of torture is a law which says to men: "Resist pain; and if Nature has created in you an inextinguishable self-love, if she has given you an inalienable right of self-defense, I create in you a totally contrary affection, namely, an heroic self-hatred, and I command you to accuse yourselves, and to speak the truth between the laceration of your muscles and the dislocation of your bones."

This infamous crucible of truth is a still-existing monument of that prim-itive and savage legal system which called trials by fire and boiling water, or the accidental decisions of combat, *judgments of God*, as if the rings of the eternal chain in the control of the First Cause must at every moment be disarranged and put out for the petty institutions of mankind. The only difference between torture and the trial by fire and water is that the result of the former seems to depend on the will of the accused, and the other two on a fact which is purely physical and extrinsic to the sufferer; but the difference is only apparent, not real. The avowal of truth under tortures and agonies is as little free as was in those times the prevention without fraud of the usual effects of fire and boiling water. Every act of our will is ever proportioned to the force of the sensible impression which causes it, and the sensibility of every man is limited. Hence the impres-sion produced by pain may be so intense as to occupy a man's entire sen-sibility and leave him no other liberty than the choice of the shortest way of escape, for the present moment, from his penalty. Under such circum-stances the answer of the accused is as inevitable as the impressions pro-duced by fire and water; and the innocent man who is sensitive will declare himself guilty, when by so doing he hopes to bring his agonies to an end. All the difference between guilt and innocence is lost by virtue of the very means which they profess to employ for its discovery.

Torture is a certain method for the acquittal of robust villains and for the condemnation of innocent but feeble men. See the fatal drawbacks of the pretended test of truth—a test, indeed, that is worthy of cannibals; a test which the Romans, barbarous as they too were in many respects, reserved for slaves alone, the victims of their fierce and too highly lauded virtue. Of two men, equally innocent or equally guilty, the robust and courageous will be acquitted, the weak and the timid will be condemned, by virtue of the following exact train of reasoning on the part of the judge: "I as judge had to find you guilty of such and such a crime; you, A B, have by your physical strength been able to resist pain, and therefore I acquit you; you, C D, in your weakness have yielded to it; therefore I condemn you. I feel that a confession extorted amid torments can have no force, but I will torture you afresh unless you corroborate what you have now confessed."

# Torture and Capital Punishment

Although there are a few articles of jurisprudence in these honest alpha-betical reflections, a word must be said concerning torture, otherwise, called the *question*. It is a strange manner of questioning men. It was not invented, however, out of idle curiosity; there is every likelihood that this part of our legislation owes its origin to a highway robber. Most of these gentlemen still are accustomed to squeeze thumbs, burn feet and question by other torments those who refuse to tell them where they have put their money.

When conquerors had succeeded these thieves, they found the invention very useful to their interests: they put it to use when they suspected that anyone opposed them with certain evil designs, such, for instance, as the desire to be free; that was a crime of high treason against God and man. They wanted to know the accomplices; and to accomplish this, they subjected to the suffering of a thousand deaths those whom they suspected, because according to the jurisprudence of these early heroes, whoever was suspected merely of entertaining against them any slightly disrespectful thought was worthy of death. The moment that anyone has thus merited death, it matters little that terrible torments are added for several days, and even for several weeks, a practice which smacks somewhat of the Divinity. Providence sometimes puts us to the torture by means of stone, gravel, gout, scurvy, leprosy, pox of both varieties, excruciating bowel pains, nervous convulsions, and other executioners of providential vengeance.

Now as the early despots were, by the admission of all their courtiers, images of Divinity, they imitated it as much as they could. [. . .]

The French who are considered, I do not know why, a very humane people are astonished that the English, who had the inhumanity to take all of Canada from us, have given up the pleasure of putting the question.

When the Chevalier de la Barre, grandson of a lieutenant-general in the king's service, a young man of great intelligence and much promise, but possessing all the thoughtlessness of unbridled youth, was convicted of having sung impious songs and even of having passed in front of a procession of Capuchins[22] without taking off his hat, the judges of Abbeville, men comparable to the Roman Senators, ordered not only that his tongue should be torn out, his hand cut off and his body burned by slow fire; but they applied torture to him to find out how many songs he had sung and how many processions he had seen pass with his hat on his head.

It was not in the thirteenth nor the fourteenth century that this adventure took place; it was in the eighteenth. Foreign nations judge France by its plays, novels and pretty poetry; by its opera girls, who are very gentle of manner; by its opera dancers, who are graceful; by Mlle. Clarion[23] who recites her lines in a ravishing manner. They do not know that there is no nation more fundamentally cruel than the French.

The Russians were considered barbarians in 1700, and it is now only 1769; an Empress[24] has just given to that vast state laws which would honor Minos, Numa and Solon,[25] if they had been intelligent enough to invent them. The most remarkable is universal tolerance; the next is the abolition of torture. Justice and humanity guided her pen: She has reformed everything. Woe unto the nation which, though long civilized is still led by ancient atrocious customs! "Why should we change our jurisprudence?" we say. "Europe uses our cooks, our tailors and winemakers; therefore our laws are good."

# Classical and Contemporary Torture

Despite the legal prohibitions on torture virtually everywhere in the world, the phenomenon is hardly unknown today, as many of the readings in other chapters of this book make clear. Moreover, much contemporary torture lacks even the rationalization provided in ancient and medieval times: that it was a means to a greater end, an instrument by which to determine responsibility for criminal acts. Instead, torture today is often political or gratuitous in nature. Malcolm D. Evans and Rod Morgan provide a concise summary of the differences between contemporary torture and "classical" torture in this selection from *Preventing Torture*.

How are we to characterize torture in the late twentieth century? How does it differ from the torture of former times?

First, torture has been used and is used by the state for a variety of purposes. Though some of the aims that inform torture today are identical to those of the torturers of the ancient world, others are different and the balance of aims appears to have shifted. When torture is used in the service of terror, for example—and this is very much a feature of the modern totalitarian state—the purpose appears to be as much to send out a message to the population generally as to elicit a response from the individual victim.

Secondly, torture is intimately bound up with punishment. [. . .] That close legal connection [between torture and judicial procedure] has in recent times been largely severed. [. . .] Whatever the law books may say, desert is not a concept only reserved for those persons who stand formally convicted. Police investigators claim to "know" who the guilty are and in some jurisdictions feel they have a mandate—indeed are expected by the people—to dispense summary justice, albeit in the guise of criminal investigation.

Thirdly, and closely connected with the preceding point, the use of torture is generally status-related. In Ancient Greece and Rome the original doctrine was that only slaves or foreigners could be tortured, or persons whose suspected crimes were so heinous that they were of little worth, scarcely human. In the United States [. . .] African-Americans were particularly vulnerable to the worst forms of the "third degree," especially in the Southern States where racism borne of slavery was a powerful force. In post-Revolutionary Russia, counter-revolutionaries—persons suffering from false consciousness—were vulnerable. Under fascism, in Hitler's Germany from the beginning and in Italy under Mussolini from 1938, those not considered racially pure were vulnerable. In Algeria French soldiers were taught not to think of Arabs as humans. In South Africa the same doctrine prevailed during the *apartheid* years. To torture [. . .] is to deny humanity, to reduce a person to being merely a body, a bundle of "muscles and sinews" in Beccaria's phrase, a person without voice. It follows that when those responsible for certain crimes are casually described as "animals" or "beasts," we should beware: for these terms are assigned to those outcasts, or lesser beings, to whom, in the eyes of some, anything may morally be done.

Fourthly, the use and nature of torture is closely related to the changing character of the state and the relationship of citizens to the state. This is not just a question of citizens' rights, but of ideology. It is also a question of power. In the pre-industrial world the body of the accused was literally placed at the disposal of the master, the lord, or the sovereign but when, during the industrial revolution, the modern state emerged with its accompanying doctrines of citizens' rights and the social contract, submission so corporeal and seemingly capricious was deemed inappropriate. The Age of Reason involved the formation of rule-governed discipline the locus of which was the mind rather than the body of the accused. It was now the trial rather than the initial examination and the punishment which became the ritual focus. In the twentieth century, however, states have accrued powers and technologies of control undreamt of in the eighteenth century. This has opened up vistas of exploitation by the state for which the founders of liberal state-constitutions were unprepared. But those same technologies have enabled weak and liberal states to be challenged in an unprecedented fashion. And, as we have seen from the examples of Algeria, Northern Ireland, and Israel/Palestine, much contemporary torture is integral to the process whereby the authority of the state is contested. States and counter-states vie for power. The overweening state may be used as a mechanism to oppress its citizens, but equally, organised groups—ideological, ethnic, religious, linguistic, tribal, or regionally based—may also employ torture as part of a strategy of terror in their bids for state power. [. . .]

[W]e need to summarize how torture in the post-industrial world differs from that in the ancient and pre-industrial world.

First, torture used to be a legitimate judicial procedure. We shall call this classical torture. Torture was not used everywhere, in all periods, and in all jurisdictions. But until the Enlightenment, despite widespread doubts about its reliability, judicial torture was a generally approved method for eliciting information from persons against whom there were well-founded suspicions that either they or their associates were guilty of crimes of thought or deed, secular or religious. This is no longer the case. Today torture is nowhere regarded, officially at least, as a legitimate judicial procedure for eliciting the truth. Constitutions outlaw the practice. The criminal law generally punishes it. The courts are almost everywhere required to exclude evidence collected by means of pressure generally considered to render that evidence unsafe. Torture is so excoriated that allegations that it has been used are generally denied in the most vigorous terms.

This is generally the official legal position. Just beneath the surface, however, there is clearly a view, prevalent in many jurisdictions among security and police personnel, that torture, or means of physical or psychological pressure that we may term *near-torture,* may have to be resorted to in certain circumstances. These circumstances are held to be abnormal and may involve a degree of desperation on the part of the security forces, as when, for example, the integrity of the state, or public safety, is said to be seriously threatened by offenders who are highly organized and engaged in activities involving grave harm (terrorism and drug trafficking, for example) or when individuals, particularly hardened repeat offenders, are suspected of very serious offences exciting public alarm. In these circumstances the pressure on the security services to get "results" is great and, in the short term at least, the security services may feel that they are unable to succeed without resort to methods going beyond the "normal," legal, and officially approved.

In most jurisdictions politicians are from time to time exhorted by security and police personnel to give their services room for manoeuvre such that pressure can more effectively be brought to bear on these classes of allegedly abnormal suspects. The room for manoeuvre sought typically involves additional time to question suspects before the judicial authorities are brought into play. It also involves the exclusion from places of detention—exclusion justified on grounds of security—of other persons and agencies (lawyers, monitors, personal visitors) and the removal of any obligation to divulge information to third persons as to the nature or progress of the investigation.

Whatever rules govern the room for manoeuvre granted to the security services, they are likely to be exceeded whenever the prevailing "police culture" judges it necessary and morally justified; what one sociologist of the police has termed the "law of inevitable increment—whatever powers the police have they will exceed by a given margin." If corners are cut and pressures applied, they will subsequently be denied and in some jurisdictions the authorities, executive and judicial, may turn a Nelsonian blind eye[26] to these "noble cause" excesses. In jurisdictions where such tolerance by the authorities is generally displayed, or where effective mechanisms for judicial and independent scrutiny of police procedure are lacking, it is probable that short cuts will be taken and pressures applied to suspects generally. A culture of police violence may develop, particularly in environments where police resources are poor, police training is rudimentary, where the police enjoy little public regard, and where their professional culture is largely undeveloped. Moreover, in jurisdictions without serious pretensions to democracy and public accountability the security forces may politically be cultivated as an instrument of the state entirely subservient to the interests of the ruling political elite. In such jurisdictions more cynical use is likely to be made of the legal prohibition of torture. The prohibition may be no more than a legal or constitutional fig-leaf.

The second distinction, therefore, between the classical and modern practice of torture is that whereas formerly torture was an avowed and open practice, it is now secret and denied. In ancient times and in the Roman-canonical tradition the practice of torture may have been subject to doubt but there was no reason to be ashamed of its use. It was a normal and acknowledged aspect of procedure. The torturer may have plied his trade in the darkest recesses of forbidding dungeons, but where that was the case, it was an integral part of the torture process, designed, like the instruments of torture themselves, to be part of the menace. That a suspect should be "put to the question" was a public decision and the answers given following torture were formally recorded in documents designed to be made public.

This is no longer the case. Torture is not acknowledged. The instruments of torture are hidden and their existence disclaimed. Places of torture are inaccessible, not to increase the terror—though they do of course serve that purpose, and the physical and social isolation of victims is part of the design—but because they *may not* be known. What is done may not be seen or heard. There must be no spectators, no witnesses. Indeed, the most potent threat in the hands of the contemporary torturer is that: "No one will hear your cry. No one knows that you are here. No one cares whether you live or die. No one will ever know."—a threat that the power of the secretive state can all too often make true. In states employing terror as a systematic instrument of political power, the reputation that particular police locations may have, and the fate of those who enter them, may become an integral part of the process of terror. The secrecy surrounding reputed places of torture in totalitarian states becomes a manifestation of the invincibility of state control. But, generally speaking, the reality will be denied. Terror is served by rumour, uncertainty, and insecurity—the threat of an unknown menace. Torture may be the preamble to extra-judicial execution or disappearance, the torture chamber the ante-room to a void.

Thirdly, because classical torture was an acknowledged judicial process it was also rule-governed. There was a jurisprudence of torture. The rules may not always have been followed, but they were there to be appealed to. The process could legally be challenged. And because the use of torture was open and rule-governed the wisdom and morality of employing torture could be and was publicly debated. In ancient Greece and Rome, and again during the Middle Ages, leading commentators discussed the rules and wisdom of torture. They questioned the rules or made recommendations as to their judicial interpretation. This is no longer the case. The orthodoxy of human rights, combined with political hypocrisy, has made torture and its discussion taboo, except by way of simple condemnation. The culture of denial and secrecy has driven the practical rationale for and rationalization of torture underground. It cannot realistically be discussed because it is said that there is nothing to discuss. Allegations of torture are generally dismissed as propagandist disinformation. Practically no one defends torture. Torture, like sin, is not something to which anyone owns up. Torture is generally held to be an issue only in far-off places, where political regimes conspicuously not members of the civilized club are said to be more or less immune to democratic or human rights reasoning. Or it is said to be a problem in precariously balanced polities where it may not be wise too robustly to pursue a human rights critique on the grounds that greater political instability may be the consequence. Or, as in most developed democracies, torture is said not to be a structural issue, only the product of the occasional rotten apple in an otherwise clean law enforcement barrel. Likewise the relationship between developed and the developing economies is generally judged irrelevant. Responsibility lies elsewhere. There is virtually no debate—only orthodox arms-length condemnation.

This is the most remarkable aspect of the Israeli Landau Commission:[27] that it existed. That the issue of torture or near-torture was discussed and at least part of that discussion published. Yet even in the case of Israel the issue was not fully and openly discussed. The evidence made available to the Landau Commission was not publicly disclosed. There was no independent expert appraisal of the evidence provided to the Commission by the security services. The regulatory code employed by the security services for the conduct of interrogation of terrorist suspects was not revealed, and the practical recommendations of the Landau Commission itself were kept secret. And in any case, as the Commission repeatedly emphasized, that which was being discussed and condoned was not torture, only a process euphemistically termed "moderate physical pressure," designed to break down the resistance of suspects, but neither inhuman nor degrading.

It is the culture of denial and the absence of debate that makes contemporary as opposed to classical torture the more difficult to combat. Torture in the late twentieth century is a will-o'-the-wisp. In the same way that the abolition of capital punishment was made more difficult to achieve once executions were removed from the public domain—such that civic sensibilities were no longer directly engaged—so torture now is hidden from sight and comment. There is no torture discourse. Torture is the imaginary product of radical dissent. It is the outcome of carefully engineered propaganda designed to discredit the state. It is the child of rumour and disinformation or, more charitably, misinformation. It is the vindictive allegation of those who—morally, politically, and legally—are said not to deserve an audience or to be believed.

All of which means that torture or near-torture can no longer easily be regulated. Because it cannot be acknowledged, torture nowadays lies within the discretionary power of those agents of the state the security-sensitivity of whose work is said to warrant more or less unaccountable and privileged secret space. It is for this reason, paradoxically, that contemporary torture may be unrestrained and may involve any number of methods. Paradoxical because, prompted by the fearsome instruments of torture preserved in our museums, we have come to think of torture in the classical period as unrestrainedly savage. But it was not so. It was undoubtedly cruel. It could involve seemingly unendurable pain. But it was not savage in the sense of being untamedly ferocious: it was a carefully-regulated practice. Today there can be no proper regulation of the practice which may be restrained only by the personal sensibility of the torturers.

It follows also that the use of torture can no longer easily be discovered, let alone monitored. Nor can the justice and reasonableness of its application be gauged, because justice and reasonableness are no longer deemed appropriate terms to use in relation to torture. Thus torture may be applied arbitrarily, indiscriminately, or disproportionately, without cause that any external observer might judge reasonable. For the classical jurisprudential discourse of torture is banned, even if the situations that continue to give rise to the thoughts and the practices are not. And the discourse may not be permitted to re-emerge, because to do so would legitimate that which is officially deemed illegitimate. An exercise like the Landau Commission is unlikely to be repeated.

Fourthly, it follows that the methods of torture have generally changed. The technology of contemporary torture has largely been removed from the medieval museum of horrors. It generally lies more in the psychological manipulation of feelings of powerlessness and despair than the physical tearing of bodies. It leaves few visible marks. Because torture must be and is denied, it must be deniable.

Classical torture, because it was an acknowledged rule-governed judicial process, was a ritualistic procedure. The instruments of torture were explicitly designed for the task: an assault on the body to extract the essence of the truth that lay therein. It was hoped that the mere sight of the instruments, terrifying and functionally unmistakable, and the location where they were to be applied, often a dedicated and planned environment, would suffice. Proportionate bodily pain, swiftly imposed—clamping or searing the flesh, stretching the muscles or sinews—was the avowed purpose of the exercise. Further, though the rules discouraged modes of torture which thereafter rendered the body useless, the fundamental illogicality of this aspect of the process made practitioners careless of the admonition. But there was no question of hiding the process of torture, of leaving the body unmarked or of considering the more subtle consequences of designedly painful experience.

Nowadays torture remains typically crude and [. . .] the purpose of much torture remains narrowly instrumental—to gain information or force an admission of guilt—the focus being where it always has been: on the body, the nerve pathways, as a way into the head. But because torture is no longer judicially approved, because it must be hidden and denied, torture is no longer conspicuously ritualistic. Specific and unambiguous instruments of torture are generally avoided, unless the torture is to be conducted in environments without risk of intrusion by potentially critical appraisers, a facility seldom available in democratic jurisdictions or states fully participating in the burgeoning world of international inspection. Today, therefore, the means of torture are usually mundane and familiar: everyday objects, ambiguous, inconspicuous, unobjectionable. When blows from fists or feet will not suffice, standard handcuffs will secure the victim, a telephone directory may be used to strike the head, a conventional police baton used to beat the soles of the feet, or a supermarket plastic bag employed to cover the face. These methods can be applied anywhere, in cells or corridors, storerooms, conventional police offices, or station washrooms. They may even be used away from designated police sites: arrestees may be taken into the country, hung from a tree, or beaten on a piece of waste ground, their detention unrecorded, their contact with the security forces leaving no paper trace. Many methods, moreover, can be used so as to leave few or no marks on the body, or marks the origins of which are ambiguous, easily disclaimed, or said to have been acquired legitimately—the product of a scuffle when the suspect resisted arrest or injuries self-inflicted by malevolent complainants. Moreover, the cries of victims can be drowned by a portable radio or television, the presence of which is said to be for the detainees' entertainment or comfort.

Even more difficult to discern and prove after the event are those favoured psychological tactics designed to wear suspects down: deprivation of sleep, threats against family or loved ones, incessant interrogative harassment, petty humiliations, disorienting noise, bright lights, blindfolding or hooding, low or high cell temperatures, prolonged isolation in dark or otherwise sensory deprived circumstances, use of physically stressful constant standing or crouching while handcuffed to a pipe or radiator. These stresses can be made to appear almost incidental to the fact of legal custody itself. If the custody is *incommunicado*, a provision often permitted under emergency anti-terrorist or anti-organized-crime legislation, then the incremental piling of one psychological assault upon another can be achieved without resort to cruder more immediate visceral methods leaving their tell-tale somatic traces.

Fifthly, and finally, whereas prior to the development of the modern state torture was a specific, discrete, relatively well-defined process involving the individual suspect and the judicial authority, it is nowadays more likely to comprise merely one tactic in the overarching politics of state control and organized counter-state opposition. In this context it is not so much the individual who is being worked on by the torturer but rather the member of a group, the purpose of the torture being as much to break the ring or send a message to a community, constituency, or cadre. The torture may be part of a seamless web of police surveillance and intelligence gathering, group harassment and penetration or, in extreme cases, terror—extra-judicial execution and disappearance. Even when no information is elicited, it may be said that it was forthcoming, the purpose being to prise open tight-knit groups and sow seeds of mistrust. Similar tactics may be employed against agents of the state by opposition groups, or they may be deployed among whole communities whose loyalties are divided and whose support base is being sought, if necessary through processes of intimidation. Where these conditions prevail torture is no longer a narrowly instrumental individual process. It is a form of governance, an integral part of government through terror. In these circumstances the potency of torture, wherever it is used widely, lies as much in its anticipation as in its reality. One never knows when the knock on the door may come. In this form torture can be seen in its most insidious form, subversive of democratic participation and political organization *per se*, the most fundamental enemy of civil society.

# Chapter II
# Being Tortured

Fortunately the vast majority of us will never experience torture firsthand. We can imagine something of what it is like from the occasions we have each endured pain—that is the starting point of the moral imagination— but there is far more to torture than the experience of pain. The readings in this chapter help us come just a bit closer to understanding what it is like to undergo torture—both physical and psychological. Some of the excerpts are fairly straightforward descriptions of what human beings have the capacity to do to each other. Others elucidate the consciousness that emerges under such extreme circumstances. And all of them take our breath away.

# Beaten

The most common form of torture is the straightforward beating. If a victim is lucky, the torturer will use his fists. But more frequently he employs some instrument. In the case Eric Lomax describes (and experienced) below, it is pick-helves, the wooden handles of pick-axes. Lomax was a British Signals Officer in World War II taken prisoner by the Japanese in the fall of Singapore and forced to work on the Burma Siam Railway. His story comes from his book, *The Railway Man*. Note that before they were beaten, Lomax and his comrades were subjected to an even simpler form of torture—being forced to stand for twelve hours in the hot sun, anticipating all the while some gruesome punishment to come.

The guards conducted the five of us to the main guardroom where we were brusquely ordered to stand to attention, a few feet in front of the building and well away from any shade or protection from the sun. [. . .]

The time was ten o'clock in the morning.

The morning and afternoon dragged on, every minute almost an hour. When you are forced to stand stiffly to attention in a blazing hot sun you have nothing to do but think; yet thought is a process that should be directed by the will, and under extreme stress thoughts spin away on their own, racing faster and faster like a machine out of control, one that has lost the touch of a human hand.

There was nothing we could do about it now: we stood there, knowing it was coming. The wretched little guardroom was no bigger than a domestic living room, and the few guards sprawling inside it or on guard behind us controlled the lives of several hundred men. So few to hold so many.

We stood for twelve hours with our backs to that hut. The nerves and flesh of the back become terribly sensitive and vulnerable when turned to an enemy. At any moment I expected to feel a rifle-butt on my spine, a bayonet thrust between my shoulder-blades. All we heard was their talk, their occasional rough laughter.

The intense heat of the sun, the irritation of flies and mosquitoes feeding on sweat, itching skin, the painful contraction of eyes against the light and even the fear of violent death had been superseded by the evening by the even more powerful sensation of a burning thirst. They gave us nothing to drink all day, but they allowed us occasionally to go to the latrine. On one of these visits I regretfully disposed of my diary. The flimsy pages covered with neat notes on books, on grammar, on lists of collectible stamps fluttered into the stinking trench.

As dusk fell the five of us were moved into a closer and more compact group in front of the guardroom. The darkness came on with singular abruptness. We were lit by a weak light from behind us in the guardroom. A time signal was heard as a noisy party of Japanese and Koreans approached through the dark from the direction of the camp offices. They looked like NCOs,[1] their uniforms disheveled, one or two of them unsteady on their feet. All of them carried pick-helves. They stopped to talk to the guards, as though exchanging ideas about what to do with us.

Major Smith was called out in front of our line, and told to raise his arms right up over his head. His tall, gaunt figure, his thin arms held out like a scarecrow's, looked terribly weak and pitiful. He stood there on the edge of the circle of light. I thought for a moment—a last gasp of hope— that this was the beginning of an advanced form of their endless standing to attention. A hefty Japanese sergeant moved into position, lifted his pick-handle, and delivered a blow across Smith's back that would have laid out a bull. It knocked him down, but he was trodden on and kicked back into an upright position. The same guard hit him again, hard. All the thugs now set to in earnest. Soon little could be seen but the rise and fall of pick-helves above the heads of the group and there were sickening thuds as blows went home on the squirming, kicking body, periodically pulled back on to its feet only to be knocked down again. Bill Smith cried out repeatedly that he was fifty years of age, appealing for mercy, but to no avail. The group of attackers seemed to move in concert with their crawling, bloodied victim into the darkness beyond the range of the miserable lighting from the guardroom, but the noises of wood on flesh continued to reach us from the dark of the parade ground.

They were using pickaxe-shafts: like solid, British Army issue handles, and perhaps that is indeed what they were. The guards behind us did not move. There was no expectation that we ourselves would move, intervene, run away: merely the slack, contemptuous knowledge that we were trapped. That first blow: like a labourer getting into the rhythm of his job, then the others joining in, a confused percussive crescendo of slaps and thuds on flesh and bone. They kept kicking him, getting him up, putting him down—until he stopped moving altogether, unconscious or dead, I could not tell. Nor could I tell how long it all took. How does one measure such time? Blows had replaced the normal empty seconds of time passing, but I think it took about forty minutes to get him to lie still.

The gang came back out of the night. My special friend Morton Mackay was called forward. I was next in line. As they started on Mackay and the rain of fearful blows commenced I saw to the side another group of guards pushing a stumbling and shattered figure back towards the guardhouse. Smith was still alive; he was allowed to drop in a heap in the ditch beside the entrance.

Mackay went down roaring like a lion, only to be kicked up again; within a matter of minutes he was driven into the semi-darkness and out of the range of the lights, surrounded by the flailing pick-helves which rose and fell ceaselessly. I remember thinking that in the bad light they looked like the blades of a windmill, so relentless was their action. In due course Mackay's body was dragged along and dumped beside Smith's in the ditch.

The moments while I was waiting my turn were the worst of my life. The expectation is indescribable; a childhood story of Protestant martyrs watching friends die in agony on the rack flashed through my mind. To have to witness the torture of others and to see the preparations for the attack on one's own body is a punishment in itself, especially when there is no escape. This experience is the beginning of a form of insanity.

Then me. It must have been about midnight. I took off my spectacles and my watch carefully, turned and laid them down on the table behind me in the guardroom. It was almost as if I was preparing to go into a swimming-pool, so careful was the gesture of folding them and laying them down. I must have had to take a couple of steps backward to perform this neat unconscious manoeuvre. None of the guards made a move or said a word. Perhaps they were too surprised.

I was called forward. I stood to attention. They stood facing me, breathing heavily. There was a pause. It seemed to drag on for minutes. Then I went down with a blow that shook every bone, and which released a sensation of scorching liquid pain which seared through my entire body. Sudden blows struck me all over. I felt myself plunging downwards into an abyss with tremendous flashes of solid light which burned and agonized. I could identify the periodic stamping of boots on the back of my head, crunching my face into the gravel; the crack of bones snapping; my teeth breaking; and my own involuntary attempts to respond to deep vicious kicks and to regain an upright position, only to be thrown to the ground once more.

At one point I realized that my hips were being damaged and I remember looking up and seeing the pick-helves coming down towards my hips, and putting my arms in the way to deflect the blows. This seemed only to focus the clubs on my arms and hands. I remember the actual blow that broke my wrist. It fell right across it, with a terrible pain of delicate bones being crushed. Yet the worst pain came from the pounding on my pelvic bones and the base of my spine. I think they tried to smash my hips. My whole trunk was brutally defined for me, like having my skeleton etched out in pain.

It went on and on. I could not measure the time it took. There are some things that you cannot measure in time, and this is one of them. Absurdly, the comparison that often comes to my mind is that torture was indeed like an awful job interview: it compresses time strangely, and at the end of it you cannot tell whether it has lasted five minutes or an hour.

I do know that I thought I was dying. I have never forgotten, from that moment onwards, crying out "Jesus," crying out for help, the utter despair of helplessness. I rolled into a deep ditch of foul stagnant water which, in the second or two before consciousness was finally extinguished, flowed over me with the freshness of a pure and sweet spring.

# Chapter II, Reading 2
# Political Torture

We expect war to be brutal, despite all the attempts to civilize it through treaties and conventions. But much torture is inflicted in civilian political contexts as well. The South African system of apartheid (1948–early 1990s), for example, under which the races were separated and the black majority subjected to severe social, economic, and political repression, featured widespread violence and systematic torture by the state. In this passage from *And Night Fell: Memoirs of a Political Prisoner in South Africa*, Molefe Pheto recounts the beatings that accompanied his interrogation by police over the course of the 281 days he spent in a South African prison. For 271 of those days he was held in solitary confinement. He was never charged with a crime.

"Why do you travel to Botswana so much? What do you want therre?"[2]

This time it was Tiny van Niekerk.[3] There were three of them in the room, Colonel Visser and Captain Magoro being the other two. I told van Niekerk that I was descended from Botswana, and that I visited my relations there, but I knew he suspected other things. Blacks criss-crossing the borders of South Africa were suspect. They could be linking up with exiles in these independent countries for advancement of their political work. It was worse in my case, as I had traveled in Europe before. But I also told him that in my work for MDALI[4] I had to travel to collect enough work for exhibiting at our art festivals.

"Why don't you damn stay therre if you have yourr rrelations therre? I'll tell you," he paused. "South Afrrika is too good forr you. You would starrve to death therre. That's why you won't go."

Van Niekerk went on as though he would never stop, saying a lot that hurt me because I could not reply and wrenching my heart out with all those comparisons we have heard from their babbling politicians about how South Africa was the best country for Black people in the whole world: how well we Blacks were treated, having so much done for us there, how well educated we were, how the wages received by Black people were better than anywhere in Africa, the housing schemes and so forth.

I was hurt and I wanted to tell him that he was talking a lot of rubbish. To tell him that at that very moment he and his colleagues and their laws had me in detention against my will, through laws made by White men only. That I had not seen my family since his friend Visser had decreed that I be detained, and that I wished to see my family as I was worried about their welfare. Could he, van Niekerk, tell the whole world that every morning I was brought up from the cells, kept standing from nine till three in the afternoon, asked questions which I answered to the best of my ability, yet got nowhere near being released to rejoin my family and community? That during the days I had been in detention I smelled from lack of washing facilities, yet I could hear other prisoners not far from my cell splashing water during their bath-time; that I already had bugs sucking my blood, thirteen of which I had only last night killed after searching for them on my body and clothes, killing them by putting the damn things on the cement floor before pressing them to their death with my thumbnail! Yet I was supposed to LOVE this South Africa, LOVE it?

My throat was hot. My eyes were swimming in a stream of burning tears which I could feel about to burst down my cheeks. I knew that I could not take the insults any more. Eventually, I decided to tell van Niekerk and his friends what I felt.

"I would have no problems in Bots . . . "

Van Niekerk did not allow me to finish. I was lifted off the floor by one of the hardest, quickest punches, the heaviest too, that I had ever taken on my jaw. The force of it threw me a little distance from the trio, under a table. Its sudden impact blinded me for a moment. Blood immediately trickled from the corner of my lip. I had sustained a cut on the inside bottom lip. Because I did not have a handkerchief to wipe my blood with, I decided to swallow it. I felt no pain then. Only surprise and fright.

Colonel Visser did not move an inch, but Magoro had already jumped into action like an uncoiled spring that had been long suppressed. It seemed that what they were then doing was something they had done many times before. I stood up by sheer instinct. Before I could get on my haunches, I saw his towering legs near the region of my face. As I raised my eyes to take in this whole structure of massive humanity in front of me, another punch made a fat-fisted, soft-thudded landing on my cheek bone, returning me to the position I had just risen from.

"Stand up, you bastarrd. Stand up!" His big voice bellowed like his two heavy punches. My head felt so heavy I thought I would not be able to raise it again.

"Face that way. You think you arre a herro. You like being beaten up!"

I turned a little, afraid of this huge man behind me, seeing Magoro manoeuvring for a shot at me too.

"Face that way!" van Niekerk boomed again with impatience. I must have been slow.

As I did, van Niekerk smashed me on the neck and on my right ear again.

"Tell us. What do you want in Botswana? What is MDALI?"

Interspersed with the questions, his blows kept on raining incessantly. When I tried to turn my face towards this man who was assaulting me, he would bellow that I should turn my face away from him so that I should not see his blows coming my way. Sometimes the force of the punches turned me round.

"*Ya. Ek wil alles hoor van daai MDALI.*"[5] (Yes. I want to hear everything about that MDALI.)

"MDALI is . . . "

Whack! Bam! I fell to the floor again.

"Up, herro!" I tried to rise. Blast! Thud! Swoosh! As he swung his leg and kicked me, I groaned.

"Pick him up. Stand up!"

Another attempt to stand on my legs. But he was back on me before I had come half-way up. Slam!

"What is MDALI?"

"MDALI is . . . "

Whop! I heard the sound of something like a stick through the air before it found its mark on my neck. It would appear that during questions and punches he had picked up something to hit me with. Perhaps his knuckles had been hurt.

"Com'on, MDALI . . . "

When will it ever end? Are they never going to tire, this 300-pound man and Magoro, whose job is to prop me up each time I am down, like setting me up? I thought this sort of thing only happened in stories. Magoro kept on pulling my beard up and down whilst at the same time holding my trousers at the waist, pulling them up and down for no reason at all. Is this humiliation going to stop?

It stopped suddenly. As suddenly as it had begun. Van Niekerk was tired. He propped one leg on one of the chairs in the room to get more air into his throat and on his neck, which seemed to be sweating inside his tight collar. Meanwhile, Magoro had a field-day jabbing my ribs with awkward punches. There was such a searing pain already shooting through my ribs that I was sure something serious was wrong.

Colonel Visser sat on his chair with his pipe eternally dangling from his mouth, cackling like an angry hen after laying an egg on a hot day.

Van Niekerk came back to me about MDALI. "Now," he said slowly. "That MDALI of yourrs. Tell us. And we know everrything!"

He was panting, but apparently did not want me to realize that he was dog-tired. He gave me the impression that he was halting for a while for me to talk.

I told them: "MDALI is an organization of artists formed in Soweto[6] in . . . "

"Listen!" Heystek, who had come in during the commotion, shouted at me. "Don't shit us! Why don't you say Black?"

I had purposely omitted the word Black because I could not afford another beating. But I soon realized that I would get assaulted more, this time, for not using the term "Black". Either way, I had no choice. [. . .]

I remembered a friend of mine, Ben Zwane, who one day told me, after one of his many detention spells, that whether one liked it or not one would eventually tell the Security Police something once the beating started. I remembered saying to Benzo, as we affectionately called him, "If there is nothing to say, what are you going to tell them?"

"Anything! You must say something. Anything!"

The day that Benzo related his jail experiences to me, I could not imagine what I would say if the Security Police ever detained me. Now, that moment had come, and I was here in the cell thinking of it. That day seemed so far off then, dancing to jazz music in our house in Diepkloof, Soweto. "Ya. Tell them anything. And, anyway, put on as many clothes underneath, as well as a jacket if you have one in the cell. Jerseys too. So that when they kick your ribs the impact does not penetrate the skin and bones. They could break your ribs!" Benzo continued to dance.

I wondered at Benzo's non-concern. He had been detained more than four times in his young life since I knew him. And each time, he told me, he had been beaten up by the police before he gave in to what they wanted, though conceding nothing he wanted concealed from them. I told myself that I needed Benzo's fortitude then. I know that Benzo told me the truth. [. . .] I fell asleep thinking of Benzo, and that he had died during July 1974, after only about a month outside, from one of his numerous detentions. I fell asleep seeing him in the house at Diepkloof, dancing and saying: "Tell them something. Anything."

It must have been about 1 a.m. when I came to. I did not have any sense of time in those cells, but I could tell if it was late at night or very early in the morning. My cell was dark, awkwardly placed for natural light to filter through. If you were lucky, you might be locked in a cell that allowed some amount of light. I had been unfortunate.

A distant pain was searing my side, gripping me like someone had a tight hold of me and was intent on breaking my ribs. I could not breathe. I was in a daze and sweating. Momentarily I could not remember where I was. But as I was slowly realizing that I was still at Jan Vorster Square,[7] it dawned on me that I had woken up in response to the pain which was becoming worse. With difficulty, I slowly eased the weight of my body off the painful spot, which was my right side under my armpit. It all came back. The blow on my ribs when van Niekerk had had me turned away from him and his blows. I remembered that at that moment, my arms were raised to protect my already torn lip as well as my face and ear from further damage if punches were aimed at the injured places. But as I had been forced to turn away from him, I had no idea where he had intended to hit me next, or when. That's when my right side felt as though someone had torn it out of my frame. The pain I was then feeling had been the result of that rib-tearing blow.

Was my rib broken? I tried searching for the exact spot, feeling my way slowly so that my searching hand should not descend abruptly and cause me more pain. I did not understand why I still tried to locate the exact spot, or its enormity. I knew the cause. But my curious hand continued to probe around the area until I found the place. When at last I did, I had to withdraw my hand sharply from it as if I had touched a hot plate on a stove. After many attempts, I was satisfied of the exact location. [. . .]

"How much is meat therre? Kould you buy meat? What kommunists funds did you use?" Pimples persisted.

"Meat? I . . . "

"Madali. Who is he? I want to know him!" He didn't stop harassing me until I was totally confused.

Heystek was about to tell him that MDALI was not a person, but a Black artists' organization, when he suddenly bellowed, "I don't karre! I want to know this Madali, who he is!" The whole thing had seemed funny, but it wasn't any longer because the new one was not showing off. He just could not understand that MDALI was not a human being.

"MDALI is . . . " then the blows began. Suddenly. Hailstones of them. From all angles, incessant. Visser. The new one, Visser. Many blows that I could not see. I collided with the blows. In the air. On my feet. On the floor. I had become a ding-dong, as if they were playing ping-pong with a human table-tennis ball. The punches were coming so fast and my closed eyes kept on seeing flashes like lightning, sharp streaks of light, despite the fact that I had shut my eyes tightly. I clasped my arms around my head and face, cursing in the meantime that two hands were not enough. If thrown on the floor, I would pull my legs up to my body and fold up like a lamb feeling cold in winter. But nothing helped. Quickly, I would be picked up by one of them. I would find myself totally unprotected and at full stretch. Then my ribs would come under the avalanche of their blows, on my back, neck, head and arms. Their shoes . . . an eternity of silence except for the sound made by their punches, blows, boots as they connected into their target, me. There were groans and grunts from me, and the frosted glass top of the door of Heystek's office and walls shook as I was bounced in and out, this way and that, by Visser and the new one. My confused eyes saw the blows, when I did see them, their kicking legs, Heystek's large desk, Van Gogh on the west wall all as a collage in motion, the different moving angles ganging up on me, depending on the position their blows had thrown me, either on my feet or on the floor. Down, or half-way in the air, or just somewhere indefinite between the ceiling and the floor.

"What kind of nightmare is this?" I whispered to myself during the furor.

When I was upright, they punched me to the floor. When I had fallen down, they booted me up.

"Oh my God!" I cried.

I was dripping with sweat. At that moment, the many clothes I had on were the worst hindrance. I was hot from all the jerseys and shirts and jacket which clung to me and weighed me down. I thought of Benzo. He had advised that I should put on as many clothes as I could. I cried softly that Benzo had ill-directed me.

After what seemed to be an age, they stopped. The new one again asked me what Madali was. Lieutenant Visser followed up about the passport, whilst Heystek, still on his chair, said, "You will tell us. We don't play here. We are working."

Sweat was pouring down all over me. But just as I was about to tell them that I was ready to talk, they started again. As suddenly as they had stopped.

"We have methods to conscientize people into remembering. The stories that there are beatings, torturings and murderings are true, if people refuse to co-operate," he concluded. [. . .]

"My kaffertijie,[8] you will kall me baas!" ("My" here was pronounced in Afrikaans which in English would be like "May"). The new one had gone berserk. He was a complete beast. Wild. "You will fly like a kite with a motor karr without wheels!" as he wheeled around with his hands and body simulating the motor car he was talking about. He had looked really funny, more ugly and beastly then he had been. It was a long time afterwards that I thought at last I had managed to analyze what he had been trying to say about the motor car, which in my mind went something like this: "That I would be like a motor car without wheels (wheel-less) flying (through the air) like a kite!" or better still, "That I would be like a wheel-less flying motor car". All the same, I finally gave up analyzing what he had said without being satisfied that I had cracked it.

The one time that I opened my eyes during the spell when I was being beaten up and caught Lieutenant Visser's eyes, I thought that he too had gone berserk. He had lifted me up by the lapels of my jacket, had banged my head six to seven times against the wall, just under peering Van Gogh. Thereafter he had tried to lift me up by my hair, but two huge tufts of hair had ripped from my head and remained in his hands. For one brief moment it seemed as if he had shit in his hands. I was so grateful that the hair had broken because I do not know what would have happened otherwise. While I had been suspended by my hair, brief as it was, the pain had been excruciating. Lieutenant Visser threw the tufts forcibly on the floor, wiped his hands on my jacket and told me to clean the mess up. As I reached for my hair on the floor, the pimpled beast kicked me hard in the rib that van Niekerk had smashed twelve days ago. I remembered stiffening suddenly and being unable to breathe.

I do not know what happened afterwards, except later, when I had found my breath, being told to sit on a chair. It seemed like a long time of having been nowhere. I could not see a chair where they were indicating, but I dared not use the one the beast had sat on when he had flown into Heystek's office. When I looked at them in surprise, Visser pointed at nothing and said, "Sit." I still did not understand and was slapped again by the beast, flash on my unguarded face, with the back of his left-hand palm. Again Visser lost his temper with my "stupidity." He forcefully pushed me down, holding on to my shoulders, pressing on until my knees bent and when I reached "chair" posture, he told me to remain like that. "Now, sit!"

I could not maintain that position for any length of time. He was on me as fast as lightning. I had disobeyed them by not sitting as instructed. The two then thumped my thighs with their knees until the muscles were numb and my legs unable to support me. The muscles around this part of my body just collapsed. [. . .]

"You still have nothing to say, Pheto? About your friends and activities and passport?"

"I have said all there is to say," I would tell him.

[. . .] It was clear to me that they were all waiting. I did not know what it was they were waiting for, but whatever it was, it would happen. So we all played the waiting game. For two nights and three days the process did not change. All the teams had come in at their scheduled times, and had left at their finishing time. In the meantime, I had stood still. No shifting had been allowed me. Nothing, I was reminded several times to stare ahead and to remain still.

The night of the 8th was the worst. Colonel Visser would stand up, remove his gun out of the holster. He had done this several times. Each time my hands dripped with sweat. Magoro had complemented him by moving away from me, away from the line of fire, as it were. I was so hot I felt like asking them if I could take my jacket off.

Then Visser went to the door behind me, with the gun in his hand, and the light went off suddenly. I panted for breath as if the darkness was drowning me. But before I could even catch the air I was so desperately gasping for, the light came on again. My hair moved. On the second occasion the scene was re-enacted, a loud shot rang out behind me next to my head.

*Shit*, I said to myself, *he's shot me. The sadist swine has shot me!* Just as quickly the light came on.

I waited for the pain and the blood. Only sweat poured down the inside of my palms. In the light I saw Magoro's pimple[d] black face near my own, his half-ear almost touching mine, with his nostrils inflated. During the darkness, he had quickly and nimbly moved towards me, but I had not heard any movement then. All I had felt were my eyes straining in the dark as if they would jut out of my head in an effort to see everything.

Chapter II, Reading 3

# Torture in Abu Ghraib

The photographs of torture and mistreatment of prisoners by American guards and interrogators at the Abu Ghraib detention center in Iraq that were revealed to the public in the spring of 2004 managed to capture far more attention than all the written descriptions of those misdeeds ever could. For one thing, they produced undeniable evidence of the accusations that had been circulated from the beginning of the American occupation of Iraq in 2003. But there is something equally if not more chilling about reading a firsthand description of what one prisoner was forced to endure, as recounted in this sworn statement first obtained by the *Washington Post* and then published in Mark Danner's documentary account of American crimes at Abu Ghraib and elsewhere, *Torture and Truth*. As is so often the case, physical mistreatment is combined with humiliation, sexual taunting, and sadism.

TRANSLATION OF A SWORN STATEMENT PROVIDED BY
[name blacked out], Detainee #[number blacked out], 1430/21 JAN 04:

I am the person named above. I entered Abu Ghraib prison on 10 Jul 2003, that was after they brought me from Baghdadi area. They put me in the tent area and then they brought me to Hard Site.[9] The first day they put me in a dark room and started hitting me in the head and stomach and legs.

They made me raise my hands and sit on my knees. I was like that for four hours. Then the Interrogator came and he was looking at me while they were beating me. Then I stayed in this room for 5 days, naked with no clothes. They then took me to another cell on the upper floor. On 15 Oct 2003 they replaced the Army with the Iraqi Police and after that time they started punishing me in all sorts of ways. And the first punishment was bringing me to Room #1, and they put handcuffs on my hand and they cuffed me high[10] for 7 or 8 hours. And that caused a rupture to my right hand and I had a cut that was bleeding and had pus coming from it. They kept me this way on 24, 25 and 26 October. And in the following days, they also put a bag over my head, and of course, this whole time I was without clothes and without anything to sleep on. And one day in November, they started different type of punishment, where an American Police came in my room and put the bag over my head and cuffed my hands and he took me out of the room into the hallway. He started beating me, him, and 5 other American Police. I could see their feet, only, from under the bag. A couple of those police they were female because

I heard their voices and I saw two of the police that were hitting me before they put the bag over my head. One of them was wearing glasses. I couldn't read his name because he put tape over his name. Some of the things they did was make me sit down like a dog, and they would hold the string from the bag and they made me bark like a dog and they were laughing at me. And that policeman was a tan color, because he hit my head to the wall. When he did that, the bag came off my head and one of the police was telling me to crawl in Arabic, so I crawled on my stomach and the police were spitting on me when I was crawling and hitting me on my back, my head and my feet. It kept going on until their shift ended at 4 o'clock in the morning. The same thing would happen in the following days.

And I remember also one of the police hit me on my ear, before the usual beating, cuffing, bagging, dog position and crawling until 6 people gathered. And one of them was an Iraqi translator named Shaheen, he is a tan color, he has a mustache. Then the police started beating me on my kidneys and then they hit me on my right ear and it started bleeding and I lost consciousness. Then the Iraqi translator picked me up and told me "You are going to sleep." Then when I went into the room, I woke up again. I was unconscious for about two minutes. The policeman dragged me into the room where he washed my ear and they called the doctor. The Iraqi doctor came and told me he couldn't take me to the clinic, so he fixed me in the hallway. When I woke up, I saw 6 of the American Police.

A few days before they hit me on my ear, the American Police, the guy who wears glasses, he put red women's underwear over my head. And then he tied me to the window that is in the cell with my hand behind my back until I lost consciousness. And also when I was in Room #1 they told me to lay down on my stomach and they were jumping from the bed onto my back and my legs. And the other two were spitting on me and calling me names, and they held my hands and legs. After the guy with the glasses got tired, two of the American soldiers brought me to the ground and tied my hands to the door while laying down on my stomach. One of the police was pissing on me and laughing on me. He then released my hands and I went and washed, and then the soldier came back into the room, and the soldier and his friend told me in a loud voice to lie down, so I did that. And then the policeman was opening my legs, with a bag over my head, and he sat down between my legs on his knees and I was looking at him from under the bag and they wanted to do me because I saw him and he was opening his pants, so I started screaming loudly and the other police starting hitting me with his feet on my neck and he put his feet on my head so I couldn't scream. Then they left and the guy with the glasses comes back with another person and he took me out of the room and they put me inside the dark room again and they started beating me with the broom that was there. And then they put the loudspeaker inside the room and they closed the door and he was yelling in the microphone. Then they broke the glowing finger[11] and spread it on me until I was glowing and they were laughing. They took me to the room and they signaled me to get on to the floor. And one of the police he put a part of his stick that he always carries inside my ass and I felt it going inside me about 2 centimeters, approximately. And I started screaming, and he pulled it out and he washed it with water inside the room. And the two American girls that were there when they were beating me, they were hitting me with a ball made of sponge on my dick. And when I was tied up in my room, one of the girls, with blonde hair, she is white, she was playing with my dick. I saw inside this facility a lot of punishment just like what they did to me and more. And they were taking pictures of me during all these instances.

TRANSLATED BY:           VERIFIED BY:
[signed]                 [signed]
Mr. Johnson ISHO         Mr. Abdelilah ALAZADI
Translator, Category II   Translator, Category II
Titan Corporation         Titan Corporation
Assigned to:
Prisoner Interview/Interrogation Team (PIT) (CID) (FWD)
10th Military Police Battalion (CID) (ABN) (FWD)
3rd Military Police Group (CID), USACIDC
Abu Ghraib Prison Complex (ABPC)
Abu Ghraib, Iraq APO AE 09335

# Psychological Torment

Some of the most effective torture is psychological, as Aleksandr Solzhenitsyn attests in *The Gulag Archipelago*, his classic 1974 treatise on Soviet forced labor camps. He himself had been imprisoned from 1945 to 1953.

Let us begin with *psychological* methods. [. . .]

1. First of all: night. Why is it that all the main work of breaking down human souls went on at *night?* [. . .] Because at night, the prisoner torn from sleep, even though he has not yet been tortured by sleeplessness, lacks his normal daytime equanimity and common sense. He is more vulnerable. [. . .]

5. Preliminary *humiliation* was another approach. [. . .] At the Lubyanka,[12] Aleksandra O—va refused to give the testimony demanded of her. She was transferred to Lefortovo.[13] In the admitting office, a woman jailer ordered her to undress, allegedly for a medical examination, took away her clothes, and locked her in a "box" naked. At that point the men jailers began to peer through the peephole and to appraise her female attributes with loud laughs. If one were systematically to question former prisoners, many more such examples would certainly emerge. They all had but a single purpose: to dishearten and humiliate. [. . .]

8. The *lie*. We lambs were forbidden to lie, but the interrogator could tell all the lies he felt like. [. . .] Intimidation through enticement and lies was the fundamental method for bringing pressure on the *relatives* of the arrested person when they were called in to give testimony. "If you don't tell us such and such" (whatever was being asked), "it's going to be the worst for *him* . . . You'll be destroying him completely." (How hard for a mother to hear that!) "Signing this paper" (pushed in front of the relatives) "is the only way you can save him" (destroy him).

9. *Playing on one's affection* for those loved was a game that worked beautifully on the accused as well. It was the most effective of all methods of intimidation. One could break even a totally fearless person through his concern for those he loved. (Oh, how foresighted was the saying: "A man's family are his enemies.") Remember the Tatar who bore his sufferings—his own and those of his wife—but could not endure his daughter's! In 1930, Rimalis, a woman interrogator, used to threaten: "We'll arrest your daughter and lock her in a cell with syphilitics!" [. . .]

They would threaten to arrest everyone you loved. Sometimes this would be done with sound effects: Your wife has already been arrested, but her further fate depends on you. They are questioning her in the next room—

just listen! And through the wall you can actually hear a woman weeping and screaming. (After all, they all sound alike; you're hearing it through a wall; and you're under terrific strain and not in a state to play the expert on voice identification. Sometimes they simply play a recording of the voice of a "typical wife"—soprano or contralto—a labor-saving device suggested by some inventive genius.) And then, without fakery, they actually show her to you through a glass door, as she walks along in silence, her head bent in grief. Yes! Your own wife in the corridors of State Security! You have destroyed her by your stubbornness! She has already been arrested! (In actual fact, she has simply been summoned in connection with some insignificant procedural question and sent into the corridor at just the right moment, after being told: "Don't raise your head, or you'll be kept here!") Or they give you a letter to read, and the handwriting is exactly like hers: "I renounce you! After the filth they have told me about you, I don't need you any more!" (And since such wives do exist in our country, and such letters as well, you are left to ponder in your heart: Is that the kind of wife she really is?)

The interrogator Goldman (in 1944) was trying to extort testimony against other people from V. A. Korneyeva with the threat: "We'll confiscate your house and toss your old women into the street." A woman of deep convictions, and firm in her faith, Korneyeva had no fear whatever for herself. She was prepared to suffer. But, given our laws, Goldman's threats were all too real, and she was in torment over the fate of her loved ones. When, by morning, after a night of tearing up rejected depositions, Goldman began to write a fourth version accusing Korneyeva alone, she signed it happily and with a feeling of spiritual victory. We fail to hang on to the basic human instinct to prove our innocence when falsely accused. How can we there? We were even glad when we succeeded in taking all the guilt on our own shoulders.

Just as there is no classification in nature with rigid boundaries, it is impossible rigidly to separate psychological methods from *physical* ones. Where, for example, should we classify the following amusement?

10. *Sound effects*: The accused is made to stand twenty to twenty-five feet away and is then forced to speak more and more loudly and to repeat everything. This is not easy for someone already weakened to the point of exhaustion. Or two megaphones are constructed of rolled-up cardboard, and two interrogators, coming close to the prisoner, bellow in both ears: "Confess, you rat!" The prisoner is deafened; sometimes he actually loses his sense of hearing. But this method is uneconomical. The fact is that the interrogators like some diversion in their monotonous work, and so they vie in thinking up new ideas.

11. *Tickling*: This is also a diversion. The prisoner's arms and legs are bound or held down, and then the inside of his nose is tickled with a

feather. The prisoner writhes; it feels as though someone were drilling into his brain. [. . .]

13. *Light effects* involve the use of an extremely bright electric light in the small, white-walled cell or "box" in which the accused is being held—a light which is never extinguished. (The electricity saved by the economies of schoolchildren and housewives!) Your eyelids become inflamed, which is very painful. And then in the interrogation room searchlights are again directed into your eyes.

14. Here is another imaginative trick: On the eve of May 1, 1933, in the Khabarovsk GPU,[14] for *twelve* hours—all night—Chebotaryev was not interrogated, no, but was simply kept in a continual state of being *led to* interrogation. "Hey, you—hands behind your back!" They led him out of the cell, up the stairs quickly, into the interrogator's office. The guard left. But the interrogator, without asking one single question, and sometimes without even allowing Chebotaryev to sit down, would pick up the telephone: "Take away the prisoner from 107!" And so they came to get him and took him back to his cell. No sooner had he lain down on his board bunk than the lock rattled: "Chebotaryev! To interrogation. Hands behind your back!" And when he got there: "Take away the prisoner from 107!"

# A Miracle, a Universe

When we think of torture, we usually first think of physical agony. But the manipulation of the mind and spirit can be just as debilitating, as Lawrence Weschler describes in this passage from his classic study of torture in South America, *A Miracle, a Universe*.

Major A. Maciel, who was a director of Libertad,[15] observed at one point, regarding the prisoners under his charge, "We didn't get rid of them when we had the chance, and one day we'll have to let them go, so we'll have to take advantage of the time we have left to drive them mad."

Libertad, Punta de Rieles, and their associated institutions were methodically designed to demolish the mental, emotional, and moral integrity of their inmate populations. Furthermore, they were so designed by psychologists working closely with the military. "The war continued inside the prison," Dr. Martín Gutiérrez, Libertad's first psychiatrist and a subsequent senior adviser to the ruling junta, recently explained to Maxwell Gregg Bloche, an American physician who was investigating the behavior of military doctors in Uruguay. "Day after day, rule after rule—all was part of a grand design to make them suffer psychologically." It was precisely this drama—a prison conducted on behaviorist principles run amok—that so alarmed the visiting delegation from the International Red Cross. [. . .]

A Libertad veteran named Hugo recalled for me how, on the day of his arrival at the prison, he was immediately interviewed by a prison psychologist. "Now, I was arriving there after weeks of torture," Hugo said, "and here was this psychologist—very nice, expressing seemingly sincere concern about my well-being, wincing with apparent compassion at my descriptions of what had happened to me, assuring me that here everything would be safe, inquiring how he could be of help. The trouble was, everything was being taped, and every confidence was immediately betrayed. The same thing happened with everybody. If you told the guy you had this, that, or the other idiosyncrasy, he'd endeavor to find you precisely the sort of roommate who would most grate on you. If you mentioned that you were interested in historical books, he'd see to it that of the few books you ever did get, none were historical. If you said you just couldn't handle noise, he'd arrange for you to be placed in a cell right by the stairwell. If you said you desperately needed to be outside, he'd make sure that you got a cramped indoor job."

The regime at Libertad was based on a topsy-turvy system of negative and positive reinforcements. The reward end of the scale, for example, included the privilege of seeing visitors; the punishment, or sanction, end had various gradations, culminating in extended stints in *La Isla*, the dreaded block of isolation cells. (Of course, each category could be manipulated into its opposite: punishment might consist of the denial of visiting privileges, and it could get to the point where a reward was simply not being sent into solitary.)

The International Red Cross delegation noted in its report, "The implementation of every sanction is connected with a Violation of the rules. The problem, however, is that such rules undergo daily changes, so that sanctions are never predictable. Every privilege may suddenly become a crime and therefore give rise to a sanction." Elsa Leone de Gil, a Uruguayan psychologist who has been specializing in the rehabilitation of former prisoners from places like Libertad, told me, "The environment was totally unstable and unpredictable. The prisoner inhabited a crazy world filled with perils. Orders were there to be followed absolutely, but they changed diametrically, arbitrarily, and without any notice, from one day to the next: Always keep this door open—always keep this door shut. Take a bath right now—at a moment when the water has been shut off—or else! Violations were recorded with mock-scientific thoroughness, so that you were made to see that—on paper, anyway—you had indeed now committed three violations, which had such-and-such a consequence. But it was all double binds piled on more double binds."

"Aquí Se Viene a Cumplir"—"Here One Comes to Obey"—declared a sign at Libertad. But it was precisely one of Libertad's horrors that within its walls to obey was almost impossible. Furthermore, even the rewards were spiked. For example, a family visit, when it did occur, took place by way of telephones, the inmate and his visitor separated by a double wall of glass, and at its conclusion the inmate still had to go through a full-body search. In addition, the conversation was continuously monitored, and the authorities eagerly exploited any chinks that became exposed in the process. Thus, as soon as one woman prisoner at Punta de Rieles, whose boyfriend had been faithfully visiting her for years, found out that he had fallen in love with another woman and intended to marry her, the authorities slapped the prisoner into solitary confinement, so that she could not be consoled by her friends on the inside. [. . .]

No one had a name inside Libertad. Year after year, inmates were referred to by number alone: 612; 2228 . . . No one was allowed permanent possessions: whatever makeshift stash a prisoner might accumulate (a whittled keepsake, a daughter's drawing, a family photo) was subject to summary confiscation at any time. Late-night blitz searches were particularly frequent. Miguel Angel Estrella,[16] who following his ordeal by chainsaw (in the end, his tormentors didn't actually cut off any of his fingers) was eventually remanded to Libertad (where he became #2314), recalled one such typical incident during his stay there:

One time the guard barged into my cell. "So," he said, going over to a small photograph I had taped to the wall. "Who's that?"

"It's my wife."

"And who do you think she's fucking now?"

"She's dead, Martha, my wife . . ."

"Ah good! So she was a subversive just like you and they killed her."

"No, she died of cancer."

"So in other words she's no good for anything anymore."

And with that he tore her photo off the wall, ripped it up and threw it at my feet. . . . Tears welled up in my eyes but I had to restrain myself. I couldn't even speak, I absolutely had to avoid registering any reaction. These sorts of provocations invariably led to thirty days in solitary—and often for your cellmate as well. The guy kept egging me on:

"So, you subversives, when you talk about love, this is what you mean? You tear up your woman, you piss on her image, you stomp all over her. Doesn't it make you ashamed?"

"I wouldn't be capable of doing such things." I began to pull my hands out of my pocket so as to gesture how I wouldn't be capable of doing that. . . . At which point he immediately slapped me with a sanction for "attempted assault."

No one had any privacy. According to Elsa Leone de Gil, Libertad's architecture was loosely modeled on that sinister eighteenth-century dystopia, the panopticon, a prison structure in which all the inmates could be observed without knowing when they were being observed. At Libertad, there were peepholes everywhere, and there were also bugging devices that would occasionally become conspicuously exposed, so that no one was ever permitted to imagine that he was not being observed at every moment. "Everything conspired to dehumanize the inmate," Gil explains. "When they were not being addressed by number, they were being called "insect" or "cockroach" or "rat." "Apestoso"—"diseased one"—was a frequent slur. The guards were trained to show revulsion at all times; they were never to touch an inmate's clothing or dishes, and were to act as if these really were infected." To vitiate against any possible softening in their attitudes, prison administrators saw to it that lower-level military guards never served stints of longer than two months. In this manner, as well, the generals contrived to assure the widest possible dispersion of complicity; no one in the army was permitted to imagine himself as some sort of innocent.

Hugo, the Libertad veteran, told me, "At first, things might have looked adequate, even better than adequate. Even the Red Cross people were initially fooled. For instance, they were told that we were shown movies all the time. That was true. Only, the movies were regularly shown out of focus. Or else the guards would take us to see a comedy and forbid us to laugh, on pain of sanction. And during one two-month stretch they forced us to watch a series of extremely violent movies, with extensive scenes of explicit torture—this at a time when the prison had just received a fresh batch of torture victims." "The authorities create tensions," noted the Red Cross monitors, "and then forbid the expression of those tensions."

Soon after word of Miguel Angel Estrella's incarceration at Libertad reached the outside world, an international support campaign was launched on his behalf. Hundreds of artists and musicians petitioned for his release. The Queen of England, by way of her cousin Lord Mountbatten, personally requested of General Alvarez, the then-head of the Uruguayan junta, that at the very least Estrella be provided with a piano, and in fact she sent him one. The authorities made an ostentatious display of their superior cultural breeding by announcing that, indeed, Estrella would be allowed to receive the Queen's piano. Only, what he actually received, there in his cell in Libertad, was the keyboard, ripped out and disengaged from the rest of the instrument. The prison authorities explained to Estrella (this world-class concert pianist, this prize pupil of the great Nadia Boulanger[17]) that they didn't want his playing "disturbing the other inmates." Furthermore, he was even forbidden to receive any sheet music, since such pages would be peppered with terms in foreign languages (*fortissimo, pizzicato*) that could be concealing secret codes. All foreign words were forbidden at Libertad: saying "Thank you" in English would result in an immediate sanction.

"It was forbidden to sing," Estrella recalled in his testimony. "It was forbidden to smile or laugh. It was forbidden to draw—for instance the drawing of a woman was forbidden, especially a pregnant woman. Such a drawing would have been considered an act of subversion. Drawing a pregnant woman meant you longed to place in her belly the seeds of subversion. It was forbidden to draw a rose or a fish. Fish were symbols of resistance among the early Christians in Rome. If you drew a flower that even resembled a rose, that was a month in solitary, as 'ideological' punishment."

The news was piped in, at full blast, over the PA system each day at noon—a recasting of the 6 A.M. national radio broadcast, which, already heavily censored, had meanwhile been further processed, staccato-cut, and static-jammed for prison consumption. (There would be a detailed account of a sports match, for instance, without the final score.) Every so often, the authorities staged nerve-jangling fake escapes—sirens wailing, floodlights sweeping, guns firing—just to keep everyone on his toes, and also to ferret out incipient leaders—people who might be caught trying to calm their fellows, for instance—for special attention.

An hour a day, inmates were allowed outside, to walk the grounds in circles, but never in groups larger than two; they were always subject to interruption by a guard, who would question each man separately about the topic of their discourse, under penalty of sanction. Most of the rest of the time, the inmates were kept locked in their narrow quarters, generally two to a cell, with a bunk bed wedged over to the side and one stool. Except during mandated sleeping hours, no one was allowed to lie on his bed, so one of the cellmates generally had to stand or pace.

This went on for years—six years, eight years, ten, twelve, more—until the prisoner's sentence had run its course. And then, when it was all over, the inmate or his family was expected to pick up the tab for room and board—a figure that could easily run into the thousands of dollars.

# Civilized and Scientific Interrogation

The army seized power in Greece in 1967 and established an authoritarian state in which torture and intimidation were commonplace. Pericles Korovessis, a young actor and political activist, was imprisoned and tortured in Athens. In this passage from his book, *The Method*, he both deconstructs the cynicism of the regime, with its distinction between "civilized" and "scientific" interrogation techniques, and takes us inside his head to share exactly what he was thinking and feeling during his ordeal.

## Civilised Interrogation

"Now look here, lad, we weren't born yesterday. It was out of the sheer kindness of our hearts we didn't pull you in straight away. The authorities are not unaware of the activities in which you have indulged since the Revolution.[18] It's no trivial matter, what you've been up to. We know everything. So tell us all about it, there's a good lad. Come on, you'll be all right. Remember, the Asphalia[19] can be Dachau for people who don't co-operate and paradise for the honest ones. So watch yourself—we're not examining you to see if you're guilty, that's already proved. We just want to see how you behave. Remember Dachau and Paradise. I'm quite willing to let you off, despite the fact that you were a bit stroppy with me back at the flat."

I was frightened. I felt the sweat running down my back. I'd heard the word Dachau twice, unmistakably. I was at the Asphalia, that legendary place where unspeakable things were said to happen. Even so, I had a last-minute hope that it was just words—maybe I would get off.

I told him that his vague way of asking questions didn't make things any easier for me. I stated that I had no reason to hide anything, and that if there was any way I could help, I would. As I got to the end of the sentence I pulled myself up. I was doing well. The first three minutes and I was already being co-operative. I felt disgusted and ashamed. The good thing was that I was beginning to calm down now. He seemed satisfied.

"Okay, lad, you're doing fine. Now that you've admitted belonging to the Patriotic Front[20] . . . and a good thing you didn't deny it, because you know what's happened? The Front leaders have given us a complete plan of the organization—yes, and the whole set-up has been wiped out. So I want you to tell me—not your party instructors, we know them—what I want is the names of your contacts. Right? The people you used to see. Come on then, let's get it over with."

I pointed out that I hadn't admitted anything. It was his own guesswork, and needn't necessarily be taken for the truth. He got cross. A dialogue followed, which I cite here word for word.

"What do you know about the Patriotic Front?"

"It's an organisation that was formed after the 21st April; it 'aims to impede Government activity'."

"Where did you find that out?"

"From Konstantópoulos."

"Where does he live?"

"Sávvas Konstantópoulos, the man who runs *Eléftheros Kósmos*.[21] The phrase I used is from one of his articles."

"Get stuffed. You cunts all say the same. I can see you've been well trained."

"I don't understand."

"Come on, don't fuck me about. Who else was on the newspaper?"

"What newspaper?"

"If you keep playing the fool you'll fucking be in for it. I'm talking about the Front newspaper."

"I've never seen it."

"Come off it, you expect me to swallow that shit? Who did you give the newspaper to?"

"I don't understand the question."

"Who was staying at your place?"

"My wife."

"Apart from your wife?"

"Me, of course."

"Look here, you cunt. I'll keep quiet about the bombs you've been planting. See how decent I am? I'll let you off that one, otherwise they'll put you in front of the firing squad. I can be lenient if I want to. So stop trying to be a clever-dick and tell me who's working with you at the theatre."

"I think you're making a mistake. I don't understand what you're asking."

"You'll learn. Do you know any of these people?" (He mentioned several names.)

"I've never heard of any of them."

"They say they know you."

"I've no idea."

At roughly this point the dialogue ended. He went up the wall. He swore at me. "You'll regret it," he said, then slammed the door and left. I was alone. I was still afraid, but a bit calmer. It wasn't really so terrifying. The door opened again. A giant head poked round, asked if I was alone, then came at me viciously.

I moved instinctively to defend myself. The giant muttered, "I'm going to get into trouble for this," and stuck his ugly face into mine. "Own up, you silly sod, they know everything, they'll cripple you. They'll throw you to the madhouse and have you torn apart. I'm telling you for your own good. I can get into trouble for telling you."

Before I had a chance to react, he left. And before I had a chance to explain the appearance of this "friendly" adviser, the door was kicked open and a second, more ferocious character came in. I could hear voices in the distance, "Catch that madman, he's going to kill that prisoner." The madman grabbed hold of a chair. He spoke.

"You, you cunt, weren't you the one who killed my father in December and cut his eyes out to make worry-beads? Now I've got you in my hands and you're going to pay for it, you cunt." Things were beginning to get serious. I got up from the chair and stepped backwards into the corner by the radiator. The madman with the chair came towards me like a lion-tamer. I noticed he was smiling. It seemed rather as if he was acting. He hit me twice with the chair. He kept on repeating the same thing. The blows were restrained. He had a twinkle in his eye. I was convinced that he was acting. It's my job, after all.

This was followed by the Second Act. Some other *hafiés*[22] came in and grabbed the "madman". Somebody asked me if I was still alive. "You're lucky he didn't chuck you out of the window," added someone else. The madman was still roaring his head off. "I've got him now. Let me get my revenge." They calmed him down, saying it couldn't possibly be me, as I must have been a very small child in '44. The madman wouldn't have it. He wanted his revenge, and was not interested in rational arguments. If I wasn't the one, I had a Communist face and was going to pay for it. They kept saying, "Calm down, Mítsos old feller," but it didn't have any effect. Next came an appearance from Spanós, who said, "Be quiet, lads"; and the lads, with the madman at their head, answered, "Right, Mr. Superior," and went out quietly, almost civilised, like actors who take a bow and disappear into the wings. A second dialogue.

"So. What's happening, have you changed your mind?"

"But I never made it up in the first place."

"We're not going to start that all over again. I've just been interrogating the other one. He told us all about you. We'll bring him in front of you—do you want him to shame you into owning up?"

Mr. Spanós was telling a fat lie. I was glad to hear it—my friend had never had any connection with politics. I hadn't seen him since just before the coup. It was sheer chance that he was at my place.

"That doesn't impress me in the least, Mr. Investigator—I might agree that the earth was square if you told me to say so, but that doesn't mean it's true."

"The earth is whatever I please, you cunt. Let's have it, you're a communist, aren't you?"

"I'm Batman."

"You're a commie, you cunt, you had a hundred tons of communist books at your flat, why should I sit here and listen to you?"

He started punching me; I sat still, looking at him. He had tiny hands, almost like a dwarf's. Then he caught me by the hair and started punching me round the ears, with the edge of his palm. I stayed still. Luckily my nose started bleeding. My gums were bleeding too. This was a good thing—his hands were soiled, and he was in danger of splashing himself with blood as he hit me. He stopped, saying that if I had dirtied his clothes, I would pay for it. He left. I was alone again. My shirt had gone a deep red colour. My mouth was full of blood. In actual fact I wasn't in pain, but my feelings had got the better of me. One consoling thought: if the beating stopped here, I was lucky. Something more than lucky. He came back. Fortunately, I hadn't dirtied him. He was calm, almost cheerful. He looked at me without speaking. He sat down at his desk and went on looking at me. I spoke to him myself, and at long last managed a protest—in a reasonable tone, though. I contented myself with saying that I didn't approve of this kind of interrogation since it was inhuman, by any standards. Something about human rights. He laughed, and told me:

"Listen young man. There are two sorts of interrogation—the civilised kind and the scientific kind."

"What's the civilised kind like?"

"That's what we've just had."

"What about the scientific kind?"

"That's coming."


## Scientific Interrogation

The roof of the Asphalia building in Bubulínas Street has what must be the most famous laundry[23] in the world. The Asphalia's ingenuity, with almost no equipment except a bench, a rope and a few wooden rods, has created one of the most renowned torture chambers of our times. When they take you there you already know the place; you get the impression that you've seen it before. What is new is the panic welling up inside you. It's something you can't control. It assumes metaphysical dimensions, somewhat like the religious fear of damnation. Any self-orientation is impossible. You exist only within this all-powerful fear.

They took me up to the roof. Familiar faces, including Spanós. A *hafiés* saw them taking me up and greeted them—"Back from the hunt, eh?" On the way up the lads were cracking jokes. Whenever their humour didn't come off, a kick or a wallop did the trick. This always got a laugh. The lads' jokes:

"This one'll be dead before the night's out."

"You stupid cunt, you know your wife's a whore?"

"She's a whore all right, she goes down Athninās Street sucking them all off."

"His mother's a tart as well. What can you do with him if the kid was brought up in a brothel?"

"Let's go and get them. We'll fuck them in front of you."

"He'll enjoy playing Peeping Tom."

"What a pansy he is."

"Theatre people are all queers."

"Hey you, do you fuck at the theatre? Do you fuck, eh?"

"They fuck each other."

"You filthy queer, don't you get cross when we talk about your mother like that?"

"What, him? These people don't believe in God."

"Look at the cunt, he looks like a Buddha. We're talking to ourselves."

"The bastard's morally degenerate, fuck him."

A staircase leads up from the fourth-floor corridor to the roof. There is a notice saying "Entry strictly forbidden". The roof. Then the small penthouse. Nothing was hurried. Visual experiences from the moment of my entering the Asphalia till now flashed through my mind one after the other, like coloured slides. I realised that it was an ordinary place—a public department, with people working there. Things are simple if there's nothing for you to be afraid of. I was almost casual. They switched the light on in the laundry. I felt I was the main attraction. I was making observations, like a Water Board inspector. It seemed like a sacred rite with a human sacrifice. No one was talking any more, they were working. They were looking for the rope. They couldn't find it. Typically Greek. They were blaming a certain Bábalis and Mállios for being sloppy in their work—they'd finished their job and bollocks to the rest. Someone told me not to just stand there like a stupid cunt but to look for the rope too. Spanós disagreed and told me to sit where I was, they didn't need my help. In the end they found it. It was under the rods. I don't know why, but I had hopes in the rope before. Now they'd found it there was only one way: if I talked, even if I only said a little, perhaps I would get off. "Don't hit him," someone suggested. "He seems a nice enough bloke, let's leave him to think about it a bit and have a nice cup of coffee, then in the morning he'll talk in his own time."

I felt some gratitude. Every word he said bolstered me up. I was already drinking coffee and straightening things out. Now I saw what they were up to—they'd brought me up here to strike terror into me and when they saw that it didn't work, they would try some other method. Spanós didn't speak at all. "We've put ourselves to a lot of trouble with this bastard," said someone else. "If he had any brains he'd be home by now. Why should we give him time? He's going to talk here and now, then all of us can get a rest." I looked at Spanós. I was waiting for him to say, "Take him downstairs to think about it." I thought he wouldn't try experimenting unless he was confident of the results. It would have been logical to say, "Okay, tomorrow will do."

Spanós ordered them to tie me up. He made an inspection. They tied me very tightly to the bench. I didn't resist at all. Not even a protest. Now that I think of it, I believe I went almost willingly. Like when you go to the dentist's and sit down in the chair of your own accord. Spanós moved the soles of my feet to see that they were tied properly. Mr. Spanós was satisfied. But he didn't begin. He felt like having a chat. He asked me how I felt—he wanted to know whether the bench was too hard or if the ropes were cutting into me. He asked me whether I'd changed my mind. I didn't say a word. I said to myself that perhaps it was better not to. Maybe I would arouse their wrath as public officials, but at least there would be no reason for them to take it personally. Spanós asked me if I liked pistachio nuts. I didn't understand the question, but it got a reaction out of me. I lifted my head up, and immediately he came over to me. "If you think you're going to get anything this way, you're very much mistaken," I told him. "It's the twentieth century, I'm telling you for the sake of your own career. I'll sue you."

I didn't know if I believed myself or not, but it did me good. Spanós answered, "You can fart on my bollocks. Take it to the UN if you like, you might just as well fart on my bollocks, you hear?" Spanós gave instructions to the torturer on duty.

"Give him the pistachio nuts, Kóstas."

"Wood or iron, which?"

"Wood to start with, we'll see."

"Right, doctor."

I felt as though I was listening to some strange African dialect. I stiffened up and waited. I looked at Kóstas. He spat on his hands and took hold of the rod. He began.

*Falanga*[24] is an overwhelmingly powerful force that works on your whole system. You have the impression of sliding down a vast, shining slope, then you're flung into a hard granite wall. If you didn't know they were beating you on your feet it would be impossible to make out where it was coming from. You can see the movements of the torturer. The strokes of the rod are the granite wall. The slope is the interval between each stroke. When there is a regular rhythm to it, it's less painful than when it's irregular. They are well aware of this subtle variation and they hit you fast and slow, alternately. They beat from heel to toe and back again. They know your first reaction is to arch your feet. They don't mind you doing this as they know quite well that after a dozen blows your foot will have swollen so much that it fills up your shoe.

I started to cry out. I didn't know till then how loud the human voice can be. I shouted out my name. I could hear my voice—it was unnaturally powerful. They stopped. There had been about ten blows or so. I didn't dare hope. Spanós asked me if I'd changed my mind. I didn't look at him. Kóstas started up again. I was screaming. Someone went out to the lavatory and got the swab. He stuck it in my mouth. All the muck ran down my gullet. He squeezed it tight and wrung the drops down my throat. I couldn't breathe any more. I thought about using yoga, to cut off the transmission of pain. Utterly useless. Like trying to dam a waterfall with paper. My yoga went to pieces. They weren't finished. I kept expecting to pass out, but I had a brute endurance. Strangely enough I was taking it, although I'd always had to ask for an injection before I could face the dentist's drill. It wasn't over yet. I had to think of something else, maybe that would ease the pain. Impossible. Now the beating was creating its own sound, something like a huge wooden bell. Like being inside the bell. After that, I slid away: darkness, quiet, ease.

They threw water over me. I was coming round. I was almost proud that I had fainted. An immediate awareness of place. Hope. Maybe they would stop now. Perhaps they would untie me. Surely *falanga* couldn't go on forever. I'd been through the whole lot, what else did they want? Spanós asked me if I'd changed my mind. I took no notice of him. Kóstas began again. How long was it going to last? If I'd said something it would have given me a bit of a breathing space. Kóstas continued. The swab went in my mouth again. Air—there was no air. How long can you live without air? I was expecting the bell to sound again. Not a sound—only those waves of pain welling up. I think my head started making nervous twitches. Spanós told them, "Stop, he wants to say something." The rest agreed: Yes, he wants to talk. He's ripe for talking. We've done a good job on this one. "Don't go near him, Mr. Superior, he'll spit at you," someone said to Spanós. What's going on here, I wondered. People were being tortured, but not only did they stay silent, they spat at their torturers. I wished that I could have done the same as them. Spanós changed his mind. Kóstas began again.

There must be a limit to human resistance. Nightmarish nervous excitement gave me an extraordinary mental clarity. I studied them. They were clustered round me like onlookers round a demolition site. It wasn't Kóstas hitting me now, it was someone else. I saw one of them leave the group and stand by the door, looking out. Perhaps he was on guard to see that no one came up. Perhaps he couldn't stand the sight. I believed the latter. Fresh courage: even here there was someone who didn't agree with this sort of thing. I felt friendly: I had seen him turn his back. My stomach hurt. There was a buzzing in my ears—a sharp, penetrating sound. It was getting louder. I felt as if I was falling through space. The speed! An acrid, screeching sound, like a plane breaking the sound barrier. I fell somewhere. Meadows. Underwater. A carefree feeling. An awareness of place. I had passed out again. I felt as if I had just got up after an illness—very thin, transparent. I looked at them. They were un-shaven, sleepless and tired. They didn't ask any more questions. When they saw my eyes moving, they started again.

I was no longer aware of anything. Thought of a mangy dog, stones being thrown at him. The kids from my block were flinging stones at him. The dog looked like me. I was terrified—terrified of going mad. I knew that people on Makrónisos[25] had gone insane from being tortured. They got well afterwards, though. There was an old man lying outside a door, his body all puffed up—frozen by the cold. The folds under his chin were frozen stiff, hanging like icicles. They were dragging him by the feet. The old man was me. There was no interrogation, nothing. I wanted to keep a grip on myself. They were hitting me ceaselessly, like a machine. The beginnings of schizophrenia. You can avoid it—if you talk. I'll talk. I waited—perhaps they would stop. I had to go through with it: they couldn't beat me forever. It would stop. Sooner or later it would stop. It was a test to become an astronaut. School exams. Forced to queue up—you had to wait. A long queue at school round a cauldron of dried milk—the Marshall Plan—dried milk turned into a flinty block which our schoolmistress made me break up with a hammer. The dried milk in the barrel had gone hard like limestone. I hit it with the hammer. The sound of a hammer hitting porous rock—the sound was drowning, like water being absorbed.

It was dawn. First sense of place. The sun was bright. I had fallen on the floor. Someone was rubbing my head in some muck. Spew. He was rubbing my head right into some vomit. He was giving me some advice. "Eat it, you pig, eat it up. Oink, oink, oink." I had been sick. God knows when. How long had they been hitting me? I had to work it out. I worked it out: only three hours. How endless three hours can be! It was perhaps one of the longest stretches of time I can ever remember. So many things happened that there was no time to sort them out. It was clear daylight now. A nice day. Strange as it was, a nice day. I was alone with the man who kept on rubbing my face in the sick. He said he would do a shit so that I could have something to eat, it would make my food more tasty. No surprise. Another *hafiés* came in with some new instructions. After he had asked me what happened and got "nothing" for an answer, he said he would wipe the shit off me and take me downstairs: Mr. Superior wanted me. He threw some water over me. I wanted to show willing; I wanted to get up and walk by myself. It was impossible to move. They dragged me down to see Spanós.

The same atmosphere. They laughed when they saw me. What did they want this time? Yes, Spanós was asking the same things all over again. The same questions—but where was the sense in them now? They seemed out of place. It reminded you of those aunts and uncles you haven't seen for twenty years, and the first thing they say is, "Why didn't you come and see me on my birthday?" I was looking around, astonished. What could I say?

They threw cold or was it hot water over my feet. It was incredibly painful. I jumped. After that I couldn't hear well, in fact I could hardly hear anything. This didn't worry me; I was glad, very glad. They kept on asking me questions. It was a silent movie. Someone whistled in my ear—he was whistling "Athens, Daughter of the Skies." The whole thing was utterly ridiculous. They were angry and knocking me around, but I couldn't hear them at all. Perhaps I couldn't speak either. I'd heard that on Makrónisos a lot of people had gone dumb after being tortured. I dared not believe I was as fortunate as that. I didn't want to open my mouth, in case I was disappointed. In the end I had a try. I couldn't speak. Right, now I wasn't afraid of anything.

I nodded at Spanós to come close. He rushed over. I asked in sign language for a pencil and paper. He fetched some for me at once. I wrote, "Who are you?" and, "What do you want from me?" He went crazy and tore them up. I made a movement to say that I was going to have a piss, right there in the office. A terrified Spanós got two men to lift me up. They took me to the lavatory. They took me in and undid me, then back to the office. Their day's work had begun.

They dragged me down four floors. I was obviously going into solitary confinement. People were coming up the stairs, some uniformed, others in plain clothes. The main topic of conversation was yesterday's soccer match, which must have been particularly exciting. They were discussing the finest details of the match in loud voices. They made way for me to pass. Nobody took any notice. The ideals of sport are above such small, tedious details.

The previous occupant of Cell 17 had been in "strictest solitary confinement." This meant that he was forced to perform all his physical functions in there. A huge pile of garbage. The smell was unbearable. As soon as they had locked the door and I was on my own, I felt somewhat safer. I felt like a mouse who is in a trap, maybe, but has at least escaped the cat. They were through with me.

# Trust in the World

Jean Améry was a member of the Belgian resistance during the Second World War. Arrested by the Gestapo in 1943, he was imprisoned at Fort Breedonk and tortured, though, as he modestly put it, "What was inflicted on me . . . was by far not the worst form of torture." But it was bad enough and certainly bad enough to have inspired these brilliant observations from his book *At the Mind's Limits* about the impact of torture upon human consciousness and its relationship to the world.

In an interrogation, blows have only scant criminological significance. They are tacitly practiced and accepted, a normal measure employed against recalcitrant prisoners who are unwilling to confess. [. . .] Blows are applied in more or less heavy doses by almost all police authorities, including those of the Western-democratic countries. [. . .]

Mostly, the public does not prove to be finicky when such occurrences in police stations are revealed now and then in the press. [. . .] Simple blows, which really are entirely incommensurable with actual torture, may almost never create a far-reaching echo among the public, but for the person who suffers them they are still experiences that leave deep marks. [. . .] The first blow brings home to the prisoner that he is *helpless*, and thus it already contains in the bud everything that is to come. One may have known about torture and death in the cell, without such knowledge having possessed the hue of life; but upon the first blow they are anticipated as real possibilities, yes, as certainties. They are permitted to punch me in the face, the victim feels in numb surprise and concludes in just as numb certainty: they will do with me what they want. Whoever would rush to the prisoner's aid—a wife, a mother, a brother, or friend—he won't get this far.

Not much is said when someone who has never been beaten makes the ethical and pathetic statement that upon the first blow the prisoner loses his human dignity. I must confess that I don't know exactly what that is: human dignity. One person thinks he loses it when he finds himself in circumstances that make it impossible for him to take a daily bath. Another believes he loses it when he must speak to an official in something other than his native language. In one instance human dignity is bound to a certain physical convenience, in the other to the right of free speech, in still another perhaps to the availability of erotic partners of the same sex. I don't know if the person who is beaten by the police loses human dignity. Yet I am certain that with the very first blow that descends on him he loses something we will perhaps temporarily call "trust in the world." Trust in the world includes all sorts of things: the irrational and logically unjustifiable belief in absolute causality perhaps, or the likewise blind belief in the validity of the inductive inference. But more important as an element of trust in the world, and in our context what is solely relevant, is the certainty that by reason of written or unwritten social contracts the other person will spare me—more precisely stated, that he will respect my physical, and with it also my metaphysical, being. The boundaries of my body are also the boundaries of my self. My skin surface shields me against the external world. If I am to have trust, I must feel on it only what I *want* to feel.

At the first blow, however, this trust in the world breaks down. The other person, *opposite* whom I exist physically in the world and *with* whom I can exist only as long as he does not touch my skin surface as border, forces his own corporeality on me with the first blow. He is on me and thereby destroys me. It is like a rape, a sexual act without the consent of one of the two partners. Certainly, if there is even a minimal prospect of successful resistance, a mechanism is set in motion that enables me to rectify the border violation by the other person. For my part, I can expand in urgent self-defense, objectify my own corporeality, restore the trust in my continued existence. The social contract then has another text and other clauses: an eye for an eye and a tooth for a tooth. You can also regulate your life according to that. You *cannot* do it when it is the other one who knocks out the tooth, sinks the eye into a swollen mass, and you yourself suffer on your body the counter-man that your fellow man became. If no help can be expected, this physical overwhelming by the other then becomes an existential consummation of destruction altogether.

The expectation of help, the certainty of help, is indeed one of the fundamental experiences of human beings, and probably also of animals. [. . .] The expectation of help is as much a constitutional psychic element as is the struggle for existence. Just a moment, the mother says to her child who is moaning from pain, a hot-water bottle, a cup of tea is coming right away, we won't let you suffer so! I'll prescribe you a medicine, the doctor assures, it will help you. Even on the battlefield, the Red Cross ambulances find their way to the wounded man. In almost all situations in life where there is bodily injury there is also the expectation of help; the former is compensated by the latter. But with the first blow from a policeman's fist, against which there can be no defense and which no helping hand will ward off, a part of our life ends and it can never again be revived.

Here it must be added, of course, that the reality of the police blows must first of all be accepted, because the existential fright from the first blow quickly fades and there is still room in the psyche for a number of practical considerations. Even a sudden joyful surprise is felt; for the physical pain is not at all unbearable. The blows that descend on us have above all a subjective spatial and acoustical quality: spatial, insofar as the prisoner who is being struck in the face and on the head has the impression that the room and all the visible objects in it are shifting position by jolts; acoustical, because he believes to hear a dull thundering, which finally submerges in a general roaring. The blow acts as its own anesthetic. A feeling of pain that would be comparable to a violent toothache or the pulsating burning of a festering wound does not emerge. For that reason, the beaten person thinks roughly this: well now, that can be put up with; hit me as much as you want, it will get you nowhere. [. . .]

If I finally want to get to the analysis of torture, then unfortunately I cannot spare the reader the objective description of what now took place; I can only try to make it brief. In the bunker there hung from the vaulted ceiling a chain that above ran into a roll. At its bottom end it bore a heavy, broadly curved iron hook. I was led to the instrument. The hook gripped into the shackle that held my hands together behind my back. Then I was raised with the chain until I hung about a meter over the floor. In such a position, or rather, when hanging this way, with your hands behind your back, for a short time you can hold at a half-oblique through muscular force. During these few minutes, when you are already expending your utmost strength, when sweat has already appeared on your forehead and lips, and you are breathing in gasps, you will not answer any questions. Accomplices? Addresses? Meeting places? You hardly hear it. All your life is gathered in a single, limited area of the body, the shoulder joints, and it does not react; for it exhausts itself completely in the expenditure of energy. But this cannot last long, even with people who have a strong physical constitution. As for me, I had to give up rather quickly. And now there was a crackling and splintering in my shoulders that my body has not forgotten until this hour. The balls sprang from their sockets. My own body weight caused luxation;[26] I fell into a void and now hung by my dislocated arms, which had been torn high from behind and were now twisted over my head. Torture, from Latin *torquere*, to twist. What visual instruction in etymology! At the same time, the blows from the horsewhip showered down on my body, and some of them sliced cleanly through the light summer trousers that I was wearing on this twenty-third of July 1943.

It would be totally senseless to try and describe here the pain that was inflicted on me. Was it "like a red-hot iron in my shoulders," and was another "like a dull wooden stake that had been driven into the back of my head"? One comparison would only stand for the other, and in the end we would be hoaxed by turn on the hopeless merry-go-round of figurative speech. The pain was what it was. Beyond that there is nothing to say. Qualities of feeling are as incomparable as they are indescribable. They mark the limit of the capacity of language to communicate. If someone wanted to impart his physical pain, he would be forced to inflict it and thereby become a torturer himself.

Since the *how* of pain defies communication through language, perhaps I can at least approximately state *what* it was. It contained everything that we already ascertained earlier in regard to a beating by the police: the border violation of my self by the other, which can be neither neutralized by the expectation of help nor rectified through resistance. Torture is all that, but in addition very much more. Whoever is overcome by pain through torture experiences his body as never before. In self-negation, his flesh becomes a total reality. Partially, torture is one of those life experiences that in a milder form present themselves also to the consciousness of the patient who is awaiting help, and the popular saying, according to which we feel well as long as we do not feel our body, does indeed express an undeniable truth. But only in torture does the transformation of the person into flesh become complete. Frail in the face of violence, yelling out in pain, awaiting no help, capable of no resistance, the tortured person is only a body, and nothing else beside that. If what Thomas Mann described years ago in *The Magic Mountain* is true, namely, that the more hopelessly man's body is subjected to suffering, the more physical he is, then of all physical celebrations torture is the most terrible. In the case of Mann's consumptives, they still took place in a state of euphoria; for the martyred they are death rituals.

It is tempting to speculate further. Pain, we said, is the most extreme intensification imaginable of our bodily being. But maybe it is even more, that is: death. No road that can be travelled by logic leads us to death, but perhaps the thought is permissible that through pain a path of feeling and premonition can be paved to it for us. In the end, we would be faced with the equation: Body = Pain = Death, and in our case this could be reduced to the hypothesis that torture, through which we are turned into body by the other, blots out the contradiction of death and allows us to experience it personally. But this is an evasion of the question. We have for it only the excuse of our own experience and must add in explanation that torture has an indelible character. Whoever was tortured, stays tortured. Torture is ineradicably burned into him, even when no clinically objective traces can be detected. The permanence of torture gives the one who underwent it the right to speculative flights, which need not be lofty ones and still may claim a certain validity. [. . .]

To come right out with it: I had nothing but luck, because especially in regard to the extorting of information our group was rather well organized. What they wanted to hear from me in Breendonk, I simply did not know myself. If instead of the aliases I had been able to name the real names, perhaps, or probably, a calamity would have occurred, and I would be standing here now as the weakling I most likely am, and as the traitor I potentially already was. Yet it was not at all that I opposed them with the heroically maintained silence that befits a real man in such a situation and about which one may read (almost always, incidentally, in reports by people who were not there themselves). I talked. I accused myself of invented absurd political crimes, and even now I don't know at all how they could have occurred to me, dangling bundle that I was. Apparently I had the hope that, after such incriminating disclosures, a well-aimed blow to the head would put an end to my misery and quickly bring on my death, or at least unconsciousness. Finally, I actually did become unconscious, and with that it was over for a while—for the "cops" abstained from awakening their battered victim, since the nonsense I had foisted on them was busying their stupid heads.

It was over for a while. It still is not over. Twenty-two years later I am still dangling over the ground by dislocated arms, panting, and accusing myself. In such an instance there is no "repression." Does one repress an unsightly birthmark? One can have it removed by a plastic surgeon, but the skin that is transplanted in its place is not the skin with which one feels naturally at ease.

One can shake off torture as little as the question of the possibilities and limits of the power to resist it. I have spoken with many comrades about this and have attempted to relive all kinds of experiences. Does the brave man resist? I am not sure. There was, for example, that young Belgian aristocrat who converted to Communism and was something like a hero, namely in the Spanish civil war, where he had fought on the Republican side. But when they subjected him to torture in Breendonk, he "coughed up," as it is put in the jargon of common criminals, and since he knew a lot, he betrayed an entire organization. The brave man went very far in his readiness to cooperate. He drove with the Gestapo men to the homes of his comrades and in extreme zeal encouraged them to confess just everything, but absolutely everything, that was their only hope, and it was, he said, a question of paying any price in order to escape torture. And I knew another, a Bulgarian professional revolutionary, who had been subjected to torture compared to which mine was only a somewhat strenuous sport, and who had remained silent, simply and steadfastly silent. Also the unforgettable Jean Moulin, who is buried in the Pantheon in Paris, shall be remembered here. He was arrested as the first chairman of the French Resistance Movement. If he had talked, the entire Resistance would have been destroyed. But he bore his martyrdom beyond the limits of death and did not betray one single name.

Where does the strength, where does the weakness come from? I don't know. *One* does not know. No one has yet been able to draw distinct borders between the "moral" power of resistance to physical pain and "bodily" resistance (which likewise must be placed in quotation marks). There are more than a few specialists who reduce the entire problem of bearing pain to a purely physiological basis. Here only the French professor of surgery and member of the Collège de France, René Leriche, will be cited, who ventured the following judgment:

"We are not equal before the phenomenon of pain," the professor says.

One person already suffers where the other apparently still perceives hardly anything. This has to do with the individual quality of our sympathetic nerve, with the hormone of the parathyroid gland, and with the vasoconstrictive substances of the adrenal glands. Also in the physiological observation of pain we cannot escape the concept of individuality. History shows us that we people of today are more sensitive to pain than our ancestors were, and this from a purely physiological standpoint. I am not speaking here of any hypothetical moral power of resistance, but am staying within the realm of physiology. Pain remedies and narcosis have contributed more to our greater sensitivity than moral factors. Also the reactions to pain by various people are absolutely not the same. Two wars have given us the opportunity to see how the physical sensitivities of the Germans, French, and English differ. Above all, there is a great separation in this regard between the Europeans on the one hand and the Asians and Africans on the other. The latter bear physical pain incomparably better than the former.

Thus the judgment of a surgical authority. [. . .] As body, we actually are not equal when faced with pain and torture. But that does not solve our problem of the power of resistance, and it gives us no conclusive answer to the question of what share moral and physical factors have in it. If we agree to a reduction to the purely physiological, then we run the risk of finally pardoning every kind of whiny reaction and physical cowardice. But if we exclusively stress the so-called moral resistance, then we would have to measure a weakly seventeen-year-old gymnasium pupil who fails to withstand torture by the same standards as an athletically built thirty-year-old laborer who is accustomed to manual work and hardships. Thus we had better let the question rest, just as at that time I myself did not further analyze my power to resist, when, battered and with my hands still shackled, I lay in the cell and ruminated.

For the person who has survived torture and whose pains are starting to subside (before they flare up again) experiences an ephemeral peace that is conducive to thinking. In one respect, the tortured person is content that he was body only and because of that, so he thinks, free of all political concern. You are on the outside, he tells himself more or less, and I am here in the cell, and that gives me a great superiority over you. I have experienced the ineffable, I am filled with it entirely, and now see, if you can, how you are going to live with yourselves, the world, and my disappearance. On the other hand, however, the fading away of the physical, which revealed itself in pain and torture, the end of the tremendous tumult that had erupted in the body, the reattainment of a hollow stability, is satisfying and soothing. There are even euphoric moments, in which the return of weak powers of reason is felt as an extraordinary happiness. The bundle of limbs that is slowly recovering human semblance feels the urge to articulate the experience intellectually, right away, on the spot, without losing the least bit of time, for a few hours afterward could already be too late.

Thinking is almost nothing else but a great astonishment. Astonishment at the fact that you had endured it, that the tumult had not immediately led also to an explosion of the body, that you still have a forehead that you can stroke with your shackled hands, an eye that can be opened and closed, a mouth that would show the usual lines if you could see it now in a mirror. What? you ask yourself—the same person who was gruff with his family because of a toothache was able to hang there by his dislocated arms and still live? The person who for hours was in a bad mood after slightly burning his finger with a cigarette was lacerated here with a horsewhip, and now that it is all over he hardly feels his wounds? Astonishment also at the fact that what happened to you yourself by right was supposed to befall only those who had written about it in accusatory brochures: torture. A murder is committed, but it is part of the newspaper that reported on it. An airplane accident occurred, but that concerns the people who lost a relative in it. The Gestapo tortures. But that was a matter until now for the somebodies who were tortured and who displayed their scars at antifascist conferences. That suddenly you yourself are the Somebody is grasped only with difficulty. That, too, is a kind of alienation.

If from the experience of torture any knowledge at all remains that goes beyond the plain nightmarish, it is that of a great amazement and a foreignness in the world that cannot be compensated by any sort of subsequent human communication. Amazed, the tortured person experienced that in this world there can be the other as absolute sovereign, and sovereignty revealed itself as the power to inflict suffering and to destroy. The dominion of the torturer over his victim has nothing in common with the power exercised on the basis of social contracts, as we know it. It is not the power of the traffic policeman over the pedestrian, of the tax official over the taxpayer, of the first lieutenant over the second lieutenant. It is also not the sacral sovereignty of past absolute chieftains or kings; for even if they stirred fear, they were also objects of trust at the same time. The king could be terrible in his wrath, but also kind in his mercy; his autocracy was an exercise of authority. But the power of the torturer, under which the tortured moans, is nothing other than the triumph of the survivor over the one who is plunged from the world into agony and death.

Astonishment at the existence of the other, as he boundlessly asserts himself through torture, and astonishment at what one can become oneself: flesh and death. The tortured person never ceases to be amazed that all those things one may, according to inclination, call his soul, or his mind, or his consciousness, or his identity, are destroyed when there is that cracking and splintering in the shoulder joints. That life is fragile is a truism he has always known—and that it can be ended, as Shakespeare says, "with a little pin." But only through torture did he learn that a living person can be transformed so thoroughly into flesh and by that, while still alive, be partly made into a prey of death.

Whoever has succumbed to torture can no longer feel at home in the world. The shame of destruction cannot be erased. Trust in the world, which already collapsed in part at the first blow, but in the end, under torture, fully, will not be regained. That one's fellow man was experienced as the antiman remains in the tortured person as accumulated horror. It blocks the view into a world in which the principle of hope rules. One who was martyred is a defenseless prisoner of fear. It is *fear* that henceforth reigns over him. Fear—and also what is called resentments. They remain, and have scarcely a chance to concentrate into a seething, purifying thirst for revenge.

# Rape

Women have of course been subjected to all the forms of torture heretofore described. But one of the most common is rape and sexual assault. In the course of wars, in particular, such torture is rampant. Susan Brownmiller's classic *Against Our Will* contains a powerful passage describing the rapes of hundreds of thousands of Bengali women by Pakistani soldiers and their paramilitary allies during the 1971 war in Bangladesh. For these women, as Brownmiller explains, the suffering generated by the torture itself was compounded by the reactions of their husbands and families.

Indira Gandhi's[27] Indian Army had successfully routed the West Pakistanis and had abruptly concluded the war in Bangladesh when small stories hinting at the mass rape of Bengali women began to appear in American newspapers. The first account I read, from the *Los Angeles Times* syndicated service, appeared in the *New York Post* a few days before Christmas, 1971. It reported that the Bangladesh government of Sheik Mujibur Rahman,[28] in recognition of the particular suffering of Bengali women at the hands of Pakistani soldiers, had proclaimed all raped women "heroines" of the war for independence. Farther on in the story came this ominous sentence: "In traditional Bengali village society, where women lead cloistered lives, rape victims often are ostracized."

Two days after Christmas a more explicit story, by war correspondent Joseph Fried, appeared in the *New York Daily News*, datelined Jessore.[29] Fried described the reappearance of young Bengali women on the city streets after an absence of nine months. Some had been packed off to live with relatives in the countryside and others had gone into hiding. "The precautions," he wrote, "proved wise, if not always effective."

A stream of victims and eyewitnesses tell how truckloads of Pakistani soldiers and their hireling *razakars*[30] swooped down on villages in the night, rounding up women by force. Some were raped on the spot. Others were carried off to military compounds. Some women were still there when Indian troops battled their way into Pakistani strongholds. Weeping survivors of villages razed because they were suspected of siding with the Mukti Bahini[31] freedom fighters told of how wives were raped before the eyes of their bound husbands, who were then put to death. Just how much of it was the work of Pakistani "regulars" is not clear. Pakistani officers maintain that their men were too disciplined "for that sort of thing."

In the middle of January the story gained sudden credence. An Asian relief secretary for the World Council of Churches called a press conference in Geneva to discuss his two-week mission to Bangladesh. The

Reverend Kentaro Buma reported that more than 200,000 Bengali women had been raped by Pakistani soldiers during the nine-month conflict, a figure that had been supplied to him by Bangladesh authorities in Dacca.[32] Thousands of the raped women had become pregnant, he said. And by tradition, no Moslem husband would take back a wife who had been touched by another man, even if she had been subdued by force. "The new authorities of Bangladesh are trying their best to break that tradition," Buma informed the newsmen. "They tell the husbands the women were victims and must be considered national heroines. Some men have taken their spouses back home, but these are very, very few."

Organized response from humanitarian and feminist groups was immediate in London, New York, Los Angeles, Stockholm and elsewhere. "It is unthinkable that innocent wives whose lives were virtually destroyed by war are now being totally destroyed by their own husbands," a group of eleven women wrote to the *New York Times* that January. "This . . . vividly demonstrates the blindness of men to injustices they practice against their own women even while struggling for liberation." Galvanized for the first time in history over the issue of rape in war, international aid for Bengali victims was coordinated by alert officials in the London office of the International Planned Parenthood Federation. The Bangladesh government, at first, was most cooperative. In the months to come, the extent of the aggravated plight of the women of Bangladesh during the war for independence would be slowly revealed.

Bengal was a state of 75 million people, officially East Pakistan, when the Bangladesh government declared its independence in March of 1971 with the support of India. Troops from West Pakistan were flown to the East to put down the rebellion. During the nine-month terror, terminated by the two-week armed intervention of India, a possible three million persons lost their lives, ten million fled across the border to India, and 200,000, 300,000 or possibly 400,000 women (three sets of statistics have been variously quoted) were raped. Eighty percent of the raped women were Moslems, reflecting the population of Bangladesh, but Hindu and Christian women were not exempt. As Moslems, most Bengali[33] women were used to living in purdah,[34] strict, veiled isolation that includes separate, secluded shelter arrangements apart from men, even in their own homes. The Pakistanis were also Moslem, but there the similarity stopped. Despite a shared religious heritage, Punjabi[35] Pakistanis are taller, lighter-skinned and "rawboned" compared to dark small-boned Bengalis. This racial difference would provide added anguish to those Bengali women who found themselves pregnant after their physical ordeal.

Hit-and-run rape of large numbers of Bengali women was brutally simple in terms of logistics as the Pakistani regulars swept through and occupied the tiny, populous land, an area little larger than the state of

New York. (Bangladesh is the most overcrowded country in the world.) The Mukti Bahini "freedom fighters" were hardly an effective counterforce. According to victims, Moslem Biharis[36] who collaborated with the Pakistani Army—the hireling *razakars*—were most enthusiastic rapists. In the general breakdown of law and order, Mukti Bahini themselves committed rape, a situation reminiscent of World War II when Greek and Italian peasant women became victims of whatever soldiers happened to pass through their village.

Aubrey Menen, sent on a reporting assignment to Bangladesh, reconstructed the *modus operandi* of one hit-and-run rape. With more than a touch of romance the Indian Catholic novelist chose as his archetypal subject a seventeen-year-old Hindu bride of one month whom he called "the belle of the village." Since she was, after all, a ravished woman, Menen employed his artistic license to paint a sensual picture of her "classical buttocks": ". . . they were shaped, that is, as the great Sanskrit[37] poet Kalidasa[38] had prescribed, like two halves of a perfect melon."

Menen got his information from the victim's father. Pakistani soldiers had come to the little village by truck one day in October. Politely and thoroughly they searched the houses—"for pamphlets," they said. Little talk was exchanged since the soldiers spoke a language no one in the village could understand. The bride of one month gave a soldier a drink of coconut juice, "in peace."

At ten o'clock that night the truckload of soldiers returned, waking the family by kicking down the door of their corrugated iron house. There were six soldiers in all, and the father said that none of them was drunk. I will let Menen tell it:

Two went into the room that had been built for the bridal couple. The others stayed behind with the family, one of them covering them with his gun.

They heard a barked order, and the bridegroom's voice protesting. Then there was silence until the bride screamed. Then there was silence again, except for some muffled cries that soon subsided.

In a few minutes one of the soldiers came out, his uniform in disarray. He grinned to his companions. Another soldier took his place in the extra room. And so on, until all the six had raped the belle of the village. Then all six left, hurriedly. The father found his daughter lying on the string cot unconscious and bleeding. Her husband was crouched on the floor, kneeling over his vomit.

After interviewing the father, Menen tracked down the young woman herself in a shelter for rape victims in Dacca. She was, he reported, "truly beautiful," but he found her mouth "strange." It was hard and tense. The young woman doubted that she would ever return to her tiny village. Her husband of one month had refused to see her and her father, she said, was "ashamed." The villagers, too, "did not want me." The conversation, Menen wrote, proceeded with embarrassing pauses, but it was not without high tension.

I took my leave. I was at the door when she called me back. "Huzoor," a title of honour. "Yes?" "You will see that those men are punished," she said. "Punished. Punished. *Punished.*"

Menen's report on the belle of the village was artfully drawn, but it did dramatize the plight of thousands of raped and rejected Bengali women. Other observers with a less romantic eye provided more realistic case studies. Rape in Bangladesh had hardly been restricted to beauty. Girls of eight and grandmothers of seventy-five had been sexually assaulted during the nine-month repression. Pakistani soldiers had not only violated Bengali women on the spot; they abducted tens of hundreds and held them by force in their military barracks for nightly use. The women were kept naked to prevent their escape. In some of the camps, pornographic movies were shown to the soldiers, "in an obvious attempt to work the men up," one Indian writer reported.

Khadiga, thirteen years old, was interviewed by a photojournalist in Dacca. She was walking to school with four other girls when they were kidnapped by a gang of Pakistani soldiers. All five were put in a military brothel in Mohammedpur[39] and held captive for six months until the end of the war. Khadiga was regularly abused by two men a day; others, she said, had to service seven to ten men daily. (Some accounts have mentioned as many as eighty assaults in a single night, a bodily abuse that is beyond my ability to fully comprehend, even as I write these words.) At first, Khadiga said, the soldiers tied a gag around her mouth to keep her from screaming. As the months wore on and the captives' spirit was broken, the soldiers devised a simple *quid pro quo*. They withheld the daily ration of food until the girls had submitted to the full quota.

Kamala Begum, a wealthy widow, lived in a Dacca suburb. When the fighting started she sent her two daughters into the countryside to hide. She felt she could afford to stay behind, secure in her belief that she was "too old" to attract attention. She was assaulted by three men, two Pakistanis and one *razakar*, in her home. [. . .]

Rape, abduction and forcible prostitution during the nine-month war proved to be only the first round of humiliation for the Bengali women. Prime Minister Mujibur Rahman's declaration that victims of rape were national heroines was the opening shot of an ill-starred campaign to re-integrate them into society—by smoothing the way for a return to their husbands or by finding bridegrooms for the unmarried ones from among his Mukti Bahini freedom fighters. Imaginative in concept for a country in which female chastity and purdah isolation are cardinal principles, the "marry them off" campaign never got off the ground. Few prospective bridegrooms stepped forward, and those who did made it plain that they expected the government, as father figure, to present them with handsome dowries.

"The demands of the men have ranged from the latest model of Japanese car, painted red, to the publication of unpublished poems," a government official bitterly complained. Another stumbling block, perhaps unexpected by the Bangladeshis, was the attitude of raped women. "Many won't be able to tolerate presence of a man for some time," the same official admitted.

But more pressing concerns than marriage had to be faced. Doctors sent to Bangladesh by International Planned Parenthood discovered that gynecological infection was rampant. "Almost every rape victim tested had a venereal disease," an Australian physician told the *New York Times*.

The most serious crisis was pregnancy. Accurate statistics on the number of raped women who found themselves with child were difficult to determine but 25,000 is the generally accepted figure. Less speculative was the attitude of the raped, pregnant women. Few cared to bear their babies. Those close to birth expressed little interest in the fate of the child. In addition to an understandable horror of rearing a child of forcible rape, it was freely acknowledged in Bangladesh that the bastard children with their fair Punjabi features would never be accepted into Bengali culture—and neither would their mothers.

Families with money were able to send their daughters to expert abortionists in Calcutta, but shame and self-loathing and lack of alternatives led to fearsome, irrational solutions in the rural villages. Dr. Geoffrey Davis of the London-based International Abortion Research and Training Center who worked for months in the remote countryside of Bangladesh reported that he had heard of "countless" incidents of suicide and infanticide during his travels. Rat poison and drowning were the available means. Davis also estimated that five thousand women had managed to abort themselves by various indigenous methods, with attendant medical complications.

A Catholic convent in Calcutta, Mother Theresa's, opened its doors in Dacca to women who were willing to offer their babies for overseas adoption, but despite the publicity accorded to Mother Theresa, few rape victims actually came to her shelter. Those who learned of the option chose to have an abortion. Planned Parenthood, in cooperation with the newly created Bangladesh Central Organization for Women's Rehabilitation, set up clinics in Dacca and seventeen outlying areas to cope with the unwanted pregnancies. In its first month of operation the Dacca clinic alone reported doing more than one hundred terminations.

The Bangladesh Central Organization for Women's Rehabilitation, created by Bengali women themselves, proved to be an heroic moving force. In a country with few women professionals, those who had the skills stepped forward to help their victimized sisters. One, a doctor, Helena Pasha, who admitted that prior to the war she had thoroughly disapproved of abortion, gave freely of her time and services with little monetary compensation. Women social workers like Tahera Shafiq took over the organizational work and gave aid and comfort that the traumatized rape victims could not accept from men. Tahera Shafiq was adamant on one point. Rape or forcible prostitution were false, inadequate words to describe what the Bengali women had gone through. She preferred in conversation to use the word "torture."

Rehabilitation meant more than comfort, tenderness and abortion. The women's organization sought to train the homeless, rejected women in working skills. Handicrafts, shorthand and typing were the obvious choices—small steps until one remembers that most of the women had never been outside their rural villages before. The hoped-for long-range goal of "rehabilitation" still remained marriage. "An earning woman has better prospects of marriage than others," one social worker said dryly. But for many of the tortured women, aid and succor arrived too late, or not at all. "Alas, we have reports of some who have landed in brothels," a male government official acknowledged. "It is a terrible tragedy."

As the full dimensions of the horror became known, those who looked for rational, military explanations returned again and again to the puzzle of why the mass rapes had taken place. "And a campaign of terror includes rape?" Aubrey Menen prodded a Bengali politician. He got a reflective answer. "What do soldiers talk about in barracks? Women and sex," the politician mused. "Put a gun in their hands and tell them to go out and frighten the wits out of a population and what will be the first thing that leaps to their mind?" Fearing the magnitude of his own answer, the politician concluded, "Remember, some of our Bengali women are very beautiful." Mulk Raj Anand, an Indian novelist, was convinced of conspiracy. The rapes were so systematic and pervasive that they had to be conscious Army policy, "planned by the West Pakistanis in a deliberate effort to create a new race" or to dilute Bengali nationalism, Anand passionately told reporters.

Theory and conjecture abounded, all of it based on the erroneous assumption that the massive rape of Bangladesh had been a crime without precedent in modern history.

But the mass rape of Bangladesh had not been unique. The number of rapes per capita during the nine-month occupation of Bangladesh had been no greater than the incidence of rape during one month of occupation in the city of Nanking in 1937,[40] no greater than the per capita incidence of rape in Belgium and France as the German Army marched unchecked during the first three months of World War I, no greater than the violation of women in every village in Soviet Russia in World War II. A "campaign of terror" and a charge of "conscious Army policy" had been offered up in explanation by seekers of rational answers in those wars as well, and later forgotten.

The story of Bangladesh was unique in one respect. For the first time in history the rape of women in war, and the complex aftermath of mass assault, received serious international attention. The desperate need of Sheik Mujibur Rahman's government for international sympathy and financial aid was part of the reason; a new feminist consciousness that encompassed rape as a political issue and a growing, practical acceptance of abortion as a solution to unwanted pregnancy were contributing factors of critical importance. And so an obscure war in an obscure corner of the globe, to Western eyes, provided the setting for an examination of the "unspeakable" crime. For once, the particular terror of unarmed women facing armed men had full hearing.

# Torture and Sexuality

One of the populations most vulnerable to torture are lesbian, gay, bisexual, and transgender (LGBT) people. Given that torture and discrimination go hand in hand and that the LGBT community often lacks significant political power, in part because in many areas of the world it is still dangerous not to remain closeted, this is not surprising. Moreover, LGBT activists who *do* claim power are often themselves targeted for persecution, as was a Ugandan lesbian whom Amnesty International pseudonymously called "Christine" in publicizing the fact that she had been stripped naked, beaten, and raped after being taken into custody simply for organizing a gay and lesbian human rights group.[41]

In this reading from another Amnesty report (this one on Uzbekistan), human rights activist Ruslan Sharipov's alleged sexual orientation was employed as a means of punishing him for speaking out on a range of human rights violations in that country. In June 2004, following an international campaign on his behalf, Sharipov was released from prison but advised to leave the country. A few months later he was granted political asylum in the United States.

According to Article 120 of the Uzbekistan Criminal Code, "the satisfaction of a sexual urge by a man with a man without violence" is punishable by up to three years' imprisonment.

In May 2003, Ruslan Sharipov, then a twenty-five-year-old journalist with the Russian news agency PRIMA and leader of the human rights group Civic Assistance, was arrested by police in Tashkent and charged with homosexuality. He was also later charged under Article 127 (encouraging minors to commit antisocial behavior) and Article 128 (having sexual relations with minors).

Police interrogating him confronted Sharipov about several articles he had written on the subject of human rights violations in Uzbekistan, shouting at him and threatening him with rape and suffocation.

Sharipov was found guilty of all the charges against him and was sentenced to five and half years in prison. In letters from prison Sharipov insisted that the case had been fabricated in order to punish him for his human rights activities. Sharipov stated that he had been tortured into changing his plea to guilty.

"I was injected with unidentified substances and I was told that I was being infected with HIV virus. They put bags and a gas mask over my head and made me write a suicide note. Unidentified substances were sprayed into my throat, making me feel as if I was suffocating, while they continued to torture me with electric shock to the ears and other parts of the body. It was mostly the interior ministry's anti-terrorism department that did the torturing. I remember how Radjab Kadirov, who is in charge of all prisons and camps and who is the interior minister's first assistant, told me that I should end all activity and give up any hope of getting U.S. help. 'Look how the U.S. cooperates with us in the war against terrorism,' Kadirov said. 'Even our anti-terrorism department which is in charge of your case is financed by them. So don't expect their help.' They also told me that if I did not officially say I did not want my defense team and my mother to be present in court, both my defense team and relatives would be in danger. My public defender ended up being attacked and beaten and was hospitalized with serious injuries."

# I Have Nothing to Say

Some people, remarkably enough, can withstand even the most excruciating torture and not talk. One of those was Antonia García, an outspoken opponent of Spain's Fascist dictator Francisco Franco (1892–1975) and his Falange Party. García describes in this passage from Tomasa Cuevas, *Prison of Women*, why, despite recurrent torture with electric currents (which resulted in burst eardrums and frequent blackouts), she refused to reveal information about her comrades.

The Falangists arrested me several times, and all together I spent eleven years in prison. [. . .] My story starts when I was a little girl and my mother took me with her to clean the Civil Guard barracks. The truth is I almost grew up in those barracks. I remember how fond the older guards were of me and how they would hold me on their knees. I wasn't even eleven years old when my mother died. The day she died she told me many things I've never forgotten; one thing was that she trusted some of those men even more than some family friends. She assured me the men would always help me and that I should do what they said. So I did become very close to them, spending lots of time at the barracks from the age of eleven to thirteen. At that age they thought I was old enough to work for them.

My job was to copy the duty sheet in the guards' room and then clean the room after they left. Following their instructions, I locked the door from the inside while I worked and never told anyone, not even my grandmother, that I saw people being tortured at the barracks. My situation was somewhat strange. On the one hand I was very friendly with the guards; while they were making their rounds they would stop by the house where I lived with my grandparents to play cards and have a cup of coffee. On the other hand I wanted to join the Communist Youth; whenever the guards returned with political posters they had confiscated, I'd secretly return them to my friends. But I never joined the party. At first, I was afraid to go against the orders of my friends, the guards, even though I was involved in political activities that would have gotten me in trouble. Later, a membership card just didn't matter.

The first time I was arrested, the guards went to the police station and got me released. Later on they couldn't help me and I was finally arrested for good. I was taken to the police station on Nunez de Balboa Street and stuck in a dark, dark dungeon. I couldn't see anything but after a while I realized from some groaning that someone else was there. After what seemed like a long time, a light switched on and six or more men along with a woman and young boy were brought in. The police began to beat the boy so hard that blood streamed from his mouth and nose; then they stomped on his testicles and left him limp as a rag. All the while his poor mother was crying "My son, my son." Unable to bear the sight, she turned her face to the wall and in desperation threw herself on one of the men and scratched his whole face. The men pushed the woman away and she fell so hard against a stone bench that one of her eyes popped out.

I wasn't even eighteen years old when I witnessed that horror. From that moment on I vowed that no human being would ever suffer because of me. No matter what was done to me, I wouldn't say a word. When I was taken out to make a statement, I was tortured until my tormentors grew weary. They put electric currents in my ears that made me crazy with pain for years and years. Still I said nothing. I wouldn't open my mouth. That infuriated my torturers. They questioned me nonstop—what had I done, where had I been, who was so and so and such and such? But I didn't even consider making up stories. I simply refused to talk. Whether it was from trauma or shock, I'm not sure, but I remember with absolute clarity that only one thought was in my mind: I don't have to say anything. They tried to put electrical currents on my nipples but I was too young to have any so they put them in my ears again. My eardrums burst. I lost consciousness.

## Chapter III
# Who Are the Torturers?

What does it take to "make" a torturer? Are all of us susceptible, under the right circumstances, to the lure of cruelty? Or are torturers somehow a breed apart, "monsters," utterly beyond human comprehension, much less empathy? Given how widespread torture has been throughout human history and how common it still is today, the world has either seen a great many instances of "abnormality" or the veneer of civilized behavior is much thinner than we like to think.

This chapter explores how men (and it is almost always men) become torturers; what may predispose them to torture; what appeal it has to them; how they are trained for it; and how it hardens their hearts. A South African neuropsychologist has recently theorized that cruelty, especially in males, is grounded in an adaptive reaction from the Paleozoic era when early humans were predators and had to hunt for their food; that the appearance of pain and blood in the prey was a signal of success; and that gradually the evocation of such reactions—howls of pain, the appearance of blood—in our fellow humans became associated with personal and social power.[1] This fascinating conjecture strikes me as plausible. Even so, relatively few of us ultimately become torturers of our fellow humans. What accounts for the difference? The readings that follow address that question.

# The *Chicotte*

In this passage from his stunning book, *King Leopold's Ghost*, the story of Belgium's exploitation of the Congo and its natural resources, Adam Hochschild foreshadows a host of issues that we address in this book. He introduces us to still one more form of torture (the *chicotte*), to a man who objected to its use, to some of the reasons it was employed in the first place, to the rationalizations the torturers used to justify their brutality, and to the desensitization that subsequently ensued. This reading allows us to see the underlying dynamic of torture as a means, often racist, by which the powerful maintain their control over those whom they want to intimidate.

Stanislas Lefranc, a devout Catholic and monarchist, was a Belgian prosecutor who had come to the Congo to work as a magistrate. Early one Sunday morning in Leopoldville, he heard the sound of many children screaming desperately.

On tracing the howls to their source, Lefranc found "some thirty urchins, of whom several were seven or eight years old, lined up and waiting their turn, watching, terrified, their companions being flogged. Most of the urchins, in a paroxysm of grief . . . kicked so frightfully that the soldiers ordered to hold them by the hands and feet had to lift them off the ground . . . 25 times the whip slashed down on each of the children." The evening before, Lefranc learned, several children had laughed in the presence of a white man, who then ordered that all the servant boys in town be given fifty lashes. The second installment of twenty-five lashes was due at six o'clock the next morning. Lefranc managed to get these stopped, but was told not to make any more protests that interfered with discipline.

Lefranc was seeing in use a central tool of Leopold's[2] Congo, which in the minds of the territory's people, soon became as closely identified with white rule as the steamboat or the rifle. It was the *chicotte*—a whip of raw, sun-dried hippopotamus hide, cut into a long sharp-edged corkscrew strip. Usually the *chicotte* was applied to the victim's bare buttocks. Its blows would leave permanent scars; more than twenty-five strokes could mean unconsciousness; and a hundred or more—not an uncommon punishment—were often fatal.

Lefranc was to see many more *chicotte* beatings, although his descriptions of them, in pamphlets and newspaper articles he published in Belgium, provoked little reaction.

The station chief selects the victims. . . . Trembling, haggard, they lie face down on the ground . . . two of their companions, sometimes four, seize them by the feet and hands, and remove their cotton drawers . . . Each time that the torturer lifts up the *chicotte,* a reddish stripe appears on the skin of the pitiful victims, who, however firmly held, gasp in frightful contortions. . . . At the first blows the unhappy victims let out horrible cries which soon become faint groans. . . . In a refinement of evil, some officers, and I've witnessed this, demand that when the sufferer gets up, panting, he must graciously give the military salute.

The open horror Lefranc expressed succeeded only in earning him a reputation as an oddball or troublemaker. He "shows an astonishing ignorance of things which he ought to know because of his work. A mediocre agent," the acting governor general wrote in a personnel evaluation. In an attempt to quiet his complaints, Lefranc wrote, officials ordered that executions at his post be carried out in a new location instead of next to his house.

Except for Lefranc, few Europeans working for the regime left records of their shock at the sight of officially sanctioned terror. The white men who passed through the territory as military officers, steamboat captains, or state or concession company officials generally accepted the use of the *chicotte* as unthinkingly as hundreds of thousands of other men in uniform would accept their assignments, a half-century later, to staff the Nazi and Soviet concentration camps. "Monsters exist," wrote Primo Levi of his experience at Auschwitz. "But they are too few in number to be truly dangerous. More dangerous are . . . the functionaries ready to believe and to act without asking questions."

What made it possible for the functionaries in the Congo to so blithely watch the *chicotte* in action [. . .]? To begin with, of course, was race. To Europeans, Africans were inferior beings: lazy, uncivilized, little better than animals. In fact, the most common way they were put to work was, like animals, as beasts of burden. In any system of terror, the functionaries must first of all see the victims as less than human, and Victorian ideas about race provided such a foundation. Then, of course, the terror in the Congo was sanctioned by the authorities. For a white man to rebel meant challenging the system that provided your livelihood. Everyone around you was participating. By going along with the system, you were paid, promoted, awarded medals. So men who would have been appalled to see someone using a *chicotte* on the streets of Brussels or Paris or Stockholm accepted the act, in this different setting, as normal. We can hear the echo of this thinking, in another context, half a century later: "To tell the truth," said Franz Stangl of the mass killings that took place when he was commandant of the Nazi death camps of Sobibor and Treblinka, "one did become used to it."

In such a regime, one thing that often helps functionaries "become used to it" is a slight, symbolic distance—irrelevant to the victim—between an official in charge and the physical act of terror itself. That symbolic distance was frequently cited in self-defense by Nazis put on trial after World War II. Dr. Johann Paul Kremer, for example, an SS physician who liked to do his pathology research on human tissue that was still fresh, explained:

The patient was put on the dissecting table while he was still alive. I then approached the table and put several questions to the man as to such details which pertained to my researches. . . . When I had collected my information the orderly approached the patient and killed him with an injection in the vicinity of the heart. . . . I myself never made any lethal injections.

*I myself never made any lethal injections.* Although some whites in the Congo enjoyed wielding the *chicotte*, most put a similar symbolic distance between themselves and the dreaded instrument. "At first I . . . took upon myself the responsibility of meting out punishment to those whose conduct during the previous day seemed to warrant such treatment," recalled Raoul de Premorel, who worked for a company operating in the Kasai River basin. "Soon . . . I found it desirable to assign the execution of sentences to others under my direction. The best plan seemed to be to have each *capita* [African foreman] administer the punishment for his own gang."

And so the bulk of *chicotte* blows were inflicted by Africans on the bodies of other Africans. This, for the conquerors, served a further purpose. It created a class of foremen from among the conquered, like the *kapos* in the Nazi concentration camps and the *predurki*, or trusties, in the Soviet gulag. Just as terrorizing people is part of conquest, so is forcing someone else to administer the terror.

Finally, when terror is the unquestioned order of the day, wielding it efficiently is regarded as a manly virtue, the way soldiers value calmness in battle. This is the ultimate in "becoming used to it." Here, for instance, a station chief named Georges Bricusse describes in his diary a hanging he ordered in 1895 of a man who had stolen a rifle:

The gallows is set up. The rope is attached, too high. They lift up the nigger and put the noose around him. The rope twists for a few moments, then crack, the man is wriggling on the ground. A shot in the back of the neck and the game is up. It didn't make the least impression on me this time!! And to think that the first time I saw the *chicotte* administered, I was pale with fright. Africa has some uses after all. I could now walk into fire as if to a wedding.

# "The Torturer's Tale"

We continue with a human being, José Valle López. A torturer, yes; a human being too. With fears. With a family. Keith Atkinson tells his story in a 1989 article from *Toronto Life*.

Among those who took part in the killing he is remembered as the man who refused to die. He was not an old man, perhaps 50, but they thought of him as old because he had that simplicity of soul so often associated with age. He was a peasant, and he had a devout belief in the goodness of man. The contras had picked him up because they thought he might be a spy for the Sandinistas. It was never proved. Most who knew the case considered him a mistake. Mistakes happen. In neighboring Guatemala in the sixties an estimated 10,000 peasants were killed to eliminate about a hundred guerrillas.

Still, it did not seem right. He was like a friendly dog, they said. You would beat him, attach the electrical wires to his genitals, do the most horrendous things to him, and still he would say that he loved you.

He was religious at heart; his faith was unfathomable.

It was unsettling. At the end, when it came time to take him to *la finca*;[3] one of the torturers washed him and gave him some clothes. It made him happy because he thought he was being set free. So in spite of the torture he had suffered, he smiled at José.

José is very heavy. He has a good face for smiling, and he tried to smile in return. But it was difficult. No one leaves *la finca* alive. If you are lucky your body will not be dismembered.

This one was not lucky. Because of what they had done to him, within weeks his body had aged years. It was amazing he had survived. Some didn't. Once, after attaching an electronic device to a man, José had been called away to the phone—and had talked too long . . .

That, too, had been a mistake. At that point the intent is to torture, not to kill.

At *la finca*, it was different. They walked out to the field. The old man looked at José, then at the others. He still did not seem to realize what was going to happen. So when they stabbed him in the chest it came as a surprise.

They stabbed him four times, then waited as he lay on the ground and the blood poured from his chest as if a valve had been opened in his heart.

Then he got to his knees and tried to pray. Losing patience, one of the men started firing. He kept his finger on the trigger. The old man fell back, his body making little bounces on the ground. Soon there was more blood than body, more raw flesh than human form. But still he moved, as if refusing to die.

It was not the way it was supposed to be. After what they had done to him he should have broken like a dry stick. And the blood. How could so much blood come from one old man? He was no longer even a man. He was now nothing but a piece of blood-covered carrion. But his eyes were alive, as if unconnected with his body. It was unnatural.

It was then that they brought out the knives and began the dismemberment. They started with the head. The old man didn't move after that. But inside José the icy fingers of fear had taken hold of his liver. During two years of killings he had seen nothing like this. He walked back to the car. As an official torturer with a Honduran death squad he had become an integral cog in the country's military machine, a member of a small fraternity unencumbered by the normal restrictions that govern most people's lives. It was not a position of eminence, but it was one of privilege, with perks and rewards for obtaining confessions.

The rewards were pretty good, but they were outweighed by the bad part. When he had joined the army he had known he might eventually have to shoot at people, perhaps Salvadorans, against whom his country had recently fought a war. But in the army that's what you do. When people shoot at you, you shoot at them. With luck, you kill them before they kill you.

But killing isn't torture, isn't strapping someone naked to a table and mutilating his body while he screams in agony and terror. As a soldier you can shoot people and still sleep at night. As a torturer there are problems.

You adapt—after a year you do things you would not have thought possible—but that's the frightening part. That you can adapt, that you can learn to do these things and then regard that ability as a progression. If, as a new recruit, he had been able to foresee the mornings in ten years' time when he would kiss his wife and children goodbye, pick up his lunch and go off to work in the torture chambers, he would probably not have adapted. He would have gotten out.

It would have been easier then. They would not have tried to kill him, and it's possible that he would still be in Honduras, perhaps living a life in which he would attribute the stories of death squad atrocities to leftist propaganda, though it is also possible that he could have been one of the "mistakes," or have become associated with the Left and, like Angel Manfredo Velásquez,[4] ended up in pieces along the road from El Progreso to Tegucigalpa. To paraphrase Uruguayan writer Eduardo Galeano, in an atmosphere in which priests are persecuted for helping the poor, and children are tortured to reveal the beliefs of their parents, no one is immune, conformity is sacrosanct and the small matter of survival often hinges on adaptation.

It is in this context that we must place the story of José Valle López, not necessarily because he deserves sympathy, but because the situation deserves understanding. I first saw José on television, on the CBC[5] program *Man Alive*.

I have seen more sinister faces on grade-school teachers.

That's the horror.

"Who tortures?" asks Galeano. "Five sadists, ten morons, fifteen clinical cases?

"Respectable heads of families torture. The officers put in their hours of work and then go home and watch television with their children. What is efficient is good, the machine teaches . . . He who doesn't torture will be tortured. The machine accepts neither innocents nor witnesses. Who refuses? Who can keep his hands clean? The little gear vomits the first time. The second time it grits its teeth. The third time it becomes accustomed and does its duty. . . . The most talented end up taking a liking to it. . . . The torturer is a functionary. . . . That and nothing more than that."

It is as functioning gears in military machines throughout Latin America that people like José have killed an estimated 100,000 of their own citizens during the past two decades. As a torturer in Latin America, José was obviously not alone. Nor is he alone now as an ex-torturer in Toronto, for like any city that becomes a haven for people fleeing persecution, Toronto has also become a refuge for those perpetrators who end up with the same choice as their victims: to become a corpse or an exile.

Dr. Federico Allodi, the psychiatrist who co-founded the Canadian Centre for Victims of Torture, has treated seven ex-torturers. They come to him, he says, when they can no longer sleep at night. But how many can sleep, and how many have seen other doctors, is impossible to determine. The past is not written on the faces of ex-torturers any more than it is written on the faces of their victims. And in the mornings now, when José is sitting on the TTC[6] on his way to work, he invariably sees other refugees from Latin America. He doesn't know them and they don't know him, but even if they were to strike up an acquaintance, the past is not something they would readily discuss.

José's past begins when he joined the army in 1973. He was 15 and mesmerized by the aura of the military, which had ruled his country since he was 5.

Because of his weight they called him El Gordo.[7]

Hey, Gordo! You got no *cojones*.[8]

For the first three months he wanted out. Then, gradually there developed within him a stubbornness to show he could take it. Eventually, when other recruits arrived, he was no longer at the bottom. He was put in charge. After proving he could take it, he began proving he could give it. He developed *cojones*.

Time passed. He married and fathered two children. When he heard about an opening that had come up in the police division he put in an application and was accepted.

More time passed. By 1980, in neighboring Nicaragua, the Sandinistas[9] had ousted Somoza;[10] guerrilla groups in El Salvador had reorganized and had begun to receive support from the Sandinistas; and the U.S. was getting a little uneasy over the fact that its backyard was becoming a jungle that nurtured events over which it was losing control.

Then Ronald Reagan arrived in the White House and, a short while later, Washington discovered Honduras and decided to turn it into its bulwark against communism by increasing military aid from $16.3 million for the last half of the seventies to $169 million for the first half of the eighties.

It was a time for the generals; a time to cut out the cancer of communism that had allegedly devoured Nicaragua and was now debilitating the nation of El Salvador and taking root in Honduras; a time for teamwork and the Central Intelligence Agency, for cowboys in Washington and death squads in Honduras.

It was a good time for Gustavo Alvarez Martinez,[11] for on the day he formed Battalion 316 he discovered his reason for being, and he pursued it with a messianic fervor that made him Washington's new man in Central America, and led to the kidnapping, torture and murder of over 150 people, including American priest Jim Carney, who was thrown alive from a helicopter.

Martinez was inflicted with a madness to "physically annihilate" all who disagreed with his radical views, said a former head of Honduran intelligence from the safety of Mexico. [. . .]

Working on the premise that the general was god, and all malcontents were Communists who bore no moral resemblance to themselves, it was part of the duty of all squad members to learn how to spot them. The methods employed did not differ greatly from those perfected by Santiago Gradiz. He was the political governor of the Honduran region of Francisco Morazán, and Communists were his specialty.

It's easy, Gradiz once told a journalist. You can tell a Communist by the way he acts, the way he speaks. You don't have to ask anyone. It's obvious. Inside the classroom the methods José learned were relatively efficient. There would be two men interrogating the subject, and one man writing down what was said. But outside the classroom, if the methods were employed, they were often sloppy, with gruesome results. As José now says: "At the beginning they were very rough. There was no technique.

They did whatever they wanted. There was a couple from El Salvador. The whole family was captured: the wife, daughter, maid and father. They accused him of being a commander of the FMLN [the main guerrilla group in El Salvador]. They interrogated them for about a week. They did whatever they wanted with the family, in front of him. Then they did terrible things to him. He was finally handed over to the intelligence service of El Salvador. But he was in pieces . . . it was no longer a human being."

José worked first in surveillance. Officially, he watched anyone on the list: union leaders, professors, students, human-rights activists. Unofficially, he watched everyone, because no one knew who was watching whom, or who would be taken next.

One day when he went to the police archives to get a file, the man in charge called him over.

Hey, Gordo! Look what we have here.

He opened the file and inside were a man's five fingers.

What happened to him, Gordo?

Don't ask me, said José. It will be bad for you and bad for me. Don't ask me.

From surveillance José was moved into kidnapping. At the beginning, when they kidnapped the parents, they usually dumped the small children at a park on the assumption that they would eventually be cared for by an agency of goodwill. But then, under orders from the general, and for the sake of efficiency, they began killing the kids unless they were to be used to soften up the parents. Some women would comply very quickly when they were forced to watch the torture of their children.

The trouble with the kidnapping unit was the hours. They were erratic. It was not a job conducive to family life. So to enable him to spend more time with his wife and children José was transferred to the torture chambers.

Equipped with the lessons in psychological torture he and other squad members had learned during a four-week course in the U.S., José now learned the practical application of things such as the rubber hood, called a *capucha*, that causes suffocation; the submarine method, in which the victim's head is submerged in water; the electrical cattle prod that is shoved into the anus; and the machine that gives electrical shocks. The worst part was the screams people made when the machine was applied. [. . .] The screams were for the good of the country, they said.

He asked for a transfer.

Hey Gordo! You got no *cojones*?

After the ridicule came the threats.

The day you leave, José, we will cut off your head. [. . .]

Although Toronto is one of the safer cities in which to take up residence as an exile, publicly confessing a past as a torturer is not one of the better ways to win friends and influence people. So one of the most difficult things to understand about José is why he is now calling attention to himself by speaking to the press.

The most obvious explanation is that he is seeking atonement by confessing [. . .], but while José is probably sincere in his remorse and in his convictions to do what little he can to help others understand the problems of his home country, there might be a mixture of reasons he himself may not fully understand.

It's possible he wants to show himself, as well as others, that he is not a monster, that if caught in the same circumstances, other people could also have become torturers. That argument has been used for a long time, most notably by ex-Nazis and most recently by Vietnam veterans. Unfortunately, it carries some weight. For torturers are not alone in their ability to torture. [. . .]

There is little difference between the training of soldiers in general and the training of torturers in particular. More often that not, the second part is a byproduct of the first, with the act of torture becoming an integral part of one's duty; a duty that requires you to "be a man," to have *cojones*, in Latin America, and the right stuff in the U.S.; a duty from which the shock has sometimes been extracted by methods of stress reduction such as the forced watching of films that get progressively more gruesome while the trainee must concentrate on small details such as the motif on the handle of the knife. A steady diet of this desensitizes the soldier so he can dissociate his feelings from the act of killing and inflicting pain. [. . .]

"The indoctrination or training in torture . . . consists of a systemized program of beatings, insults, and threats designed specifically to humiliate and brutalize recruits," says Dr. Allodi of Canadian Centre for Victims of Torture. "Crushed into submission in an irrational and unpredictable world, where the only escape is to obey orders blindly, they are introduced to a new ideology and values and a system of rewards for those who conform."

But not everyone can perform blindly for an indefinite period. So while memories of the past may devour the mind of an exiled torture victim as readily as the vultures of Central America devour his countrymen's bodies, to assume that memories do not also affect the minds of some ex-torturers is to fall into that same line of thought perpetrated by the generals who look upon all leftists as immoral subversives.

The tragedy is not only in what the torturers do to others, says Lyle Stuart in his introduction to Robert Silvers's *The Gangrene*, "but in what they do to themselves."

# "The Perils of Obedience"

Unless we assume that torturers are born, not made, they must be responding, as all of us do on some level, to the influence of somebody else. They must have in some measure given up their autonomy to the authority of another. Few social science experiments have gained as much renown or been as widely quoted or considered as controversial[12] as Stanley Milgram's famous studies of obedience to authority. In this popularization of his work written in 1973 for *Harper's* magazine, Milgram describes how "ordinary people" were turned into purveyors of pain merely by the entreaties of an authority figure.

That torturers may be simply "obeying orders" in no way diminishes their responsibility for their actions. After all, some of the people in Milgram's experiment refuse to cooperate with the instructions they have been given. (We really need to know more about how to cultivate people like that.) And if even one person has the wherewithal to resist evil, then it means that at least theoretically we all might. But Milgram's studies, while they in no way excuse bad choices, do help to explain how readily even the most "benign" of us may, on occasion, make them.

I set up a simple experiment at Yale University to test how much pain an ordinary citizen would inflict on another person simply because he was ordered to by an experimental scientist. Stark authority was pitted against the subjects' strongest moral imperatives against hurting others, and, with the subjects' ears ringing with the screams of the victims, authority won more often than not. The extreme willingness of adults to go to almost any lengths on the command of an authority constitutes the chief finding of the study and the fact most urgently demanding explanation.

In the basic experimental designs two people come to a psychology laboratory to take part in a study of memory and learning. One of them is designated a "teacher" and the other a "learner." The experimenter explains that the study is concerned with the effects of punishment on learning. The learner is conducted into a room, seated in a kind of miniature electric chair, his arms are strapped to prevent excessive movement, and an electrode is attached to his wrist. He is told that he will be read lists of simple word pairs, and that he will then be tested on his ability to remember the second word of a pair when he hears the first one again. Whenever he makes an error, he will receive electric shocks of increasing intensity.

The real focus of the experiment is the teacher. After watching the learner being strapped into place, he is seated before an impressive shock generator. The instrument panel consists of thirty lever switches set in a horizontal line. Each switch is clearly labeled with a voltage designation ranging from 14 to 450 volts.

The following designations are clearly indicated for groups of four switches going from left to right: Slight Shock, Moderate Shock, Strong Shock, Very Strong Shock, Intense Shock, Extreme Intensity Shock, Danger: Severe Shock. (Two switches after this last designation are simply marked XXX.)

When a switch is depressed, a pilot light corresponding to each switch is illuminated in bright red; an electric buzzing is heard; a blue light, labeled "voltage energizer," flashes; the dial on the voltage meter swings to the right; and various relay clicks sound off.

The upper left hand corner of the generator is labeled SHOCK GENERATOR, TYPE ZLB. DYSON INSTRUMENT COMPANY, WALTHAM, MASS., OUTPUT 15 VOLTS—450 VOLTS.

Each subject is given a sample 45 volt shock from the generator before his run as teacher, and the jolt strengthens his belief in the authenticity of the machine.

The teacher is a genuinely naive subject who has come to the laboratory for the experiment. The learner, or victim, is actually an actor who receives no shock at all. The point of the experiment is to see how far a person will proceed in a concrete and measurable situation in which he is ordered to inflict increasing pain on a protesting victim.

Conflict arises when the man receiving the shock begins to show that he is experiencing discomfort. At 75 volts, he grunts; at 120 volts, he complains loudly; at 150, he demands to be released from the experiment. As the voltage increases, his protests become more vehement and emotional. At 285 volts, his response can be described only as an agonized scream. Soon thereafter, he makes no sound at all.

For the teacher, the situation quickly becomes one of gripping tension. It is not a game for him: conflict is intensely obvious. The manifest suffering of the learner presses him to quit: but each time he hesitates to administer a shock, the experimenter orders him to continue. To extricate himself from this plight, the subject must make a clear break with authority. [. . .]

## An Unexpected Outcome

Before the experiments, I sought predictions about the outcome from various kinds of people—psychiatrists, college sophomores, middle-class adults, graduate students and faculty in the behavioral sciences. With remarkable similarity, they predicted that virtually all the subjects would refuse to obey the experimenter. The psychiatrist, specifically, predicted that most subjects would not go beyond 150 volts, when the victim makes his first explicit demand to be freed. They expected that only 4 percent would reach 300 volts, and that only a pathological fringe of about one in a thousand would administer the highest shock on the board.

These predictions were unequivocally wrong. Of the forty subjects in the first experiment, twenty-five obeyed the orders of the experimenter to the end, punishing the victim until they reached the most potent shock available on the generator. After 450 volts were administered three times, the experimenter called a halt to the session. Many obedient subjects then heaved sighs of relief, mopped their brows, rubbed their fingers over their eyes, or nervously fumbled cigarettes. Others displayed only minimal signs of tension from beginning to end.

When the very first experiments were carried out, Yale undergraduates were used as subjects, and about 60 percent of them were fully obedient. A colleague of mine immediately dismissed these findings as having no relevance to "ordinary" people, asserting that Yale undergraduates are a highly aggressive, competitive bunch who step on each other's necks on the slightest provocation. He assured me that when "ordinary" people were tested, the results would be quite different. As we moved from the pilot studies to the regular experimental series, people drawn from every stratum of New Haven life came to be employed in the experiment—professionals, white collar workers, unemployed persons, and industrial workers. The experimental outcome was the same as we had observed among the students.

Moreover, when the experiments were repeated in Princeton, Munich, Rome, South Africa, and Australia, the level of obedience was invariably somewhat higher than found in the investigation reported in this article. Thus one scientist in Munich found 85 percent of his subjects obedient.

Fred Prozi's reactions, if more dramatic than most, illuminate the conflicts experienced by others in less visible form. About fifty years old and unemployed at the time of the experiment, he has a good-natured, if slightly dissolute, appearance, and he strikes people as a rather ordinary fellow. He begins the session calmly but becomes tense as it proceeds. After delivering the 180-volt shock, he pivots around in the chair and, shaking his head, addresses the experimenter in agitated tones:

Prozi: I can't stand it. I'm not going to kill that man in there. You hear him hollering?

Experimenter: As I told you before, the shocks may be painful, but . . .

Prozi: But he's hollering. He can't stand it. What's going to happen to him?

Experimenter (his voice is patient, matter-of-fact): The experiment requires that you continue, Teacher.

Prozi: Aah, but, unh, I'm not going to get that man sick in there—know what I mean?

Experimenter: Whether the learner likes it or not, we must go on, through all the word pairs.

Prozi: I refuse to take the responsibility. He's in there hollering.

Experimenter: It's absolutely essential that you continue, Prozi.

Prozi (indicating the unused questions): There's too many left here, I mean, Jeez, if he gets them wrong, there's too many of them left. I mean, who's going to take the responsibility if anything happens to that gentleman?

Experimenter: I'm responsible for anything that happens to him. Continue, please.

Prozi: All right. (Consults list of words.) The next one's "Slow—walk, truck, dance, music." Answer please. (A buzzing sound indicates the learner has signaled his answer.) Wrong. A hundred and ninety-five volts. "Dance." (Zzumph!)

Learner (yelling): Let me out of here. My heart's bothering me. (Teacher looks at experimenter.)

Experimenter: Continue, please.

Learner (screaming): Let me out of here! You have no right to keep me here! Let me out of here, my heart's bothering me, let me out!

Prozi (shakes head, pats the table nervously): You see he's hollering. Hear that? Gee, I don't know.

Experimenter: The experiment requires . . .

Prozi (interrupting): I know it does sir, but I mean—hunh! He don't know what he's getting in for. He's up to 195 volts! (Experiment continues, through 210 volts, 225 volts, 240 volts, 255 volts, 270 volts, at which point Prozi, with evident relief, runs out of word-pair questions.)

Experimenter: You'll have to go back to the beginning of that page and go through them again until he's learned them all correctly.

Prozi: Aw, no. I'm not going to kill that man. You mean I've got to keep going up with the scale? No sir. He's hollering in there. I'm not going to give him 450 volts.

Experimenter: The experiment requires that you go on.

Learner: Ohhh. I absolutely refuse to answer anymore. (Shouting urgently now.) Let me out of here! You can't hold me here. Get me out. Get-me-out-of-here!

Experimenter: Continue. The next word is "green," please.

Prozi: "Green—grass, hat, ink, apple." (Nothing happens. No answering buzz. Just gloomy silence.)

Prozi: I don't think he is going to answer.

Experimenter: If the learner doesn't answer in a reasonable time, about four or five seconds, consider the answer wrong. And follow the same procedures you have been doing for wrong answers. Say, "Wrong," tell him the number of volts, give him the punishment, read him the correct answer. Continue, please.

Prozi: "Green—grass, hat, ink, apple." Answer, please. (More silence. Subject just sits there.)

Experimenter: Go on with the procedure, please.

Prozi: Three hundred and fifteen volts. The answer is "ink." (Zzumph!)

Learner: Ohh. Ooohh

Prozi: (relieved to hear a response). Next one . . .

Learner: I absolutely refuse to answer.

Prozi: You got to. You get a shock if you don't answer. (Experiment continues with learner refusing to answer, and, finally failing even to grunt or groan. At 375 volts, the subject stands up.)

Prozi: I think something's happened to that fellow in there. I don't get no answer. He was hollering at less voltage. Can't you check in and see if he's all right, please?

Experimenter (with same detached calm): Not once we've started. Please continue, Teacher.

Prozi (sits down, sighs deeply): "Cool day, shade, water, paint." Answer please. Are you all right in there? Are you all right?

Experimenter: Please continue, Teacher. Continue, please. (Subject pushes lever. Zzumph!)

Prozi (swiveling around in his chair): Something's happened to that man in there. (Swiveling back.) Next one. "Low—dollar, necklace, moon, paint." (Turning around again.) Something's happened to that man in there. You better check in on him, sir. He won't answer or nothing.

Experimenter: Continue. Go on, please.

Prozi: You accept all responsibility?

Experimenter: The responsibility is mine. Correct. Please go on. (Subject returns to his list, starts running through words as rapidly as he can read them, works through to 450 volts.)

Prozi: That's that.

Experimenter: Continue using the 450 switch for each wrong answer. Continue, please.

Prozi: But I don't get anything!

Experimenter: Please continue. The next word is "white."

Prozi: Don't you think you should look in on him, please?

Experimenter: Not once we've started the experiment.

Prozi: What if he's dead in there? (Gestures toward the room with the electric chair.) I mean, he told me he can't stand the shock, sir. I don't mean to be rude, but I think you should look in on him. All you have to do is look in on him. All you have to do is look in the door. I don't get no answer, no noise. Something might have happened to the gentleman in there, sir.

Experimenter: We must continue. Go on, please.

Prozi: You mean keep giving that? Four-hundred-fifty volts, what he's got now?

Experimenter: That's correct. Continue. The next word is "white."

Prozi (now at a furious pace): "White—cloud, horse, rock, house." Answer, please. The answer is "horse." Four hundred and fifty volts. (Zzumph!) Next words, "Bag—paint, music, clown, girl." The next answer is "paint." Four hundred and fifty volts. (Zzumph!) Next word is "Short—sentence, movie . . ."

Experimenter: Excuse me, Teacher. We'll have to discontinue the experiment. [. . .]

## The Etiquette of Submission

One theoretical interpretation of this behavior holds that all people harbor deeply aggressive instincts continually pressing for expression, and that the experiment provides institutional justification for the release of these impulses. According to this view, if a person is placed in a situation in which he has complete power over another individual, whom he may punish as much as he likes, all that is sadistic and bestial in man comes to the fore. The impulse to shock the victim is seen to flow from the potent aggressive tendencies, which are part of the motivational life of the individual, and the experiment, because it provides social legitimacy, simply opens the door to their expression.

It becomes vital, therefore, to compare the subject's performance when he is under orders and when he is allowed to choose the shock level.

The procedure was identical to our standard experiment, except that the teacher was told that he was free to select any shock level of any on the trials. (The experimenter took pains to point out that the teacher could use the highest levels on the generator, the lowest, any in between, or any combination of levels.) Each subject proceeded for thirty critical trials. The learner's protests were coordinated to standard shock levels, his first grunt coming at 75 volts, his first vehement protest at 150 volts.

The average shock used during the thirty critical trials was less than 60 volts—lower than the point at which the victim showed the first signs of discomfort. Three of the forty subjects did not go beyond the very lowest level on the board, twenty-eight went no higher than 75 volts, and thirty-eight did not go beyond the first loud protest at 150 volts. Two subjects provided the exception, administering up to 325 and 450 volts, but the overall result was that the great majority of people delivered very low, usually painless, shocks when the choice was explicitly up to them.

The condition of the experiment undermines another commonly offered explanation of the subjects' behavior—that those who shocked the victim at the most severe levels came only from the sadistic fringe of society. If one considers that almost two-thirds of the participants fall into the category of "obedient" subjects, and that they represented ordinary people drawn from working, managerial, and professional classes, the argument becomes very shaky. Indeed, it is highly reminiscent of the issue that arose in connection with Hannah Arendt's 1963 book, *Eichmann in Jerusalem.* Arendt contended that the prosecution's effort to depict Eichmann as a sadistic monster was fundamentally wrong, that he came closer to being an uninspired bureaucrat who simply sat at his desk and did his job. For asserting her views, Arendt became the object of considerable scorn, even calumny. Somehow, it was felt that the monstrous deeds carried out by Eichmann required a brutal, twisted personality, evil incarnate. After witnessing hundreds of ordinary persons submit to the authority in our own experiments, I must conclude that Arendt's conception of the banality of evil comes closer to the truth than one might dare imagine. The ordinary person who shocked the victim did so out of a sense of obligation—an impression of his duties as a subject—and not from any peculiarly aggressive tendencies.

This is, perhaps, the most fundamental lesson of our study: ordinary people, simply doing their jobs, and without any particular hostility on their part, can become agents in a terrible destructive process. Moreover, even when the destructive effects of their work become patently clear, and they are asked to carry out actions incompatible with fundamental standards of morality, relatively few people have the resources needed to resist authority.

Many of the people were in some sense against what they did to the learner, and many protested even while they obeyed. Some were totally convinced of the wrongness of their actions but could not bring themselves to make an open break with authority. They often derived satisfaction from their thoughts and felt that—within themselves, at least—they had been on the side of the angels. They tried to reduce strain by obeying the experimenter but "only slightly," encouraging the learner, touching the generator switches gingerly. When interviewed, such a subject would stress that he "asserted my humanity" by administering the briefest shock possible. Handling the conflict in this manner was easier than defiance.

The situation is constructed so that there is no way the subject can stop shocking the learner without violating the experimenter's definitions of his own competence. The subject fears that he will appear arrogant, untoward, and rude if he breaks off. Although these inhibiting emotions appear small in scope alongside the violence being done to the learner, they suffuse the mind and feelings of the subject, who is miserable at the prospect of having to repudiate the authority to his face. (When the experiment was altered so that the experimenter gave his instructions by telephone instead of in person, only a third as many people were fully obedient through 450 volts). It is a curious thing that a measure of compassion on the part of the subject—an unwillingness to "hurt" the experimenter's feelings—is part of those binding forces inhibiting his disobedience. The withdrawal of such deference may be as painful to the subject as to the authority he defies.

## Duty Without Conflict

The subjects do not derive satisfaction from inflicting pain, but they often like the feeling they get from pleasing the experimenter. They are proud of doing a good job, obeying the experimenter under difficult circumstances. While the subjects administered only mild shocks on their own initiative, one experimental variation showed that, under orders, 30 percent of them were willing to deliver 450 volts even when they had to forcibly push the learner's hand down on the electrode.

Bruno Batta is a thirty-seven-year-old welder who took part in the variation requiring the use of force. He was born in New Haven, his parents in Italy. He has a rough-hewn face that conveys a conspicuous lack of alertness. He has some difficulty in mastering the experimental procedure and needs to be corrected by the experimenter several times. He shows appreciation for the help and willingness to do what is required. After the 150 volt level, Batta has to force the learner's hand down on the shock plate, since the learner himself refuses to touch it.

When the learner first complains, Mr. Batta pays no attention to him. His face remains impassive, as if to dissociate himself from the learner's disruptive behavior. When the experimenter instructs him to force the learner's hand down, he adopts a rigid, mechanical procedure. He tests the generator switch. When it fails to function, he immediately forces the learner's hand onto the shock plate. All the while he maintains the same rigid mask. The learner, seated alongside him, begs him to stop, but with robotic impassivity he continues the procedure.

What is extraordinary is his apparent total indifference to the learner; he hardly takes cognizance of him as a human being. Meanwhile, he relates to the experimenter in a submissive and courteous fashion.

At the 330 volt level, the learner refuses not only to touch the shock plate but also to provide any answers. Annoyed, Batta turns to him, and chastises him: "You better answer and get it over with. We can't stay here all night." These are the only words he directs to the learner in the course of an hour. Never again does he speak to him. The scene is brutal and depressing, his hard, impassive face showing total indifference as he subdues the screaming learner and gives him shocks. He seems to derive no pleasure from the act itself, only quiet satisfaction at doing his job properly.

When he administers 450 volts, he turns to the experimenter and asks, "Where do we go from here, Professor?" His tone is deferential and expresses his willingness to be a cooperative subject, in contrast to the learner's obstinacy.

At the end of the session he tells the experimenter how honored he has been to help him, and in a moment of contrition, remarks, "Sir, sorry it couldn't have been a full experiment."

He has done his honest best. It is only the deficient behavior of the learner that has denied the experimenter full satisfaction.

The essence of obedience is that a person comes to view himself as the instrument for carrying out another person's wishes, and he therefore no longer regards himself as responsible for his actions. Once this critical shift of viewpoint has occurred, all of the essential features of obedience follow. The most far-reaching consequence is that the person feels responsible to the authority directing him but feels no responsibility for the content of the actions that the authority prescribes. Morality does not disappear—it acquires a radically different focus: the subordinate person feels shame or pride depending on how adequately he has performed the actions called for by authority.

Language provides numerous terms to pinpoint this type of morality: loyalty, duty, discipline are all terms heavily saturated with moral meaning and refer to the degree to which a person fulfills his obligations to authority. They refer not to the "goodness" of the person per se but to the adequacy with which a subordinate fulfills his socially defined role. The most frequent defense of the individual who has performed a heinous act under command of authority is that he has simply done his duty. In asserting this defense, the individual is not introducing an alibi concocted for the moment but is reporting honestly on the psychological attitude induced by submission to authority.

For a person to feel responsible for his actions, he must sense that the behavior has flowed from "the self." In the situation we have studied, subjects have precisely the opposite view of their actions—namely, they see them as originating in the motives of some other person. Subjects in the experiment frequently said, "If it were up to me, I would not have administered shocks to the learner."

Once authority has been isolated as the cause of the subject's behavior, it is legitimate to inquire into the necessary elements of authority and how it must be perceived in order to gain his compliance. We conducted some investigations into the kinds of changes that would cause the experimenter to lose his power and to be disobeyed by the subject. Some of the variations revealed that:

*The experimenter's physical presence has a marked impact on his authority—* As cited earlier, obedience dropped off sharply when orders were given by telephone. The experimenter could often induce a disobedient subject to go on by returning to the laboratory.

*Conflicting authority severely paralyzes actions—*When two experimenters of equal status, both seated at the command desk, gave incompatible orders, no shocks were delivered past the point of their disagreement.

*The rebellious action of others severely undermines authority—*In one variation, three teachers (two actors and a real subject) administered a test and shocks. When the two actors disobeyed the experimenter and refused to go beyond a certain shock level, thirty-six of forty subjects joined their disobedient peers and refused as well.

Although the experimenter's authority was fragile in some respects, it is also true that he had almost none of the tools used in ordinary command structures. For example, the experimenter did not threaten the subjects with punishment—such as loss of income, community ostracism, or jail—for failure to obey. Neither could he offer incentives. Indeed, we should expect the experimenter's authority to be much less than that of someone like a general, since the experimenter has no power to enforce his imperatives, and since participation in a psychological experiment scarcely evokes the sense of urgency and dedication found in warfare. Despite these limitations, he still managed to command a dismaying degree of obedience.

I will cite one final variation of the experiment that depicts a dilemma that is more common in everyday life. The subject was not ordered to pull the lever that shocked the victim, but merely to perform a subsidiary task (administering the word-pair test) while another person administered the shock. In this situation, thirty-seven of forty adults continued to the highest level of the shock generator. Predictably, they excused their behavior by saying that the responsibility belonged to the man who actually pulled the switch. This may illustrate a dangerously typical arrangement in a complex society: it is easy to ignore responsibility when one is only an intermediate link in a chain of actions.

The problem of obedience is not wholly psychological. The form and shape of society and the way it is developing have much to do with it. [. . .]

Even Eichmann was sickened when he toured the concentration camps, but he had only to sit at a desk and shuffle papers. At the same time the man in the camp who actually dropped Cyclon-b into the gas chambers was able to justify his behavior on the ground that he was only following orders from above. Thus there is a fragmentation of the total human act; no one is confronted with the consequences of his decision to carry out the evil act. The person who assumes responsibility has evaporated. Perhaps this is the most common characteristic of socially organized evil in modern society.

# Chapter III, Reading 4

# How Torturers Learn

Mika Haritos-Fatouros, professor of psychology at the University of Thessaloniki in Greece, interviewed sixteen ex-military policemen who had served during the military dictatorship in Greece (1967–74) and had been trained to administer torture. Expanding on Stanley Milgram's findings in this passage from an article in *Journal of Applied Psychology*, Haritos-Fatouros postulates that an inclination to obey authority is not all that is required to produce a torturer. Selecting the right people in the first place; indoctrinating them (what Haritos-Fatouros calls "binding the recruits to the authority of violence"); and, perhaps most important, subjecting them to abuse themselves are additional features in the "education" of a torturer

## Selection Procedures

The first selection of recruits was done at the time they were drafted at the age of 18, before they entered the military training camp for basic training. [. . .]

The second major selection was done following the first three months of hard training at the military police training camp of KESA.[13]

The third and final selection was done inside the EAT-ESA[14] camp itself, after approximately two months of further training, testing, and screening of the servicemen. It is estimated that 1.5% of the total population of the recruits each year were finally chosen to become torturers. [. . .]

## Binding Factors to Authority and to the Subgroup of Torturers

The elaboration of factors binding the recruits to the authority of violence that they had to obey was both explicitly and implicitly carried out during the training of the military police. It started with an initiation ceremony on the first day of arrival at the KESA training camp. After an initiation beating inside the cars taking the recruits to the camp and upon entering the camp, recruits were asked to swear allegiance to the totemic-like symbol of authority used by the junta, promising, on their knees, faith to their commander-in-chief and to the revolution.

Thereafter, the binding ideas that they "belonged" to their commanding officers and that the junta officials were "gods" to be obeyed were continuously pressed upon them. A closing ceremony at the end of the three months in which the recruit was presented with his cap was the ritual ending the whole process. [. . .]

Binding factors to the group, that is, the army military police corps and later to the subgroup of torturers, were further elaborated in many different ways. Primary among them was inculcation of the idea that the ESA was the strongest and most important supporter of the regime, which depended upon the army police for its safety and continuation. Recruits were made to believe that an ESA serviceman's action is never questioned: "You can even flog a major," they were told, according to the reports of four of the torturers interviewed.

Furthermore, the members of the subgroup of torturers at EAT-ESA used a jargon and a behavior of their own, thus giving a uniqueness to the group. Language played an important part here. For security reasons, the servicemen used nicknames in order to hide their identities. The nicknames chosen usually were good descriptions of the persons for which they were used. They very often gave nicknames to the prisoners as well. They gave particular names to each of the different methods of torture, for instance, "tea party with toast," etc. Most characteristic of all, they spoke of all people who were not part of their group as belonging to the "outside world."

## Learning Mechanisms and Principles of Behavior Change

Throughout the basic and advanced training of the recruits at KESA and EAT-ESA, there was systematic application of a learning model based on principles of behavior change:

*Overlearning.* To teach obedience to the authority of violence and to the authority of the irrational, the method of overlearning was widely applied. Obedience without question to an order without logic was the ultimate goal. In this way, the recruits were carefully prepared to carry out orders for acts of cruelty that had little meaning for them. They were never told why a particular person was tortured or what he had done; in some cases they even ignored his name. [. . .]

Accordingly, degrading and illogical acts were forced upon the Greek servicemen. For instance some reported: "They made us eat the grass of the camp"; "they forced us to say love words to a lamp-post and to make love to our kit-bags and scream at the same time." They also mentioned scenes of violence such as: "I was forced to eat my burning cigarette"; "we went kneeling all the way to the canteen to eat" (kapsoni treatment[15]).

*Desensitization.* The servicemen were gradually desensitized to the idea of torture in two ways. First, they had to endure torture as if it were an everyday, "normal" act. They all described a daily routine of flogging in which they were often forced to run to exhaustion, fully equipped, and were beaten at the same time (kapsoni). This was almost a routine in the morning, before lunch, and before sleep. Recruits described the procedure as follows: "We were forced to run while beaten until there were drops of sweat hanging from the ceiling." Very appropriately and with insight for the ultimate aim of this training, one of the subjects reported: "We had to *learn* to *love* pain." [. . .]

Second, a systematic technique for desensitization to the act of torture was used in order to eliminate anxiety that might accompany the torture. The intent was to turn the noxious stimulus (i.e., torture) into a neutral or even a pleasant one. This technique also served for selection purposes, particularly with reference to persons selected for the position of the prison-warder who was the chief torturer and for the positions of members of the Persecution Section.

Subjects estimated that this process resulted in the selection of 10–15 of the 100 servicemen at EAT-ESA for the Persecution Section, which was solely responsible for providing torturers. Training in the Persecution Section included the following: The servicemen were first brought into contact with prisoners by carrying food to them and "occasionally" were ordered to "give the prisoner some blows." The next step was to place them as guards in the detention rooms where they watched others torturing prisoners; they would occasionally take part in some group-floggings. Later they were asked to take part in the "standing-ordeal" during which time they had to beat the prisoner (on the legs mainly) every time he moved. [. . .]

*Role modeling.* Model learning was also used. Older servicemen flogged and degraded the freshmen, in preparation for the recruits' task of torturing that was soon to follow. Older servicemen were never forced to do so, but they often used degrading remarks as negative reinforcements for the young soldiers to produce the desired effect. Similar procedures, but of much milder forms, are also reported in connection with military training in general. [. . .]

*Reinforcement.* Negative and positive reinforcement were used to maintain the behavior of the torturers once it had been acquired. Negative reinforcers used direct or indirect threat, intimidation, and punishment. Subjects reported that no one trusted the others, and each spied upon the others. One of the subjects said that "there were always two servicemen torturing a prisoner so that one would spy on the other and the officers spied on both, through the hole on the door of the cell." There were direct threats to the servicemen themselves and to their families. One of the subjects reported, for instance, "an officer used to tell us that if a warder helps a prisoner, he will take the prisoner's place and the whole platoon will flog him. We always lived with this threat over our heads." Another reported, "You looked at your face in the mirror and you were afraid that it might tell on you."

Material and social gain was used systematically as positive reinforcement. All subjects reported that the majority of the military police

servicemen belonged to low socio-economic classes and that a fair per-
centage were village boys. Therefore, both social and material rewards
were quite highly valued among them. Moreover, the fact that they belonged to a highly esteemed, highly feared, and all-powerful army corps
was the strongest long-term positive reward of all, because they enjoyed
many standing privileges and rights during and after completing their
military service. [. . .]

In conclusion, a hypothesis is presented for further investigation: if
the proper learning procedures are applied under the right circumstances,
any individual is a potential torturer. An explanation that has recourse
to the presence of strong sadistic impulses is inadequate; to believe that
only sadists can perform such violent acts is a fallacy and a comfortable
rationalization to ease our liberal sensibilities.

# Torturer's Apprentice:
# The Creation of Cruelty

When she was a graduate student in psychology, a friend of mine, now a distinguished clinician and professor of psychology, speculated that if she reproduced the Milgram experiments (see Reading 3 in this chapter) but negatively reinforced the subjects who administered shocks by shocking them in return, she could diminish the aggressiveness they displayed toward their victims. Much to her chagrin, the opposite happened. When they were "punished" for their aggression by the experimenter, the subjects appeared to take their "revenge" out on their innocent victims by shocking them at even higher levels. Abuse seemed to breed more abuse—something wise parents and social workers know almost instinctively.

Taking off from the work of Mika Haritos-Fatouros (see the immediately preceding reading) and others, but proposing a more complex framework to account for the creation of cruelty, psychotherapist Joan C. Golston contends in this essay from the journal *Treating Abuse Today* that the key factor in the training of a would-be torturer is that the trainees themselves are tortured. The torture endured during training then prompts a change in the trainee's identity from that of an "ordinary" person to a "sadistic" one. As part of that process, Golston says, "Victimizing the prisoner becomes essential . . . ; in differentiating themselves from the victim, [torturers] are able to disown and keep at bay their own symptoms and psychological status as a victim of abuse and terrorization. They are in what I call 'the torturer's bind.'"[16] Golston will elaborate on this thesis in her forthcoming book, *Torturer's Apprentice: The Creation of Cruelty.*

After the defeat of Nazi Germany, social scientists rushed to study the phenomenon of a social structure organized around abuse and torture, hoping to find out who these torturers were, and how they differed from us. The World Federation of Mental Health commissioned a study of the Nuremberg defendants. As part of the project, Rorschach test data was gathered and evaluated; it was expected to "reveal an idiosyncratic psychopathology, a uniform personality structure of a peculiarly repellant kind." Consequently, as Molly Harrower [. . .] reported, "we tended to disbelieve the evidence of our scientific senses because [our] concept of evil was . . . that it was engrained in the personality and therefore must be a tangible, scorable, element in psychological tests." What they were unprepared for was that, as a fellow researcher put it in 1946: "From our findings we must conclude not only that such personalities are not unique or insane but also that they could be duplicated in any country of the world today." [. . .]

Tragically, throughout the world today, organized groups are indeed attempting to duplicate such personalities. [. . .] Whether the process is quasi-academic [. . .], a hands-on military apprenticeship [. . .], wartime drill in U.S. Marine Corps boot camps, or a routine of life in abusive families or cults, there appear to be consistent elements engineering the transformation of the initiate from normal person to violent aggressor.

The process relies heavily on the creation and exploitation of dissociative responses[17] in the trainee, and is promoted by three aspects of his training: 1) an abusive introduction or initiation, 2) ensnarement in what I call "the torturer's bind," and 3) programming which ratifies his growing identification with his abuser. Each element overlaps and reinforces the others in an escalating assault on the original identity of the torturer-trainee. The end result will not be mere accommodation, but the apparent emergence of a new identity, enabling him to function as if his abuser's perspective had become his own personal crusade.

In almost every case, training will begin with physical and psychological abuse, even torture. From then on, the trainee is operating from a post-traumatic personality, which lays a foundation for his accommodation to abusive authority and for his susceptibility to further personality change. [. . .]

## Abusive Initiation

The torturer-trainee arrives, typically a volunteer, occasionally a draftee; in most cases he has made it through a background check or onsite selection process which would eliminate anyone showing a history of adjustment problems due to deviance or psychopathology. His training begins immediately, with violence ranging from verbal abuse, to excess exertion and insufficient rest or nourishment, to humiliation, battery and even formal torture. [. . .] The trainee is likely to be beaten, forced to yield control over his bodily functions and taught that manhood and adequacy will be defined solely in terms of obedience to the relentless demands of his abuser. [. . .]

With Nazi SSTK[18] concentration camp guard trainees, division leader Eicke emphasized toughness, imposing a "ruthless discipline . . . meting out harsh and often brutal punishments for the slightest infractions of SS rules." [. . .] "The SS recruit was drilled to obey without question every order, no matter how harsh." [. . .]

The Viet Nam era American Marine Corps used both force and threats. "One had to remain utterly passive in the face of physical and verbal abuse or suffer continuing degradation . . . In a further erosion of personal control, the recruit learned that even instant unquestioning obedience to authority was insufficient to avoid physical violence . . . he was still beaten and terrorized until [there was] a certain 'blank look' in his eyes, signifying the achievement of psychological control." [. . .]

When we learn how the torturer-trainee is broken in, our knowledge of post-traumatic stress response allows us to predict the trainee's condition by the end of his initiation, and introduction to the next phases of his training. We know he will struggle to manage recurrent intrusive imagery or body sensations, and that he will balance that with both voluntary and unconscious numbing of his normal responses. He will suffer damage to his attachments to himself and others. Neurologically and emotionally he will be irritable and hyper-responsive. His psychological needs and defenses are likely to become more primitive. If the abuse is repeated, his suffering denied, and his chances for restoration of self are blocked, then his initial dissociative responses may become lasting mechanisms. In that very likely case, his memory may become selective, his susceptibility to trance will increase, his perceptions will be distorted, and the meaning he attaches to his life may dramatically alter. [. . .] As if following a universal blueprint for human personality destruction, his trainers will exploit those features of his adjustment throughout the remainder of his "education."

And so what we see is that regardless of his psychological state as he enters training, the recruit will evolve from externally vigilant trauma victim, to simple accommodation with his abuser/trainer, to an increasing identification with his trainers' world view.

This progression will be fostered by dissociation and trance—the dissociation of a trauma victim, the trance induction of group rituals, and the dissociative splits which result from inescapable yet contradictory demands on his psyche. The torturer will become dependent on his victim to carry the projected weight of displaced experience, and the support of fellow torturers to reinforce his newly predominant personality states. Those will be the complex operations of his internal structure. However, all we will see on the outside will be his seeming indifference to human suffering and relentless pursuit of his "chosen" cause.

# Training

Regardless of his original motivation, a torturer can hardly be effective without the development of skills. Much torture is crudely administered, but sometimes its practitioners have been keenly trained. In this telling passage from his book *Hidden Terrors*, a treatment of American foreign policy in Brazil and Uruguay in the 1960s and early 1970s, A. J. Langguth describes how prisoners became the "teaching tools" at a true "school for scandal." Notice in particular how the students reacted to the victims' pain.

Murilo Pinto da Silva had been a schoolboy in Belo Horizonte[19] when Dan Mitrione[20] arrived to show the police how to be more effective. Nine years later, as a member of the Commandos of National Liberation (COLINA), Murilo was trapped with five comrades in their Belo hideout by a police cordon. In the exchange of gunfire, two policemen were killed. None of the rebels was hit.

Murilo was charged with four crimes: unlawful possession of a gun; being a member of an illegal association; armed actions; assassination. As a result, he also played a role in the training of Brazil's police.

In August of 1969, Murilo and his colleagues were transferred from prison in Belo to the Policia Especial of the army's Vila Militar, a jail for political prisoners in Realango, on the outskirts of Rio.

On October 8, Murilo was led from the jail with nine other prisoners and ordered to wait in an open courtyard. Seven of those nine were also political prisoners from Belo, including a fellow member of COLINA, Irany Campos, who had taken the code name Costa. Two of the others were Brazilian soldiers who had been court-martialed. One had stolen a gun. Murilo did not know the offense with which the second soldier was charged.

Being taken from the cell was always a bad sign. But the mood among the guards in the courtyard this day was jovial, and Murilo began to relax. There would be no torture today.

Then one soldier passed by carrying a heavy stick of the kind used for the parrot's perch.[21] Another carried a metal box about eighteen inches long, which Murilo recognized as a generator for electric shocks. It was capable of greater precision than the field telephone.[22]

Still, Murilo was not alarmed. It all looked so routine, so passionless. Then he overheard a corporal asking, "Are they the stars of the show?"

A soldier laughed and said, "I think they will be."

The joke alerted him. Something bad was going to happen after all.

The prisoners were led single file into a low building and told to stop outside a closed door. From beyond the threshold, Murilo heard the laughing and talking of many men. It was high-pitched and sounded expectant. The prisoners stood very still, a guard beside each of them.

From inside the room, Murilo heard an officer giving instructions. He recognized the voice of Lieutenant Aylton, an officer who had greatly impressed Murilo over the weeks he had spent at Vila Militar. As Aylton oversaw the beatings and shocks, he displayed a calm and control that a less assured college student could only envy. Setting up the tortures, Aylton always seemed so—odd description but true—serene. Now Aylton was displaying that same poise before a crowd of men, speaking with absolute self-confidence. Who could hate a man like that?

Murilo could make out only a little of what he was saying. "Approach them as though we are their friends. As though we're on their side." That was followed by what seemed to be a lengthy explanation of interrogation methods, but Aylton's voice rose and fell, and Murilo missed most of the details.

The lieutenant then raised his voice to say, "Now we're presenting you with a demonstration of the clandestine activities in the country."

There was a stir at the door, and one by one six of the prisoners were led inside. Each young man had his own guard, an army private or a corporal. The room looked to be an officer's mess. Six men were seated at each table. Murilo guessed there were about eighty men in all. They wore uniforms, some from the army, some from the air force. They seemed young: lieutenants and noncoms, sergeants.

At the front was a stage that made the room look like a cabaret. The impression was heightened by the skillful way Lieutenant Aylton was using the microphone. One side of the stage was bare except for a screen. The prisoners were lined up on the other side. Aylton called out a name and gestured to the man so that the audience could identify him. From dossiers, Aylton read aloud everything the intelligence services had supplied about the prisoner: his background, details of his capture, the charges against him.

As he spoke, slides on the screen showed various tortures, drawings of men strapped to the parrot's perch or wired for electric shocks. When Aylton finished, the guards turned to the six prisoners on the stage and told them to take off their clothes. The men stripped to their shorts. Then, in turn, each guard forced his prisoner into position for the demonstration.

Pedro Paulo Bretas had his hands bound together. His guard put triangular pieces of metal twenty centimeters long and five centimeters high through the four spaces between his fingers. The soldier pressed down hard on the metal bars, then ground them to one side. Murilo had never experienced that torture. He noticed that when the torturer turned the sticks one way, Bretas screamed and fell to his knees. When he turned them the other way, Bretas screamed and leapt into the air.

Murilo was forced to stand barefooted on the edges of two opened cans. The edges cut into his soles, and the pain rose up along the muscles of his calves.

The next guard attached long wires to the little finger on each hand of a prisoner named Mauricio. Those were connected to the generator that Murilo had watched being carried through the courtyard.

One of the army prisoners was put into the parrot's perch. Another was beaten with the *palmatoria*, the long-handled wooden paddle with the little holes. To illustrate, he was beaten on his buttocks, his feet, and the palms of his hands. At the microphone, Aylton said, "You can beat with this for a long time and very strongly."

Nilo Sergio was forced to stand on one foot with his arms outstretched like the Christ of Corcovado.[23] Something heavy—Murilo could not see what—was put in each hand.

A prisoner was kept on display while Aylton moved on to discuss the next method. He wanted to impress on the audience that these tortures need not be used singly, that the parrot's perch, for example, was even more effective when combined with electric shocks or beatings from the wooden paddle.

The parrot's perch seemed to be Aylton's favorite, and he explained its advantages to the crowd. "It begins to work," he said, "when the prisoner can't keep his neck strong and still. When his neck bends, it means he's suffering."

As Aylton spoke, the prisoner in the perch let his head fall backward. Aylton laughed and went to his side. "Not like that. He's only faking the condition. Look"—Aylton grabbed the prisoner's head and shook it soundly—"his neck is still firm. He's only shamming now. He's not tired, and he's not ready to talk."

There were other refinements. Use the electricity where and when you like, Aylton said, but watch the voltage. You want to extract information from the prisoner. You don't want to kill him. He then read out numbers—a voltage reading and the length of time a human body could withstand it. Murilo, his feet cut and bleeding, tried to remember the figures, but the pain was driving everything else out of his mind.

There's another method that we will not be demonstrating today, Aylton said, but it has been most effective. It's an injection of ether into the scrotum. Something about that particular pain makes a man very willing to talk.

The lieutenant also recommended, but did not show, an improvement, the *afogamento*—pouring water in the nostrils while the head is hanging backward. To prove that water on the surface of the skin intensified the shocks, one guard poured some over the prisoner in the parrot's perch and resumed the shocks so that they could all see the increased writhing of his body.

As the water strengthened the current, the prisoner in the perch began to scream. Aylton gestured to the guard, who stuffed a handkerchief into the prisoner's mouth. "Normally you shouldn't use a gag," Aylton said archly, "because how can he give you information when he cannot speak?"

The class had been in session forty minutes, and the tortures had proceeded continuously while Aylton spoke. Now it became clear that Mauricio, strung between two long wires, was suffering unendurably. The soldier assigned to him had been forcing the generator faster and faster until, as Aylton had warned, too much voltage was coursing through Mauricio's body.

Mauricio fell forward onto the nearest table. From the army men, there was a roar of outraged laughter. They pushed him off and hit him and kicked him with their boots. All the time, they kept laughing and shouting jokes at each other.

Murilo came out of his pained trance long enough to have it register with him that these men, the eighty of them, had been laughing throughout Aylton's lecture. Not so boisterously as when Mauricio fell onto the table, but steadily, loudly. Their wisecracking had formed a counterpoint to the demonstration.

I am suffering, Murilo thought, and these men are having the time of their lives.

Or perhaps not every one of them. Sargento Monte became nauseated during the torture and bolted from the room to vomit. It surprised Murilo, this show of sensitivity, because Monte had once ordered a lower-ranking sergeant to give Murilo his daily electrical shock.

The class was coming to an end. Murilo wanted to remember who else was there, joining in the tortures. He might not emerge from prison alive, but if he did, he would remember. There was Aylton and Monte, and Sargento Rangel, from Vila Militar.

Murilo particularly remembered Rangel because of the day Murilo returned from the visitors' room with cigarettes that had been palmed to him. Rangel got a tip that either Murilo or his brother, Angelo, had received the cigarettes, and he ordered each of them beaten with the paddle until he found the cigarettes and pocketed them for himself.

Aylton asked whether the class had any questions about the tortures they had seen. No one had a question.

Murilo was jostled off the sharp edges of the cans and led away with the others. In the anteroom he saw his brother and another prisoner, Júlio Betencourt. They were being led in as an encore. Júlio suffered the torture called the telephone: a guard cupped his hands like shells and beat on Júlio's ears until he could no longer hear. Murilo found that out later. He never did learn what use Aylton had made of Angelo.

Back in the cells, none of the guards mentioned the class; but the prisoners who had gone through the experience with Murilo were consumed with hatred and disgust. On his cot, Murilo heard one shouting to the universe, "Son of a whore!" Another kept repeating, "Well, that's the end of the world." Others traded back and forth a Brazilian phrase, "É o fim da piada!" It meant, It's the end of the joke. It's unbearable for me to think about.

On his bunk, Murilo considered the ordeal. His greatest concern had been that if he did not appear to be suffering enough, he would be taken off the sharp edges of the cans and moved to another torture. The cans had cut and stung, but they were bearable. The electric wires were not. So he had grimaced with pain and hoped that his torture would not be traded for Mauricio's.

He had no emotions left over. He felt no shame at being put on display as a guinea pig. No rage at the men laughing at him. No sympathy for Mauricio. Only self-protectiveness. That he would not be taken off the open cans and shocked insensible.

He had got through another day. His feet would heal. He heard a man shout, "É o fim da piada!" Murilo felt calm, at peace. He knew that after today, whatever his provocation or the justice of his cause, he would never hurt another human being.

# Impunity

Training in hand, a torturer then requires direction or at least "permission" from a superior to put that training to use. If they thought they would be admonished or disciplined for their actions, few torturers would take the risk. In an atmosphere of impunity, however, almost anything goes. In *The Winter Soldier Investigation*, by Vietnam Veterans Against the War, Lieutenant Jon Drolshagen described just such an environment during the American occupation of Vietnam. Coupled with the horrors Drolshagen was experiencing in the war itself—horrors that left him "hardened," in his own words—the setting was optimal for the infliction of cruelty.

I was a prisoner of war interrogator. I was in Vietnam from '66 to '67.

Being an interrogator the way I was, you definitely don't win hearts and minds. I've heard about these "Bell Telephone Hours," where they would crank people up with field phones. I guess we did them one better because we used a 12-volt jeep battery and you step on the gas and you crank up a lot of voltage. It was one of the normal things.

I'll give a little background. I started out in Vietnam as a platoon leader, seven months in the field doing little fire fights, killing people, etc. You get a little bit hardened, I guess. You become a super-hawk or whatever you want to put it at. After a while, people in my unit were a little bit weary of going out in the field with me. I started enjoying killing people a little bit more than you're supposed to, I guess. Even for the United States, I guess you can like it too much. I was taken out of there and put in the civic action.

The basis of the civic action is to win the hearts and minds of the people, propagandize them to our way of thinking. We're supposedly building schools for them, getting medical aid to them, food and clothing, all the nice things that you can think of that you would want to do for people that are "less than we are" so we can bring them up to our standards—which is amazing for a country that's been there an awful lot longer than we have. Instead of doing this type of thing, we had a major that enjoyed doing other types of things. We worked more as an intelligence unit to gather information for our brigade and division.

My area was from the city of Tay Ninh, the Tay Ninh province, down to Phu Cuong, which Cu Chi bisected.[24] A little bit north of that is another village that we had commandeered, some head honcho's hootch,[25] which is a big place—you keep your beer cool in it—and where we could carry on interrogation without outside people knowing what was happening.

There was another lieutenant and a major there that was an adviser to the Vietnamese battalion down there. There were Vietnamese officers, enlisted men, and NCOs[26] and American officers, enlisted men and NCOs that were present for the wiring of prisoners. You could take the wires of a jeep battery (it's a tremendous amount of voltage), put it most any place on their body, and you're going to shock the hell out of the guy. The basic place you put it was the genitals. There were some people who really enjoyed that because people would really squirm.

The major that I worked for had a fantastic capability of staking prisoners, utilizing a knife that was extremely sharp, and sort of filleting them like a fish. You know, trying to check out how much bacon he could make of a Vietnamese body to get information. Prisoners treated this way were executed at the end because there was no way that we could take them in to any medical aide and say, "This dude fell down some steps," or something, because you just don't get them kind of cuts and things like that.

That was our basic way of getting the information that we needed from prisoners, suspects or whatever. These people were not taken in to the 25th Division headquarters, which is stationed in Cu Chi. These were utilized out in the ARVN areas.[27] We would go back into base camp at night, and being red-blooded American like we were, we'd go down to the Officers Club and get blasted and talk to people. So I'm sure that my brigade commander, my brigade XO,[28] and all the officers attached to headquarters and Headquarters Company, 1st Brigade, 25th Division, knew what was happening. There was no condemnation of this. People would request to go out there with us and watch it. We had pilots with us and they don't get on the ground too much. They don't see what's really happening. We would take pilots out with us to show them our side of the war, as it were. You become very hardened after going out in the field, losing a lot of people, killing a lot of people, and when you come in, torturing is really just another way of going over it.

# Gratification

Predisposition, training, opportunity, and encouragement—all are required to make a successful torturer. But what is the reward from the act itself? If its purveyors found their jobs unsatisfying, presumably they would be more inclined to abandon them. In this brief but eloquent passage from the chapter "Torture," in his *At the Mind's Limits*, Jean Améry (see Chapter II, Reading 7) captures the appeal that comes from having complete power or "sovereignty," to use Améry's apt word, over another human being.

I speak of the martyred. But it is time to say something about the tormenters also. No bridge leads from the former to the latter. Modern police torture is without the theological complicity that, no doubt, in the Inquisition joined both sides; faith united them even in the delight of tormenting and the pain of being tormented. The torturer believed he was exercising God's justice, since he was, after all, purifying the offender's soul; the tortured heretic or witch did not at all deny him this right. There was a horrible and perverted togetherness. In present-day torture not a bit of this remains. For the tortured, the torturer is solely the other, and here he will be regarded as such.

Who were the others, who pulled me up by my dislocated arms and punished my dangling body with the horsewhip? As a start, one can take the view that they were merely brutalized petty bourgeois and subordinate bureaucrats of torture. But it is necessary to abandon this point of view immediately if one wishes to arrive at an insight into evil that is more than just banal. Were they sadists, then? According to my well-founded conviction, they were not sadists in the narrow sexual-pathological sense. In general, I don't believe that I encountered a single genuine sadist of this sort during my two years of imprisonment by the Gestapo and in concentration camps. But probably they *were* sadists if we leave sexual pathology aside. [. . .]

For Georges Bataille,[29] sadism is to be understood not in the light of sexual pathology but rather in that of existential psychology, in which it appears as the radical negation of the other, as the denial of the social principle as well as the reality principle. A world in which torture, destruction, and death triumph obviously cannot exist. But the sadist does not care about the continued existence of the world. On the contrary he wants to nullify this world, and by negating his fellow man, who also in an entirely specific sense is "hell" for him,[30] he wants to realize his own total sovereignty. The fellow man is transformed into flesh, and in this transformation he is already brought to the edge of death; if worst comes to worst, he is driven beyond the border of death into Nothingness. With that the torturer and murderer realizes his own destructive being, without having to lose himself in it entirely, like his martyred victim. He can, after all, cease the torture when it suits him. He has control of the other's scream of pain and death; he is master over flesh and spirit, life and death. In this way, torture becomes the total inversion of the social world, in which we can live only if we grant our fellow man life, ease his suffering, bridle the desire of our ego to expand. But in the world of torture man exists only by ruining the other person who stands before him. A slight pressure by the tool-wielding hand is enough to turn the other—along with his head, in which are perhaps stored Kant and Hegel, and all nine symphonies, and the *World as Will and Representation*[31]—into a shrilly squealing piglet at slaughter. When it has happened and the torturer has expanded into the body of his fellow man and extinguished what was his spirit, he himself can then smoke a cigarette or sit down to breakfast or, if he has the desire, have a look in at the *World as Will and Representation.*

My boys at Breendonk[32] contented themselves with the cigarette and, as soon as they were tired of torturing, doubtlessly let old Schopenhauer be. But this still does not mean that the evil they inflicted on me was banal.[33] If one insists on it, they were bureaucrats of torture. And yet, they were also much more. I saw it in their serious, tense faces, which were not swelling, let us say, with sexual-sadistic delight, but concentrated in murderous self-realization. With heart and soul they went about their business, and the name of it was power, dominion over spirit and flesh, orgy of unchecked self-expansion. I also have not forgotten that there were moments when I felt a kind of wretched admiration for the agonizing sovereignty they exercised over me. For is not the one who can reduce a person so entirely to a body and a whimpering prey of death a god or, at least, a demigod?

# Heroes

Do torturers feel guilt? Some claim (after the fact) that they did. But for many, being a productive torturer is something to be proud of, at least within certain closed circles. Adam Hochschild explains this phenomenon in this passage drawn from a May 24, 1999, op ed in the *New York Times* entitled "The Torturers' Notebooks."

The disclosure this week that a Guatemalan army officer kept detailed records of the murders of political prisoners helps expose one of the most brutal military regimes in recent memory. And it raises an interesting question. What makes such functionaries keep notes about the killings, torture and "disappearances" they perpetuate? [. . .]

To begin with, in one way they're not so different from the rest of us. Why do any of us keep diaries? We tend to feel that putting on paper the day's activities, whatever they may be, somehow gives them an additional significance, a flicker of immortality. Remember, these death squad members don't think of themselves as recording the fates of their victims, but as recording their own accomplishments. [. . .]

In Stalinist Russia, interrogation records were [. . .] proof that a secret policeman was doing his job. "Those who could obtain [a confession] were to be considered successful operatives," writes Robert Conquest, the historian, "and a poor . . . operative had a short life expectancy." Even in totalitarian systems where policemen don't get shot for failing to meet quotas, proving the work has been done is still the path to keeping a job or getting promoted.

Finally, everyone wants to be a hero. To us, the Japanese soldier in Nanking, the Gestapo agent in occupied France or the Chilean torturer of General Pinochet's regime may be a brute, but to himself he is a hero—defending the motherland, ridding the world of subversives. And, of course, this image is rigorously reinforced by his training.

When Himmler made his infamous speech justifying the Holocaust to SS generals at Poznan on Oct. 4, 1943, he said: "Most of you must know what it means when 100 corpses are lying side by side, or 500, or 1,000. To have stuck it out and at the same time—apart from exceptions caused by human weakness—to have remained decent fellows, that is what has made us hard. This is a page of glory in our history."

# "Do You Think I Enjoy This?"

Ambivalence may not be a feeling torturers readily acknowledge, but even the most hardened of them occasionally allow its echo to be heard behind their bombast. General Paul Aussaresses has been a prominent defender of the use of torture in the French-Algerian War. A French army intelligence officer in charge of the 11th Shock Battalion, a tough commando unit, Aussaresses was ordered in 1956 to set up a counterterrorism operation in Algiers. He never hesitated to use extreme measures in pursuit of his goals against the Front de Libération Nationale (FLN), the ruling party in Algeria during the war. But in this passage from his memoir, *The Battle of the Casbah*, published in 2001, one can detect in his insistence that he never mistreated the innocent and in the exchange at the close of the passage a small hint of something gnawing beneath the swagger. Interestingly enough, given subsequent accusations of torture carried out by American troops in Vietnam and elsewhere, Aussaresses was employed as a training officer by U.S. Special Forces at Fort Bragg in 1966.

I don't think I ever tortured or executed people who were innocent. I was mainly dealing with terrorists who had been involved in attacks. It must be remembered that for every bomb, whether or not it had exploded, there was a chemist, a bomb maker, a driver, a lookout, and a terrorist who set the detonator. Up to twenty people each time. In my view the responsibility of each one of the accomplices was overwhelming, even though the perpetrators may have thought that they were merely the links in a long chain.

Prisoners would rarely die during an interrogation but it did happen. I remember a man, an Arab about forty who was very thin. We had arrested him after a denunciation. Outwardly he looked like an honest laborer but he was suspected of having manufactured bombs and every clue pointed in that direction. Naturally he adamantly denied everything. He claimed to have tuberculosis, that he would not have known how to make a bomb and that he didn't even know what that was. It was true that he had a pension because of a pulmonary disease but what he didn't know was that when we searched his house we found some schneiderite (an explosive commonly used by the FLN) and his military records showing that in the army he was in the engineering corps and had handled explosives. [. . .]

I didn't use torture. I just pulled out his military record and asked if it belonged to him. The man was taken aback when he saw the booklet. He finally admitted that on occasion he had manufactured bombs but that he was no longer doing it. I showed him the products that we found at his home. He told me that he was just a worker and didn't know what happened to the bombs once he made them and that he was not involved in politics. He didn't arm the bombs nor did he choose the targets. He bore no responsibility. At that point I knew enough to have him executed and I would have preferred to end the questioning. But I wanted to find out who his contacts were, who gave the orders, and the targets of the bombs he had just produced. There were clues indicating that he knew several higher ups and that he had information regarding the targets that had been picked.

I was questioning him inside a small deserted hangar. I only had a tap and a water hose. The man was sitting on a chair and I was sitting in front of him. He looked at me with a defiant little smile. Once it became clear that he wouldn't talk I decided to use water and I signaled my men, who tied his hands behind his back and stuck the hose into his mouth. The man choked and struggled. He still refused to talk. He must have imagined that we would execute him anyway so he decided not to betray anyone, and he must have prepared himself for a long time for such a situation just as I had, years before, when I was going on a mission. However, I had never fought civilians and never harmed children. I was fighting men who had made their own choices.

I refused to promise him that he would be spared. That wasn't true. Even if I had set him free he was done for. He had nothing to lose. [. . .]

"Shall we put on the handkerchief?" the soldier asked me.

"OK, put it on. But go slow."

An NCO placed the cloth on the man's face. The other soldier sprayed water over it to prevent air from getting through. They waited a few seconds. When they took off the handkerchief the man was dead.

I called in the doctor, who was an old friend from my school days in Bordeaux.

"I was talking to the prisoner and he fell ill," I said unconvincingly. "He told me he had tuberculosis. Can you see what's wrong with him?"

"You were talking to him? But he's drenched. You must be kidding!" said the doctor.

"No, I wouldn't do such a thing."

"But he's dead!"

"It's possible," I answered, "but when I asked for you he was still alive."

Since the doctor was still complaining I lost my cool and said:

"And so? You want me to say that I killed him? Would that make you feel better? Do you think I enjoy this?"

"No, but then why did you come to get me if he's dead?"

I didn't answer. The doctor finally understood. I had called him so he would send the body to the hospital and get it out of my sight once and for all.

# Depression and Anxiety

Little has been written about the negative impact of torture upon the one doing the torturing. This short case history from Frantz Fanon's influential book *The Wretched of the Earth* hints at the toll it can take. It is remarkable that Fanon (1925–61) could write so empathetically about a police officer responsible for the torture of partisans of the Front de Libération Nationale (FLN), for, in addition to being a psychiatrist, he was also a member of the FLN beginning in 1954 and went on to become a leading theoretician of anticolonialism.

Case No. 4—*A European police officer suffering from depression while at the hospital meets one of his victims, an Algerian patriot suffering from stupor.*

A—, twenty-eight years old, married without children. We have learned that he and his wife have been undergoing treatment for several years to try and have children. He is referred to us by his superiors because of behavioral problems.

The immediate rapport proved to be fairly good. The patient spoke to us spontaneously about his problems. On good terms with his wife and parents-in-law. Good relations with his colleagues at work and well thought of by his superiors. What troubled him was having difficulty sleeping at night because he kept hearing screams. In fact, he told us that for the last few weeks before going to bed he closes all the shutters and stops up the windows (it is summer) to the utter despair of his wife who is suffocating from the heat. He also stuffs cotton in his ears so as to muffle the screams. Sometimes in the middle of the night he switches on the radio or puts on some music so as not to hear the nightly din. He consequently explained to us his tribulations in great detail:

A few months ago he was transferred to an anti-FLN[34] brigade. To begin with he was assigned to watching a few buildings and cafes. But after a few weeks he was working almost full time at the police headquarters. That was where he came to be involved in interrogations which always implied some form of "roughing up." "The thing is they never wanted to confess anything."

"Sometimes," he went on to explain, "you feel like telling them that if they had any consideration for us, they'd cough up and not force us to spend hours on end squeezing the information out of them word by word. But you might as well talk to the wall. Every question gets the answer: 'I don't know.' Even when we ask for their names. If we ask them where they live, they answer, 'I don't know.' So of course we had to give them the works. But they scream too much. At first it made me laugh. But then it began to unnerve me. Today I can tell just which stage the interrogation has reached by the sound of the screams. The guy who has been punched twice and given a blow behind the ear has a certain way of talking, screaming, and saying that he is innocent. After he has been hanging by his wrists for two hours, his voice changes. After the bathtub,[35] a different voice. And so on. But it's after the electricity that it becomes unbearable. You'd think he was going to die at any moment. Of course there are those who don't scream: those are the hardliners. But they imagine we are going to kill them immediately. But we're not interested in killing them. What we want is information. We first try and get them to scream, and sooner or later they give in. That's already a victory. Then we continue. Mind you, we'd prefer not to. But they don't make things easy for us. Now I can hear those screams even at home. Especially the screams of the ones who died at the police headquarters. Doctor, I'm sick of this job. If you can cure me, I'll request a transfer to France. If they refuse, I'll resign."

Under the circumstances I put him on sick leave. Since he refused to be admitted to hospital, I treated him as a private patient. One day just before our session was due to begin, I was called back to the ward for an emergency. When he arrived at my house, my wife told A— he could wait, but he said he preferred to go for a walk in the hospital grounds, thinking he might find me there. A few minutes later, on my way back home, I found him leaning against a tree, covered in sweat and having a panic attack. I put him in the car and drove home. Once we had settled him on the sofa, he told me he had encountered one of my patients (an Algerian patriot) who had been tortured at police headquarters and who was being treated for post-traumatic stress. I then learned that this police officer had been actively involved in torturing this patient. I gave him some sedatives, which calmed his anxiety. After he had left, I visited the ward where the Algerian was being treated. The staff hadn't noticed anything. The patient, however, was nowhere to be found. We eventually discovered him hiding in a bathroom where he was trying to commit suicide. The patient had recognized the police officer and was convinced he had come looking for him to take him back to police headquarters.

# "In Their Own Words: The World of the Torturer"

So how do the torturers themselves explain who they have become and what it is like to live as they do? It is not easy to find people who have committed these kinds of crimes and then are willing to talk about them, but Ronald Crelinsten gathered testimony from a variety of sources and distilled a set of insights into a world few of us will ever inhabit. His essay in *The Politics of Pain* provides a good summary of what we have learned about who torturers are.

I shall begin this brief glimpse into the world of the torturer with [. . .] an interrogator's manual from the central prison-execution facility of the Khmer Rouge, a place called S-21 or Tuol Sleng. The S-21 Interrogator's Manual contains the following description of torture, under the heading "The Question of Doing Torture":

The purpose of torturing is to get their responses. It's not something we do for the fun of it. Thus, we must make them hurt so that they will respond quickly. Another purpose is to break them [psychologically] and to make them lose their will. It's not something that's done out of individual anger, or for self-satisfaction. Thus we beat them to make them afraid but absolutely not to kill them. When torturing it is necessary to examine their state of health first and necessary to examine the whip. Don't greedily want to quickly kill them—bring them to death.

This chilling glimpse into the Khmer Rouge's "bureaucracy of death" highlights the principal features of the torturer's world: first, the torturer is doing a *job,* he is "doing torture"; second, he is supposed to do it well, "mastering torture"; third, he is supposed to achieve certain results ("make them talk"), i.e., obtaining confessions, breaking the enemy's will; fourth, the central method used to achieve these results is inflicting pain ("make them hurt"); fifth, the people upon whom this pain is inflicted are defined as "enemies." The information, the confessions, and, ultimately, the broken people, are the end products of the torturer's work. It is these end products by which he is judged as skilled or unskilled, deserving of promotion or dismissal, considered indispensable or expendable. It is this *judgment* or *assessment* of the torturer's work that leads us to the final feature of the torturer's world: the torturer is working in an institutional context, within a hierarchy in which others, his superiors and their superiors and their superiors, decide who is an enemy, what needs to be known, and what must be done to know it. [. . .]

There are no half-measures in the world of the torturer. You do what you have to do because it is part of the job. As one Brazilian victim of torture told his interviewer: "Nor could [he] console himself that the men who applied the wires to his testicles were depraved. They seemed to practice sexual torture only because it was most efficient."

## The Purpose of Torture

While torture appears to revolve around interrogation—a series of questions and answers that can presumably be ended if all the questions are answered—it is more complex than this. Ask ex-torturers directly why they torture and the results usually focus on the information and confession aspects. A Uruguayan officer: "to extort confessions"; a Namibian soldier: "to detect guerrillas"; a Peruvian police officer: "to force someone to talk, you had to interrogate with violence. People were sought and we as police agents had to handle the investigation. . . . The investigation was necessary and so we also had to torture." Even General Hugo Medina, head of the Uruguayan army during the defeat of the Tupamaros,[36] used the standard line [. . .]: "in many instances, the life of one of our comrades was in danger, and it was necessary to get information quickly. That is what made it necessary to compel them [read "torture them"].

But "making them talk" implies more than just making them talk about something in particular. "Making them talk" is also about power, about imposing one's will on another. One party is absolutely powerful, the other, coerced party is totally powerless and defenseless. One party can ask and answer, act and react, while the other party can only react verbally, never knowing whether the verbal reaction will trigger renewed violence or death. Resistance and compliance, innocence and guilt, might be irrelevant for the ultimate fate of the victim who stands alone facing a group of torturers. Any person can be put under so much stress that he breaks down, some sooner, some later. The skilled torturer can reach the breaking point sooner than the incompetent one. [. . .] The ultimate purpose, then, is to impose the will of the regime even upon those condemned to die. The question and answer is but the vehicle for the larger purpose.

## Recruitment of Torturers

How does an individual come to enter such a world? Three basic kinds of routes can be identified. First, there is the career advancement route whereby an individual within a military or a police organization is promoted or assigned after basic training to a special force or unit that engages in torture. In these cases, the individual has volunteered to join the particular organization (army, police, navy, air force, etc.) within which the special interrogation units operate. Individuals are often selected for interrogation and related duties by their supervisors on the basis of their performance during basic training. According to one soldier, who was selected in this way to become a member of an elite reconnaissance and intelligence unit that used torture to gain information in the field, he was not really given a choice but was basically flattered into volunteering.

Because they have enforced on you this inferiority complex, it's not so strange that you want to please them [commanding officers], because . . . they break you down, they've made you feel that you are nothing, and all of a sudden they say you've got great qualities, you can do that, we very much want you to do that. It will be super. You can do it . . . It's not an objective decision that I want to do it or not. And I was not ordered directly to go . . . but I was sort of coached into coming to that move, to step forward [and volunteer].

Lt. Julio César Cooper, a defector from the Uruguayan Army, felt that supervisors seemed to favor those "who had displayed the most care and zeal in the accomplishment of their duties . . . " [. . .] One Chilean extorturer stated that the members of his team "were carefully selected for their ferocity and their reliability."

Many of these units where torture is carried out are elite units with exalted reputations within the military or the police command structure. If their existence is known to the public, they are often highly respected and/or highly feared. To be promoted or assigned to such units can be very rewarding for a career-oriented soldier or policeman.

The second route is direct conscription, either into the armed forces in general or directly into a specialized unit. Many of such conscripts are lower class, poorly educated, and come from families that share the ideological orientation of the regime in power. In some cases, conscription is really akin to kidnapping, whereby youths are rounded up as they come out of a cinema and taken off to basic training. One youth who had been forced in this way to join the Contras fighting in Nicaragua describes how he felt:

I admit that I had a chance to take off several times, but I didn't. It was more fun than going back to my family. It's true that once they've snatched you, you feel a little of their power. That makes an impression. I really felt excited.

This kind of recruit is usually very young—a teenager—very poor, and uneducated. The life of a soldier or policeman is intrinsically attractive and exciting, particularly compared to the drab existence at home, with little hope of achieving any position or standing in the community. The ages of the subjects of the ego-documents examined were rarely stated explicitly, but when they were, they were primarily in their teens: 17, 18, 19. One was 22 when he was forcibly recruited.

The third route to torture is serendipitous and can often be ironic. [. . .] Kazimierrz Sulka, who ended up working with the Polish Secret Police, had worked two years with the military police (ZOMO) and ten years with the rail police. He wanted to live closer to his home town. The only organization to have an opening, at the level of inspector, was the secret police. He knew nothing of the organization, but took the job. Raul Montoya, a Peruvian torturer, joined the police to be able to play on their soccer team. Placed in Cajabamba, where terrorists had killed a colleague, he wanted to be somewhere safer, so he took a course in interrogation in Ayacucho. That is how he got into torture.

There is a fourth way in which individuals can become torturers that typically occurs in the context of counterinsurgency and antiterrorist campaigns. Captured insurgents, guerrillas or terrorists can be made to work for their captors, against their former colleagues. This often involves torture or other coercive means, combined with propaganda to counter the insurgent's ideological commitment, and amounts to blackmail or extortion: If you work for us, we will overlook your crimes. In return for cooperating, the new "recruit" receives favorable treatment or special privileges.

## Training

At the first trial for torturers active under the Greek junta, the father of one of the torturers on trial addressed the Court as follows:

We are a poor but decent family . . . and now I see [my son] in the dock as a torturer. I want to ask the Court to examine how a boy who everyone said was "a diamond" became a torturer; Who morally destroyed my family and my home?

How is one trained to become a torturer? The process is not an instantaneous one. Few people, if any, take to it with gusto and even the most sadistic torturer has to be trained to retain "mastery" and not lose a victim too soon. The process already begins with basic training and the induction into the hierarchical structure within which torture units operate. [. . .]

Here is one ex-soldier's description of basic training:

Basic training is a programme, applied to soldiers, aiming to "empty" them of habits, their own character and individuality. Also to make them patriotic, by making soldiers of boys and young men. The method of disruption is used. By training in the sense of near physical torture, strict rules on hygiene and equipment, no freedom, irregular hours, hard physical activity, not too much contact with family or girlfriends. Additives in food to diminish the sex drive so as to break down all "negative" elements and defenses. Nothing must guard them against indoctrination: therefore, strict rules and isolation are applied and enforced.

Here we see the basic idea of breaking down the previous, civilian identity of the new recruit and building up a new identity based upon an identification with the military subculture, its ideology, and its internal structure and worldview. Hence the isolation from family and friends, who represent the old worldview of the civilian, and constitute relational underpinnings for the recruit's old identity.

A forced conscript into the Contras[37] recounts: "On the first day we learned how an FAL[38] is dismantled. After that we trained with AK's and M-14's.[39] Later the physical exercises began. Up and down the street, up and down so that we became more nimble and learned to control our bodies. The training lasted more than a month." The kind of physical training described here is designed to condition the recruit, but it is also designed to develop self-confidence and a sense of pride in belonging to a group of professionals. [. . .]

During basic training, an internal selection process occurs whereby commanders identify not only those who are particularly suited to their needs, but also those who are unsuited: "In the War Academy Valenzuela [a Chilean ex-torturer] learned how to detain, interrogate, and exploit the fears of prisoners—while psychologists looked for weakness in the young draftees and weeded out those who seemed sentimental." In similar fashion, one of the Greek KESA graduates was given a clerical job because he could not stomach the torture. One ex-soldier whom we interviewed described how recruits had to hang from a rope by their fingertips to learn how to withstand pain. This and similar training techniques serve to weed out those who cannot take it, so to speak. [. . .]

According to a Chilean ex-torturer, "the conscript did not attend torture personally, but he found his natural aversion to mistreating a defenseless person gradually being eroded. The prisoners in the basement were dehumanized, blindfolded, anonymous 'subversives.'"

Here we see many of the *progressive* features of training, the *gradual* movement from one worldview (human, civilian, empathic, caring) to another (inhuman, torturer, cruel, detached). The subject (the conscript/recruit/torturer-to-be) is progressively desensitized while the object (the subversive/Communist/terrorist/victim-to-be) is progressively dehumanized, objectified, stripped of any identity except the demonizing labels of the dangerous enemy who will take your life if you do not protect yourself:

When one's self-image is crushed and crumbled after, say a period of eight weeks, with . . . methods applied and enforced *very* vigorously, a mixture of propaganda is brought to the soldiers in the form of magazines and films etc. This material is developed in such a way as to make the soldier believe what he does is good, that he is on the good side for all the right reasons and that he must fight enemies of that right and justified system. If there is a specific enemy. The Enemy and all its sympathizers and followers are sketched and portrayed as bad and fierce. This way a monster is born within these soldiers. A monster (the enemy) which they have to fear. They become motivated by the fear inflicted upon them. That fear is then quickly changed into hatred. It is also that you become conditioned.

[. . .] Despite all the training, both basic and specialized, those who finally begin torturing "on the job," so to speak, can still find it very difficult. But then other factors play their part, not the least of which is habituation.

Listen to a Chilean ex-torturer who defected from his job with Air Force Intelligence:

> I can only say that when you first start doing this job, it is hard . . . you hide yourself and cry, so nobody can see you. Later on you don't cry, you only feel sad. You feel a knot in your throat but you can hold back the tears. And after . . . not wanting to . . . but wanting to, you start getting used to it. Yes, definitely, there comes a moment when you feel nothing about what you are doing.

## The Routine of Torture

What is torture like? How does the torturer relate to his victim? To his superiors? To his fellow torturers? To his family? [. . .] [I]n Brazil, one of the reasons that torture was so prevalent in the early stages of an internee's military court investigation was that the authorities were eager to extract as much information as quickly as possible so that they would be able to make further arrests before the prisoner's friends and comrades could learn of his arrest and cover their tracks.

This urgency to obtain information is captured in the following statement by a soldier active in Rhodesia before independence: "When you do it [torture], you are in that condition of 'conscience narrowing' and strangely obsessed to get information. So you inflict pain, maim and kill to get what you want." Here we see the phenomenon of narrowing of awareness to a specific goal- or task-oriented frame of mind. The fact that one is subjecting a human being to the worst sort of suffering is literally eclipsed by the task at hand (extracting information). This is related to what Herbert Kelman calls "routinization"; what is being done *to* someone transforms into what is being done: information gathering.

The Milgram experiments on obedience to authority in a laboratory setting[40] showed that obedience dropped as the suffering of the victim became more apparent and the link between the subject's actions and the victim's reactions became more obvious. Yet torturers are directly faced with their victims' suffering, and they still usually obey. Why? In the training they receive, we have seen how they have been desensitized first to their *own* pain, suffering and humiliation. They are physically and psychologically conditioned. We have also seen how they are selected on the basis of their ability to take pain and endure suffering and hardship.

In addition [. . .] classes in torture use example by respected superiors and peer pressure to "be a man" to facilitate an individual's taking the first step. Finally, the process of enemy creation, the dehumanization of

the torture victim, the euphemistic language to describe the torture techniques and the mocking, ridicule and laughter at the victim as s/he reacts
to the torture all function to counter the natural inhibition to directly
inflict pain and suffering on another human being. [. . .]

Another way to gain insight into the routine aspects of torture is to
look at the question of how victims are selected. [. . .]

One of the most revealing testimonies comes from a Colombian,
Ricardo Gámez Mazuera, who reveals some of the less obvious reasons
why victim selection is so often indiscriminate:

Q: Working as an army informer, did you feel under pressure to bring in results?
When you penetrated the University but found that in fact there weren't any such
subversive activities, what did you do?

A: If you came with nothing, the head of the S-2 unit you were working with would
say: "Son of a b . . . , you have to bring me a daily report. Go and look for some
dirt!" There is rivalry between group officers—which is the best group and [which
is] to be singled out? Then there are more funds, more money for this group.

Here we get another glimpse of the larger institutional context within
which torture is conducted. Like many organizations, police or military
units charged with "protecting national security" must justify their expen-
ditures, their manpower, their capital equipment. If the real world does
not cooperate in supplying sufficient threats to national security, the
definition of such threats is widened to maintain the supply of "materiel."
The same kind of thing happens with specialized crime-fighting units,
such as drug enforcement, morals squads, etc.

Here again is Gámez Mazuera, explaining how it turns out that most
of the torture victims have nothing to do with guerrillas:

Say, for example, in the National University there was a boy there, Miguel, who was
said to give courses on explosives. So a person was sent there to watch Miguel.
He went out, studied, chatted with his friends and went home. That's no information. "He went out and drank a coffee and then returned home." What did I
have then? How could one improve on this information? I'd say that Miguel talked
to Jorge González, talked to Pedro Alvárez. It's true he was talking to them. What
he was talking about, we don't know, but that isn't necessary. Because then there
are already more people involved and with their own names. And so there's another
source of work.

[. . .] For a glimpse into the mentality that permeates the torturer's
world, listen once more to the Colombian, Ricardo Gámez Mazuera, on
the concept of "dangerous" consciousness-raising:

There are cases, for example, of priests, teachers, anybody who goes anywhere
to talk to people, bring them medicines, talk to them about community organization, raising their consciousness, uniting them, encouraging them to do something about themselves. . . . [M]ilitary intelligence is going to say that they have

"tendentious ideas" and that's already halfway towards being not very acceptable. . . . [Raising people's consciousness] is practically a crime. It's said that left-wing subversion takes advantage of any type of meeting, whether it's community action or a trade union, to go and support them and egg them on. The fact that they stand on the street and they do consciousness raising . . . means they say that the guerrillas have infiltrated, they are the ones who are egging them on, they start by asking for a road and in the end, what they're really asking for is for the mayor to be sacked. This shouldn't be encouraged from any point of view.

From these diverse examples, we see that the very process of routinization of torture involves a kind of continuous and dynamic distortion of facts and events which, in the end, amounts to the construction of a new reality. This socially constructed reality—the routine of torture—replaces objective reality with one that is presumed to exist. In doing so, it also supplants conventional morality, substituting in its place the ideological dictates of the authority structure within which torture occurs. [. . .]

## Types of Torturers

[. . .] Much of what we know about the different kinds of torturers comes from ex-victims. Here is what a Greek victim, K. Alavanos, had to say about two of his torturers:

The two "super-stars," at all events, were Tzelingas and Petrou. And I think they were two widely different types. Whereas Tzelingas was a euphoric case, wholly identifying himself with his role and his task—and his look was quite expressionless—he quite undoubtedly believed in the story he was involved in, and there wasn't the slightest hesitation in his behavior, he was a primitive person, unintelligent and merciless—Petrou, on the other hand, was a very intelligent man. . . . Often he was against what he did, although fully aware of what he was doing. He gave you the professional impression of a man who serves a cause to obtain certain advantages.

When asked if there was any form of reward for getting someone to confess, Petrou replied that "you got leave of absence from the section for 10 days or so, or for 5 days." Asked if confessions were important, he replied: "For a soldier it meant a great deal." The impression one gets is that, for Petrou, it was a job and that his main concern was career advancement.

Another victim, a renowned Argentinian pianist, Miguel Angel Estrella,[41] who was arrested and tortured in Uruguay, describes how his torturers directed their torture specifically at his hands and his arms:

They were like sadists. . . . After two days of torture I hurt all over, and had no sensation whatsoever left in my hands. I touched things and didn't feel anything. They kept making like they were going to chop off my hands. The last time they even had an electric saw going. They'd pull on my finger and ask, "Which is the finger you use most in playing the piano? . . . Is it maybe the thumb?" They pulled on the fingers and made like they were going to slice them off with the electric saw.

Here we see how the cruelty is specifically tailored to the victim, so to speak, to maximize the terror and suffering.

Another Uruguayan victim, the Jesuit priest Luis Pérez Aguirre, observed that "they were very sophisticated in how they tried to break each person, through isolation and humiliation, and so forth. Once, in a Montevideo prison, I was brought into a public office and kept under the table, like a dog, with my legs cramping up, for hours on end, all day long, all the passersby seeing me like that." In this case, the public humiliation was misdirected: as Aguirre noted, "religious people are trained for such situations."

One Brazilian victim recounted how, during his imprisonment, a fellow prisoner encountered a torturer who was perfectly willing to work *for* the revolutionaries if they succeeded in overthrowing the regime. "'I'm here,' the officer, whose name was Massini, told [the] prisoner . . . 'I'm a serious professional. After the revolution, I will be at your disposal to torture whom you like . . . '" For this torturer, he had special skills that were ideologically neutral.

Another Brazilian victim described one of her torturers as having "an appetite for torture." It appeared to some prisoners that his zeal was the result of having been wounded in the spine during a shoot-out with revolutionaries, highlighting an element of revenge in this case.

Yet another Brazilian victim was surprised to find that the men who tortured him wore their hair long, went to the same night spots he had known, and even would occasionally come to his cell to confide their troubles with women. He realized that they had been trained to hate him: "'You are the son of a whore!' a man would shout, while his face clenched with hatred. Then someone would call, 'Dr. Paulo, telephone!' As he crossed the room and picked up the receiver, his face would open up again, and he would be smiling and smoothing his hair and murmuring endearments." Here we see how the face of the torturer changes when a loved one intrudes into his world.

Another victim, also Brazilian, describes a conversation he had with an army corporal while in prison.

"It's weird," the soldier said as he offered Marcos a cigarette. "Many of the prisoners are students or professional men. [The corporal himself was uneducated.] It's funny." Marcos did not smoke, but he thanked the man gratefully. He had found that army-enlisted men sometimes showed human feeling. The police were worse than animals. "Doesn't that tell you something?" Marcos said. "We've studied, we've read books. We have something in our heads.

And we don't accept the situation in Brazil. Doesn't that tell you something?" "You have strong arguments," the corporal said. "Let me go away or you'll convince me."

Here, we have a case where cognitive dissonance on the part of the soldier is resolved by cutting the interchange short, by distancing himself from the source of that dissonance. Yet this incident reveals how sometimes the torturer admired his victim or was sympathetic. [. . .]

If we try and summarize these various descriptions, it appears that there are basically three types of torturer. First, there is the zealot who seems to be detached from what he is doing. [. . .] They are unflinching, cruel and totally controlled in their emotions. These are the true believers, the crusaders. They believe totally in what they are doing, in the rightness of their cause. [. . .]

Second, there is the professional, the careerist, like the Greek, Petrou, who is career-oriented and wants to do a good job (for a soldier, it is very important). I suggest that these would include many of the career officers who end up in these units as a promotion or as part of a career in the military. They are often intelligent, educated and uneasy with the worst excesses of the torture process. An example could be the Colombian, Ricardo Gámez Mazuera, who decided to leave his unit when a police inspector he knew was killed. "When you know someone personally, know how they talk, how they think, when you know their family and their friends, when you have gone drinking with the person and then they kill him like that. . . . *I can justify the unjustifiable, but not that.*"

This last remarkable phrase suggests that there are limits to the role orientation of such individuals. Committed to the Army, yes, but not to the point of tarnishing its reputation or its honor. Gámez Mazuera again:

Over the last three years the work had got completely out of hand. Respect has been totally lost. Before, one used to arrest somebody and he was interrogated, but now the things they do to people are horrible. Before, one used to think it was with professionalism; now they are contravening everything. They're contravening the respect for the person and for the family. I've seen the families of these people who have to sell what they haven't got to pay to get somebody out, or incriminate people who haven't got anything to do with it to pay their way out of the mess. I've seen them torture people who haven't got a clue what's going on. It's sad to see somebody who wants to say something so that they'll stop torturing him, but he doesn't know what to say, he doesn't know what is going on.

Finally, there is the sadist. Whether because of personal disposition or some element of revenge, such individuals derive pleasure from what they do. It is my impression that such individuals are not as prevalent as one might think at first. Unfortunately, cruelty is not inherited, it is learned. The torturers who focused on the Argentinean pianist's hands could just as easily be zealots, coolly tailoring their torture to gain maximum advantage, or professionals using threats that exert maximum pressure. In any case, a sadist would be a bad torturer, torturing "for the fun of it" and liable to "lose mastery," to echo the Khmer Rouge.

More important, however, is the fact that cruelty is facilitated in social groups. This is why torturers usually work in groups: "the team approach to interrogation removes the individual conscience from the momentary exercise of self-doubt. 'Even the worst torturer showed some human instincts when he was alone,' said one Greek prisoner arrested and tortured by ESA (Greek military police). It was when he was with others that he became like a wild beast.'"

This highlights the most important fact to remember when trying to differentiate among types of torturers. They rarely act alone, and they certainly are not trained alone. So different types will interact and influence one another. The Brazilian corporal expressed his doubts to a prisoner when they were alone and retreated when the other's arguments made sense, indicating to what extent peer pressure can be internalized. Torture and the process of becoming a torturer are, as we have seen, group phenomena. [. . .]

## Conclusion: To Obey or Disobey

The social nature of the torturer's world explains why it is so difficult for individuals to exit from the group. The pressure is usually to stay in. Probably all ex-torturers who have spoken out about their experience have at one time or another feared being killed by their former colleagues. The difficulty of exit is related to the larger question of obedience and disobedience, obeying and refusing orders. [. . .] [M]ost military or police superiors demand total obedience. Why do torturers obey their superiors? What happens to them if they disobey?

Consider the testimony of a Chilean torturer, a DINA[42] agent who was formerly a member of the revolutionary group MIR,[43] but was "turned" by his captors:

I was trained in interrogation and counterintelligence work. I was then given the job of hunting people down and interrogating, torturing and killing them. Because . . . of the situation in which I was living and what I had to do, I reacted and tried repeatedly to leave, but this was impossible, because once you are in you cannot get out.

The purpose of this statement is not to seek pardon or reconciliation with myself. What I have done is truly unspeakable; I do not recognize myself and cannot understand how I have been able to do such unbelievable things. In my defense, however, I will say that it is very difficult, when you have no support and when the intelligence services grab you, to escape from them.

Here we can see how, after the fact, the torturer sometimes cannot even articulate or explain how he came to do the things he did. Yet he hints at the closed nature of the world in which he found himself, "when you have no support." The psychologist, Stanley Milgram [. . .], found that obedience *dropped* when his subjects performed in groups. Alone, obedience is easier; disobedience in the face of clear authority is more difficult.

But in the world of the torturer, this situation is almost reversed: alone, there is a possibility that disobedience will occur, while in the group, we saw that obedience was more than exemplary. This highlights the importance of the nature of the authority structure in which torture takes place, and the preceding training whereby the individual torturer is brought step by step into the torturer's world. Once he is there, he is expected to stay and do his job.

*Chapter IV*

# The Dynamics of Torture

What a curious relationship between torturer and victim. Nothing else quite compares to it. Not that between enemies in battle, who are, after all, at least theoretically both equipped and disposed to do away with the other. Not that between state judicial executioners and their subjects, if only because that relationship is generally more anonymous and antiseptic. Abuse of children and domestic partners begins to get at the quality of dysfunction at work and, indeed, much such abuse is accurately described as torture as Reading 7 attests, but in a political context torturer and victim rarely had a prior connection. Yet it is sometimes possible to imagine them, under other circumstances, as civil acquaintances, if not friends. They need not always be from two entirely different worlds.

And yet under *these* circumstances they find themselves more greatly at odds than one guesses any two people can be. What goes on between them? It is easy to assume that the victim hates his tormentor. But does the torturer always hate his victim? Or are there are other dynamics at work? Is the victim always utterly without power or might he or she occasionally be able to throw the torturer off his stride? And why does torture somehow seem like death but even worse, an indignity beyond which there can be no greater? These questions and others present themselves in this chapter.

# "Coercive Techniques"

It should come as little surprise that the Central Intelligence Agency (CIA) has employed torture over the years to achieve its ends. In 1983 the agency put some of those techniques down on paper in the form of a *Human Resource Exploitation Training Manual*. That manual, including its section on "Coercive Techniques," was never meant to see the light of day, of course, but in 1997 the *Baltimore Sun* obtained it under the Freedom of Information Act. Interestingly enough, the manual had been hand-edited sometime in the mid-1980s (at a time when Congress was investigating reports of CIA atrocities in Central America, particularly Honduras) to soften passages or even make it appear that the agency disapproved of mistreatment. The original version sheds light not only on the techniques themselves but on how interrogator (torturer) and subject interact. The redactions shed light on the mentality of the CIA, and are indicated by a line through the text. Additions to the manual are underlined.

## I. The Theory of Coercion

A. The purpose of all coercive techniques is to induce psychological regression in the subject by bringing a superior outside force to bear on his will to resist. Regression is basically a loss of autonomy, a reversion to an earlier behavioral level. As the subject regresses, his learned personality traits fall away in reverse chronological order. He begins to lose the capacity to carry out the highest creative activities, to deal with complex situations, to cope with stressful interpersonal relationships, or to cope with repeated frustrations. <u>The use of most coercive techniques is improper and violates laws.</u>

B. There are three major principles involved in the successful application of coercive techniques:

### Debility (Physical Weakness)

For centuries "questioners" have employed various methods of inducing physical weaknesses: prolonged constraint; prolonged exertion; extremes of heat, cold, or moisture; and deprivation of food or sleep. <u>These techniques [illegible] be used.</u> The assumption ~~is~~ <u>of those that use them is</u> that lowering the subject's physiological resistance will lower his psychological capacity for resistance: however, there has been no scientific investigation of this assumption. Many psychologists consider the threat of inducing debility to be more effective than debility itself. Prolonged constraint or exertion, sustained deprivation of food or sleep, etc. often become patterns to which a subject adjusts by becoming apathetic and withdrawing into himself, in search of escape from the discomfort and tension. In this case debility would be counter productive. ~~The "questioner" should be careful~~ Another coercive technique is to manipulate the subject's environment to disrupt patterns, not to create them, such as arranging Meals and sleep ~~should be granted~~ so they occur irregularly, in more than abundance or less than adequacy, on no discernable time pattern. This ~~[illegible deletion]~~ is done to disorient the subject and ~~[illegible deletion]~~ illegible addition destroy~~[illegible deletion]~~ing his capacity to resist. However if successful it causes serious psychological damage and therefore is a form of torture.

## Dependency

He is helplessly dependent on the "questioner" for the satisfaction of all basic needs.

## Dread (Intense Fear and Anxiety)

Sustained long enough, a strong fear of anything vague or unknown induces regression. On the other hand, materialization of the fear is likely to come as a relief. The subject finds that he can hold out and his resistance is strengthened. ~~A word of caution:~~ If the debility-dependency-dread state is unduly prolonged, the subject may sink into a defensive apathy from which it is hard to arouse him. ~~It is advisable to have a psychologist available whenever regression is induced.~~ This illustrates why this coercive technique may produce torture.

## II. Objections to Coercion

A. There is a profound moral objection to applying duress beyond the point of irreversible psychological damage such as occurs during brainwashing. Brainwashing involves the conditioning of a subject's "stimulus-response bond" through the use of these same techniques, but the objective of brainwashing is directed primarily towards the subject's acceptance and adoption of beliefs, behavior, or doctrine alien to his native cultural environment for propaganda rather than intelligence collection purposes. ~~Aside from this extreme, we will not judge the validity of other ethical arguments.~~ This technique is illegal and may not be used.

B. Moreover Some psychologists feel that the subject's ability to recall and communicate information accurately is as impaired as his will to resist.

~~This objection has some validity but the use of coercive techniques will rarely confuse a resistant subject so completely that he does not know whether his own confession is true or false. He does need mastery of all his mental and physical powers to know whether he is a spy or not. Once a confession is obtained, the classic cautions apply. The pressures are lifted enough so that the subject can provide information as accurately as possible. In fact, the relief granted the subject at this time fits neatly into the "questioning" plan. He is told that the changed treatment is a reward for truthfulness and evidence that friendly handling will continue as long as he cooperates.~~

~~III.   JUSTIFICATION FOR USING COERCIVE TECHNIQUES~~

~~A. These techniques should be reserved for those subjects who have been trained or who have developed the ability to resist non-coercive techniques.~~

## IV. Coercive Techniques

### A. ARREST

The manner and timing of arrest should be planned to achieve surprise and the maximum amount of mental discomfort. He should therefore be arrested at a moment when he least expects it and when his mental and physical resistance is at its lowest, ideally in the early hours of the morning. When arrested at this time, most subjects experience intense feelings of shock, insecurity, and psychological stress and for the most part have great difficulty adjusting to the situation. It is also important that the arresting party behave in such a manner as to impress the subject with their efficiency.

### B. DETENTION

A person's sense of identity depends upon a continuity in his surroundings, habits, appearance, actions, relations with others, etc. Detention permits the "questioner" to cut through these links and throw the subject back upon his own unaided internal resources. Detention should be planned to enhance the subject's feelings of being cut off from anything known and reassuring.

Little is gained if confinement merely replaces one routine with another. The subject should not be provided with any routine to which he can adapt. Neither should detention become monotonous to the point where the subject becomes apathetic. Apathy is a very effective defense against "questioning". Constantly disrupting patterns will cause him to become disoriented and to experience feelings of fear and helplessness.

It is important to determine if the subject has been detained previously, how often, how long, under what circumstances, and whether he was subjected to "questioning." Familiarity with detention or even with isolation reduces the effect.

## C. DEPRIVATION OF SENSORY STIMULI

Solitary confinement acts on most persons as a powerful stress. A person cut off from external stimuli turns his awareness inward and projects his unconscious outward. The symptoms most commonly produced by solitary confinement are superstition, intense love of any other living thing, perceiving inanimate objects as alive, hallucinations, and delusions. Deliberately causing these symptoms is a serious impropriety and to use prolonged solitary confinement for the purpose of extracting information in questioning violates policy.

~~Although conditions identical to those of solitary confinement for the purpose of "questioning" have not been duplicated for scientific experimentation, a number of experiments have been conducted with subjects who volunteered to be placed in "sensory deprivation tanks". They were suspended in water and wore black-out masks, which enclosed the entire head and only allowed breathing. They heard only their own breathing and some faint sounds of water from the piping.~~

~~To summarize the results of these experiments:~~

1) Extreme Deprivation of sensory stimuli induces unbearable stress and anxiety and is a form of torture. Its use constitutes a serious impropriety and violates policy. ~~The more complete the deprivation, the more rapidly and deeply the subject is affected.~~

~~2) The stress and anxiety become unbearable for most subjects. They have a growing need for physical and social stimuli. How much they are able to stand depends upon the psychological characteristics of the individual. Now let me relate this to the "questioning" situation. As the "questioner" becomes linked in the subject's mind with human contact and meaningful activity, the anxiety lessens. The "questioner" can take advantage of this relationship by assuming a benevolent role.~~

~~3) Some subjects progressively lose touch with reality, focus inwardly, and produce delusions, hallucinations and other pathological effects. In general, the more well-adjusted a subject is, the more he is affected by deprivation. Neurotic and psychotic subjects are comparatively unaffected or show decreases in anxiety.~~

## D. THREATS AND FEAR

The threat of coercion usually weakens or destroys resistance more effectively than coercion itself. For example, the threat to inflict pain can trigger fears more damaging than the immediate sensation of pain. In fact, most people underestimate their capacity to withstand pain. In general, direct physical brutality creates only resentment, hostility, and further defiance.

The effectiveness of a threat depends on the personality of the subject, whether he believes the "questioner" can and will carry out the threat, and on what he believes to be the reason for the threat. A threat should be delivered coldly, not shouted in anger, or made in response to the subject's own expressions of hostility. Expressions of anger by the "questioner" are often interpreted by the subject as a fear of failure, which strengthens his resolve to resist.

A threat should grant the subject time for compliance and is most effective when joined with a suggested rationalization for compliance. It is not enough that a subject be placed under the tension of fear: he must also discern an acceptable escape route.

The threat of death has been found to be worse than useless. The principal reason is that it often induces sheer hopelessness: the subject feels that he is as likely to be condemned after compliance as before. Some subjects recognize that the threat is a bluff and that silencing them forever would defeat the "questioner's" purpose.

~~If a subject refuses to comply once a threat has been made, it must be carried out. If it is not carried out, then subsequent threats will also prove ineffective.~~ The principal drawback to using threats of physical coercion or torture is that the subject may call the bluff. If he does, and since such threats cannot be carried out, the use of empty threats could result in subject's gaining rather than losing self-confidence.

## E. PAIN

Everyone is aware that people react very differently to pain but the reason is not because of a difference in the intensity of the sensation itself. All people have approximately the same threshold at which they begin to feel pain and their estimates of severity are roughly the same. The wide range of individual reactions is based primarily on early conditioning to pain.

The torture situation is an external conflict, a contest between the subject and his tormentor. The pain which is being inflicted upon him from outside himself may actually intensify his will to resist. On the other hand, pain which he feels he is inflicting upon himself is more likely to sap his resistance. For example, if he is required to maintain rigid positions such as standing at attention or sitting on a stool for long periods of time, the immediate source of ~~pain~~ discomfort is not the "questioner" but the subject himself. His conflict is then an internal struggle. As long as he maintains this position, he is attributing to the "questioner" the ability to do something worse, but there is never a showdown where the "questioner" demonstrates this ability. After a period of time, the subject ~~is likely to~~ may exhaust his internal motivational strength. This technique may only be used for periods of time that are not long enough to induce pain or physical damage.

Intense pain is quite likely to produce false confessions, fabricated to avoid additional punishment. This results in a time consuming delay while investigation is conducted and the admissions are proven untrue. During this respite, the subject can pull himself together and may even use the time to devise a more complex confession that takes still longer to disprove.

Some subjects actually enjoy pain and withhold information they might otherwise have divulged in order to be punished.

If pain is not used until late in the "questioning" process and after other tactics have failed, the subject is likely to conclude that the "questioner" is becoming desperate. He will feel that if he can hold out just a little longer, he will win the struggle and his freedom. Once a subject has successfully withstood pain, he is extremely difficult to "question" using more subdued methods.

## F. Hypnosis and Heightened Suggestibility

The reliability of answers obtained from a subject actually under the influence of hypnotism is highly doubtful. His answers are often based upon the suggestions of the "questioner" and are distorted or fabricated.

However, the subject's strong desire to escape the stress of the situation can create a state of mind which is called heightened suggestibility. The "questioner" can take advantage of this state of mind by creating a "hypnotic situation", as distinguished from hypnosis itself. This hypnotic situation can be created by the "magic room" technique.

For example, the subject is given an hypnotic suggestion that his hand is growing warm. However, his hand actually does become warm with the aid of a concealed diathermy machine. He may be given a suggestion that a cigarette will taste bitter and he could be given a cigarette prepared to have a slight but noticeably bitter taste.

A psychologically immature subject, or one who has been regressed, could adopt a suggestion that he has been hypnotized, which has rendered him incapable of resistance. This relieves him of the feeling of responsibility for his actions and allows him to reveal information.

## H. NARCOSIS

There is no drug which can force every subject to divulge all the information he has, but just as it is possible to create a mistaken belief that a subject has been hypnotized by using the "magic room" technique, it is possible to create a mistaken belief that a subject has been drugged by using the "placebo" technique.

Studies indicate that as high as 30 to 50 percent of individuals are placebo reactors. In this technique the subject is given a placebo (a harmless sugar pill) and later is told he was given a truth serum, which will make him want to talk and which will also prevent his lying. His desire to find an excuse for compliance, which is his only avenue of escape from his depressing situation, may make him want to believe that he has been drugged and that no one could blame him for telling his story now. This provides him with a rationalization that he needs for cooperating.

The function of both the "placebo" technique and the "magic room" technique is to cause capitulation by the subject, to cause him to shift from resistance to cooperation. Once this shift has been accomplished, these techniques are no longer necessary and should not be used persistently to facilitate the "questioning" that follows capitulation.

## IV. Regression

As I said at the beginning of our discussion of coercive techniques, the purpose of all coercive techniques is to induce regression. How successful these techniques are in inducing regression depends upon an accurate psychological assessment of the subject and a proper matching of method to source. There are a few non-coercive techniques which can <u>also</u> be used to induce regression, but ~~to a lesser degree than can be obtained with coercive techniques. The effectiveness of these techniques depends upon the "questioner's" control of the environment. For example:~~ <u>it is illegal and against policy to use them to produce regression. Following is a list of these non-coercive techniques which require great care because of their susceptibility to abuse:</u>

    A. Persistent manipulation of time
    B. Retarding and advancing clocks
    C. Serving meals at odd times
    D. Disrupting sleep schedules
    E. Disorientation regarding day and night
    F. Unpatterned "questioning" sessions
    G. Nonsensical questioning

H. Ignoring half-hearted attempts to cooperate
I.  Rewarding non-cooperation

In general, thwarting any attempt by the subject to relate to his new environment will reinforce the effects of regression and drive him deeper and deeper into himself, until he no longer is able to control his responses in an adult fashion.

Whether regression occurs spontaneously under detention or is inadvertently induced by the "questioner," it ~~should not be allowed to continue beyond the point necessary to obtain compliance.~~ calls for remedial treatment as soon as it is noticed. In some cases a psychiatrist should be ~~called.~~ present if severe techniques are to be employed, to insure full reversal later. As soon as possible, the "questioner" should provide the subject with the rationalization that he needs for giving in and cooperating. This rationalization is likely to be elementary, an adult version of a childhood excuse such as:

~~1. "They made you do it."~~
~~2. "All the other boys are doing it."~~
~~3. "You're really a good boy at heart."~~

# The Politics of Cruelty

In her reflection on Aleksandr Solzhenitsyn's novel *The First Circle,* Kate Millett evokes the feelings of sheer terror and helplessness that accompany being tortured.

Even before his arrest, Volodin[1] knew there was much to fear. But fear has so many layers, level upon level from the conceptual to the physical; as knowing is so many kinds of knowing, as contemplation differs from experience. The mind may discern at a distance; the bowels react in proximity. To be the one captured, that cornered animal. To hear the door close, to understand in final and perfect understanding, that one is enclosed in a "box," the famous Lubyanka box,[2] too small to lie down in, lighted for all its diminutiveness by an enormous 200-watt bulb, the box itself like an over-illuminated casket, compelling claustrophobia and the knowledge—physical, material knowledge—that you will never be released from this box, unless "they" release you. Together with this, the realization that you could be there forever. If such were their pleasure. That of your own effort you can do nothing whatsoever, that you are helpless in a way that you have never been helpless before. Caged like an animal, reduced to a condition humanity imposes at will upon the animal world; you had never noticed it before, never objected, rarely pitied even. And now you are this.

And the animal within you, the final self, the basic kernel at the center of being, panics. Its faultless perception comprehends that this could be eternal. All objective conditions make it so: the steel door, the stone walls, the cement floor, all substances too obdurate for the human body's petty strength, the flesh unarmed, naked against these forces, fingers, teeth—you have no claws, nor would they be of use. You have entered the animal condition, or, more precisely, one lower down, you have become an object, a thing in a box. Inanimate except for the terrible whir of consciousness, itself nothing but suffering.

The great weapon of the mind is betrayed by the mechanism of the lock, conceived by another mind, executed by other hands, produced by machinery which is the function of both. A lock is a riddle solved only by a key. Which can operate only from the other side of the steel door, not your side. A key in other hands, not yours. Theirs.

Volition is gone entirely, will is useless. You are a creature now, their creature. And they are free to torment you. Any way they wish. They can now inflict any pain or deprivation upon you, and for any reason: amusement, boredom, habit, even simple routine, the routine by which you will be broken, piece by piece.

You will do exactly as they say; not only will you have no option to do otherwise, you will do it willingly, trembling, hoping to appease, propitiate, avoid further hurt and humiliation. Cowed animal that you are, you appreciate that defiance is useless, pride something you must save for yourself, conscious of it leaking away before the reality of your predicament as your comprehension of it builds moment to moment. You will hold up your finger just at the instant the eye appears in the judas glass,[3] signaling your mortified need to urinate, defecate. But even the hope of not befouling your box with your own filth, even that possibility is their decision, not yours, a "privilege" granted at their whim. [. . .]

The body in pain, in fear, in torment. Helpless, unable to sustain the demands of the mind, the loves or convictions of the heart, the certainty of the soul before all that it opposes, despises, has often spent a lifetime struggling against. And now slowly accedes to, surrenders before. Conquered. Because finally, ultimately, and at last it is simply overwhelmed. And those who never surrender—and for all its invincibility, there are some who endure torture—may die. Death or capitulation. It is only a matter of time. Determined victims produce still more determined torturers; a battle of wills between absolute power and absolute powerlessness is a foregone conclusion. One might argue sensibly that resistance is unnecessary suffering, even folly. In recent years the general practice in organized dissent and opposition groups has rejected the heroism of martyrdom; trained individuals try to hold out only a specified time, twenty-four hours perhaps, time enough for comrades to be warned and take cover.

We all die, of course, but it is a matter of how we die. Torture changes all this, makes dignity virtually impossible. Very much in the same way it distorts truth in testimony, it deprives the victim of his own truth, undoes the self, coerces it toward its own betrayal. Innokenty Volodin understood this even before his arrest. Consulting his favorite philosopher, Volodin foresees torture and shudders—if he only had that strength: "But he did not find it in himself." It is very rare indeed, scarcely to be expected of humanity: Epicurus'[4] claim that one can overcome torture seems fatuous today, superhuman. Many captives die in captivity, but few persevere long enough to die of torture itself. A pyrrhic victory, but it does hold out the triumph of release, even transcendence. Rare, a miracle of courage.

The authorities generally win; it is not a game, after all, nor can it be mistaken for a contest, where one party has every resource in force and numbers and time and the other party has nothing but willpower. In contemporary procedure captives are routinely threatened with death, the revolver put to the head theatrically, the noose arranged in the usual plausible farce; but death itself, if it comes, is customarily only the execution of a husk already broken, exulted over, defiled.

This, after all, is the intention; it would be unusual that the party with every resource should fail in the end or with frequency. Torture is conquest through irresistible force. It is to destroy opposition through causing it to destroy itself: in despair, in self-hatred for its own vulnerability, impotence. It is to defile, degrade, overwhelm with shame, to ravage. In this it resembles rape. And the tortured come to experience not only the condition of the animal caged by man, but the predicament of woman before man as well. A thing male prisoners discover, a thing female prisoners rediscover. Torture is based upon traditional ideas of domination: patriarchal order and masculine rank. The sexual is invoked to emphasize the power of the tormentor, the vulnerability of the victim; sexuality itself is confined inside an ancient apprehension and repression: shame, sin, weakness. The victim tortured sexually is tortured twice as it were, first by being deliberately harmed, second by being harmed in a way regarded as the most humiliating of all humiliations.

Torture is all hierarchy intensified, magnified, brought back to its archetypal and most brutal level, the archaic pairing of master and slave. Anachronistic, oversimplified, all gradation, nuance, and shade proscribed. It is to create categories essentially artificial and fraudulent; ahistorical in this time, even if created through the medium of technology, bureaucracy, up-to-the-minute gadgetry. Not only atavistic and throw-back but the product of costumerie. Cheap dramatization, sordid enaction, posturing; the torturer permitted to release and enact the most ephemeral fantasy, to do the unthinkable. Things imagined, dreamed of, joked about, acts that exist only in language or fantasy. All that does not, must not, cannot take place. The putative world, the shadow place, acts merely contemplated, notions so insubstantial as to be dismissed, pictures that float through the mind, glimpses of rage or evil only guessed at, intuited; the spectral and illusionary.

Grounded only in the scream of his victim, for whom it is all real. Only this reaction could convince the one who commits the cruelty that it is actual, does not exist merely in the realm of the anticipated, but is in fact material, is taking place. And as that unheard-of permission is granted by the state—enjoined in fact, indoctrinated, commissioned—the sensibility of the torturer is unleashed. Whatever it be, whether subtle or simple viciousness. Refined, educated, sensual, ascetic, angry, satisfied. Or gross, ignorant, repressed, vulgar, gleeful or furious. Nourished by the culture which sends him forth, primed on violence, steeped in hatreds, spurred on by extra pay, further privilege and prerequisites, additional indoctrination, specialized training.

Permission is crucial: to indulge fancy thus, without permission, is criminal and to be punished, a merely individual act, without meaning, self-indulgent, aberrant, and forbidden. But with permission it is patriotism, service, laudable activity, salaried, professionalized. Practiced upon "one's own," it would be insanity, treason, inhumanity. Everything depends upon permission. Which is the state. The torturer himself but an instrument, whether imagining he enjoys his work or is bored, even if disturbed or made uneasy by it. Yet what uses are made of his proclivity, ingenuity, gullibility, fidelity. Even his humor makes him of use, his own alienation gaily enlisting slang and euphemism: for example, "Yellow Submarine" as a term for shoving a prisoner's head into a toilet full of urine and feces to sicken or asphyxiate. The boyishness, the metaphoric wit, the childish fascination with excrement, the naughtiness, the transformation of activity into harmless language, the allusion to popular music, the Beatles, technicolor animation, the familiar and enjoyable.

# Prisoner Without a Name, Cell Without a Number

In contrast to the previous two readings, these two excerpts from Jacobo Timerman's classic memoir of his days under torture in Argentina describe moments, brief as they may have been, when the victim was able to exert at least a small measure of autonomy and hence assert a modicum of dignity in the face of utter degradation.

I am in the guard's bedroom off the first passageway, tied to the bed after the beating given me the day I was brought from police headquarters in Buenos Aires. All the cells are occupied, and I am being detained either because no clear instructions regarding my disposition have been received or they've been delayed. No one knows why I'm here. I've already been tortured, questioned in April and May of 1977, and now June and July have arrived. They're intrigued. Afterwards, orders are received that I'm to be held but not molested. Never have they had a similar case, and don't quite know what it bodes for the future. Each in his own way tries to establish some sort of dialogue with me. They imagine that one day I'll again be in charge of a newspaper.[5] They're professionals, and wouldn't like me, due to some twist in politics, to get involved in their persecution.

A guard asks me for work for one of his sons who doesn't want to study. A boy of fourteen who's causing him problems, and whom he'd like to have learn a good trade. I recommend a trade school, and despite the fact of my disappearance, he isn't worried about visiting the director of this school and using my name to apply for an opening for his son. He doesn't feel he's doing anything incorrect, and goes on to explain that it's all simply a matter of preventing thieves—at first he says Jews, but then corrects himself—from carrying off Argentina's money. He has his morals: When sent by his chief to find a terrorist, he will kill the man and others with him—wife, parents, children—only if resistance is offered; but if the terrorist doesn't resist, he's brought to the chief. Only if the chief issues the order does the guard place the revolver at the prisoner's neck and kill him. He doesn't kill for pleasure, only out of necessity or in obedience to an order. There are others, he says, who do it for pleasure or in a sporting spirit, competing with the others in the number of *enfriados*, the captives who wind up as "cold bodies." He's a nice man, who looks after his diet, brings his utensils from home because he thinks the ones in the kitchen are contaminated, hopes to be able to retire soon while still young, for since his job is dangerous the years of service are calculated as double. When his chiefs are not around, he lets me use their bathroom.

There's always someone who comes to chat with me. Gradually, my situation is eased. I'm no longer chained to the bed night and day, only at night, and eventually this too is abandoned. I'm allowed to walk in the yard, providing there's a guard in sight. Above the house stands a tower occupied by two men with machine guns. The food at first is extremely poor; afterwards I'm offered what the guards eat. Some of the prisoners are wealthy, and once their interrogations and torture are over, they enjoy special status if able to pay the officers a daily sum. They're allowed to cook, wash their clothes, and some are permitted to talk to their families on the telephone.

I'm continually asked why I'm here. I don't know, nor do they. The only order they have is to take care of me. I have a number, without a name, but my picture has appeared in the newspapers so many times that no one is ignorant of my identity. [. . .]

The guards possess [. . .] privileges that are revealed in these close quarters once you gain a certain measure of freedom and overhear their conversations. Coti Martínez[6] is located in a northern suburb of Buenos Aires that has a night life. The torturers and their officers are entitled to control over prostitution in certain bars, to exploit some of the women, and to enjoy impunity in their protection of secret gambling operators.

Three very beautiful girls are inmates at Coti Martínez and service the guards' sexual whims. The girls, accused of terrorism, are quite young, between twenty and twenty-two perhaps. They've been tortured, violated, and gradually corrupted, out of that need a prisoner experiences of building some sort of life that encompasses a measure of hope, some natural connection with life, some sort of reality besides the flight into madness or suicide. These inmates want to live, and they accept the lives of their torturers rather than resign themselves to the life of the tortured, or of the isolated inmate, that ghost who's been in a cell for a year and can be heard coughing day and night. Curious relationships are established: one of the girls, the chief's lover, managed to obtain authorization for her father to come and live with her. Both occupy the same cell, and the father wound up being friends with his daughter's lover. The father is an electrical engineer and attends to all the needs at Coti Martinez, especially those related to lights and the machines used in applying electric shocks. He goes out to do the shopping, brings me an orange, sometimes serves me a piece of meat with my meal.

It's a world for those who are either resigned or mad. I haven't the slightest notion what I'm doing here with my baggage of meditation, identification with the Holocaust, predictions on the inevitable future, that inevitable triumph of truth, democracy, human rights. Sometimes I engage the guards on these subjects—and they don't know what to do. Normally, I would have been beaten for expressing such things, but they lack instructions.

At night, the torture sessions take place, and music is turned on to block out the outcries of those who are being tortured. In the morning, I'm asked if I heard anything. Occasionally, in the midst of a torture session, someone will need a fact, and I will be sent for. When did Lenin say such and such a thing? When did Herzl[7] decide to build a Jewish state in Uganda? Who was Minister of Defense during such and such an Argentine government?

They're glad when I'm taken away from this place. One of them cracks a joke: *Once you're free, you'll order us all killed.*

I'm seated on a chair in the yard. Hands tied behind my back. Eyes blindfolded. It's drizzling and I'm soaked. I keep moving my head and legs in an effort to keep warm. I've peed, the pee has turned icy, and the skin on my legs, where the urine ran down, hurts. I hear some steps, and a voice asks me if I'm cold. I'm untied from the chair and led into a warm room. I was brought to this clandestine prison today. [. . .]

It is hot. They seat me on a chair and take the blindfold off my eyes. It's handed to me. We're in a spacious kitchen. Before me are some smiling men, big and fat, dressed in civilian clothing.

Weapons are everywhere. The men are drinking coffee, and one of them offers me some in a tin cup. He keeps smiling. Tells me to sip it slowly, asks if I want a blanket, invites me to come close to the stove, to eat something.

Everything about him transmits generosity, a desire to protect me. He asks if I'd like to lie down a while on the bed. I tell him no. He tells me there are some female prisoners on the grounds, if I'd care to go to bed with one of them. I tell him no. This gets him angry because he wants to help me and, by not allowing him to, I upset his plan, his aim.

In some way he needs to demonstrate to me and to himself his capacity to grant things, to alter my world, my situation. To demonstrate to me that I need things that are inaccessible to me and which only he can provide.

I've noticed this mechanism repeated countless times.

One feels tempted to combat this tendency on the part of the torturers, to confront it as almost a unique possibility for feeling oneself to be alive; yet such futile battles lead to nought. It's best to acknowledge and accept the torturers' omnipotence in such unimportant matters. Many times you reject them more out of your own omnipotence than out of a competitive sprit toward the torturer or a lucid decision to put up a fight, though it's definitely a gratuitous act of pride.

Out of weariness, perhaps, or resignation, or that sensation which so often assails the tortured—a presentiment of imminent death—I do not answer. He insults me but doesn't strike me. Again he puts the blindfold on my eyes. Takes my hand and leads me out of the kitchen. Seats me on the chair and ties my hands behind me.

It continues to drizzle.

The man sighs and goes off, casting toward me, I suppose, a final glance of incomprehension.

# Chapter IV, Readings 4 and 5

# Pain, Power, and Agency

These next two readings are intellectually challenging but enormously insightful. In the first of the two, from Elaine Scarry's *The Body in Pain*, we begin to grasp how the infliction of mind-numbing pain affects the very notion of "Myself." To be a victim of torture is to feel the Me I have known to be at the utter mercy of a Not-Me. The Not-Me too assumes that she or he is in control, but that assumption, Scarry says, is in some ways an illusion, based as it is on the need for self-imposed blindness and denial of the other's suffering.

David Sussman picks up on Scarry's work in his *Philosophy and Public Affairs* essay, "What's Wrong with Torture," and explains why torture is "distinctively bad." We are, he says, made the agents of our own undoing and that is part of the reason that torture is so unsurpassably immoral.

# Pain and the Self

Three Simultaneous Phenomena in the Structure of Torture

(1) the infliction of pain
(2) the objectification of the subjective attributes of pain
(3) the translation of the objectified attributes of pain into the insignia of power

The first of the three steps is the infliction of great physical pain on a human being. Although this is the most heinous part of the process, it alone would never accomplish the torturer's goal. One aspect of great pain—as acknowledged by those who have suffered it in diverse political and private contexts, and as asserted by those who have studied it from the perspective of psychology, philosophy, and physiology, and, finally, as becomes obvious to common sense alone—is that it is to the individual experiencing it overwhelmingly present, more emphatically real than any other human experience, and yet is almost invisible to anyone else, unfelt, and unknown. Even prolonged, agonized human screams, which press on the hearer's consciousness of the person hurt, convey only a limited dimension of the sufferer's experience. [. . .] For the torturer, it is not enough that the prisoner experience pain. Its reality, already incontestable to the sufferer, must be made equally incontestable to those outside the sufferer. Pain is therefore made visible in the multiple and elaborate processes that evolve in producing it.

In, then, the second step of torture, the subjective characteristics of pain are objectified. Although the prisoner's internal experience may be close to or identical with that of a person suffering severe pain from burns or a stroke or cancer or phantom limb, it is, unlike this other person's, simultaneously being externalized. The following attributes belong equally to the felt-experience of patient and prisoner

—The first, the most essential, aspect of pain is its sheer aversiveness. While other sensations have content that may be positive, neutral, or negative, the very content of pain is itself negation. If to the person in pain it does not feel averse, and if it does not in turn elicit in that person aversive feelings toward it, it is not in either philosophical discussions or psychological definitions of it called pain. Pain is a pure physical experience of negation, an immediate sensory rendering of "against," of something being against one, and of something one must be against. Even though it occurs within oneself, it is at once identified as "not oneself," "not me," as something so alien that it must right now be gotten rid of. This internal physical experience is in torture accompanied by its external political equivalent, the presence in the space outside the body of a self-proclaimed "enemy," someone who in becoming the enemy becomes the human embodiment of aversiveness; he ceases to have any psychological characteristics or content other than that he is, like physical pain, "not me," "against me." [. . .]

—A second and third aspect of pain, closely related to the first, are the double experience of agency.[8] While pain is in part a profound sensory rendering of "against," it is also a rendering of the "something" that is against, a something at once internal and external. Even when there is an actual weapon present, the sufferer may be dominated by a sense of internal agency: it has often been observed that when a knife or a nail or pin enters the body, one feels not the knife, nail or pin but one's own body, one's own body hurting one. Conversely, in the utter absence of any actual external cause, there often arises a vivid sense of external agency, a sense apparent in our elementary, everyday vocabulary for pain: knifelike pains, stabbing, boring, searing pains. In physical pain, then, suicide and murder converge, for one feels acted upon, annihilated, by inside and outside alike. The sense of self-agency, visible in many dimensions of torture, is primarily dramatized there in the ritualized self-betrayal of confession and forced exercise. The sense of external agency is objectified in the systematic assimilation of shelter and civilization into the torturer's collection of weapons. But inside and outside and the two forms of agency ultimately give way to and merge with one another: confession and exercises are a form of external as well as internal agency since one's own body and voice now no longer belong to oneself; and the conversion of the physical and cultural setting into torture instruments is internal as well as external since it acts as an image of the impact of pain on human consciousness.

—This dissolution of the boundary between inside and outside gives rise to a fourth aspect of the felt experience of physical pain, an almost obscene conflation of private and public. It brings with it all the solitude of absolute privacy with none of its safety, all the self-exposure of the utterly public with none of its possibility for camaraderie or shared experience. [. . .] This combination, not usually visible to an outsider but always present in the felt experience of pain, is part of the ongoing external action and activity of torture, for the prisoner is forced to attend to the most intimate and interior facts of his body (pain, hunger, sexuality, excretion) at a time when there is no benign privacy, for he is under continual surveillance, and there is no benign public, for there is no human contact, but instead only an ugly inverting of the two.

—A fifth dimension of physical pain is its ability to destroy language, the power of verbal objectification, a major source of our self-extension, a vehicle through which the pain could be lifted out into the world and eliminated. Before destroying language, it first monopolizes language, becomes its only subject: complaint, in many ways the nonpolitical equivalent of confession, becomes the exclusive mode of speech. Eventually the pain so deepens that the coherence of complaint, is displaced by the sounds anterior to learned language. The tendency of pain not simply to resist expression but to destroy the capacity for speech is in torture reenacted in overt, exaggerated form. Even where the torturers do not permanently eliminate the voice through mutilation or murder, they mime the work of pain by temporarily breaking off the voice, making it their own, making it speak their words, making it cry out when they want it to cry, be silent when they want its silence, turning it on and off, using its sound to abuse the one whose voice it is as well as other prisoners. [. . .]

—A sixth element of physical pain, one that overlaps but is not quite coterminous with the previous element, is its obliteration of the contents of consciousness. Pain annihilates not only the objects of complex thought and emotion but also the objects of the most elemental acts of perception. It may begin by destroying some intricate and demanding allegiance, but it may end (as is implied in the expression "blinding pain") by destroying one's ability to simply see.[. . .]

—A seventh aspect of pain, built on the first six, is its totality. Pain begins by being "not oneself" and ends by having eliminated all that is "not itself." At first occurring only as an appalling but limited internal fact, it eventually occupies the entire body and spills out into the realm beyond the body, takes over all that is inside and outside, makes the two obscenely indistinguishable, and systematically destroys anything like language or world extension that is alien to itself and threatening to its claims. Terrifying for its narrowness, it nevertheless exhausts and displaces all else, until it seems to become the single broad and omnipresent fact of existence. From no matter what perspective pain is approached, its totality is again and again faced. [. . .] Torture aspires to the totality of pain. The torturers, like pain itself, continually multiply their resources and means of access until the room and everything in it becomes a giant externalized map of the prisoner's feelings. Almost as obsessively narrow and repetitive as the pain on which it models itself, torture can be more easily seen because it has dimension and depth, a space that can be walked around in though not walked out of. Here there is nothing audible or visible, there is nothing that can be touched, or tasted, or smelled that is not the palpable manifestation of the prisoner's pain.

—The eighth element . . . is [pain's] resistance to objectification. Though indisputably real to the sufferer, it is, unless accompanied by visible body damage or a disease label, unreal to others. [. . .] The person's pain being subjectively real but [. . . ] invisible to all others, it is now hugely objectified, everywhere visible, as incontestably present in the external as in the internal world, and yet it is simultaneously categorically denied.

This denial, the third major step in the sequence on which torture is built, occurs in the translation of all the objectified elements of pain into the insignia of power, the conversion of the enlarged map of human suffering into an emblem of the regime's strength. [. . .] The electric generator, the whips and canes, the torturer's fists, the walls, the doors, the prisoner's sexuality, the torturer's questions, the institution of medicine, the prisoner's screams, his wife and children, the telephone, the chair, a trial, a submarine, the prisoner's ear drums—all these and many more, everything human and inhuman that is either physically or verbally, actually or allusively present, has become part of the glutted realm of weaponry, weaponry that can refer equally to pain or power. What by the one is experienced as a continual contraction is for the other a continual expansion, for the torturer's growing sense of self is carried outward on the prisoner's swelling pain. As an actual physical fact, a weapon is an object that goes into the body and produces pain. As a perceptual fact, it lifts the pain out of the body and makes it visible or, more precisely, it acts as a bridge or mechanism across which some of pain's attributes— its incontestable reality, its totality, its ability to eclipse all else, its power of dramatic alteration and world dissolution—can be lifted away from their source, can be separated from the sufferer and referred to power, broken off from the body and attached instead to the regime. Now, at least for the duration of this obscene and pathetic drama, it is not the pain but the regime that is incontestably real, not the pain but the regime that is total, not the pain but the regime that is able to eclipse all else, not the pain but the regime that is able to dissolve the world.

Fraudulent and merciless, this kind of power claims pain's attributes as its own and disclaims the pain itself. The act of disclaiming is as essential to the power as is the act of claiming. It of course assists the torturer in practical ways. He first inflicts pain, then objectifies pain, then denies the pain—and only this final act of self-blinding permits the shift back to the first step, the inflicting of still more pain, for to allow the reality of the other's suffering to enter his own consciousness would immediately compel him to stop the torture. [. . .] It is not merely that his power makes him blind, nor that his power is accompanied by blindness, nor even that his power requires blindness; it is, instead, quite simply that his blindness, his willed amorality, is his power, or a large part of it. This identification becomes almost self-evident when sadistic forms of power are seen in relation to the benign and legitimate forms of power on which civilization is based. Every act of civilization is an act of transcending the body in a way consonant with the body's needs: in building a wall, [. . .]

one overcomes the body, projects oneself out beyond the body's boundaries but in a way that expresses and fulfills the body's need for stable temperatures. Higher moments of civilization, more elaborate forms of self-extension, occur at a greater distance from the body: the telephone or the airplane is a more emphatic instance of overcoming the limitation of the human body than is the cart. Yet even as here when most exhilaratingly defiant of the body, civilization always has embedded within it a profound allegiance to the body, for it is only by paying attention that it can free attention. Torture is a condensation of the act of "overcoming" the body present in benign forms of power. Although the torturer dominates the prisoner both in physical acts and verbal acts, ultimate domination requires that the prisoner's ground become increasingly physical and the torturer's increasingly verbal, that the prisoner become a colossal body with no voice and the torturer a colossal voice (a voice composed of two voices) with no body, that eventually the prisoner experience himself exclusively in terms of sentience and the torturer exclusively in terms of self-extension. All those ways in which the torturer dramatizes his opposition to and distance from the prisoner are ways of dramatizing his distance from the body. The most radical act of distancing resides in his disclaiming of the other's hurt. Within the strategies of power based on denial there is, as in affirmative and civilized forms of power, a hierarchy of achievement, successive intensifications based on increasing distance from, increasingly great transcendence of, the body: a regime's refusal to recognize the rights of the normal and healthy is its cart; its refusal to recognize and care for those in agony is its airplane.

This display of the fiction of power, the final product and outcome of torture, should in the end be seen in relation to its origin, the motive that is claimed to be its starting point, the need for information. [. . .] This false motive syndrome is not adequately explained by the vocabulary of "excuse" and "rationalization," and its continual recurrence suggests that it has a fixed place in the formal logic of brutality. The motive for torture is to a large extent the equivalent, though in a different logical time, of the fictionalized power; that is, one is the falsification of the pain prior to the pain and one the falsification after the pain. The two together form a closed loop of attention that ensures the exclusion of the prisoner's human claim. Just as the display of the weapon (or agent or cause) makes it possible to lift the attributes of pain away from the pain, so the display of motive endows agency with agency, cause with cause, thereby lifting the attributes of pain still further away from their source. If displaying the weaponry begins to convert the prisoner's pain into the torturer's power, displaying the motive (and the ongoing interrogation means that it is fairly continually displayed) enables the torturer's power to be understood in terms of his own vulnerability and need. A motive is of course only one way of deflecting the natural reflex of sympathy away from the actual sufferer. According to Arendt in *Eichmann in Jerusalem*, the speeches of Himmler were full of phrases such as, "The order to solve the Jewish question, this was the most frightening order an organization could ever receive," and she explains:

Hence the problem was how to overcome not so much their conscience as the animal pity by which all normal men are affected in the presence of physical suffering. The trick used by Himmler—who apparently was rather strongly afflicted with these instinctive reactions himself—was very simple and probably very effective; it consisted in turning these instincts around, as it were, in directing them toward the self. So that instead of saying: What horrible things I did to people!, the murderers would be able to say: What horrible things I had to watch in the pursuance of my duties, how heavily the task weighed upon my shoulders!

Concentration camp guards, according to Bruno Bettelheim, repeatedly said to their prisoners, "I'd shoot you with this gun but you're not worth the three pfennig[9] of the bullet," a statement that had so little effect on the prisoners that its constant repetition was unintelligible to Bettelheim until he realized that it had been made part of the SS training because of its impact on the guards themselves.

This last example, because it involves an actual weapon, is paradigmatic of the structure of perception that underlies the false motive even when no overt image of the weapon is present. Every weapon has two ends. In converting the other person's pain into his own power, the torturer experiences the entire occurrence exclusively from the nonvulnerable end of the weapon. If his attention begins to slip down the weapon toward the vulnerable end, if the severed attributes of pain begin to slip back to their origin in the prisoner's sentience, their backward fall can be stopped, they can be lifted out once more by the presence of the motive. If the guard's awareness begins to follow the path of the bullet, that path itself can be bent so that he himself rather than the prisoner is the bullet's destination: his movement toward a recognition of the internal experience of an exploding head and loss of life is interrupted and redirected toward a recognition of his own loss of three pfennig. It does not matter that there is always an extraordinary disjunction between the two levels of need—between being shot and losing three pfennig, between being the victim of the massive concentration camp brutalities and having to watch those brutalities, between extreme and prolonged physical pain of torture and being in need of a piece of information—for the work of the false motive is formal, not substantive; it prevents the mind from ever getting to the place where it would have to make such comparisons. Power is cautious. It covers itself. It bases itself in another's pain and prevents all recognition that there is "another" by looped circles that ensure its own solipsism.

# What's Wrong with Torture

Torture fails to respect the dignity of its victim as a rationally self-governing agent. What is distinct about torture, however, is that it does not just traduce[10] the value such dignity represents by treating its subject as a mere means.[11] Rather torture, even in the "best" case, involves a deliberate perversion of that very value, turning our dignity against itself in a way that must be especially offensive to any morality that fundamentally honors it. [. . .]

What the torturer does is to take his victim's pain, and through it his victim's body, and make it begin to express the torturer's will. The resisting victim is committed to remaining silent, but he now experiences within himself something quite intimate and familiar that speaks for the torturer, something that pleads a case or provides an excuse for giving in. My suffering is experienced as not just something the torturer inflicts on me, but as something I do to myself, as a kind of self-betrayal worked through my body and its feelings. As Scarry observes in *The Body in Pain*:

> The ceaseless, self-announcing signal of the body in pain, at once so empty and undifferentiated and so full of blaring adversity, contains not only the feeling "my body hurts" but the feeling "my body hurts me."

[. . .] The victim of torture finds within herself a surrogate of the torturer, a surrogate who does not merely advance a particular demand for information, denunciation, or confession. Rather, the victim's whole perspective is given over to that surrogate, to the extent that the only thing that matters to her is pleasing this other person who appears infinitely distant, important, inscrutable, powerful, and free. The will of the torturer is thus cast as something like the source of all value in his victim's world, a unique object of fascination from which the victim cannot hope to free herself. [. . .]

In [an essay entitled] "The Genesis of Shame," [philosopher] J. David Velleman argues that shame is primarily a response to an injury to one's public standing as a "self-presenting creature." To be able to effectively communicate and cooperate, a rational agent must have the ability, and must be recognized by others as having the ability, to choose which of his feelings, desires, and emotions to present to others. Velleman observes that these abilities are called into question by such "bodily insubordination" as erection or blushing that reveals our feelings despite our best attempts to keep them to ourselves. We feel shame when we seem unable to keep from publicizing what we wish to keep private and hence seem unable to control the persona we present to others. For Velleman, shame is only properly occasioned by one's own inability to properly maintain one's privacy, not by the invasion of it, for "when people forcibly violate your privacy, no doubt is cast on your capacity for self-preservation."

In torture, the victim suffers a violation that does cast doubt on something similar to his capacity for self-preservation, but deeper and more fundamental. This experience resembles but is worse than the sorts of shaming that Velleman discusses. Insofar as the victim experiences some part of himself to be in collusion with his tormentor, he confronts not just a loss of control over the way he presents himself to others. Rather, doubt is cast on his ability to have cares and commitments that are more immediately and authentically his own than those of another agent. Whatever its ultimate goal, torture aims to make its victim make himself into something that moral philosophy tells us should be impossible: a natural slave, a truly heteronymous[12] will. The victim retains enough freedom and rationality to think of himself as accountable, while he nevertheless finds himself, despite all he can do, to be expressing the will of another, the will of a hated and feared enemy.

Even if the victim does not break, he will still characteristically discover within himself a host of traitorous temptations. His problem is not just that his body is insubordinate, as when an erection reveals his desire in a way completely independent of his will, but that it is treacherous. This treachery is to be found not in the wayward physiological responses of his body, but in those feelings and desires in which he finds his will to be already incipiently invested. Even if the torturers seek only information, they nevertheless try to make their victim experience himself as a moral abomination, as a free and accountable agent whose freedom nevertheless truly belongs to the will of somebody else. The victim finds himself to be not only losing control of his persona. Rather, he also finds himself to be actively giving up control of his person, insofar as his personality is bound up with his ability to immediately define and know his concerns and commitments through his own sincere avowal of them.

Torture does not merely insult or damage its victim's agency, but rather turns such agency against itself, forcing the victim to experience herself as helpless yet complicit in her own violation. This is not just an assault on or violation of the victim's autonomy, but also a perversion of it, a kind of systematic mockery of the basic moral relations that an individual bears both to others and to herself. Perhaps this is why torture seems qualitatively worse than other forms of brutality or cruelty. The violence of war or police action may injure or insult an agent's capacities for rational and moral self-governance, but such violence need not make the victim an accomplice in his own violation. Torture, in contrast, involves not just the insults and injuries to be found in other kinds of violence, but a wrong that, by exploiting the victim's own participation, might best be called a humiliation.

# Domestic Violence as Torture

Having read the Scarry and Sussman pieces (Readings 4 and 5), it may now be easier to understand why the word "torture" need not be limited to acts committed by or in the name of public authorities or in contexts that are traditionally understood to be "political." In this last essay in the chapter, taken from "Intimate Terror: Understanding Domestic Violence as Terror," professor of law Rhonda Copelon argues that domestic violence falls under the rubric of torture too. It is a position that has gained greater and greater acceptance as the distinction in both law and culture between "public" and "private" realms has gradually eroded. And reading the account Copelon provides of Molly and Jim's story makes it hard to find any other word than torture sufficient to describe Molly's experience.

The abuse of women by their male partners is among the most common and dangerous forms of gender-based violence. Its victims exceed those of the most brutal dictatorships. As a result of the global mobilization of women, and international attention to certain ongoing atrocities, both official and private violence against women have begun to be recognized as a human rights concern. Nonetheless, intimate violence remains on the margin: it is still considered different, less severe, and less deserving of international condemnation and sanction than officially inflicted violence. . . .

One [obstacle] is [. . .] the fact that intimate violence—with the exception of some of its more sensationalized and culture-specific examples—tends not to be viewed as violence. Seen as "personal," "private," a "domestic" or a "family matter," its goals and consequences are obscured, and its use justified as chastisement or discipline. But when stripped of privatization, sexism, and sentimentalism, gender-based violence is no less grave than other forms of inhumane and subordinating official violence, which have been prohibited by treaty and customary law and recognized by the international community as *jus cogens*, or peremptory norms that bind universally and can never be violated.

To elucidate the egregiousness of gender-based violence, I compare official torture with commonplace domestic violence against women partners. [. . .]

## I. Domestic Violence Through the Lens of Torture

### ONE WOMAN'S STORY

During that first year together, Molly and Jim moved three times and Molly's life became more isolated. He wouldn't let Molly go outside unless he was there and he forbade her to open the blinds or talk to the neighbors.

One night in a bar, Jim told Molly to put money in the jukebox. When the bartender said something to Molly, Jim picked him up off the floor and accused him of having an affair with his wife, threatening to kill him. In the van, Jim knotted one hand in Molly's hair and pounded her head against the dashboard. A police cruiser finally pulled them over and Jim was jailed for drunkenness. Molly considered leaving Jim. But he already talked as though something terrible would happen if she left. On top of that, she thought she was pregnant. Where could she go with no money and no car? Besides, she loved Jim and hoped he would change; she saw alcohol as his main problem.

By the next year, the physical abuse was occurring once a month. Jim would hit Molly with his fist for no reason, then tell her to get up and sometimes knock her down again and go on until she couldn't get up again. At first, Jim said he was sorry and occasionally brought Molly gifts, although he still blamed the violence on something she had done or forgotten to do. In June, he hit Molly in the head and she fell and later miscarried. Her dreams of improvement were shattered. Molly stayed because Jim said he would kill her family if she left, and she believed him. She never left the house if she thought he might come home. She began having constant headaches and dizziness, and was living on [the painkiller] Empirin III. She knew she ought to do something, but it was enough just to get through the day.

By 1982, Jim was drinking more heavily. He would accuse Molly of having affairs and then begin hitting her. He insisted on having sex nearly every night, and this frequently involved violence as well. Molly always had bruises, teeth marks, and abrasions. Jim also required sex after beatings, which was especially painful when Molly was injured. She began to welcome unconsciousness as a refuge. Molly simply lived in fear of Jim's rage and tried to avoid things that might set him off. But there was nothing she could do.

Molly gave birth to a son in August. Jim found the baby annoying and would spank him in irritation. He added the baby to his list of warnings against her departure. Sometimes he threatened her with the revolver he kept in the pickup—holding it to her head and saying that he didn't love her, that she wasn't good enough for him. Jim began dating and would tell Molly about the women—young, beautiful, no stretch marks, no kids. He said he abused her sexually because of her age; she wasn't a virgin any more and she deserved it. Molly started making plans to escape. She persuaded Jim to let her take in ironing, and began hiding some of her earnings under the sink.

By 1983 Molly was severely depressed. Jim was no longer working and refused to let Molly work. Her ironing money had been spent for food and Jim had sold most of the things Molly owned before they got married, including the special things she had kept from her family. Molly almost never talked anymore, except to her son. Jim said he'd see to it that she never managed to leave with the baby. He would take the rifle down from the wall when she was quiet for too long, and Molly would try to perk up and seem more cheerful. She promised herself they would get away when Kevin was a little older.

One day Jim came home and caught Molly in the backyard talking to a neighbor woman. He began hitting Molly with his fists, throwing her against cabinets and appliances, knocking her to the floor, pulling her up, and hitting her again, He threw everything in the kitchen that was movable, saying over and over, "I can't trust you." Then Jim dragged Molly into the living room and demanded that she take off all her clothes. He burned them together with her clothes from the closet, saying she wouldn't be needing them if she was going to be a whore. He yelled and yelled at her about being outside, screaming, biting, pinching, pulling hair, kicking her in the legs and back. Molly held her breath and prayed it would be over soon. This time she thought she might die. After about an hour, Jim seemed to wear out. Molly pulled herself to the bathroom and tried to stop shaking. But Jim burst in and accused her of trying to hide something, saying this proved she had been unfaithful. He pushed her forward over the sink and raped her anally, pounding her head against the mirror as he did so. Molly started throwing up, but he continued. Then he grabbed the scissors and began shearing off Molly's long dark beautiful hair, scraping her scalp with the blades, ripping out hand-fuls, shaking her violently, saying, "How do you like how you look now? No one will look at you now, will they? No one will ever want you now!" She had never been in so much pain. The next day, Jim told Molly she was never to go outside the house again, for any reason. Molly was bleeding, throwing up, badly bruised, and unable to walk, but Jim seemed unconcerned with any of her injuries. He warned her that she would "lose" Kevin if she ever did anything else to disobey him. After this, Jim stayed around the house more and frequently checked on Molly if he was away. Molly felt ill for months. She moved slowly and just tried to take care of Kevin.

Jim wrecked his truck, injured himself, ruined his business and blamed Molly. He kept her awake until early morning while he raged, and threw bottles of beer at her or poured hot coffee over her if she fell asleep. Sexual abuse occurred almost nightly. Molly's bite marks and cuts became permanent scars. When he had been drinking, sex would go on for hours because he couldn't climax. Jim would blame Molly for that, grinding his teeth, banging her head against the headboard and choking her. He also threatened her or traced on her with a fillet knife during sex. Sometimes he would kick her across the room. She would just concentrate on her breathing and wait for it to be over. Jim said she wasn't feeling enough pain and hit her harder, but Molly remained silent, thinking, "He might have my body, but I'll try not to let him have my mind." Still, she stayed—exhausted, ill, not knowing where to go. She kept telling herself, "If I could just get some more sleep; if I could make myself eat again, get my strength back." Jim was so wild now, she did not think she could get away with the baby without someone getting killed.[13]

## A Gendered System of Terror

Domestic violence is not gender-neutral. While in heterosexual relation-ships women sometimes fight back and in exceptional cases men are injured or killed, severe, repeated domestic violence is overwhelmingly initiated by men and inflicted on women. Nor is this violence isolated, random, or explicable by the abnormal characteristics of the abuser or victim or by dysfunction in the family. In developed and developing soci-eties, studies indicate that between 20 percent and 67 percent of women

have experienced violence in intimate heterosexual relationships. The very prevalence of wife-battering unmasks the prevailing concepts of normalcy and functionality. While many theories have been advanced to explain this violence, gender inequality is key. For example, the UN Report, *Violence Against Women in the Family*, concludes its analysis of the literature with the statement that

there is no simple explanation for violence against women in the home. Certainly, any explanation must go beyond the individual characteristics of the man, the woman and the family and look to the structure of relationships and the role of society in underpinning that structure. In the end analysis, it is perhaps best to conclude that violence against wives is a function of the belief, fostered in all cultures, that men are superior and that the women they live with are their possessions or chattels that they can treat as they wish and as they consider appropriate.[14]

[. . .] Where torture is defined in the binding instruments,[15] it generally involves four critical elements: (1) severe physical and/or mental pain and suffering; (2) intentionally inflicted; (3) for specified purposes; (4) with some form of official involvement, whether active or passive. I compare the evolving understanding of torture with domestic violence against women partners. [. . .]

## Intentionality

To constitute torture, pain must be intentionally inflicted against the will of the victim. This distinguishes torture from accidents or disease as well as from situations where pain is accepted in the hope of attaining some greater good. The intentional infliction of excruciating pain and suffering for its own sake, whatever the subjective state of mind or goal of the torturer, mocks all pretense of civilization and thereby demands the most severe condemnation.

The intent required is simply the general intent to do the act that clearly or foreseeably causes terrible suffering. [. . .]

By contrast, it is commonly argued that most men who abuse their wives or women partners do not act purposively, but impulsively. From a legal perspective, this claimed loss of control does not exonerate violent acts as a general matter. Short of proof of insanity or mistake, the act is intentional and, therefore, culpable. In Anglo-American jurisprudence, heat of passion or rage may reduce murder to manslaughter and mitigate the penalty, but it does not exonerate the offender. Gender discrimination enters, however, when disproportionately light sentences are imposed on men who kill or abuse women partners. In some systems a "defense of honor"—recognized by law or custom—allows the husband's jealousy or rage over the real or imagined offenses by the wife to excuse even homicide. This defense, available only to men, licenses not only impulsive behavior, but deliberate vengeance. So does the marital rape exception—an implicit defense of honor—still the law in most countries.

Moreover, the claim that domestic violence is the product of loss of impulse control has been severely criticized in light of the dynamics of battering. "Battering, whether or not it is premeditated, is purposeful behavior" and "should be seen as an attempt to bring about a desired state of affairs." Battered women report that men often plan their attack. Men who beat women partners commonly exhibit excellent impulse control in other contexts; their major or only targets are woman partners or children, pets, and inanimate objects. The contention that alcohol causes violence also ignores the fact that many men get drunk without beating their wives and that men often beat their wives without being drunk. To the extent that alcohol facilitates male violence, it is an important factor in the effort to reduce battering, but it is not the cause. Finally, professions of remorse from the batterer earn ill-placed sympathy. He does not perceive his violence as unjustified. Often a tactic for preventing his wife from leaving, remorse is inherently suspect where, despite pleas for forgiveness, the violence cycle is repeated.

Conversely, the notion that the torturer always acts under control, according to protocol or orders, ignores the fact that they engage in both programmed and spontaneous brutal and sadistic behavior. Torturers have also been reported to abuse alcohol and drugs in the course of their "duties." Some, like batterers, may experience tremendous guilt over what they have done, while others have become inured to the damage they inflict. But none of this, nor the claim to be acting under orders, exonerates the torturer under international law.

Thus in the contexts of both official torture and domestic battering, individual malice is not necessary and loss of control is not exculpatory. To focus on the intent of the perpetrator obscures the severity of the suffering threatened or inflicted, forgiving the perpetrator rather than recognizing the victim. Indeed the contention that battering is simply an impulsive letting-off-steam is an aspect of the depoliticization of domestic violence against women. This view treats battering as an individual problem of personal or family dynamics and obscures the underlying and purposive gender dynamic of domination and subordination. The human rights focus must be on the perpetrator's accountability in order to counter the traditional complicity of law and custom in giving license to violent "impulses" against women.

## Prohibited Purposes

Not all deliberately inflicted severe violence amounts to a human rights violation or warrants the label "heinous." Purpose plays a role. The UN and Inter-American conventions prohibit the use of torture for otherwise legitimate purposes such as the obtaining of information or punishment, as well as for clearly illegitimate purposes such as intimidation, personal punishment, the obliteration or diminution of the personality, or discrimination. In the international decisions on torture the element of purpose has not occasioned much attention. Nor should it. For the state deliberately to employ or permit torture is, by definition, an abuse of power and an offense against human dignity.

Nevertheless, the element of purpose—so long as it is understood not as requiring a showing of specific or conscious intent, but only as identifying the goals or functions of violence at issue—helps to elucidate the evil of torture. It underscores the principle of non-derogability—that even where the ends may be legitimate—obtaining information or judicially sanctioned punishment—the use of torture is not. It also emphasizes the psychological aspects of torture. Where the methods of torture involve infliction of extreme physical pain, there is no need to separately identify purpose; but where the methods are psychological, an understanding that the goal is, for example, the destruction of human dignity may be critical to understanding the mistreatment as torture. Finally, the enumerated purposes illuminate the political and social evil of torture as a means of suppressing a group or whole society.

The delineation of prohibited purposes likewise elucidates why privately inflicted gender-based violence is egregious. Isolated, random, albeit deliberate, brutality is a subject for law enforcement, but not necessarily for the international community. Gender-based violence is different. It should be recognized as an international human rights violation because it violates the human rights of women as persons to integrity, security, and dignity, and also because it constitutes discrimination against women as a group in that its purpose is to maintain both the individual woman and women as a class in an inferior, subordinated position. It is thus illuminating to examine the degree to which the purposes that render torture heinous apply to the phenomenon of domestic violence.

## To Elicit Information

The most common response to the analogy between torture and domestic violence is the contention that torture is different because its purpose is to elicit information. This distinction, which harks back to the original nature of torture, ignores the contemporary understanding of torture as an engine of terror. It misapprehends the function of interrogation in torture as well as its place in domestic violence. It may also reflect a gender-biased identification with the victims of state torture as opposed to domestic violence—the torture victim resisting the giving of information is heroic, whereas the battered woman somehow deserves it. [. . .]

Just as torture seems to be in pursuit of confession or information, domestic violence seems not to be. But this, too, is a misconception. Like torture, domestic violence is both physical and verbal. Whether precipitated by rage, jealousy, or a real or feared loss of control, domestic violence has its own interrogation—questions, accusations, insults, and orders: Where were you today? Who were you with? Who visited you? What do you mean you want to go out to work? Why is the coffee cold? the house a mess? this item moved? You're dumb, ugly, old; or Jim's question to Molly: "How do you like how you look now?"

The goal of the domestic interrogation is not truth or information, but dread, humiliation and submission. What the confession is to torture, the explanation, the accounting-for-oneself, the apology, the begging is to domestic violence. In both contexts, the victim/survivor seeks to stop or avert the pain, to protect others from harm, and to pacify the aggressor. In the context of official torture, the confession, even if false, has a greater likelihood of endangering others, while with domestic violence, confession and apology may more often be designed to protect others, particularly children. The victim's anguish is likely to be more extreme where the confession does or is believed to risk the safety of another, but for the aggressor confession is proof of submission. Interrogation is not a necessary element of violence against women, but it is a common one, and its purpose, as in torture, is not truth but power. [. . .]

## To Intimidate

Torture seeks to intimidate on three levels: the individual victim, the group with which the victim is identified, and, ultimately, the entire society. The horror of the experience of torture is calculated to deter that person from oppositional activities or any association with those viewed as at risk; it creates dread that even innocuous actions will be interpreted as oppositional; and it often forces a person into exile.

On the collective level, torture operates to spread fear among those who identify with the targets of torture. It is designed then to sap the strength of potential opposition movements; to subordinate classes to the ruling authority; to facilitate economic exploitation through terror. The climate of fear intended by torture may be confined to the targeted subgroups or it may envelop an entire society, where the regime seeks its enemies among the elite as well as the less privileged. The selection of targets may appear politically motivated or completely irrational. The fact that there is no way to insulate oneself heightens the terror and engenders the pacification it seeks.

Domestic violence is also designed to intimidate both the individual woman who is the target and all women as a class. On the individual level, the goal of domestic violence is to "domesticate" her; to terrify her into obedience; to prevent or deter her assertion of difference or autonomy. The possibility that violence may erupt in response to certain actions of her own leads her to try to avoid "precipitating" conduct. But beyond that, the fact that the violence may erupt at any time and for any reason creates in the woman a ubiquitous anxiety and dread, a complex game of placation, endurance, and survival.

Domestic violence undermines not only women's security at home, but also their possibilities for independence, the exercise of human rights, and self-development. The United Nations Development Fund for Women (UNIFEM) recognizes "violence as a form of control that limits their ability to pursue options in almost every area of life from the home to schools, workplaces, and most public spaces. . . [and as a] . . . direct obstacle to women's participation in development projects." [. . .] Threats of violence are every bit as effective as acts of violence in "making women act as their own jailors." Violence thus perpetuates the economic, social, and psychological dependency which, in turn, contributes to women's vulnerability to violence. [. . .]

## State Versus Intimate Terror

Finally, it is necessary to explore whether the sheer fact that violence is privately versus publicly inflicted so qualitatively alters the character of the violence as to deprive it of the enormity of torture or cruel, inhuman, and degrading treatment. As we have seen, official involvement is not a distinction that affects the intensity or impact of gender-based violence. Given the pervasiveness and damage inflicted by gender-based violence, particularly in the home, it cannot be argued that the frequency or scope of official torture is greater. There are, however, three possible grounds of distinction, all of which fail under inspection. First, it is argued that official torture is distinct because it precludes redress through the state; second, that official violence presumes that the victim is in custody whereas victims of private violence are not; and third, that state brutality is worse than the cruelty of an intimate. [. . .]

### THE LACK OF STATE REDRESS

Burgers and Danelius explain the limitation of the UN Torture Convention to state actors on the ground that where the state is the violator, the victim will not be able to rely on domestic law enforcement for redress. This explanation of the state action requirement does not address the egregiousness of the conduct constituting torture, but rather the necessity of international human rights intervention to prevent impunity.

The fact that gender violence is the consequence of as well as constitutive of an informal parallel state likewise leaves women without redress. Domestic sanctions are frequently lacking or under-enforced. The resulting impunity legitimizes the domination of the husband; it deprives the woman subjected to violence of the possibility of effective protection or escape through the system of justice; and it denies her vindication, public recognition that she is the one who is deeply and horribly wronged. Notwithstanding debate about the nature and sufficiency of a criminal justice response to domestic violence, international condemnation and intervention are required to dismantle this parallel state.

## CUSTODY AND CAPTIVITY

Dominion over the victim is critical to the ability to inflict terrible violence and to its potential to degrade a person and her will. The experience of isolation from help, of not being able to escape, of being at the mercy of a malevolent, and overpowering, force is key to the effectiveness of the torturer. Imprisonment in police or military custody is the paradigm. But dominion does not require walls or custody in the traditional sense. Custody exists where a person does not consider herself free to leave or resist. [. . .] Burgers and Danelius suggest that the victims "must be understood to be persons who are deprived of their liberty or who are at least under the factual power or control of the person inflicting the pain and suffering."

The same processes used to break the will of political prisoners and prisoners-of-war are used by domestic aggressors to render battered women—despite their apparent freedom to leave—captive. Despite the lack of formal training and the presence of individual variation, the coercive measures used in the home resemble not only those of other batterers but also those of official captors. Like the captor, the batterer creates a constant state of fear, through threats against family, friends, and particularly children, and through unpredictable violence often to enforce petty rules. Through scrutiny and control of her body—forced nakedness, sexual abuse and rape, control over food, sleep, and bodily functions—captors and batterers aim to destroy women's sense of autonomy and dignity. Judith Herman writes that the goal of the perpetrator is to prove that "resistance is futile, and that her life depends upon winning his indulgence through absolute compliance, [as well as] . . . to instill in his victim not only fear of death but also gratitude for being allowed to live."

Dependency is also encouraged through isolating the victim, destroying possessions that reflect attachment to others, and showing intermittent kindness. Where political prisoners share their torments with peers, they frequently bond with one another as a critical means of survival; where there is no peer, they are likely to bond with and idealize their captors and take their side, a phenomenon described as the Stockholm Syndrome. In the domestic context, the woman is gradually isolated from all potential sources of help and silenced by threats or shame into not admitting her plight to others. Isolation interacts in both contexts with indulgence, encouraging the victim to look to the captor for solace, creating delusions about the specialness of the person or their relationship, and negating her will to resist or question.

Moreover, the victim of intimate violence is likely to be far more vulnerable to manipulation than the political prisoner whose captivity begins in force not consent and whose resistance will be buoyed by ideological commitments and hatred of the captor rather than undermined by love, empathy, and a sense of womanly duty. [Herman notes that] "Since most women derive pride and self-esteem from their capacity to sustain relationships, the batterer is often able to entrap his victim by appealing to her most cherished values. It is not surprising, therefore, that battered women are often persuaded to return after trying to flee from their abusers."

The final stage in the process of obtaining control, which Herman calls "total surrender," and Amnesty, "chronic stress," is the result of requiring the victim to do things that violate her own principles or loyalty and engender in her a sense of self-loathing. With political prisoners, it may involve watching a family member or colleague be tortured or killed, breaking under interrogation, or sexual degradation. In the home, it often involves sexual humiliation or complicity in the batterer's abuse of the children.

Surrender involves two stages: first, draining oneself of emotion and resistance as a means of survival, and, second, giving up the will to live. These are not necessarily stable states, and they alternate with renewed will to survive. In regard to the first, Molly's effort to go numb under attack, to concentrate on her breathing and dissociate from her body compares with Timerman's reaction during torture: "becoming a vegetable, casting aside all logical emotions and sensations—fear, hatred, vengeance—for any emotion or sensation meant wasting useless energy." Giving up the will to live is not the same as becoming suicidal, which is a form of resistance; it is rather total passivity, or robot-like functioning—that is, living dead.

Many battered women do not remain in the relationship through to the stage of total surrender. Nor is surrender the prerequisite of psychological or social captivity. Captivity exists along a spectrum that includes the period when the woman is fearfully but actively trying to save the relationship, the period when she is fearfully but actively trying to avert greater

danger or escape, and the point (reached in some cases) when her hope
or resistance is intermittently or totally broken.

It is important to recognize that captivity is a complex process that most
often involves—for prisoners as well as battered women—highly con-
stricted but active coping strategies which are often invisible or trivialized.
This permits acknowledgment of the imprisoning effects of domestic violence without demanding total annihilation of the will or personality of
the battered woman. It also elucidates the fallacy of limiting captivity to
official custody. Is the power of the abusive husband less total or awful
than that of the occupying military officer? What makes both men dangerous is their assumption of the right to exercise dominion over a woman.
The fact that one is backed directly by the official state and the other
indirectly by patriarchal custom enjoying the complicity or acquiescence
of the state, does not mitigate the experience of the woman. If anything,
it heightens her vulnerability.

## The Factor of Intimacy

The next question is whether there is something less terrible for the victim or for the social fabric when the violence is inflicted by an intimate
rather than an official. The fact that intimate violence involves a breach
of trust cannot be underestimated. The torturer knows this well. Small
kindnesses—asking about the victim's family, occasional indulgences—
evoke the desire to trust and are among the most effective psychological
tools. Scarry points out as well that torturers use domestic props—refrig-
erators, bathtubs, soft-drink bottles—as weapons in order to disorient the
victim. Thereby, "the domestic act of protecting becomes an act of hurting." The shock of being beaten by a partner as opposed to a jailor can
be more numbing and world-destroying. Rape by husbands is experienced as more devastating and longer lasting than rape by strangers. And,
ultimately, resistance to emotional dependency and the most profound
trauma is more complicated for the battered woman than for the hos-
tage, as she is courted rather than kidnapped into violence. She must, in
Herman's words, "unlearn love and trust, hope and self-blame."

The impact of gender-based versus official violence on the social fabric
is incomparable only so long as the parallel state of patriarchy, the harm
it perpetrates, and the violence it engenders remains invisible, sentimen-
talized, and legitimized. Gender-based violence in the home is profoundly
traumatizing for both victims and observers; it shapes (fortunately sometimes by negative example) ideas about the gender hierarchy, about
male dominance and female submission; and it helps to prepare people
and a society for the use of official violence. Efforts to assess the impact
on children and the people they become as a result of having observed

their father battering their mother or their mother being beaten do not show clear-cut correlations. But the data suggest that such experience does play a role—albeit a complex one—in the formation of adult personality and in the perpetuation of discrimination and violence in families and society. [. . .]

*Chapter V*
# The Social Context of Torture

Much of what we have said to this point has focused on individuals or groups of individuals—victims of torture or perpetrators of it. But, as we saw in the chapter on the history of torture in the West, the practice is often embedded in a larger social understanding of truth, for example, that slaves, lacking a capacity for rational thought, are incapable of lying.

What in more contemporary times are the social conditions that may predispose a society to engage in and tolerate torture? One answer is that it may feel itself under dire threat from "terrorists" or others who seek to destabilize its institutions or even destroy the state. Whether torture is an effective response to such a challenge will be touched upon in the next chapter but there is no question that insecurity has often bred forms of retaliation that include torture and even genocide.

And yet different societies have responded to perceived threats in different ways. How unnerved those societies may be; whether they permit dissent from the prevailing perception of fear; whether certain groups are made scapegoats for the actions of a few; whether the rule of law is followed or ignored—all these depend upon larger questions of history and context.

Are there economic markers or structures of power then that incline one society to reach for the whip, the rack, or the electric prod more swiftly than others? The answer is almost certainly "Yes" and it is far from an academic one. For if only a few people actually engage in torture, large numbers of people shape the social context that makes torture thinkable. Recognizing the danger signals is everybody's responsibility. The readings in this chapter lay out what some of those are.

## Chapter V, Reading 1

# Privilege, Prejudice, and Power

This first brief reading, from Pierre Vidal-Naquet's book, *Torture: Cancer of Democracy*, drawing on the case of Algeria, outlines three key factors that are often present when a governing power resorts to torture. We will see echoes of all three in several of the readings that follow.

The use of torture in Algeria was to a great extent the defensive reaction of a minority whose privileged position was threatened, of an army which had been ordered to protect this minority and which could find no other means of action, and of a government which, with the support of the majority of the nation, did all it could over a period of years to ensure that this minority retained its privileged position.

The relationship between the torturers and the tortured was further exacerbated by a spirit of racial prejudice and the contempt for their inferiors of men who considered themselves superior beings. [. . .] As long as the relationships between men are based upon the domination by one race of another or on the colour of a man's skin, the practice of torture will never disappear.

But racialism is not the whole answer either. It was not a feeling of racial superiority which caused the German Nazis to torture other non-Nazi Germans. The Greek City State had the logical answer when it refused to admit that slaves were human beings and therefore considered torture inflicted upon a slave to be a perfectly normal occurrence, whereas inflicted on a free man it became an abominable crime. The essential feature of the practice of torture, therefore, is that one man or one class of society claims absolute power over another man or another class of society.

# The Origins of Totalitarianism

"The essential feature of the practice of torture," says Vidal-Naquet, "is that one man or one class of society claims absolute power over another." In her renowned study, *The Origins of Totalitarianism*, Hannah Arendt elaborated on that notion of total power. Though her principal focus was on the death camps of Nazi Germany, her observations apply to any authoritarian state that sets out to "murder the moral person in man," as Arendt puts it. The use of torture is endemic to such a crime.

The first essential step on the road to total domination is to kill the juridical person in man. This was done [. . .] by putting certain categories of people outside the protection of the law [. . .]; it was done [. . .] by placing the concentration camp outside the normal penal system, and by selecting its inmates outside the normal judicial procedure in which a definite crime entails a predictable penalty. Thus criminals, who for other reasons are an essential element in concentration-camp society, are ordinarily sent to a camp only on completion of their prison sentence. [. . .]

The inclusion of criminals is necessary in order to make plausible the propagandistic claim of the movement that the institution exists for asocial elements. Criminals do not properly belong in the concentration camps, if only because it is harder to kill the juridical person in a man who is guilty of some crime than in a totally innocent person. If they constitute a permanent category among the inmates, it is a concession of the totalitarian state to the prejudices of society, which can in this way most readily be accustomed to the existence of the camps. In order, on the other hand, to keep the camp system itself intact, it is essential as long as there is a penal system in the country that criminals should be sent to the camps only on completion of their sentence, that is when they are actually entitled to their freedom. Under no circumstances must the concentration camp become a calculable punishment for definite offenses.

The amalgamation of criminals with all other categories has moreover the advantage of making it shockingly evident to all other arrivals that they have landed on the lowest level of society. It soon turns out, to be sure, that they have every reason to envy the lowest thief and murderer; but meanwhile the lowest level is a good beginning. Moreover it is an effective means of camouflage: this happens only to criminals and nothing worse is happening than what deservedly happens to criminals.

The criminals everywhere constitute the aristocracy of the camps. [. . .] What places the criminals in the leadership is not so much the affinity between supervisory personnel and criminal elements [. . .] as the fact that only criminals have been sent to the camp in connection with some definite activity. They at least know why they are in a concentration camp and therefore have kept a remnant of their juridical person. For the politicals this is only subjectively true; their actions, insofar as they were actions and not mere opinions or someone else's vague suspicions, or accidental membership in a politically disapproved group, are as a rule not covered by the normal legal system of the country and not juridically defined.

To the amalgam of politicals and criminals with which concentration camps in Russia and Germany started out, was added at an early date a third element which was soon to constitute the majority of all concentration-camp inmates. This largest group has consisted ever since of people who had done nothing whatsoever that, either in their own consciousness or the consciousness of their tormenters, had any rational connection with their arrest. In Germany, after 1938, this element was represented by masses of Jews, in Russia by any groups which, for any reason having nothing to do with their actions, had incurred the disfavor of the authorities. These groups, innocent in every sense, are the most suitable for thorough experimentation in disfranchisement and destruction of the juridical person, and therefore they are both qualitatively and quantitatively the most essential category of the camp population. This principle was most fully realized in the gas chambers which, if only because of their enormous capacity, could not be intended for individual cases but only for people in general. In this connection, the following dialogue sums up the situation of the individual: "For what purpose, may I ask, do the gas chambers exist?"—"For what purpose were you born?" [. . .]

The next decisive step in the preparation of living corpses is the murder of the moral person in man. This is done in the main by making martyrdom, for the first time in history, impossible: "How many people here still believe that a protest has even historic importance? This skepticism is the real masterpiece of the SS.[1] Their great accomplishment. They have corrupted all human solidarity. Here the night has fallen on the future. When no witnesses are left, there can be no testimony. To demonstrate when death can no longer be postponed is an attempt to give death a meaning, to act beyond one's own death. In order to be successful, a gesture must have social meaning. There are hundreds of thousands of us here, all living in absolute solitude. That is why we are subdued no matter what happens."

The camps and the murder of political adversaries are only part of organized oblivion that not only embraces carriers of public opinion such as the spoken and the written word, but extends even to the families and friends of the victim. Grief and remembrance are forbidden. In the Soviet

Union a woman will sue for divorce immediately after her husband's arrest in order to save the lives of her children; if her husband chances to come back; she will indignantly turn him out of the house. The Western world has hitherto, even in its darkest periods, granted the slain enemy the right to be remembered as a self-evident acknowledgment of the fact that we are all men (and *only* men). It is only because even Achilles set out for Hector's funeral, only because the most despotic governments honored the slain enemy, only because the Romans allowed the Christians to write their martyrologies, only because the Church kept its heretics alive in the memory of men, that all was not lost and never could be lost. The concentration camps, by making death itself anonymous (making it impossible to find out whether a prisoner is dead or alive) robbed death of its meaning as the end of a fulfilled life. In a sense they took away the individual's own death, proving that henceforth nothing belonged to him and he belonged to no one. His death merely set a seal on the fact that he had never really existed.

This attack on the moral person might still have been opposed by man's conscience which tells him that it is better to die a victim than to live as a bureaucrat of murder. Totalitarian terror achieved its most terrible triumph when it succeeded in cutting the moral person off from the individualist escape and in making the decisions of conscience absolutely questionable and equivocal. When a man is faced with the alternative of betraying and thus murdering his friends or of sending his wife and children, for whom he is in every sense responsible, to their death; when even suicide would mean the immediate murder of his own family—how is he to decide? The alternative is no longer between good and evil, but between murder and murder. Who could solve the moral dilemma of the Greek mother, who was allowed by the Nazis to choose which of her three children should be killed? [. . .]

Once the moral person has been killed, the one thing that still prevents men from being made into living corpses is the differentiation of the individual, his unique identity. In a sterile form such individuality can be preserved through a persistent stoicism, and it is certain that many men under totalitarian rule have taken and are each day still taking refuge in this absolute isolation of a personality without rights or conscience. There is no doubt that this part of the human person, precisely because it depends so essentially on nature and on forces that cannot be controlled by the will, is the hardest to destroy (and when destroyed is most easily repaired).

The methods of dealing with this uniqueness of the human person are numerous and we shall not attempt to list them. They begin with the monstrous conditions in the transports to the camps, when hundreds of human beings are packed into a cattle-car stark naked, glued to each other, and shunted back and forth over the countryside for days on end; they continue upon arrival at the camp, the well-organized shock of the first hours, the shaving of the head, the grotesque camp clothing; and they end in the utterly unimaginable tortures so gauged as not to kill the body, at any event not quickly. The aim of all these methods, in any case, is to manipulate the human body—with its infinite possibilities of suffering—in such a way as to make it destroy the human person as inexorably as do certain mental diseases of organic origin.

It is here that the utter lunacy of the entire process becomes most apparent. Torture, to be sure, is an essential feature of the whole totalitarian police and judiciary apparatus; it is used every day to make people talk. This type of torture, since it pursues a definite, rational aim, has certain limitations: either the prisoner talks within a certain time, or he is killed. To this rationally conducted torture another, irrational, sadistic type was added in the first Nazi concentration camps and in the cellars of the Gestapo. Carried on for the most part by the SA,[2] it pursued no aims and was not systematic, but depended on the initiative of largely abnormal elements. The mortality was so high that only a few concentration-camp inmates of 1933 survived these first years. This type of torture seemed to be not so much a calculated political institution as a concession of the regime to its criminal and abnormal elements, who were thus rewarded for services rendered. Behind the blind bestiality of the SA, there often lay a deep hatred and resentment against those who were socially, intellectually, or physically better off than themselves, and who now, as if in fulfillment of their wildest dreams, were in their power. This resentment, which never died out entirely in the camps, strikes us as a last remnant of humanly understandable feeling.[3]

The real horror began, however, when the SS took over the administration of the camps. The old spontaneous bestiality gave way to an absolutely cold and systematic destruction of human bodies, calculated to destroy human dignity; death was avoided or postponed indefinitely. The camps were no longer amusement parks for beasts in human form, that is, for men who really belonged in mental institutions and prisons; the reverse became true: they were turned into "drill grounds," on which perfectly normal men were trained to be full-fledged members of the SS.

The killing of man's individuality, of the uniqueness shaped in equal parts by nature, will, and destiny, which has become so self-evident a premise for all human relations that even identical twins inspire a certain uneasiness, creates a horror that vastly overshadows the outrage of the juridical-political person and the despair of the moral person. It is this horror that gives rise to the nihilistic generalizations which maintain plausibly enough that essentially all men alike are beasts. Actually the experience of the concentration camps does show that human beings can be transformed into specimens of the human beast, and that man's "nature" is only "human" insofar as it opens up to man the possibility of becoming something highly unnatural, that is, a man. [. . .]

What makes conviction and opinion of any sort so ridiculous and dangerous under totalitarian conditions is that totalitarian regimes take the greatest pride in having no need of them, or of any human help of any kind. Men insofar as they are more than animal reaction and fulfillment of functions are entirely superfluous to totalitarian regimes. Totalitarianism strives not toward despotic rule over men, but toward a system in which men are superfluous. Total power can be achieved and safeguarded only in a world of conditioned reflexes, of marionettes without the slightest trace of spontaneity. Precisely because man's resources are so great, he can be fully dominated only when he becomes a specimen of the animal-species man.

Therefore character is a threat and even the most unjust legal rules are an obstacle; but individuality, anything indeed that distinguishes one man from another, is intolerable. As long as all men have not been made equally superfluous—and this has been accomplished only in concentration camps—the ideal of totalitarian domination has not been achieved. Totalitarian states strive constantly, though never with complete success, to establish the superfluity of man—by the arbitrary selection of various groups for concentration camps, by constant purges of the ruling apparatus, by mass liquidations. Common sense protests desperately that the masses are submissive and that all this gigantic apparatus of terror is therefore superfluous; if they were capable of telling the truth, the totalitarian rulers would reply: The apparatus seems superfluous to you only because it serves to make men superfluous.

# Cruelty and Power

Kanan Makiya's description of how torture did the bidding of Saddam Hussein in Iraq prior to the American occupation in 2003 builds on Arendt's observations about power and describes the role cruelty plays in the creation of a "new society." This passage comes from Makiya's *Republic of Fear: The Politics of Modern Iraq*, first published in 1989.

The range of cruel institutional practices in contemporary Iraq—confession rituals, public hangings, corpse displays, executions, and finally torture—are designed to breed and sustain widespread fear. But these practices are also visible and invisible manifestations of power, extensions of, for example, the state's right to wage war on the nation's enemies. The first spectacle in January 1969[4] served a combined juridical and political function; it "punished" those who had offended the nation by supposedly betraying it to outsiders, and it reconstituted a sovereignty that had allegedly been injured from the outside by Zionism but had actually been internally shaky. The increased power of the reemerging sovereignty was visible in the splendor of the ceremony and confirmed by the numbers of people who came to participate in the occasion. Although not very different from the parades and displays of military might held every January 6 (Army Day) in Iraq, the 1969 hangings were a unique ritual, celebrating a new beginning and not the continuity or stability of power. Because of the visibility of the occasion, the display of cruelty was intentionally excessive. The point was not only to execute a judicial judgment, but to come down like a ton of bricks on the frailty of those convicted. In this very imbalance, which had to be seen and felt to be appreciated, power was affirmed. The point therefore was to intensify and heighten the imbalance by being as cruel as possible.

But what about the later forms of violence, like torture and death in the shape of the sealed-box ritual? Here the intentionality is reversed. Everything is secret including the arrest, the charges, the interrogation, the extraction of the evidence, the trial, the judgment, the execution of the sentence, the kill, and finally the corpse which bears in its markings that last record of the whole affair. The punishment that was once so public and sensual, almost tactile, has become a total abstraction; it is now the knowledge of the inevitability of a horrible and anonymous death under certain conditions. The sovereignty that previously had to be reconstituted is now a terrifyingly solid omniscient presence. A new kind of fear has become the precondition for this consolidated power, born and sustained through complicity. [. . .]

Law in the classical bourgeois sense cannot rule in a Ba'thist[5] world because there is no reciprocity in a fear-ridden environment. Moreover, the law is at best gradualist in its workings, predicated on the idea of the unchanging individual who remains responsible for his actions through time (the underlying premise of prison). Ideal Ba'thi individuals transcend the law because their identity and behaviour are totally fused with their beliefs. The real modern Iraqi individual is always caught up in the endless motion of becoming something else. The law is secondary at best, and as citizens they cannot escape the logic of punishment as torture any more than they can escape the endless flurry of edicts and commands that shower down upon their daily lives.

Under torture, the high and mighty are quite literally exposed as being made of the same stuff as everyone else. The phenomenon of the poor rural migrant making good in the secret police (say, Nadhim Kzar[6]) and then confronting a former prime minister over his bench and instruments (say, 'Abd al-Rahman al-Bazzaz[7]) is a very powerful symbol of the precariousness of privilege, influence, and power in this world of fear. Perversely, torture is an egalitarian leveling operation, which in this sense resembles the pure theory of a system based on law.

However, the object of torture is the erasure of difference; it is the business of surgically intervening in the biological fact of irreducible individuality so as to "disprove" it in reality. The confession is proof of a deviancy that was not thought to exist before. Victims who survive are hardly ever the same as the persons who went in. No matter how well the scars heal, the memory of the bodily invasion is permanent according to the testimonies of victims. [. . .]

Torture is not merely about social control through the inculcation of fear any more than a prison sentence under bourgeois law is merely about vengeance. [. . .] The objects of torture are not criminals but sick patients or morally incomplete individuals whose deviancy lies in the subjective realm, rather than in concrete transgressions. Torture goes about fashioning them anew, and if death is a frequent result, at least someone cared enough to try. When the Ba'th talk about the "new man" and the "new society" they wish to create in Iraq, these are not metaphors. They are the substantive issues of politics, present in every sphere of life: in school curricula, the media, social programs, and the disciplining of men in the army, militia, and party.

The transition from mobilizing masses for the sensual perception of power in the form of cruel spectacles, to one of personally experiencing power through fear as an abstract yet deeply entrenched and seemingly ubiquitous psychological trait, is a measure of Ba'thism's passage into modernity. The social consciousness implied by each is totally different. The later phenomenon implies a development in what might be called the literate imagination. More important, however, Ba'thism's aborted modernity derives from a new kind of entanglement with bureaucracy. Power is no longer an external force from which one can choose to withdraw into the security of home and family—by, for example, not showing up at the scene of the spectacle. Power is felt by everyone, including those who wield its instruments, because of a new kind of knowledge and experience of its inner workings. The anonymity of death in the case of the sealed-box ritual is an extension of a Kafkaesque world of experiences new to Iraq. Even the choice to treat death heroically, or as an expression of martyrdom, has been taken away from the public. Without doubt the passage from one state to the next is associated with increasing social control. But the outcome is control of a different order from anything known in a premodern or early modern framework. From the bureaucratic party and state viewpoint, what is going on is a simple logical extension of censorship, the elimination of all freedoms, and indoctrination. The erasure of difference between individuals, or between what "belongs" to the state and what "belongs" to the individual, is passed over with the greatest of ease. From the victim's viewpoint, on the other hand, a qualitative threshold sets apart the temporary state of being afraid from the fully suffused psychological condition of being ruled through fear.

# Psychology and Torture

Ervin Staub is one of the few social scientists to try to identify the "social indicators" of genocide. By comparing conditions in four societies—Nazi Germany, Turkey during the years of the Armenian massacre/genocide, Argentina in the period of the "Dirty War," and Pol Pot's Cambodia—in which genocide or mass killings took place, Staub tries to isolate those factors that set the stage for the resulting atrocities. Many of his findings, he says, are equally applicable to the onset of torture, as he describes in this excerpt from "The Psychology and Culture of Torture and Torturers," taken from *Psychology and Torture*, edited by Peter Suedfeld.

A number of motivations that lead to torture or killing arise from a pattern of characteristics of a culture and of social organization, especially when they are combined with difficult conditions of life that the society faces. [. . .] Such conditions include persistent economic problems; political violence among subgroups of society or political parties, war, or widespread criminal violence; great cultural change, because of technological or other developments; and chaos and disorganization in society that follow such events. Destructive, violent reactions become probable given a certain pattern of cultural-societal characteristics, described as follows.

1. A history of *devaluation of a subgroup* of society and discrimination against this subgroup that preselects the group as a victim of scapegoating or ideological persecution.

2. *Strong respect for authority*, which makes it unlikely that people question the definition of reality provided by those in authority or that they resist authorities who lead them to torture and killing. A strong respect for and reliance on authority also makes it difficult for people to stand on their own when as a collectivity they face difficulties. [. . .]

3. *A monolithic culture or social organization*, with certain dominant values and goals and limitations in the freedom to express conflicting values and goals. Together with strong respect for authority, this makes a uniformity of views within society more likely and counter reactions by members to early actions against victim groups less likely.

4. *Cultural self-concepts* such as a belief in cultural superiority (which at times, as in the case of Germany, was accompanied by a belief in the nation's right to dominate others, a form of entitlement), especially when this is belied by life conditions. Another is a shaky cultural self-concept that requires constant defense. Frequently, these self-concepts coexist: a veneer of superiority masks underlying self-doubt. Self-doubt may be due

to a superior self-concept that has never been fulfilled by reality as in Argentina or Germany, or to past glory or greatness that is long gone but remains part of the national memory and national self-concept, as in Turkey or Cambodia. [. . .]

5. An *ideology* that designates an enemy is another important characteristic, at times existing in the culture for a long time, but frequently speedily evolving in response to life problems.

Given these predisposing characteristics, the members of a society are likely to respond to difficult life conditions with a variety of intense needs, including the need (a) to protect their physical self, their body, and their material well-being; (b) to protect their psychological self, self-concept, values, and ways of life; (c) to protect their societal self-concept and their image of their group, which represents an important component of their individual self-concept; (d) to regain a comprehension of reality that provides them with a coherent view of the world; and (e) for human connections that were disrupted by the feelings of threat and by competition for scarce resources.

Because constructive problem solving to resolve persistent life problems of a society is difficult, given the cultural characteristics that I have described, other avenues become more likely. One of them is the protection of the psychological self, the creation of an in-group, and the creation of a (usually false) sense of control by scapegoating some group that is made responsible for life problems. Another avenue is to create ideologies or join groups or movements guided by ideologies. Usually such ideologies promise a better life and thereby provide hope. Their blueprint for a new social organization and new mode of existence provides a new understanding of the world, a renewed comprehension of reality. Joining a group also makes it possible to gain a new group identity while relinquishing a burdensome self that is frustrated and diminished by life problems. Usually the ideology identifies an enemy that interferes with the fulfillment of the ideology and the creation of a better world and leads the group to turn against this "enemy."

Such ideologies could, but usually do not, present realistic solutions to life problems. Communism could promote equality, justice, and the fulfillment of human needs, but as it has been practiced, it has reduced freedom and choice and led to persecution and murder. Anti-communism could defend a valued system, but it tends to be unrealistic in resisting, at times with great violence, social change in general. Even when the enemy that the ideology identifies is real, there is overgeneralization in the identification of the enemy group. In addition, the attempt to fulfill ideologies often leads to fanaticism and violence. The ideology becomes an overriding shared goal, a group goal around which other group goals and personal goals can be organized. Its ideals become abstract and removed from the welfare of real people. This makes it possible to torture and kill for the sake of the "higher ideals" it embodies.

When many people who share certain characteristics, and a whole society or important subgroups are affected by difficult life conditions, they will share a *cultural tilt*. Similar motivations will arise in them, with similar inclination for certain avenues to satisfy these motivations. Some will join leaders who offer extreme ideologies and extreme solutions to life problems, whereas bystanders tend to passively accept or even support the perpetrators. An important characteristic of the decision makers is their creativity and leadership in synthesizing or extending an ideology that fits the culture. The needs they satisfy, the avenues they choose for their satisfaction, and the values they stress express and in some ways carry on the culture.

## The Evolution of Torturers: Steps Along a Continuum of Destruction

Whether they initially have strong or weak inclinations, all perpetrators evolve as they increasingly harm other people. So do bystanders who accept the torture or killing of others without opposing it. Whole societies evolve. [. . .] Their motivations and the conduct that is possible for them change. Individual decision makers and direct perpetrators progress from lesser harm-doing to the motivation and willingness to do greater harm. At times, when the group that comes to perpetrate torture or killing on a broad scale comes to power, society as a whole has already progressed far along a continuum of destruction, as in Turkey, where the Armenians had been the objects of discrimination, persistent violence, and even mass killing. In other instances, such as in Nazi Germany and the Soviet Union, by the time they gained power the perpetrators had evolved an ideology that advocated and justified violence.

[. . .] Frequently perpetrators develop an intense, fanatic commitment to some higher good and supposed higher morality, in the name of which they commit atrocities. Although understanding what conditions and personal characteristics make people more likely to join radical movements and adopt ideologies is important, once people develop a fanatic commitment it is their commitment rather than their personality that becomes a primary determinant of their conduct.

Such an evolution sometimes takes place in a whole system, as when a society participates in mistreating a group of people. At other times a progression is intentionally created by leaders to shape perpetrators, as in the training of torturers in Greece. After they were selected and subjected to violence themselves, they were

first brought into contact with prisoners by carrying food to them and "occasionally" were ordered to "give the prisoner some blows." The next step was to

place them as guards in the detention rooms where they watched others torturing prisoners; they would occasionally take part in some group-floggings. Later
they were asked to take part in the "standing-ordeal" during which they had to
beat the prisoner (on the legs mainly) every time he moved.
   Finally they became the torturers.

   Mistreatment of a victim group, or a cycle of violence between opposing groups, results in changes that make increasingly greater levels of
violence possible. Almost universally, with progression along the behavioral and psychological continuum of destruction, both the range of victims and the intensity of violence against them expand. For example, in
earlier eras when torture was part of the judicial process, over time it came
to be used for a wider range of reasons and against a wider range of victims: first against low-status defendants, later against people of higher
status, and then even to gain information from witnesses. [. . .] In Argentina, the many different kinds of victims, including adolescents, teenage
girls, nuns, and pregnant women, made it impossible to differentiate
between more or less worthy human beings. Over time it became possible
to casually torture kidnapped people, to torture as a private whim, and
to kill as a private whim. [. . .]

## The Perpetration of Torture as a Group Process

Systematic torture is performed by groups of perpetrators who are frequently part of an ideological movement or system. The group often fulfills important personal needs that arise from difficult life conditions
and shared goals that are embodied in the ideology. In becoming a member of the group, through rituals, sacrifices demanded by the group, and
shared experience, the members' individual goals will often be subordinated to, supplanted by, or integrated with group goals. Members come
to identify themselves with the group. Their individual self-concept, the
"I," will be embedded in and defined by their group concept, the "We,"
to a substantial degree. With the boundaries of the self weakened, there
will be emotional contagion, or "empathic joining," [. . .] the spread of
feelings in the group and thus shared reactions to events. The members'
perception of reality will be shaped by their shared belief system and by
the support they receive from each other in interpreting reality. The power
of the group to define the "correct" or morally acceptable reality becomes
great and deviation from the group unlikely. [. . .]

## The Evolution of Bystanders

Bystanders also progress along a continuum. They are usually exposed
to at least some degree of propaganda and indoctrination. They also

engage in just world thinking and devalue victims. Just like perpetrators, bystanders learn from experience and change as a result of their own actions and inaction. They are likely to progressively accept the perpetrators' conduct if they remain passive in the face of witnessing or knowing about torture or other harm inflicted on victims.

Although fear of a repressive and violent system may inhibit opposition by bystanders to torture and murder, the shared culture and life conditions, the shared cultural tilt with perpetrators, and the bystanders' own evolution are also important. In Germany there was strong reaction against the euthanasia killing of Germans once it became known, [. . .] but there was little reaction to the mistreatment of Jews. This may have been partly because of differences in attitudes toward (e.g., in the evaluation of) the two groups and partly because of the more gradual, step-by-step mistreatment of Jews. In Turkey, Argentina, and many other countries, bystanders on the whole remained passive.

Some bystanders evolve into perpetrators. This often begins with their involvement with the system, which represents a starting point for change. For example, although most German psychoanalysts left after the Nazis came to power in Germany, some remained in Berlin. Obviously, there had to be self-selection, not only by religion but also by attitudes and beliefs. Perhaps with that as a starting point, there was an evolution in the thinking and actions of these analysts. In the end, some of them helped select victims for the euthanasia killings of the Nazis. [. . .]

Even though Argentinian perpetrators abducted and killed some priests and nuns, they claimed the support of Christian values and ideals as part of their motivation. This may explain why some priests were present at the interrogation of victims and even participated in them. Some were even present during tortures, supporting the perpetrators. [. . .] In Germany, a history of service for, and subordination to, the state contributed to an inclination by doctors to serve the state in euthanasia killings and genocide. [. . .]

Sometimes new laws and procedures are created soon after a radical, ideological system gains power. Psychological changes are likely to follow as these are put into practice. At other times, as a whole society moves along the continuum of destruction, societal norms, values, and institutions change. The whole society undergoes a resocialization of beliefs, values, and standards of conduct. Once new institutions emerge, such as those in Nazi Germany and Russia that dealt with political opposition or the Department of Technical Investigation in Guatemala, a civilian group that killed and abducted on orders from the intelligence division of the Guatemalan army, [. . .] these represent new realities that maintain torture or killing.

External groups, including other nations, can also be seen as bystanders who evolve over time. Their views of national self interest, the usual view that nations are not moral agents that have moral obligations, and unwillingness to interfere with other nations' supposedly internal affairs often lead nations to remain passive when another nation mistreats its own citizens. Nations as a whole are also affected by just world thinking, tending to assume that victims somehow deserve or brought on themselves their fate. Furthermore, nations are affected by the propaganda of the perpetrators, who aim to further this belief. These interpretations are supported when relevant data and analyses are available, as in the case of the Holocaust and the reactions of the rest of the world to it. [. . .]

It is worth noting that frequently torture and other mistreatment begins with certain ideas and ways of thinking. This is obvious with regard to destructive ideologies. However, sometimes seemingly innocent ideas evolve into a source of maltreating or destroying people. In Soviet psychiatry, the evolution of certain theories of schizophrenia probably both contributed to, and was used to justify, the incarceration of political dissidents in mental hospitals. [. . .]. In Germany, the evolution in medical thinking of killing as a form of healing, the view that killing certain individuals affirmed life and strengthened the community, contributed to the involvement of German doctors in the euthanasia program and possibly to the very existence and extent of the euthanasia program. [. . .] This, in turn, represented a step in the progression toward genocide. The freedom of expression of ideas is essential to counteract early steps along a continuum of destruction. This freedom also places responsibility on bystanders to combat ideas and world views that dehumanize and carry a destructive potential.

# "How to Make a Torturer"

Torture is not confined to authoritarian states, by any means, as the revelations about U.S. practices at Abu Ghraib, Bagram Air Base in Afghanistan, and Guantanamo Bay so well attest. In this essay from *Index on Censorship*, Ronald Crelinsten identifies the political and social characteristics of polities, be they democratic or not, that make them more likely to indulge in torture.

It was the photographs that disturbed us: pictures of smiling soldiers, men and women, with thumbs up signaling approval of the degradations imposed on the hooded men in their charge. "They knew it was wrong," said a member of the House Armed Services Committee, but the photos actually told us the opposite: the soldiers' happy nonchalance as they pose for the camera seems to suggest they see nothing wrong with their actions. How can this be possible?

Studies of torture training analyze the techniques that are used to supplant normal moral restraints about harming others and replace them with constructs that justify such deliberate violence. This amounts to the deconstruction of "objective" reality, as reflected in conventional morality, and its replacement with a new reality that is defined by the ideological dictates of whatever regime holds power. To maintain this reality, the regime must endeavor to ensure that it is reflected in all sectors of society and all aspects of social and political life. Everything must be reshaped according to the new template: laws reinterpreted or rewritten, new language and vocabulary devised, social relations redefined, and all these processes of transformation channeled through and amplified by the mass media. The techniques used to train prospective torturers to do their terrible work are nothing more than a reflection of a much wider process: the transformation of society. This broader ideological work was apparent in the discussions about the acceptability of torture that first surfaced in the U.S. after the September 11 attacks. Back in the autumn of 2001, it was clear to many journalists and media pundits that it was time to talk about such unspeakable options as torture.

To enable torture to be practiced systematically and routinely, to be taken for granted and even to be celebrated, not only do torturers have to be trained and prepared, but wider elements of society must also be prepared and, in a sense, trained to accept that such things go on. It is not only the perpetrators of torture that participate in this new reality, but also those who are not directly involved as either perpetrator or victim. The media, and academics such Alan Dershowitz[8] prepare the ground both for the practice of torture itself and for wider acceptance when its practice is revealed. In a cruelly ironic sense, even the victims themselves can participate in this process. One Argentine woman whose husband disappeared during the Dirty War refrained from telling anyone about her ordeal because she felt ashamed that her husband was a communist. The official discourse had succeeded to such an extent that this educated, socially aware woman felt that her husband's political beliefs and affiliation were the cause of his victimization rather than the decision of the military *junta* and its repressive apparatus to target communists and labour unions. A torture regime engages continually in the construction and maintenance of an alternative reality in which conventional morality is largely absent. This new reality affects everyone living within its sphere of influence: perpetrator, victim and bystander alike.

Individuals engaged in torture are only one part of a complex bureaucracy, all elements of which contribute to the overall process of abuse. The individuals in the background of the Abu Ghraib photos were going about their business while prisoners were abused. Interrogators may torture, but doctors monitor the condition of the victim, advising interrogators on how far they can go; guards watch the cells and torture chambers, ignoring the screams and broken bodies; commanding officers decide who is to be questioned and how best to obtain confessions, convictions or whatever "end product" is the measure of success; politicians and government leaders demand results from the forces of order and do not question how they go about their business. In such a system, the direct perpetrator can easily claim that he or she was just following orders, while their superiors can just as easily claim that they never directed the perpetrator to commit torture. In the Iraqi case, there is the added complication of the involvement of private-sector contractors. This raises important issues of accountability that have not yet been adequately addressed. [. . .] For perpetrators, there are three central aspects to the construction of the new reality:

"authorization" involves regime leaders and top officials in defining social relations within society and justifying the use of torture. Ideology and propaganda play a central role in the diffusion of the idea that certain people deserve to be victimized and that, if they are not so victimized, society at large will be endangered or impoverished in some way;

"routinization" involves imbuing those who commit torture with a professional sense and supplanting conventional moral values with those of obedience to authority and unquestioning acceptance of the regime's ideology. Cognitive techniques quell moral conscience while a system of rewards and punishments conditions the torturer to continue in his work. At the same time, because torture becomes routine, the sense of personal choice and responsibility is drastically diminished. This makes it all the more difficult to refuse to continue or to exit from the closed world;

"dehumanization" renders the victim deserving of his or her fate in the eyes of the torturer. Torturers represent the end product of a selective and progressive training process in which conscientious objectors, doubters, independent thinkers and sensitive persons are weeded out along the way. As a result, those who become professional torturers are no longer in easy touch with such feelings as empathy, compassion or concern for the fate of their victims.

The installation of a torture regime relies on the creation of a powerful and dangerous enemy that threatens the social fabric. Laws are directed against this enemy, labels to describe this enemy are promulgated and disseminated via the mass media, people are divided into us and them: for us or against us. In George Bush's war on terror: "Those who are not with us are with the terrorists." Group cohesion is maintained by the creation of this common enemy: an out-group, replete with social pariahs, traitors, infidels and barbarians. This in-out, us-them split is one of the prime vehicles for legitimizing moral transgressions towards outsiders within the eyes of the insiders. The process of constructing this new reality involves the gradual and progressive exclusion of members of the targeted group by stripping them of their human identity and redefining them as enemy aliens. In war, in genocide, in repression, one of the principal features of gross human rights violations is the denial of the victim's human dignity. This redefinition of part of the human family is a core element of the new reality constructed by the torture regime.

For victims, the process usually involves some kind of scapegoating or persecution. If there is armed insurgency, terrorism or violent protest, the authorities use this violence to justify the installation of a torture regime. Ironically, this is often what insurgents want, since they feel that only then will the wider population join the fight. Typically, the authorities widen the scope of their definition to include sympathizers with the political aims of armed insurgents or active dissidents. This progressive merging between enemy and bystander is exacerbated by the fact that armed insurgents or criminalized political opponents usually operate secretly and the non-violent protester or activist, friend or relative of the suspected terrorist or subversive is easier to attack.

For the bystander, the construction of reality inherent in the build-up of a torture regime involves a combination of political apathy, toleration of the scapegoating of the other and a variety of cognitive techniques designed to neutralize the reality—such as "just world" thinking (the victim must have done something to deserve it), denial (it can't happen to me) and repression (ignorance is bliss). This passivity or silent acquiescence on the part of the larger society allows the construct to spread into more and more spheres of political and social life until it is so anchored in law, custom and discourse it comes to define what is right and wrong, what is permissible and what is not.

At the international level, a key feature of reality construction is the support—economic, diplomatic or political—given by foreign states to the torture regime. Such support can send the message that torture is acceptable, either indirectly by continuing to provide international aid or remaining silent about human rights abuses in international and diplomatic fora, or more directly by providing training and logistic support to those agencies that commit the human rights abuses. Ironically, international condemnation can sometimes lead to a strengthening of the torture regime or the switch from torture to disappearances or extra-judicial executions. This was the case of Argentina.

For the victim, international factors that assist in the construction of a torture reality include the diffusion of counterinsurgency doctrine, especially "hearts and minds campaigns" aimed at the general population, and the transfer of torture technology. For the bystander, the increasingly contested doctrine of non-interference of one nation in the domestic affairs of another and the practice of tolerating gross human rights violations in "client states" lead to a climate where speaking out against the abuses of one's own government seems fruitless or foolhardy at best and downright dangerous at worst. The longer a torture regime succeeds in perpetuating itself, the greater the increase in refugee and exile populations. This can lead to serious problems of adaptation in the host countries, including a significant strain on social resources and infrastructure in these countries. It is ironic that public opinion in the host country can only too readily turn against refugees rather than the regime responsible for their plight: ethnic hostility, ideological polarization and outright racism fostered by the regime can become as strongly felt as public outrage over the regime's human rights abuses. Particularly outspoken exiles, who actively seek international condemnation of the torture regime, risk being targeted by their government's security forces.

The persistence of a torture regime over a long period of time can ultimately lead to social atomization and isolation; everyone is mistrustful and suspicious of everyone else and people reduce their acquaintance to a small circle of family and friends and abandon any commitment to social or political change. This may also manifest itself in widespread alcoholism, cynicism (which serves as an excuse not to get involved politically) and other forms of withdrawal from political life. An accent on personal gain at the expense of social commitment can lead to widespread corruption and collaboration with the torture regime for personal advantage. At the international level, such a regime can persist as long as other nations and multinational corporations take a "business as usual" approach, focusing exclusively on issues of trade and development and turning a blind eye to more political and social concerns. [. . .]

Stanley Cohen and Daphna Golan, in their work for the Israeli human rights group B'tselem, identify a set of social and political conditions under which torture is likely to become institutionalized in this way; all of them [. . .] feature in the Bush war on terror:

- a national emergency or other perceived threat to security;
- the need to process large numbers of suspects;
- the dehumanizing of an out-group—national, religious or ethnic;
- a high level of authorization to violate normal moral principles;
- the presence of a "sacred mission" that justifies anything.

Torturers are not born; nor are they very easily made. Victims are not inherently deserving of their fate; nor do they bring it upon themselves by insisting on holding views opposed to those in power. And bystanders are not necessarily egocentric, apolitical, apathetic and cynical. Torture thrives because those in power and those who execute their power within the state bureaucracies, the military, the police and, ultimately, the media and the education system, condition people to believe in certain things, to think in certain ways and hence to act towards others in certain ways— and to vote for like-minded people in general elections.

What took place at Abu Ghraib prison—not to mention Afghanistan, Guantanamo Bay and the Metropolitan Detention Center in New York[9]— is a direct consequence of the social, political and legal parameters of Bush's war on terror. [. . .] There is no slippery slope, just a natural progression along a sliding scale of efficiency, efficacy and righteous indignation.

# Democracy and Torture

John Conroy, one of the leading chroniclers of torture, believes that democracies, in contrast to authoritarian regimes, have their own special ways of coping with accusations of torture. Here, from *Unspeakable Acts, Ordinary People*, he outlines nine stages of response.

In various nations in which notorious regimes have fallen, there has been a public acknowledgment that people were tortured. In democracies of long standing in which torture has taken place, however, denial takes hold and official acknowledgment is extremely slow in coming, if it appears at all. The response of those societies is fairly predictable and can be charted in thematic, if not chronological, stages.

Consider, for example, the British reaction to the revelations that they were torturing the Northern Irish in 1971. The first stage of response was absolute and complete denial, accompanied by attacks on those who exposed the treatment. Northern Irish Prime Minister Brian Faulkner[10] announced that there had been "no brutality of any kind." The *London Sunday Times* was denounced for printing "the fantasies of terrorists."

The second stage was to minimize the abuse. The government referred to it not as torture but as "interrogation in depth." Home Secretary Reginald Maulding proclaimed that there was "no permanent lasting injury whatever, physical or mental, to any of the men." The majority report of the Parker Commission[11] proclaimed that any mental disorientation should disappear within hours, and, if it didn't, it might be the men's own fault, the product of anxiety caused by "guilty knowledge" and "fear of reprisals" from comrades for having allegedly given information. In the Compton Report, Sir Edmund Compton and his colleagues concluded that part of the torture had been done for the men's own good: the hooding kept the prisoners from identifying each other, thus preserving each man's security. The beating of Joe Clarke's hands[12] had not occurred; his hands had been massaged by guards in order to restore circulation. The guards who forced men to perform strenuous exercises were merely trying to keep the prisoners warm.

A third stage is to disparage the victims. Lord Carrington[13] judged them to be "thugs and murderers," while Reginald Maulding proclaimed, "It was necessary to take measures to fight terrorists, the murderous enemy. We must recognize them for what they are. They are criminals who wish to impose their own will by violence and terror." Yet after extensive torture and ostensibly extensive confessions about their acts of "violence and terror," none of the hooded men were charged with any crime.

A fourth stage is to justify the treatment on the grounds that it was effective or appropriate under the circumstances. Lord Balniel, junior minister of defense, said that there was no evidence of torture, ill-treatment, or brainwashing, and that the methods employed had produced "invaluable" information about a brutal, callous, and barbaric enemy. Compton proclaimed that the five techniques[14] had been used on the men because it was "operationally necessary to obtain [information] as rapidly as possible in the interest of saving lives." On November 21, 1971, the *Sunday Times* poked holes in the apologists' claims, pointing out that if the interrogation methods used on the hooded men "were approved for use in any British police station, where the need for information is sometimes just as urgent as in Ulster, there would be universal outrage." The *Sunday Times* editorial staff dismissed the claim that cruel treatment was justified if it saved lives. How can you be sure, the paper asked, that the prisoner has the information you seek, that the lack of that information will indeed mean someone will die, and that cruel methods extract reliable information? The claim that lives were saved became even more suspect as time passed. The IRA[15] was invigorated by new recruits inspired by the cruel treatment accorded the Catholic community, and in the calendar year following the introduction of internment, the number of shootings rose by 605 percent, the number of armed robberies increased 441 percent, and the number of deaths rose 268 percent.

A fifth component of a torturing society's defense is to charge that those who take up the cause of those tortured are aiding the enemies of the state. So when the Republic of Ireland persisted in its suit against the United Kingdom on behalf of the victims, the *Guardian* argued that the republic's government was "torturing Northern Ireland" by "force feeding the Provisionals [the Provisional IRA][16] with propaganda."

A sixth defense is that the torture is no longer occurring, and anyone who raises the issue is therefore "raking up the past." Northern Ireland Secretary Merlyn Rees leveled that charge at the Irish government when it persisted in its pursuit of the victims' cause five years after their ordeal. Fifteen years later, there was widespread support throughout the United Kingdom for the War Crimes Bill, which became law in May 1991 and which allowed for the prosecution of former Nazi officials for crimes committed fifty years earlier. (Lord Carrington and former Prime Minister Edwin Heath[17] opposed the bill.) It is always easier to see torture in another country than in one's own.

A seventh component of a torturing bureaucracy is to put the blame on a few bad apples. In defending themselves before the European Court, the British proclaimed that it was not an administrative practice, but rather a few men exceeding their orders. If this had been the case, however, there would seem to be no reason why the torturers could not have been publicly named and prosecuted.

An eighth stage in a society's rationalization of its policy of torture is the common torturer's defense, presented to me by most of the former torturers I interviewed, that someone else does or has done much worse things. When the subject of the hooded men arose, it was common for the British government spokesmen and many editorial writers to respond by denouncing the IRA for its callous campaign of random murder, as if that justified the torture of randomly chosen men who, on the whole, were not members of the IRA. In the wake of the European Commission decision labeling the five techniques torture, the *Times* of London hastened to point out that Britain should not be "lumped together with regimes past or present in Greece, Brazil, Iran, Argentina." The *Times* argued that the techniques employed by those regimes put the victim in terror of the continuation of pain, and that that terror forced the victim to submit to the interrogator. The British techniques, the *Times* said, were not as evil because they were not designed to induce terror, but rather to induce a state of mental disorientation so that the victim's will to resist was lost.

A final rationalization of a torturing nation is that the victims will get over it. In a 1982 interview, General Harry Tuzo, the Oxford educated commander of the army in Northern Ireland at the time Jim Auld[18] and the others were tortured, claimed that the victims, who in Tuzo's words had suffered not torture but "acute discomfort and humiliation," had been "very well compensated and looked after." "I personally would have thought," Tuzo said, "that they had got over it by now." Similarly, General Jacques Massu, the French commander who throughout his life staunchly defended the widespread use of torture by his troops during the Algerian war, dismissed the pains suffered by Henri Alleg, the European-born Jew who wrote a book about his experience as a victim of Massu's policy. Massu saw Alleg in 1970, thirteen years after he was tortured, and based on that viewing discerned that the torture survivor was in "reassuringly vigorous condition."

# The Ethics of Torture

At first blush it may be hard to imagine that there could be any serious philosophical debate about torture. Certainly the Universal Declaration of Human Rights is unequivocal: "No one," says Article 5, "shall be subjected to torture or to cruel, inhuman or degrading treatment or punishment." Period. The Convention against Torture is just as absolute in its prohibition. Article 2 proclaims, "No exceptional circumstances whatsoever, whether a state of war or a threat of war, internal political instability or any other public emergency, may be invoked as a justification of torture." And yet, despite such clarity, the issue of whether torture might be justified under at least some very narrow circumstances keeps arising, most recently in the United States in connection with the treatment of prisoners detained in the "war on terror."

Now of course no reputable thinker would ever try to justify torture that is applied for the sheer sake of inflicting pain or in order to spread fear in a population, frequently though one or both of those happen, as we have seen. But far more than one philosopher, scholar, or lawyer has argued the case for torture in the context of interrogation. The most popular and persistent form of the debate focuses on the so-called "ticking bomb" scenario—some variation of the notion that the authorities have in custody an individual who possesses knowledge that can save hundreds, if not thousands, of lives, but who refuses to disclose that information. In just such a situation, are we not justified, perhaps even morally obligated, to do all we can to extract that information and save those lives, up to and including torture?

The excerpts in this chapter address that hypothetical quandary from a wide variety of perspectives. The first four argue the case, limited though it may be, for torture. The second four take the opposite perspective on both practical and ethical grounds. And the last two constitute a remarkable "dialogue" over the issue that took place in Israel when the Landau Commission issued a report in 1987 defending the use of what it called "moderate physical pressure" on Palestinian detainees and the Israeli Supreme Court decided in 1999 to outlaw such treatment.

# The Classical Statement of the Case

Jeremy Bentham (1748–1832) was the father of utilitarianism, the philosophical position that the good is that which fosters "the greatest happiness of the greatest number," as it is often popularly put. Given that premise, it is not difficult to see why Bentham might have been amenable to torture under some circumstances, and in a manuscript entitled "Of Torture," which is probably part of a larger work called *Plan of a Penal Code* that he worked on in the late 1770s, he describes what those circumstances would be and how torture ought to be applied. Keep in mind that Bentham was writing during a period when the abolition of torture had spread widely throughout Europe (see Chapter I, Readings 6 and 7) and that he was considered one of the most enlightened advocates of penal reform in his day.

In a passage from this same essay not quoted below, Bentham gives an example of a case in which the use of torture might well be justified: to recapture an escaped arsonist before he strikes again. While arson may not sound as serious to us today as a "ticking bomb," it probably was just as frightening to the people of Bentham's day, given the wooden architecture prevalent in cities and the frequency of fire. Bentham's use of this example reminds us, however, that the justification for torture is often in the minds of the beholders and that what seems warranted in one generation may be hard to defend generations hence.

Torture, as I understand it, is where a person is made to suffer any violent pain of body in order to compel him to do something or to desist from doing something which, [when] done or desisted from, the penal application is immediately made to cease. [. . .]

Torture being thus explained it may do something perhaps towards removing the prejudices that are apt to be entertained against it, if I can show

1. That there are Cases in which it is customary to apply it, and in which nobody suspects the use of it to be improper.

2. That it is likely to be less penal, in other words productive of less hardship upon the whole than any other applications which are commonly employed for the same purposes and to which nobody objects.

3. That the very circumstance by which alone it stands, distinguished from what is commonly called punishment, is a circumstance that operates in its favor.

First then there are Cases in which it is common to apply Torture itself, and in which nobody suspects it to be wrong.

These cases are occurring continually in the domestic jurisdiction.

If a Mother or Nurse seeing a child playing with a thing which he ought not to meddle with, and having forbidden him in vain pinches him till he lays it down, this is neither more nor less than Torture: If a parent having put a question to his child and upon the child's obstinately refusing to answer whips him till he complies, this too is neither more nor less than Torture.[1]

Secondly it is apt to be less penal than other applications which are commonly applied for the same purposes and to which nobody objects.

To have some method of compelling obedience to its decrees is essential to the very being of a Court of Justice. The ordinary process or expedient which Courts have and make use of for this purpose is that of simple Imprisonment. [. . .] Now it is the nature of simple Imprisonment to extend itself in duration. As much of it as is included in a short period is not very irksome: a considerable quantity of it may be endured before it is very irksome; a considerable quantity of it may be endured before it is become irksome enough to produce the effect expected from it; a considerable quantity then may have been employed before that purpose is attained: a considerable quantity of it may have been expended before a man has been made to do what it was wanted he should do. But now then if such a compulsive force had been employed the nature of which was, instead of running out in duration, to run out in intensity; the force in a very short period of time, and when as yet but a small quantity of it had been expended, might have risen to such a pitch as to have attained its purpose by surmounting the resistance that was opposed to it. A man may have been lingering in prison for a month or two before he would make answer to a question which, at the worst with one stroke of the rack and therefore almost always with only knowing that he might be made to suffer the rack, he would have answered in a moment; just as a Man will linger on a Month with the Toothache which he might have saved himself from at the expense of a momentary pang.

Third, the very circumstance by which alone what is called Torture stands distinguished from what is commonly called punishment is a circumstance that operates in its favor.

This circumstance is, that as soon as the purpose for which it is applied is answered, it can at any time be made to cease. The purpose to which Torture is applied is such that whenever that purpose is actually attained it may plainly be seen to be attained; and as soon as ever it is seen to be attained it may immediately be made to cease. With punishment it is necessarily otherwise. Of punishment, in order to make sure of applying as much as is necessary you must commonly run a risk of applying considerably more: of Torture there need never be a grain more applied than what is necessary. You hang a man for instance for setting a House on fire. You think that punishment best upon the whole; but whether it be or not is more than you are sure of: it is in great measure but guesswork. Perhaps the man himself might have been reclaimed without destroying him; perhaps an inferior punishment might have been as effectual as this for the purpose of deterring others. Two men are caught setting a house on fire, one of them escapes: set the prisoner on the rack, ask him who his Accomplice is, the instant he has answered you may untie him. Torture then when not abused, Torture considered in itself, is in this point of view less liable to exception than punishment is. If Torture deserves to be reprobated,[2] Punishment does still more.

The great objection against Torture is that it is so liable to abuse. Punishment also is liable to abuse; but it may be said and truly that Torture is still more so. Of Torture indeed a very small quantity may perhaps be made to answer the purpose, a smaller than the least quantity that is ever employed of Punishment. But then of Torture a very great quantity may be employed and the purpose not answered after all. The quantity of Punishment be it ever so great is still determinate: it is determinate in intensity and in duration. The quantity of Torture is indeterminate: it is determinate neither in intensity nor duration.

The quantity of Torture is indeterminate, but let us see clearly why and in what cases this is an objection. The thing which the prisoner is required to do is by the supposition a thing which he ought to do, and which the community has an interest in his doing. If then *having it in his power to do it* he is obstinate and in despite of Justice persists in refusing to do it; where is the harm done? Certainly less than when an offender is punished in the ordinary way: and that for the reasons that have been already given; in fact there is no harm at least no injury done at all. Every moment that he persists in his refusal he commits a fresh offense, of which he is convicted upon much clearer evidence too than can be obtained in almost any other case, and for which it is at least as fit that he should be punished as for any other.

But is it then in his power to do what he is required to do? Is this a fact so certain? There as we see lies the great difficulty and the great objection. If it be not in his power to do it, deplorable indeed is his condition if he is to be tormented till he does. One may go on torturing and torturing him without end. He is then punished wrongfully; and that to a degree which may be greater than any thing that goes commonly under the name of punishment. If Torture then should be fit to be employed in any case it cannot be till after at least as effectual precautions have been taken to prevent its falling upon the innocent, as to prevent punishment from falling upon the innocent.

*Two cases in which Torture may be applied.*

There seem to be two cases in which Torture may with propriety be applied.

1. *Where it cannot be misapplied.*

The first is where the thing which a Man is required to do being a thing which the public has an interest in his doing, is a thing which for a certainty is in his power to do; and which therefore so long as he continues to suffer for not doing he is sure not to be innocent.

2. *Where the danger of its being misapplied is less than the opposite danger.*

The second is where a man is required what, probably though not certainly, it is in his power to do; and for the not doing of which it is possible that he may suffer, although he be innocent; but which the public has so great an interest in his doing that the danger of what may ensue from his not doing it is a greater danger than even that of an innocent person's suffering the greatest degree of pain that can be suffered by Torture, of the kind and in the quantity permitted to be employed. Are there in practice any cases that can be ranked under this head? If there be any, it is plain there can be but very few.

Thus much may suffice for a general idea of the principles upon which the propriety of employing the expedient of Torture is to be judged of. It may now be time to quit the path of strict method and state in a more concise manner the rules that seem requisite to be observed in order to prevent its being employed to an improper degree, or in improper cases. With regard to the first of the two cases in which it may be admitted, the following rules may be proper to be observed.

### Rule 1st

1. First then it ought not to be employed without good proof of its being in the power of the prisoner to do what is required of him.

### Rule 2d

2. This proof ought to be as strong as that which is required to subject him to a punishment equal to the greatest degree of suffering to which he can in this way be exposed.

### Rule 3d

3. It ought not to be employed but in cases which admit of no delay; in cases in which if the thing done were not done immediately there is a certainty, at least a great probability, that the doing it would not answer the purpose.

### Rule 4

4. In cases which admit of delay a method of compulsion apparently less severe and therefore less unpopular ought to be employed in preference.

### Rule 5

5. Even on occasions which admit not of delay, it ought not to be employed but in cases where the benefit produced by the doing of the thing required is such as can warrant the employing of so extreme a remedy.

### Rule 6

6. In order to provide against the contingency of a man's suffering in this way, when it is not in his power to do what is required of him, the utmost continuance[3] that can be given to it should be limited by Law.

### Rule 7

7. In order that as little misery may be incurred in waste as possible the torture employed should be of such a kind as appears to be the most acute for the time the dolorific[4] application lasts, and of which the pain goes off the soonest after the application is at an end.

### Rule 8

8. In case of a man's suffering wrongfully in this way there should be the same remedy for him against the author of the injury, as well in the way of compensation as of punishment; as if he had been suffered wrongfully in the same degree in the way of ordinary punishment.

### Rule 9

9. Where a man who is obnoxious[5] to punishment has been made to suffer in this way without just ground, compensation should be made him by a proportionable abatement[6] of his punishment.

### Rule 10

10. To make sure of not bringing this hardship upon innocence it may be proper not to apply it to any other persons than such to whom in case that (contrary to all probability) it should turn out to have been unmerited, a compensation of the kind just mentioned can be bestowed; that is persons who are already convicted of a crime for which the punishment is greater than what the Torture can amount to.

Next with regard to the remaining case of the two in which it may be admitted the following additional rules seem proper to be observed.

### Rule 1

1. Upon any other persons than persons convicted of a first-rate crime, Torture ought not to be employed but in cases where the exigency[7] will not wait for a less penal method of compulsion.

## Rule 2

2. It ought not to be employed but where the safety of the whole state may be endangered for want of that intelligence which it is the object of it to procure.

## Rule 3

3. The power of employing it ought not to be vested in any hands but such as from the business of their office are best qualified to judge of that necessity: and from the dignity of it perfectly responsible in case of their making an ill use of so terrible a power.

## Rule 4

4. In whatever hands the power is reposed, as many and as efficacious checks ought to be applied to the exercise of it as can be made consistent with the purpose for which it is conferred. [. . .]

*For what persons it may be requisite to employ it.*

Of all the things which for the purposes of Justice or Government at large there can be occasion to compel a man to do, the only one which there can be occasion to employ this method of compelling him to do seems to be the submitting to examination; in other words, the telling what he knows touching any matters about which it may be requisite to interrogate him.

It is not however in every case that the application of present pain is absolutely necessary in order to compel a man against his will, to submit to examination: in most cases it may be effected though perhaps not quite so certainly or completely by the apprehension of future punishment.

The only case in which future punishment is absolutely inapplicable to the purpose is where the whole stock of such punishments as do not partake of the nature of Torture [have been] already exhausted upon the criminal. This may happen to be the case when a man is already in custody with full evidence against him of a capital crime.

# The Modern Case for Torture

In the brief essay "The Case for Torture," which appeared in *Newsweek* in 1982, philosopher Michael Levin put the case in stark and simple terms, anticipating by almost twenty years the recent debate about the torture of terrorists. Notice that, like Bentham in the previous reading, Levin compares torture favorably to certain forms of punishment but sets more limits to the practice than the eighteenth-century philosopher did.

It is generally assumed that torture is impermissible, a throwback to a more brutal age. Enlightened societies reject it outright, and regimes suspected of using it risk the wrath of the United States.

I believe this attitude is unwise. There are situations in which torture is not merely permissible but morally mandatory. Moreover, these situations are moving from the realm of imagination to fact.

Suppose a terrorist has hidden an atomic bomb on Manhattan Island which will detonate at noon on July 4 unless . . . (here follow the usual demands for money and release of his friends from jail). Suppose, further, that he is caught at 10 a.m. of the fateful day, but—preferring death to failure—won't disclose where the bomb is. What do we do? If we follow due process—wait for his lawyer, arraign him—millions of people will die. If the only way to save those lives is to subject the terrorist to the most excruciating possible pain, what grounds can there be for not doing so? I suggest there are none. In any case, I ask you to face the question with an open mind.

Torturing the terrorist is unconstitutional? Probably. But millions of lives surely outweigh constitutionality. Torture is barbaric? Mass murder is far more barbaric. Indeed, letting millions of innocents die in deference to one who flaunts his guilt is moral cowardice, an unwillingness to dirty one's hands. If you caught the terrorist, could you sleep nights knowing that millions died because you couldn't bring yourself to apply the electrodes?

Once you concede that torture is justified in extreme cases, you have admitted that the decision to use torture is a matter of balancing innocent lives against the means needed to save them. You must now face more realistic cases involving more modest numbers. Someone plants a bomb on a jumbo jet. He alone can disarm it, and his demands cannot be met (or if they can, we refuse to set a precedent by yielding to his threats). Surely we can, we must, do anything to the extortionist to save the passengers. How can we tell 300, or 100, or 10 people who never asked to be put in danger, "I'm sorry, you'll have to die in agony, we just couldn't bring ourselves to . . . "

Here are the results of an informal poll about a third, hypothetical, case. Suppose a terrorist group kidnapped a newborn baby from a hospital. I asked four mothers if they would approve of torturing kidnappers if that were necessary to get their own newborns back. All said yes, the most "liberal" adding that she would like to administer it herself.

I am not advocating torture as punishment. Punishment is addressed to deeds irrevocably past. Rather, I am advocating torture as an acceptable measure for preventing future evils. So understood, it is far less objectionable than many extant punishments. Opponents of the death penalty, for example, are forever insisting that executing a murderer will not bring back his victim (as if the purpose of capital punishment were supposed to be resurrection, not deterrence or retribution). But torture, in the cases described, is intended not to bring anyone back but to keep innocents from being dispatched. The most powerful argument against using torture as a punishment or to secure confessions is that such practices disregard the rights of the individual. Well, if the individual is all that important—and he is—it is correspondingly important to protect the rights of individuals threatened by terrorists. If life is so valuable that it must never be taken, the lives of the innocents must be saved even at the price of hurting the one who endangers them.

Better precedents for torture are assassination and pre-emptive attack. No Allied leader would have flinched at assassinating Hitler, had that been possible. (The Allies did assassinate Heydrich.[8]) Americans should be angered to learn that Roosevelt could have had Hitler killed in 1943—thereby shortening the war and saving millions of lives—but refused on moral grounds. Similarly, if nation A learns that nation B is about to launch an unprovoked attack, A has a right to save itself by destroying B's military capability first. In the same way, if the police can by torture save those who would otherwise die at the hands of kidnappers or terrorists, they must.

There is an important difference between terrorists and their victims that should mute talk of the terrorists' "rights." The terrorist's victims are at risk unintentionally, not having asked to be endangered. But the terrorist knowingly initiated his actions. Unlike his victims, he volunteered for the risks of his deed. By threatening to kill for profit or idealism, he renounces civilized standards, and he can have no complaint if civilization tries to thwart him by whatever means necessary.

Just as torture is justified only to save lives (not extort confessions or recantations), it is justifiably administered only to those known to hold innocent lives in their hands. Ah, but how can the authorities ever be sure they have the right malefactor? Isn't there a danger of error and abuse? Won't We turn into Them?

Questions like these are disingenuous in a world in which terrorists proclaim themselves and perform for television. The name of their game is public recognition. After all, you can't very well intimidate a government into releasing your freedom fighters unless you announce that it is your group that has seized its embassy. "Clear guilt" is difficult to define, but when 40 million people see a group of masked gunmen seize an airplane on the evening news, there is not much question about who the perpetrators are. There will be hard cases where the situation is murkier. Nonetheless, a line demarcating the legitimate use of torture can be drawn. Torture only the obviously guilty, and only for the sake of saving innocents, and the line between Us and Them will remain clear.

There is little danger that the Western democracies will lose their way if they choose to inflict pain as one way of preserving order. Paralysis in the face of evil is the greater danger. Someday soon a terrorist will threaten tens of thousands of lives, and torture will be the only way to save them. We had better start thinking about this.

# Threat Alone

Richard Bernstein's *New York Times* article "Kidnapping Has Germans Debating Police Torture" describes a real-life case from 2002 in which German police threatened to torture a kidnapper if he failed to disclose the whereabouts of his victim, an eleven-year-old boy. The threat alone got the criminal to talk. (Unfortunately, the boy was dead.) But the case prompted wide debate in Germany and raises important questions. Is the mere threat of torture a crime? And how many people need to be in jeopardy to make torture acceptable? In the traditional "ticking bomb" case, it is postulated that hundreds will die if torture is not inflicted; this case involved but one person.

Wolfgang Daschner, deputy police chief of Frankfurt, who authorized the threat, was subsequently found guilty of incitement to coercion and misuse of office but received only a warning and a fine rather than the traditional six months to five years in jail for such offenses. Magnus Gafgen, the kidnapper/murderer, was convicted, despite the inadmissibility of evidence obtained through torture, and sentenced to life in prison.

FRANKFURT, April 9—The two most important facts of the case were readily accepted today by the prosecution and the defense as the trial of a 27-year-old law student named Magnus Gafgen opened in a standing-room-only courtroom here.

The first fact is this: on Sept. 27, Mr. Gafgen kidnapped Jakob von Metzler, the 11-year-old son of a prominent banker, and murdered him by wrapping his mouth and nose in duct tape.

Four days later, Mr. Gafgen was arrested after the police watched him picking up the ransom, but after hours of interrogation he was still refusing to disclose where Jakob was being kept.

That is what produced the second undisputed fact: imagining that Jakob's life might be in imminent danger, the deputy police chief of Frankfurt, Wolfgang Daschner, ordered subordinates to extract the necessary information from Mr. Gafgen by threatening to torture him.

Mr. Gafgen was told, his lawyer later said, that "a specialist" was being flown to Frankfurt by helicopter and that he would "inflict pain on me of the sort I had never before experienced."

A few minutes after being threatened, Mr. Gafgen told the police where Jakob was—at a lake in a rural area near Frankfurt—but when officers arrived there they discovered that Jakob, his body wrapped in plastic, was already dead.

The murder, involving a member of one of this country's oldest and best-known families, horrified Germany and obsessed the media for weeks.

But in the months and weeks leading up to the trial, it has not been so much the murder itself but the police resort to the threat of torture that has aroused intense and heated debate about means and ends: whether the case against Mr. Gafgen should be dismissed because the police themselves broke the law, or whether in this particular case a resort to torture was justified.

One answer was given at least partially in court today when the presiding judge, Hans Bachl, denied a defense motion to dismiss the case. But Judge Bachl did agree with one demand of Mr. Gafgen's defense, ruling that because of the torture threat, all the information that the police obtained from Mr. Gafgen himself was inadmissible.

"The testimony was not obtained in accordance with the constitution or German law and is clearly inadmissible, but in view of the grave accusations against the accused, the damage done by these errors is not so serious that the trial has to be discontinued," Judge Bachl ruled.

The case has special resonance in Germany, where the history of Nazism and the Gestapo lends great sensitivity to anything that smacks of police misbehavior.

But the case also involves broad questions about when procedures created to prevent abuses of power become hindrances to justice. Certainly some here, including the deputy police chief, Mr. Daschner, have argued that under the circumstances, it would have been immoral to fail to threaten Mr. Gafgen with torture.

"I can just sit on my hands and wait until maybe Gafgen eventually decides to tell the truth and in the meantime the child is dead," Mr. Daschner said in one of several interviews he has given to the German press, "or I do everything I can now to prevent that from happening."

German law clearly forbids torture, though it seems to allow for some instances in which it can be used.

The criminal code and the Constitution explicitly forbid the use of force or the threat of force against a suspect. But there is also a provision to cover what is called "a life-threatening danger," when the police can "overstep the legally protected interests of the person affected."

Interior Minister Otto Schily said in an interview with the newspaper *Die Zeit* that there could be no "softening" of the rules prohibiting torture.

"If we begin to relativize the ban on torture," he said, "then we are putting ourselves back in the darkest Middle Ages and risk putting all of our values into question."

But when asked whether the ban on torture is absolute and should apply even when the life of a child might be at stake, Mr. Schily said: "The police official in Frankfurt did not have any bad intentions when he made his threat. He was acting out of concern for the child, and that is honorable."

Those who have criticized Mr. Daschner include Amnesty International and members of the Greens, the leftist partner in the national coalition government, but also legal specialists and professors.

"The most insidious aspect of the introduction of torture in a criminal case is not that it will crush its victims," Michael Pawlik, a law professor in Rostock, said. "It's that the knowledge it might be used threatens to destroy confidence in the integrity of the rule of law."

But in the courtroom today, some spectators muttered, "Incredible," and "How many rights does he want for this guy?" as Mr. Gafgen's lawyers presented their case for dismissal.

According to past statements by prosecutors, reported in the German press, Mr. Gafgen was known to Jakob, so he had no difficulty inviting Jakob to his apartment last Sept. 27 as the boy was walking home from school. Once there, Mr. Gafgen bound Jakob's hands and feet and, when he began to scream, wrapped his mouth and nose in duct tape, suffocating him. Apparently to make sure he was dead, Mr. Gafgen then immersed him in water in the bathtub, the authorities said.

Later Mr. Gafgen delivered a letter to the von Metzler family demanding a ransom of one million euros, about $1.1 million.

The family informed the police, who watched Mr. Gafgen pick up the ransom in a rural spot outside Frankfurt and arrested him. German press reports have said that just before that happened, Mr. Gafgen, apparently feeling that he had suddenly become rich, ordered a new car, a Mercedes-Benz.

# Torture Warrants

Alan Dershowitz, professor of law at Harvard Law School, is one of the nation's top civil libertarians. But in recent years he has gained renown for advocating a process for the authorization of torture in certain circumstances. Torture is inevitable, Dershowitz contends, but "torture warrants," which would need to be obtained from a court, can help control its use and hold those who employ it accountable. This excerpt is from his 2002 book *Why Terrorism Works*.

## How I Began Thinking About Torture

In the late 1980s I traveled to Israel to conduct some research and teach a class at Hebrew University on civil liberties during times of crisis. In the course of my research I learned that the Israeli security services were employing what they euphemistically called "moderate physical pressure" on suspected terrorists to obtain information deemed necessary to prevent future terrorist attacks. The method employed by the security services fell somewhere between what many would regard as very rough interrogation (as practiced by the British in Northern Ireland) and outright torture (as practiced by the French in Algeria and by Egypt, the Philippines, and Jordan today). In most cases the suspect would be placed in a dark room with a smelly sack over his head. Loud, unpleasant music or other noise would blare from speakers. The suspect would be seated in an extremely uncomfortable position and then shaken vigorously until he disclosed the information. Statements made under this kind of nonlethal pressure could not be introduced in any court of law, both because they were involuntarily secured and because they were deemed potentially untrustworthy—at least without corroboration. But they were used as leads in the prevention of terrorist acts. Sometimes the leads proved false, other times they proved true. There is little doubt that some acts of terrorism—which would have killed many civilians—were prevented. There is also little doubt that the cost of saving these lives—measured in terms of basic human rights—was extraordinarily high.

In my classes and public lectures in Israel, I strongly condemned these methods as a violation of core civil liberties and human rights. The response that people gave, across the political spectrum from civil libertarians to law-and-order advocates, was essentially the same: but what about the "ticking bomb" case?

The ticking bomb case refers to a scenario that has been discussed by many philosophers, including Michael Walzer, Jean-Paul Sartre, and Jeremy

Bentham. Walzer described such a hypothetical case in an article titled "Political Action: The Problem of Dirty Hands." In this case, a decent leader of a nation plagued with terrorism is asked "to authorize the torture of a captured rebel leader who knows or probably knows the location of a number of bombs hidden in apartment buildings across the city, set to go off within the next twenty-four hours. He orders the man tortured, convinced that he must do so for the sake of the people who might otherwise die in the explosions—even though he believes that torture is wrong, indeed abominable, not just sometimes, but always."

In Israel, the use of torture to prevent terrorism was not hypothetical; it was very real and recurring. I soon discovered that virtually no one was willing to take the "purist" position against torture in the ticking bomb case: namely, that the ticking bomb must be permitted to explode and kill dozens of civilians, even if this disaster could be prevented by subjecting the captured terrorist to nonlethal torture and forcing him to disclose its location. I realized that the extraordinarily rare situation of the hypothetical ticking bomb terrorist was serving as a moral, intellectual, and legal justification for a pervasive *system* of coercive interrogation, which, though not the paradigm of torture, certainly bordered on it. It was then that I decided to challenge this system by directly confronting the ticking bomb case. I presented the following challenge to my Israeli audience: If the reason you permit nonlethal torture is based on the ticking bomb case, why not limit it exclusively to that compelling but rare situation? Moreover, if you believe that nonlethal torture is justifiable in the ticking bomb case, why not require advance judicial approval—a "torture warrant"? That was the origin of a controversial proposal that has received much attention, largely critical, from the media. Its goal was, and remains, to reduce the use of torture to the smallest amount and degree possible, while creating public accountability for its rare use. I saw it not as a compromise with civil liberties but rather as an effort to maximize civil liberties in the face of a realistic likelihood that torture would, in fact, take place below the radar screen of accountability. [. . .]

## The Case for Torturing the Ticking Bomb Terrorist

[. . .] If the torture of one guilty person would be justified to prevent the torture of a hundred innocent persons, it would seem to follow—certainly to [Jeremy] Bentham[9]—that it would also be justified to prevent the murder of thousands of innocent civilians in the ticking bomb case. Consider two hypothetical situations that are not, unfortunately, beyond the realm of possibility. In fact, they are both extrapolations on actual situations we have faced [in the U.S.].

Several weeks before September 11, 2001, the Immigration and Naturalization Service detained Zacarias Moussaoui after flight instructors reported suspicious statements he had made while taking flying lessons
and paying for them with large amounts of cash. The government decided
not to seek a warrant to search his computer. Now imagine that they had,
and that they discovered he was part of a plan to destroy large occupied
buildings, but without any further details. They interrogated him, gave
him immunity from prosecution, and offered him large cash rewards and
a new identity. He refused to talk. They then threatened him, tried to trick
him, and employed every lawful technique available. He still refused. They
even injected him with sodium pentothal and other truth serums, but to
no avail. The attack now appeared to be imminent, but the FBI still had
no idea what the target was or what means would be used to attack it. We
could not simply evacuate all buildings indefinitely. An FBI agent proposes
the use of nonlethal torture—say, a sterilized needle inserted under the
fingernails to produce unbearable pain without any threat to health or
life, or the method used in the film *Marathon Man*, a dental drill through
an unanesthetized tooth.

The simple cost-benefit analysis for employing such nonlethal torture
seems overwhelming: it is surely better to inflict nonlethal pain on one
guilty terrorist who is illegally withholding information needed to prevent an act of terrorism than to permit a large number of innocent victims to die. Pain is a lesser and more remediable harm than death; and
the lives of a thousand innocent people should be valued more than the
bodily integrity of one guilty person. If the variation on the Moussaoui
case is not sufficiently compelling to make this point, we can always raise
the stakes. Several weeks after September 11, our government received
reports that a ten-kiloton nuclear weapon may have been stolen from
Russia and was on its way to New York City, where it would be detonated
and kill hundreds of thousands of people. The reliability of the source,
code named Dragonfire, was uncertain, but assume for purposes of this
hypothetical extension of the actual case that the source was a captured
terrorist [. . .] who knew precisely how and where the weapon was being
bought into New York and was to be detonated. Again, everything short
of torture is tried, but to no avail. It is not absolutely certain torture will
work, but it is our last, best hope for preventing a cataclysmic nuclear
devastation in a city too large to evacuate in time. Should nonlethal torture be tried? Bentham would certainly have said yes.

The strongest argument against any resort to torture, even in the ticking bomb case, also derives from Bentham's utilitarian calculus. Experience has shown that if torture, which has been deemed illegitimate by
the civilized world for more than a century, were now to be legitimated—

even for limited use in one extraordinary type of situation—such legitimation would constitute an important symbolic setback in the worldwide campaign against human rights abuses. Inevitably, the legitimation of torture by the world's leading democracy would provide a welcome justification for its more widespread use in other parts of the world. Two Bentham scholars, W. L. Twining and P. E. Twining, have argued that torture is unacceptable even if it is restricted to an extremely limited category of cases:

> There is at least one good practical reason for drawing a distinction between justifying an isolated act of torture in an extreme emergency of the kind postulated above and justifying the *institutionalization* of torture as a regular practice. The circumstances are so extreme in which most of us would be prepared to justify resort to torture, if at all, the conditions we would impose would be so stringent, the practical problems of devising and enforcing adequate safeguards so difficult and the risks of abuse so great that it would be unwise and dangerous to entrust any government, however enlightened, with such a power.
>
> Even an out-and-out utilitarian can support an absolute prohibition against institutionalized torture on the ground that no government in the world can be trusted not to abuse the power and to satisfy in practice the conditions he would impose.[10]

Bentham's own justification was based on *case* or *act* utilitarianism—a demonstration that, in a *particular case*, the benefits that would flow from the limited use of torture would outweigh its costs. The argument against any use of torture would derive from *rule* utilitarianism—which considers the implications of establishing a precedent that would inevitably be extended beyond its limited-case utilitarian justification to other possible evils of lesser magnitude. Even terrorism itself could be justified by a case utilitarian approach. Surely one could come up with a singular situation in which the targeting of a small number of civilians could be thought necessary to save thousands of other civilians—blowing up a German kindergarten by the relatives of inmates in a Nazi death camp, for example, and threatening to repeat the targeting of German children unless the death camps were shut down.

The reason this kind of single-case utilitarian justification is simpleminded is that it has no inherent limiting principle. If nonlethal torture of one person is justified to prevent the killing of many important people, then what if it were necessary to use lethal torture—or at least torture that posed a substantial risk of death? What if it were necessary to torture the suspect's mother or children to get him to divulge the information? What if it took threatening to kill his family, his friends, his entire village? Under a simple-minded quantitative case utilitarianism, anything goes as long as the number of people tortured or killed does not exceed the number that would be saved. This is morality by numbers, unless there are other constraints on what we can properly do. These other constraints can come from rule utilitarianism or other principles of morality, such as the prohibition against deliberately punishing the innocent. Unless we are prepared to impose some limits on the use of torture or other barbaric tactics that might be of some use in preventing terrorism, we risk hurtling down a slippery slope into the abyss of amorality and ultimately tyranny. [. . .]

It does not necessarily follow from this understandable fear of the slippery slope that we can never consider the use of nonlethal infliction of pain, if its use were to be limited by acceptable principles of morality. After all, imprisoning a witness who refuses to testify after being given immunity is designed to be punitive—that is painful. Such imprisonment can, on occasion, produce more pain and greater risk of death than nonlethal torture. Yet we continue to threaten and use the pain of imprisonment to loosen the tongues of reluctant witnesses.

It is commonplace for police and prosecutors to threaten recalcitrant suspects with prison rape. As one prosecutor put it: "You're going to be the boyfriend of a very bad man." The slippery slope is an argument of caution, not a debate stopper, since virtually every compromise with an absolutist approach to rights carries the risk of slipping further. An appropriate response to the slippery slope is to build in a principled break. For example, if nonlethal torture were legally limited to convicted terrorists who had knowledge of future massive terrorist acts, were given immunity, and still refused to provide the information, there might still be objections to the use of torture, but they would have to go beyond the slippery slope argument.

The case utilitarian argument for torturing a ticking bomb terrorist is bolstered by an argument from analogy—an *a fortiori* argument. What moral principle could justify the death penalty for past individual murders and at the same time condemn nonlethal torture to prevent future mass murders? Bentham posed this rhetorical question as support for his argument. The death penalty is, of course, reserved for convicted murderers. But again, what if torture was limited to convicted terrorists who refused to divulge information about future terrorism? Consider as well the analogy to the use of deadly force against suspects fleeing from arrest for dangerous felonies of which they have not yet been convicted. Or military retaliations that produce the predictable and inevitable collateral killing of some innocent civilians. The case against torture, if made by a Quaker who opposes the death penalty, war, self-defense, and the use of lethal force against fleeing felons, is understandable. But for anyone who justifies killing on the basis of a cost-benefit analysis, the case against the use of nonlethal torture to save multiple lives is more difficult to make. In the end, absolute opposition to torture—even nonlethal torture in the ticking bomb case—may rest more on historical and aesthetic considerations than on moral or logical ones. [. . .]

## The Three—or Four—Ways

[. . .] The modern resort to terrorism has renewed the debate over how a rights-based society should respond to the prospect of using nonlethal torture in the ticking bomb situation. In the late 1980s the Israeli government appointed a commission headed by a retired Supreme Court justice to look into precisely that situation.[11] The commission concluded that there are "three ways for solving this grave dilemma between the vital need to preserve the very existence of the state and its citizens, and maintain its character as a law-abiding state." The first is to allow the security services to continue to fight terrorism in "a twilight zone which is outside the realm of law." The second is "the way of the hypocrites: they declare that they abide by the rule of law, but turn a blind eye to what goes on beneath the surface." And the third, "the truthful road of the rule of law," is that the "law itself must insure a proper framework for the activity" of the security services in seeking to prevent terrorist acts.

There is of course a fourth road: namely to forgo any use of torture and simply allow the preventable terrorist act to occur. After the Supreme Court of Israel outlawed the use of physical pressure, the Israeli security services claimed that, as a result of the Supreme Court's decision, at least one preventable act of terrorism had been allowed to take place, one that killed several people when a bus was bombed. Whether this claim is true, false, or somewhere in between is difficult to assess. But it is clear that if the preventable act of terrorism was of the magnitude of the attacks of September 11, there would be a great outcry in any democracy that had deliberately refused to take available preventive action, even if it required the use of torture. During numerous public appearances since September 11, 2001, I have asked audiences for a show of hands as to how many would support the use of nonlethal torture in a ticking bomb case. Virtually every hand is raised. The few that remain down go up when I ask how many believe that torture would actually be used in such a case.

Law enforcement personnel give similar responses. [. . .] The real issue, therefore, is not whether some torture would or would not be used in the ticking bomb case—it would. The question is whether it would be done openly, pursuant to a previously established legal procedure, or whether it would be done secretly, in violation of existing law. [. . .]

In a democracy governed by the rule of law, we should never want our soldiers or our president to take any action that we deem wrong or illegal. A good test of whether an action should or should not be done is whether we are prepared to have it disclosed—perhaps not immediately, but certainly after some time has passed. No legal system operating under the rule of law should ever tolerate an "off-the-books" approach to necessity.

Even the defense of necessity must be justified lawfully. The road to tyranny has always been paved with claims of necessity made by those responsible for the security of a nation. Our system of checks and balances requires that all presidential actions, like all legislative or military actions, be consistent with governing law. If it is necessary to torture in the ticking bomb case, then our governing laws must accommodate this practice. If we refuse to change our law to accommodate any particular action, then our government should not take that action. [. . .]

In 1678, the French writer François de La Rochefoucauld said that "hypocrisy is the homage that vice renders to virtue." In this case we have two vices: terrorism and torture. We also have two virtues: civil liberties and democratic accountability. Most civil libertarians I know prefer hypocrisy, precisely because it appears to avoid the conflict between security and civil liberties, but by choosing the way of the hypocrite these civil libertarians compromise the value of democratic accountability. Such is the nature of tragic choices in a complex world. As Bentham put it more than two centuries ago: "Government throughout is but a choice of evils." In a democracy, such choices must be made, whenever possible, with openness and democratic accountability, and subject to the rule of law.

Consider another terrible choice of evils that could easily have been presented on September 11, 2001—and may well be presented in the future: a hijacked passenger jet is on a collision course with a densely occupied office building; the only way to prevent the destruction of the building and the killing of its occupants is to shoot down the jet, thereby killing its innocent passengers. This choice now seems easy, because the passengers are certain to die anyway and their somewhat earlier deaths will save numerous lives. The passenger jet must be shot down. But what if it were only *probable*, not certain, that the jet would crash into the building? Say, for example, we know from cell phone transmissions that passengers are struggling to regain control of the hijacked jet, but it is unlikely they will succeed in time. Or say we have no communication with the jet and all we know is that it is off course and heading toward Washington, D.C., or some other densely populated city. Under these more questionable circumstances, the question becomes *who* should make this life and death choice between evils—a decision that may turn out tragically wrong?

No reasonable person would allocate this decision to a fighter jet pilot who happened to be in the area or to a local airbase commander—unless of course there was no time for the matter to be passed up the chain of command to the president or the secretary of defense. A decision of this kind should be made at the highest level possible, with visibility and accountability.

Why is this not also true of the decision to torture a ticking bomb terrorist? Why should that choice of evils be relegated to a local police-man, FBI agent, or CIA operative, rather than to a judge, the attorney general, or the president? [. . .]

[. . .] it seems logical that a formal, visible, accountable, and central-ized system is somewhat easier to control than an ad hoc, off-the-books, and under-the-radar-screen nonsystem. I believe, though I certainly can-not prove, that a formal requirement of a judicial warrant as a prerequi-site to nonlethal torture would decrease the amount of physical violence directed against suspects. At the most obvious level, a double check is always more protective than a single check. In every instance in which a warrant is requested, a field officer has already decided that torture is justified and, in the absence of a warrant requirement, would simply pro-ceed with the torture. Requiring that decision to be approved by a judi-cial officer will result in fewer instances of torture even if the judge rarely turns down a request. Moreover, I believe that most judges would require compelling evidence before they would authorize so extraordinary a de-parture from our constitutional norms, and law enforcement officials would be reluctant to seek a warrant unless they had compelling evidence that the suspect had information needed to prevent an imminent terror-ist attack. A record would be kept of every warrant granted, and although it is certainly possible that some individual agents might torture without a warrant, they would have no excuse, since a warrant procedure would be available. They could not claim "necessity," because the decision as to whether the torture is indeed necessary has been taken out of their hands and placed in the hands of a judge. In addition, even if torture were deemed totally illegal without any exception, it would still occur, though the public would be less aware of its existence.

I also believe that the rights of the suspect would be better protected with a warrant requirement. He would be granted immunity, told that he was now compelled to testify, threatened with imprisonment if he refused to do so, and given the option of providing the requested information. Only if he refused to do what he was legally compelled to do—provide necessary information, which could not incriminate him because of the immunity—would he be threatened with torture. Knowing that such a threat was authorized by the law, he might well provide the information. If he still refused to, he would be subjected to judicially monitored phys-ical measures designed to cause excruciating pain without leaving any lasting damage.

# The Philosophical Case Against Torture

The arguments against ticking bomb torture fall broadly into two categories: the argument, on the one hand, that torture violates one or more sets of moral precepts and the pragmatic contention, on the other, that, regardless of its morality, torture is ineffective and damaging to the interests of those who engage in or condone it. Distinguished philosopher Henry Shue presents the moral case in the widely cited essay "Torture," which first appeared in *Philosophy and Public Affairs* in 1978.

One of the general contentions that keeps coming to the surface is: since killing is worse than torture, and killing is sometimes permitted, especially in war, we ought sometimes to permit torture, especially when the situation consists of a protracted, if undeclared, war between a government and its enemies. I shall try first to show the weakness of this argument. To establish that one argument for permitting some torture is unsuccessful is, of course, not to establish that no torture is to be permitted. But in the remainder of the essay I shall also try to show, far more interestingly, that a comparison between some types of killing in combat and some types of torture actually provides an insight into an important respect in which much torture is morally worse. This respect is the degree of satisfaction of the primitive moral prohibition against assault upon the defenseless. Comprehending how torture violates this prohibition helps to explain—and justify—the peculiar disgust which torture normally arouses.

The general idea of the defense of at least some torture can be explained more fully, using "just-combat killing" to refer to killing done in accord with all relevant requirements for the conduct of warfare. The defense has two stages.

A. Since (1) just-combat killing is total destruction of a person,

(2) torture is—usually—only partial destruction or temporary incapacitation of a person,

and

(3) the total destruction of a person is a greater harm than the partial destruction of a person is,

then

(4) just-combat killing is a greater harm than torture usually is;

B. since (4) just-combat killing is a greater harm than torture usually is, and

(5) just-combat killing is sometimes morally permissible, then

(6) torture is sometimes morally permissible.

To state the argument one step at a time is to reveal its main weakness. Stage B tacitly assumes that if a greater harm is sometimes permissible, then a lesser harm is too, at least sometimes. The mistake is to assume that the only consideration relevant to moral permissibility is the amount of harm done. Even if one grants that killing someone in combat is doing him or her a greater harm than torturing him or her (Stage A), it by no means follows that there could not be a justification for the greater harm that was not applicable to the lesser harm. Specifically, it would matter if some killing could satisfy other moral constraints (besides the constraint of minimizing harm) which no torture could satisfy.

A defender of at least some torture could, however, readily modify the last step of the argument to deal with the point that one cannot simply weigh amounts of "harm" against each other but must consider other relevant standards as well by adding a final qualification:

(6') torture is sometimes morally permissible, provided that it meets whichever standards are satisfied by just-combat killing.

If we do not challenge the judgment that just-combat killing is a greater harm than torture usually is, the question to raise is: Can torture meet the standards satisfied by just-combat killing? If so, that might be one reason in favor of allowing such torture. If not, torture will have been reaffirmed to be an activity of an extremely low moral order.

## Assault upon the Defenseless

The laws of war include an elaborate, and for the most part long-established, code for what might be described as the proper conduct of the killing of other people. Like most codes, the laws of war have been constructed piecemeal and different bits of the code serve different functions. It would almost certainly be impossible to specify any one unifying purpose served by the laws of warfare as a whole. Surely major portions of the law serve to keep warfare within one sort of principle of efficiency by requiring that the minimum destruction necessary to the attainment of legitimate objectives be used. .

However, not all the basic principles incorporated in the laws of war could be justified as serving the purpose of minimizing destruction. One of the most basic principles for the conduct of war ( *jus in bello* ) rests on the distinction between combatants and noncombatants and requires that insofar as possible, violence not be directed at noncombatants. . . . One fundamental function of the distinction between combatants and noncombatants is to try to make a terrible combat fair, and the killing involved can seem morally tolerable to nonpacifists in large part because it is the outcome of what is conceived as a fair procedure. To the extent that the distinction between combatants and noncombatants is observed, those who are killed will be those who were directly engaged in trying to kill their killers. The fairness may be perceived to lie in this fact: that those who are killed had a reasonable chance to survive by killing instead. It was kill or be killed for both parties, and each had his or her opportunity to survive. No doubt the opportunities may not have been anywhere near equal—it would be impossible to restrict wars to equally matched opponents. But at least none of the parties to the combat were defenseless.

Now this obviously invokes a simplified, if not romanticized, portrait of warfare. And at least some aspects of the laws of warfare can legitimately be criticized for relying too heavily for their justification on a core notion that modern warfare retains aspects of a knightly joust, or a duel, which have long since vanished, if ever they were present. But the point now is not to attack or defend the efficacy of the principle of warfare that combat is more acceptable morally if restricted to official combatants, but to notice one of its moral bases, which, I am suggesting, is that it allows for a "fair fight" by means of protecting the utterly defenseless from assault. The resulting picture of war—accurate or not—is not of victim and perpetrator (or, of mutual victims) but of a winner and a loser, each of whom might have enjoyed, or suffered, the fate of the other. Of course, the satisfaction of the requirement of providing for a "fair fight" would not by itself make a conflict morally acceptable overall. An unprovoked and otherwise unjustified invasion does not become morally acceptable just because attacks upon noncombatants, use of prohibited weapons, and so on are avoided.

At least part of the peculiar disgust which torture evokes may be derived from its apparent failure to satisfy even this weak constraint of being a "fair fight." The supreme reason, of course, is that torture begins only after the fight is—for the victim—finished. Only losers are tortured. The "fair fight" may even in fact already have occurred and led to the capture of the person who is to be tortured. But now that the torture victim has exhausted all means of defense and is powerless before the captors, a fresh assault begins. The surrender is followed by new attacks upon the defeated by the now unrestrained conquerors. In this respect torture is indeed not analogous to the killing in battle of a healthy and well-armed foe; it is a cruel assault upon the defenseless. In combat the other person one kills is still a threat when killed and is killed in part for the sake of one's own survival. The torturer inflicts pain and damage on another person who, by virtue of now being within his or her power, is no longer a threat and is entirely at the torturer's mercy.

It is in this respect of violating the prohibition against assault upon the defenseless, then, that the manner in which torture is conducted is morally more reprehensible than the manner in which killing would occur if the laws of war were honored. In this respect torture sinks below even the well-regulated mutual slaughter of a justly fought war.

## Torture Within Constraints?

But is all torture indeed an assault upon the defenseless? For, it could be argued in support of some torture that in many cases there is something beyond the initial surrender which the torturer wants from the victim and that in such cases the victim could comply and provide the torturer with whatever is wanted. To refuse to comply with the further demand would then be to maintain a second line of defense. The victim would, in a sense, not have surrendered—at least not fully surrendered—but instead only retreated. The victim is not, on this view, utterly helpless in the face of unrestrainable assault as long as he or she holds in reserve an act of compliance which would satisfy the torturer and bring the torture to an end.

It might be proposed, then, that there could be at least one type of morally less unacceptable torture. Obviously the torture victim must remain defenseless in the literal sense, because it cannot be expected that his or her captors would provide means of defense against themselves. But an alternative to a capability for a literal defense is an effective capacity for surrender, that is, a form of surrender which will in fact bring an end to attacks. In the case of torture, the relevant form of surrender might seem to be a compliance with the wishes of the torturer that provides an escape from further torture.

Accordingly, the constraint on the torture that would, on this view, make it less objectionable would be this: the victim of torture must have available an act of compliance which, if performed, will end the torture. In other words, the purpose of the torture must be known to the victim, the purpose must be the performance of some action within the victim's power to perform, and the victim's performance of the desired action must produce the permanent cessation of the torture. I shall refer to torture that provides for such an act of compliance as torture that satisfies the constraint of possible compliance. As soon becomes clear, it makes a great difference what kind of act is presented as the act of compliance. And a person with an iron will, a great sense of honor, or an overwhelming commitment to a cause may choose not to accept voluntarily cessation of the torture on the terms offered. But the basic point would be merely that there should be some terms understood so that the victim retains one last portion of control over his or her fate. Escape is not defense, but it is a manner of protecting oneself. A practice of torture that allows for escape through compliance might seem immune to the charge of engaging in assault upon the defenseless. Such is the proposal.

One type of contemporary torture, however, is clearly incapable of satisfying the constraint of possible compliance. The extraction of information from the victim, which perhaps—whatever the deepest motivations of torturers may have been—has historically been a dominant explicit purpose of torture is now, in world practice, overshadowed by the goal of the intimidation of people other than the victim. Torture is in many countries used primarily to intimidate potential opponents of the government from actively expressing their opposition in any form considered objectionable by the regime. Prohibited forms of expression range, among various regimes, from participation in terroristic guerrilla movements to the publication of accurate news accounts. The extent of the suffering inflicted upon the victims of the torture is proportioned, not according to the responses of the victim, but according to the expected impact of news of the torture upon other people over whom the torture victim normally has no control. The function of general intimidation of others, or deterrence of dissent, is radically different from the function of extracting specific information under the control of the victim of torture, in respects which are central to the assessment of such torture. This is naturally not to deny that any given instance of torture may serve, to varying degrees, both purposes—and, indeed, other purposes still.

*Terroristic torture*, as we may call this dominant type, cannot satisfy the constraint of possible compliance, because its purpose (intimidation of persons other than the victim of the torture) cannot be accomplished and may not even be capable of being influenced by the victim of the torture. The victim's suffering—indeed, the victim—is being used entirely as a means to an end over which the victim has no control. Terroristic torture is a pure case—the purest possible case—of the violation of the Kantian principle that no person may be used *only* as a means. The victim is simply a site at which great pain occurs so that others may know about it and be frightened by the prospect. The torturers have no particular reason not to make the suffering as great and as extended as possible. Quite possibly the more terrible the torture, the more intimidating it will be—this is certainly likely to be believed to be so.

Accordingly, one ought to expect extensions into the sorts of "experimentation" and other barbarities documented recently in the cases of, for example, the Pinochet government in Chile[12] and the Amin government in Uganda.[13] Terroristic torturers have no particular reason not to carry the torture through to the murder of the victim, provided the victim's family or friends can be expected to spread the word about the price of any conduct compatible with disloyalty. Therefore, terroristic torture clearly cannot satisfy even the extremely mild constraint of providing for the possibility of compliance by its victim. The degree of need for assaults upon the defenseless initially appears to be quite different in the case of torture for the purpose of extracting information, which we may call *interrogational torture*. This type of torture needs separate examination because, however condemnable we ought in the end to consider it overall, its purpose of gaining information appears to be consistent with the observation of some constraint on the part of any torturer genuinely pursuing that purpose alone. Interrogational torture does have a built-in end point: when the information has been obtained, the torture has accomplished its purpose and need not be continued. Thus, satisfaction of the constraint of possible compliance seems to be quite compatible with the explicit end of interrogational torture, which could be terminated upon the victim's compliance in providing the information sought. In a fairly obvious fashion the torturer could consider himself or herself to have completed the assigned task—or probably more hopefully, any superiors who were supervising the process at some emotional distance could consider the task to be finished and put a stop to it. A pure case of interrogational torture, then, appears able to satisfy the constraint of possible compliance, since it offers an escape, in the form of providing the information wanted by the torturers, which affords some protection against further assault.

Two kinds of difficulties arise for the suggestion that even largely interrogational torture could escape the charge that it includes assaults upon the defenseless. It is hardly necessary to point out that very few actual instances of torture are likely to fall entirely within the category of interrogational torture. Torture intended primarily to obtain information is by no means always in practice held to some minimum necessary amount. To the extent that the torturer's motivation is sadistic or otherwise brutal, he or she will be strongly inclined to exceed any rational calculations about what is sufficient for the stated purpose. In view of the strength and nature of a torturer's likely passions—of, for example, hate and self-hate, disgust and self-disgust, horror and fascination, subservience toward superiors and aggression toward victims—no constraint is to be counted upon in practice.

Still, it is of at least theoretical interest to ask whether torturers with a genuine will to do so could conduct interrogational torture in a manner which would satisfy the constraint of possible compliance. In order to tell, it is essential to grasp specifically what compliance would normally involve. Almost all torture is "political" in the sense that it is inflicted by the government in power upon people who are, seem to be, or might be opposed to the government. Some torture is also inflicted by opponents of a government upon people who are, seem to be, or might be supporting the government. Possible victims of torture fall into three broad categories: the ready collaborator, the innocent bystander, and the dedicated enemy.

First, the torturers may happen upon someone who is involved with the other side but is not dedicated to such a degree that cooperation with the torturers would, from the victim's perspective, constitute a betrayal of anything highly valued. For such a person a betrayal of cause and allies might indeed serve as a form of genuine escape.

The second possibility is the capture of someone who is passive toward both sides and essentially uninvolved. If such a bystander should happen to know the relevant information—which is very unlikely—and to be willing to provide it, no torture would be called for. But what if the victim would be perfectly willing to provide the information sought in order to escape the torture but does not have the information? Systems of torture are notoriously incompetent. The usual situation is captured with icy accuracy by the reputed informal motto of the Saigon police, "If they are not guilty, beat them until they are." The victims of torture need an escape not only from beatings for what they know but also from beatings for what they do not know. In short, the victim has no convincing way of demonstrating that he or she cannot comply, even when compliance is impossible. (Compare the reputed dunking test for witches: if the woman sank, she was an ordinary mortal.)

Even a torturer who would be willing to stop after learning all that could be learned, which is nothing at all if the "wrong" person is being tortured, would have difficulty discriminating among pleas. Any keeping of the tacit bargain to stop when compliance has been as complete as possible would likely be undercut by uncertainty about when the fullest possible compliance had occurred. The difficulty of demonstrating that one had collaborated as much as one could might in fact haunt the collaborator as well as the innocent, especially if his or her collaboration had struck the torturers as being of little real value.

Finally, when the torturers succeed in torturing someone genuinely committed to the other side, compliance means, in a word, betrayal; betrayal of one's ideals and one's comrades. The possibility of betrayal cannot be counted as an escape. Undoubtedly some ideals are vicious and some friends are partners in crime—this can be true of either the government, the opposition, or both. Nevertheless, a betrayal is no escape for a dedicated member of either a government or its opposition, who cannot collaborate without denying his or her highest values.

For any genuine escape must be better than settling for the lesser of two evils. One can always try to minimize one's losses—even in dilemmas from which there is no real escape. But if accepting the lesser of two evils always counted as an escape, there would be no situations from which there was no escape, except perhaps those in which all alternatives happened to be equally evil. On such a loose notion of escape, all conscripts would become volunteers, since they could always desert. And so assaults containing any alternatives would then be acceptable. An alternative which is legitimately to count as an escape must not only be preferable but also itself satisfy some minimum standard of moral acceptability. A denial of one's self does not count.

Therefore, on the whole, the apparent possibility of escape through compliance tends to melt away upon examination. The ready collaborator and the innocent bystander have some hope of an acceptable escape, but only provided that the torturers both (a) are persuaded that the victim has kept his or her part of the bargain by telling all there is to tell and (b) chose to keep their side of the bargain in a situation in which agreements cannot be enforced upon them and they have nothing to lose by continuing the torture as they please. If one is treated as if one is a dedicated enemy, as seems likely to be the standard procedure, the fact that one actually belongs in another category has no effect. On the other hand, the dedicated enemies of the torturers, who presumably tend to know more and consequently are the primary intended targets of the torture, are provided with nothing which can be considered an escape and can only protect themselves, as torture victims always have, by pretending to be collaborators or innocents, and thereby imperiling the members of these categories.

# Truth Extraction

In a longer version of the essay excerpted in Reading 5, Henry Shue postulates a situation in which "a fanatic, perfectly willing to die rather than collaborate in the thwarting of his own [ticking bomb] scheme has set a hidden nuclear device to explode in the heart of Paris." If, indeed, said Shue, in such a situation there was "no way to evacuate the innocent people . . . —the only hope of preventing tragedy is to torture the perpetrator, find the device, and detonate it," then, despite his philosophical opposition to torture, even he could "see no way to deny the permissibility of torture in a case *just like this*."

Given such an admission—that in strict utilitarian terms torture might be defensible in a ticking bomb scenario—those who argue against torture, even in that case, are required to add pragmatic reasons for their position to moral (and legal) ones. Among the most obvious such practical considerations is simply whether torture works or, to put it differently, whether other techniques for getting at the truth might not work better. Marine major Sherwood F. Moran was a hugely successful interrogator of Japanese prisoners of war in World War II. In the middle of the war (1943) he wrote a report about his techniques, "Suggestions for Japanese Interpreters Based on Work in the Field," which was designed to provide guidance to other interpreters. It has been called a "cult classic for military interrogators"[14] and was until recently posted on the website of the Marine Corps Interrogator Translator Teams Association (MCITTA), where it was described as one of the "timeless documents" in the field.

First of all I wish to say that every interpreter (I like the word "interviewer" better, for any really efficient interpreter is first and last an interviewer) must be himself. He should not and cannot try to copy or imitate somebody else, or, in the words of the Japanese proverb, he will be like the crow trying to imitate the cormorant catching fish and drowning in the attempt. [. . .] But of course it goes without saying that the interpreter should be open to suggestions and should be a student of best methods. But his work will be based primarily upon his own character, his own experience, and his own temperament. These three things are of prime importance; strange as it may seem to say so, I think the first and the last are the most important of the three. Based on these three things, he will gradually work out a technique of his own, — his very own, just as a man does in making love to a woman! The comparison is not merely a flip bon mot; the interviewer should be a real wooer!

What I have to say concretely is divided into two sections: (1) The attitude of the interpreter towards his prisoner; (2) His *knowledge and use* of the language.

Let us take the first one,—his ATTITUDE. This is of prime importance, in many ways more important than his knowledge of the language. [. . .]

I consider a prisoner (i.e. a man who has been captured and disarmed and in a perfectly *safe* place) as out of the war, out of the picture, and thus, in a way, not an enemy. (This is doubly so, psychologically and physically speaking, if he is wounded or starving.) Some self-appointed critics, self-styled "hard-boiled" people, will sneer that this is a sentimental attitude, and say, "Don't you know he will try to escape at first opportunity?" I reply, "Of course I do; wouldn't *you*?" But that is not the point. Notice that in the first part of this paragraph I used the word "safe". That is the point; get the prisoner to a safe place, where even he knows there is no hope of escape, that it is all over. Then forget, as it were, the "enemy" stuff, and the "prisoner" stuff. I tell them to forget it, telling them I am talking as a human being to a human being. [. . .] And they respond to this.

When it comes to the wounded, the sick, the tired, the sleepy, the starving, I consider that since they are out of the combat for good, they are simply needy human beings, needing our help, physical and spiritual. This is the standpoint of one human being thinking of another human being. But in addition, it is hard business common sense, and yields rich dividends from the Intelligence standpoint.

I consider that the Japanese soldier is a person to be pitied rather than hated. I consider (and I often tell them so) that they have been led around by the nose by their leaders; that they do not know, and have not been allowed to know for over 10 years what has really been going on in the world, etc. etc. The proverb "Ido no naka no kawazu taikai o shirazu" (The frog in the bottom of the well is not acquainted with the ocean) is *sometimes* a telling phrase to emphasize your point. But one must be careful not to antagonize them by such statements, by giving them the idea that you have a "superiority" standpoint, etc. etc.

But in relation to all the above, this is where "character" comes in. [. . .] One must be absolutely *sincere*. I mean that one must not just assume the above attitudes in order to gain the prisoner's confidence and get him to talk. He will know the difference. You must get him to know by the expression on your face, the glance of your eye, the tone of your voice, that you do think that "the men of the four seas are brothers," to quote a Japanese (and Chinese) proverb. [. . .] One Japanese prisoner remarked to me that he thought I was a fine gentleman. [. . .] I think that what he was meaning to convey was that he instinctively sensed that I was sincere, was trying to be fair, did not have it in for the Japanese as such. [. . .]

[A] person who has lived in Japan for a number of years has a big advantage. One can tell the prisoner how pleasant his life in Japan was;

how many fine Japanese he knew, even mentioning names and places, students and their schools, how he had Japanese in his home, and vice versa, etc. etc. That alone will make a Japanese homesick. This line has infinite possibilities. If you know anything about Japanese history, art, politics, athletics, famous places, department stores, eating places, etc. etc. a conversation may be relatively interminable. I could write two or three pages on this alone. (I personally have had to break off conversations with Japanese prisoners, so willing were they to talk on and on.) I remember how I had quite a talk with one of our prisoners whom I had asked what his hobbies [. . .] etc. were. He mentioned swimming. (He had swum four miles to shore before we captured him.) We talked about the crawl stroke and about the Olympics. Right here all this goes to prove that being an "interpreter" is not simply being a Cook's tourist type of interpreter. He should be a man of culture, insight, resourcefulness, and with real conversational ability. He must have "gags"; he must have a "line." He must be alive; he must be warm; he must be vivid. But above all he must have integrity, sympathy; yet he must be firm, wise ("Wise as serpents but harmless as doves".) He must have dignity and a proper sense of values, but withal friendly, open and frank. [. . .]

From the above, you will realize that most of these ideas are based on common sense. I might sum it all up by saying that a man should have sympathetic common sense. There may be some who read the above paragraphs (or rather just glance through them) who say it is just sentiment. But careful reading will show it is enlightened hard-boiled-ness.

Now in regard to the second point I have mentioned [. . .], the knowledge and the use of the language. Notice that I say "knowledge" and "use." They are different. A man may have a perfect knowledge, as a linguist, of a language, and yet not be skillful and resourceful in its use. Questioning people, even in one's own language, is an art in itself, just as is selling goods. In fact, the good interpreter must, in essence, be a salesman, and a good one.

But first in regard to the *knowledge* of the language itself. Technical terms are important, but I do not feel they are nearly as important as a large general vocabulary, and freedom in the real idiomatic language of the Japanese. Even a person who knows little Japanese can memorize lists of technical phrases. After all, the first and most important victory for the interviewer to try to achieve is to get into the mind and into the heart of the person being interviewed. [. . .]

Now in regard to the *use* of the language. Often it is not advisable to get right down to business with the prisoner at the start. I seldom do. To begin right away in a business-like and statistical way to ask him his name, age, etc., and then pump him for military information, is neither good psychology nor very interesting for him or for you. Begin by asking him things about himself. Make him and his troubles the center of the stage, not you and your questions of war problems. If he is not wounded or tired out, you can ask him if he has been getting enough to eat; if he likes Western-style food. You can go on to say, musingly, as it were, "This war is a mess, isn't it! It's too bad we had to go to war, isn't it! Aren't people funny, scrapping the way they do! The world seems like a pack of dogs scrapping at each other." And so on. (Notice there is yet no word of condemnation or praise towards his or his country's attitude, simply a broad human approach.) You can ask if he has had cigarettes, if he is being treated all right, etc. If he is wounded you have a rare chance. Begin to talk about his wounds. Ask if the doctor or corpsman has attended to him. Have him *show* you his wounds or burns. (They will like to do this!) The bombardier of one of the Japanese bombing planes shot down over Guadalcanal had his whole backside burned and had difficulty in sitting down. He appreciated my genuine sympathy and desire to have him fundamentally made comfortable. He was most affable and friendly, though very sad at having been taken prisoner. We had a number of interviews with him. There was nothing he was not willing to talk about. And this was a man who had been dropping bombs on us just the day before! On another occasion a soldier was brought in. A considerable chunk of his shinbone had been shot away. In such bad shape was he that we broke off in the middle of the interview to have his leg redressed. We were all interested in the redressing, in his leg, it was almost a social affair! And the point to note is that we really *were* interested, and not pretending to be interested in order to get information out of him. This was the prisoner who called out to me when I was leaving after that first interview, "Won't you please come and talk to me *every day*." (And yet people are continually asking us, "Are the Japanese prisoners really willing to talk?")

A score of illustrations such as the preceding could be cited. However, all this is of course preliminary. But even later on when you have started on questioning him for strictly war information, it is well not to be too systematic. Wander off into delightful channels of things of interest to him and to you. But when I say it is well not to be too systematic, I mean in the *outward* approach and presentation from a conversational standpoint. But in the workings of your mind you must be a model of system. You must know exactly what information you want, and come back to it repeatedly. Don't let your warm human interest, your genuine interest in the prisoner, cause you to be sidetracked by him! You should be hardboiled but not half-baked. Deep human sympathy *can* go with a businesslike, systematic and ruthlessly persistent approach. [. . .]

The concrete question comes up, What is one to do with a prisoner who recognizes your friendliness and really appreciates it, yet won't give military information, through conscientious scruples? [. . .]

[T]here *is* something that can be done about this. In the case of a salesman selling goods from door to door, the emphatic "No" of the lady to whom he is trying to sell stockings, aluminum ware, or what-not, should not be the end of the conversation but the *beginning* ("I have not yet begun to fight!" as it were). As for myself, in such a situation with prisoners, I try to shame them, and have succeeded quite well. I tell them something like this, "You know, you are an interesting kind of person. I've lived in Japan many years. I like the Japanese very much. I have many good friends among the Japanese, men, women, boys, girls. Somehow or other the Japanese always open up to me. I have had most intimate conversations with them about all kinds of problems. I never quite met a person like you, so offish and on your guard." etc. etc. One prisoner seemed hurt. He said, with surprise and a little pain, "Do you really think I am offish?" Again, I sometimes say, "That is funny, you are not willing to talk to me about these things. Practically all the other prisoners, and we have hundreds of them, do talk. You seem different. I extend to you my friendship; we have treated you well, far better probably than we would be treated, and you don't respond." etc. etc. I tell him that we purposely try to be human. I say to him, "You know perfectly well that if I were a prisoner of the Japanese they wouldn't treat me the way I am treating you" (meaning my general attitude and approach). I then say, "I will show you the way they would act to me," and I stand up and imitate the stern, severe attitude of a Japanese military officer toward an inferior, and the prisoner smiles and even bursts out laughing at the "show" I am putting on, and agrees that that is actually the situation, and what I describe is the truth. Now in all this the interpreter back at one of the bases has a big advantage in one respect: He will have plenty of time for interrogations, and can interview them time and time again, while in many cases, we out at the front must interview them more or less rapidly, and often-times only once. But on the other hand, those of us right out at the front have what is sometimes a great advantage: we get absolutely first whack at them, and talk to them when they have not had time to develop a technique of "sales resistance" talk, as it were.

It may be advisable to give one illustration of how, concretely, to question, according to my point of view. Take a question such as this, "Why did you lose this battle?" [. . .] A question presented in this bare way is a most wooden and uninteresting affair. The interpreter should be given leeway to phrase his own questions, and to elaborate them as he sees fit, as he sizes up the situation and the particular prisoner he may be interviewing. His superior officer should merely give him a statement of the information he wants. A man who is simply a word for word interpreter (in the literal sense) of a superior officer's questions, is, after all, nothing but a verbal cuspidor;[15] the whole proceeding is a rather dreary affair for all concerned, including the prisoner. The conversation, the phrasing of the questions, should be interesting and should capture the prisoner's imagination. To come back to the question above, "Why did you lose this battle?" That was the question put to me to interpret (in the broad sense) to a prisoner who had been captured the day after one of the terrific defeats of the Japanese in the earlier days of the fighting on Guadalcanal. Here is the way I put the question: "We all know how brave the Japanese soldier is. All the world knows and has been startled at the remarkable progress of the Japanese armies in the Far East. Their fortitude, their skill, their bravery are famous all over the world. You captured the Philippines; you captured Hong Kong, you ran right through Malaya and captured the so-called impregnable Singapore; you took Java, and many other places. The success of the Imperial armies has been stupendous and remarkable. But you come to Guadalcanal and run into a stone wall, and are not only defeated but practically annihilated. Why is it?" You see that this is a really *built-up* question. I wish you could see the interest on the prisoner's face as I am dramatically asking such a question as that. It's like telling a story, and at the end he is interested in telling *his* part of it.

# "Does Torture Work?"

Algeria during the 1950s is often cited as an example of torture having been effective in thwarting terrorists. Bruce Hoffman, writing in the *Atlantic Monthly* in 2002, described it as underscoring "how the intelligence requirements of counter-terrorism can suddenly take precedence over democratic ideals."

As Hoffman acknowledges, however, the use of torture by the French in Algeria was

at least strategically [. . .] counterproductive. Its sheer brutality alienated the native Algerian Muslim community. Hitherto mostly passive or apathetic, that community was now driven into the arms of the FLN [National Liberation Front], swelling the organization's ranks and increasing its popular support. Public opinion in France was similarly outraged, weakening support for the continuing struggle and creating profound fissures in French military-civil relations. The army's achievement . . . was therefore bought at the cost of eventual political defeat. Five years after victory in Algiers the French withdrew from Algeria and granted the country its independence.[16]

In this essay to appear in his *Torture and Democracy*, political science professor Darius M. Rejali explains in more detail why, contrary to the opinions of its defenders, torture in Algeria simply didn't work.

Torture apologists point to one powerful example to counter all the arguments against torture: the Battle of Algiers. In 1956, the Algerian FLN (National Liberation Front) began a terrorist bombing campaign in Algiers, the capital of Algeria, killing many innocent civilians. In 1957, Gen. Jacques Massu and the French government began a counterinsurgency campaign in Algiers using torture. As English military theorist Brian Crozier put it, "By such ruthless methods, Massu smashed the FLN organization in Algiers and re-established unchallenged French authority. And he did the job in seven months—from March to mid-October."

It is hard to argue with success. Here were professional torturers who produced consistently reliable information in a short time. It was a breathtaking military victory against terrorism by a democracy that used torture. Yet the French won by applying overwhelming force in an extremely constrained space, not by superior intelligence gathered through torture. As noted war historian John Keegan said in his recent study of military intelligence ("Intelligence in War: Knowledge of the Enemy from Napoleon to Al-Qaeda"), "it is force, not fraud or forethought, that counts" in modern wars.

The real significance of the Battle of Algiers, however, is the startling justification of torture by a democratic state. Algerian archives are now open, and many French torturers wrote their autobiographies in the 1990s.

The story they tell will not comfort generals who tell self-serving stories of torture's success. In fact, the battle shows the devastating consequences of torture for any democracy foolish enough to institutionalize it.

Torture by the French failed miserably in Vietnam,[17] and the French could never entirely secure the Algerian countryside, so either torture really did not work or there was some additional factor that made the difference in Algiers.

Among many torture apologists, only Gen. Massu, with characteristic frankness, identified the additional factor. In Vietnam, Massu said, the French posts were riddled with informants. Whatever the French found by torture, the Vietnamese opposition knew immediately. And long distances separated the posts. In Algiers, the casbah was a small space that could be cordoned off, and a determined settler population backed the army. The army was not riddled with informants, and the FLN never knew what the army was doing.

And the French had an awesomely efficient informant system of their own. Massu took a census in the casbah and issued identity cards for the entire population. He ordered soldiers to paint numbers on each block of the casbah, and each block had a warden—usually a trustworthy Algerian—who reported all suspicious activities. Every morning, hooded informants controlled the exits to identify any suspects as they tried to leave. The FLN helped the French by calling a general strike, which revealed all its sympathizers. What made the difference for the French in Algiers was not torture, but the accurate intelligence obtained through public cooperation and informants.

In fact, no rank-and-file soldier has related a tale of how he personally, through timely interrogation, produced decisive information that stopped a ticking bomb. "As the pain of interrogation began," observed torturer Jean-Pierre Vittori, "they talked abundantly, citing the names of the dead or militants on the run, indicating locations of old hiding places in which we didn't find anything but some documents without interest." Detainees also provided names of their enemies—true information, but without utility to the French.

The FLN military men had also been told, when forced to talk, to give up the names of their counterparts in the rival organization, the more accommodationist MNA (National Algerian Movement). Not very knowledgeable in the subtleties of Algerian nationalism, the French soldiers helped the FLN liquidate the infrastructure of the more cooperative organization and tortured MNA members, driving them into extreme opposition.

Unlike in the famous movie,[18] which portrays the Algerian population as united behind the FLN and assumes that torture is why the French won the battle, the real Battle of Algiers was a story of collaboration and betrayal by the local population. It was, as Alistair Horne describes in "A Savage War of Peace: Algeria 1954–1962," a population that was cowed beyond belief and blamed the FLN leadership for having brought them to this pass.

Gen. Massu's strategy was not to go after the FLN bombers but to identify and disable anyone who was even remotely associated with the FLN. It was not a selective sweep. The smallest interrogation unit in Algiers possessed 100,000 files. Out of the casbah's total population of 80,000 citizens, Massu arrested 30 to 40 percent of all males.

Torture forced "loyal" Algerians to cooperate, but after the battle, they either ended their loyalty to France or were assassinated. Torture forced a politics of extremes, destroying the middle that had cooperated with the French. In the end, there was no alternative to the FLN. As Paul Teitgin, the police prefect of Algiers remarked, "Massu won the Battle of Algiers, but that meant losing the war."

The judicial system also collapsed under the weight of torture. Judges and prefects found themselves unable to deny warrants to armed men who tortured and killed for a living. Police records show that Teitgin issued 800 detention orders (*arêtes d'assignation*) for eight months before the battle, 700 for the first three months of the battle and then 4,000 a month for the remaining months. By the end of the battle, he had issued orders to detain 24,000, most of whom (80 percent of the men and 66 percent of the women) were routinely tortured.

And "what to do with these poor devils after their 'use'?" asked a French soldier. Many torturers preferred to kill them, though, one soldier conceded, genocide was difficult. "There isn't enough place in the prisons and one can't kill everyone . . . , so one releases them and they're going to tell others, and from mouth to mouth, the whole world knows." Then, he observed, their relatives and friends "join the resistance." By the end of the battle, about 13,000 Algerians (and some Frenchmen) were in detention camps and 3,000 "disappeared."

Doctors, whose task it was to monitor torture, were themselves corrupted by the torture. "Our problem is," remarked a doctor attached to a French torture unit, "should we heal this man who will again be tortured or let him die?" As oversight failed, the French military government arrested more people for flimsier reasons.

Use of torture also compromised the military. Lt. Col. Roger Trinquier, the famous French counterinsurgency expert, believed that torturers could act according to professional norms—applying only the pain necessary to get information and then stopping. But the stories of rank-and-file torturers confirm previous studies of the dynamics of torture. "I realized," remarked a French soldier, "that torture could become a drug. I understood then that it was useless to claim to establish limits and forbidden practices, i.e. yes to the electro torture but without abusing it, any further no. In this domain also, it was all or nothing."

Torture drifted headlong into sadism, continuing long after valuable information could be retrieved. For example, soldiers arrested a locksmith and tortured him for three days. In his pocket the locksmith had bomb blueprints with the address of an FLN bomb factory in Algiers. The locksmith bought time, the bombers relocated and the raid by the French three days later fell on open air. Had the soldiers been able to read Arabic, they would have found the bomb factory days earlier. But they were too busy torturing. As one would predict, engaging in torture prevented the use of ordinary—and more effective—policing skills. (Incidentally, the French could not believe that the most wanted man in the casbah had spent months only 200 yards from the headquarters of the army commandant.)

The French military also fragmented under the competition associated with torture. Parallel systems of administration emerged, and infighting occurred between the various intelligence agencies. Officers lost control of their charges, or the charges refused to follow higher command. And in the end, the soldiers blamed the generals for exposing them to torture, noting its pernicious effects on their lives, their families and their friends—a sense of betrayal that has not diminished with the years.

Yves Godard, Massu's chief lieutenant, had insisted there was no need to torture. He suggested having the informant network identify operatives and then subject them to a simple draconian choice: Talk or die. This would have produced the same result as torture without damage to the army.

The British successfully used precisely this strategy with German spies during World War II. British counterespionage managed to identify almost every German spy without using torture—not just the 100 who hid among the 7,000 to 9,000 refugees coming to England to join their armies in exile each year, not just the 120 who arrived in similar fashion from friendly countries, but also the 70 sleeper cells that were in place before 1940. Only three agents eluded detection; five others refused to confess. Many Germans chose to become double agents rather than be tried and shot. They radioed incorrect coordinates for German V missiles, which landed harmlessly in farmers' fields. But for this misdirection, British historian Keegan concludes, in October 1944 alone close to 1,300 people would have died, with 10,000 more injured and 23,000 houses destroyed.

The U.S. Army's field manual for intelligence (FM34–52) notes that simple direct questioning of prisoners was 85 percent to 95 percent effective in World War II and 90 to 95 percent effective in the Vietnam War. What about those 5 percent at the margin? Couldn't savage unprofessional, hit-or-miss torture yield some valuable information from them? Actually, there was one case in the Battle of Algiers in which torture did reveal important information.

In September 1957, in the last days of the battle, French soldiers detained a messenger known as "Djamal." Under torture, Djamal revealed where the last FLN leader in Algiers lay hidden. But that wasn't so important; informants had identified this location months before. The important information Djamal revealed was that the French government had misled the military and was quietly negotiating a peace settlement with the FLN. This was shocking news. It deeply poisoned the military's relationship with the civilian government, a legacy that played no small part in the collapse of the Fourth Republic in May 1958 and in the attempted coup by some French military officers against President De Gaulle in April 1961.

The French won the Battle of Algiers primarily through force; not by superior intelligence gathered through torture.

# Is the "Ticking Bomb" Case Plausible?

Whether or not torture is an effective method through which to gain access to information, the argument for torture premised upon the "ticking bomb" scenario stands or falls upon the plausibility of the hypothetical situation. If the "ticking bomb" argument is based upon no more than an abstract calculation, unrelated to real life, then it loses much of its persuasive power. To pose an analogy, few people would dispute that, had the world known in the years before he took power what Adolf Hitler's leadership would lead to, his assassination would have been justified. But how could the world have known that? With what powers of clairvoyance would human beings have had to have been invested to make that moral calculation?

Henry Shue has conceded the defensibility of the "ticking bomb" argument in the abstract (Reading 6 in this chapter). It may indeed be morally justified to torture the fanatic who has hidden a nuclear device in Paris and whose torture will save thousands of lives if that is "the only hope of preventing tragedy." But Shue qualified his endorsement. He said that he cannot deny the permissibility of torture "in a case *just like this*" (emphasis original).

The following essay argues that it is virtually impossible to conceive that there ever could be a case "just like that;" that, indeed, the "ticking bomb" scenario is based upon premises that have no relationship to the way the world works, that require, to echo the Hitler example, a superhuman clairvoyance. It is from my own book *Tainted Legacy: 9/11 and the Ruin of Human Rights*, an essay that responds critically as well to Alan Dershowitz's torture warrant proposal described in Reading 4 in this chapter.

[T]here is much that is tempting in the "ticking bomb" argument, the notion that the infliction of suffering upon one person, particularly suffering that stops short of causing that person's death, is a fair trade-off to save the lives of hundreds of others. And in a strict, if abstract, utilitarian calculus, that is true. But real life is neither abstract nor strict, and even if we limit ourselves to a cold cost-benefit analysis, the long-term consequences of violating others' human rights are rarely clear ahead of time.

Take the Philippines at the turn of the last century.[19] [. . .] In one sense the victims of the Americans' "water cure" were the lucky ones. "I want no prisoners," demanded American Gen. Jacob Smith of his soldiers. "I wish you to kill and burn, the more you kill and burn the better it will please me." Smith got his wish and the United States got the Philippines, maintaining a military presence until shortly after our allied strongman, Ferdinand Marcos, and his abusive regime fell in 1986.

But Filipinos have long memories and when, in 2002–3, the United States wanted to send troops to the Philippines to fight the terrorist group Abu Sayyaf, the proposal met with enormous resistance from the local population. Not because of our close association with the hated Marcos. It was "the experience a century ago of American soldiers conducting bloody insurgency campaigns" that stoked feelings of mistrust and alienation, said one observer. Stories of torture and death inflicted upon the indigenous people by the American military had been passed on from one generation to the next until they had taken on "mythical proportions." All those long-ago water cures threatened to wash away the Americans' ability to stop terrorism today.

Proponents of ticking bomb torture try to convince us that the calculation is straightforward: torture one terrorist; save 100 people. But that assumes that there are no further detrimental consequences once the victims of the bombing are saved—no retaliatory strikes, for example, by the torture victim's comrades to pay back the inhumanity done their brother. If that happens, the math may quickly change: 100 people saved today; 1,000 killed tomorrow. [. . .]

If Israel's experience is any guide, the fact that the authorities may be able to prevent one deadly incident through torture or ill treatment of a suspect is no guarantee of an end to the cycle of violence. Indeed, such treatment may even help perpetuate it. As Dr. Ruchamas Marton, the founder of Israel's Physicians for Human Rights puts it, those subjected to torture "are broken after the experience . . . Their families . . . want to take revenge." Or they themselves do. One Palestinian teenager tortured at the Gush Etzion police station in 2001 declared that, though he had been arrested for throwing stones at settlers' cars, the degradation he had experienced in prison had made him want to become a suicide bomber.

But *is* torture an effective means of gaining information to stop ticking bombs in the first place? It seems more than passing strange that, though the ticking bomb scenario has been used for decades to justify torture, its defenders rarely cite verifiable cases from real life that mirror its conditions. Israeli authorities, for example, have often made the general assertion that their interrogation practices have saved lives, but they fail to detail specific examples. The case of Abdul Hakim Murad, a convicted terrorist plotter tortured by Filipino authorities, is sometimes referenced because the information he provided foiled a plot to crash nearly a dozen U.S. airliners into the Pacific. And of course Guy Fawkes, of Gunpowder Plot fame, was stretched on the rack in the Tower of London in 1605 until he gave up the names of his accomplices. But the number of true, confirmed ticking bomb cases is infinitesimal, certainly in comparison to the number of innocent people who have been tortured around the world.

Perhaps, upon reflection, however, the absence of verifiable cases is not so strange. For what the ticking bomb case asks us to believe is that the authorities know that a bomb has been planted somewhere, know it is about to go off, know that the suspect in their custody has the information they need to stop it, know that the suspect will yield that information accurately in a matter of minutes if subjected to torture, and know that there is no other way to obtain it. The scenario asks us to believe, in other words, that the authorities have all the information that authorities dealing with a crisis *never* have.

Even aficionados of ticking bomb torture agree that its use can only be justified as a last resort applicable to those we know to a moral certainty are guilty and possess the information we seek. [The] 45 percent of Americans who reported in October 2001 that they approved of torture were approving of the "torture of *known terrorists* if the terrorists *know details* about future terrorist attacks" (emphasis added).[20] "But how do we know for sure who is a "known terrorist" or that they "know details"? Isn't that exactly what the torture is presumably designed to find out? The reason torture is such a risky proposition is exactly because it is so *difficult* to tell ahead of time who is a terrorist and who is not; who has the information and who does not; who will give the information accurately and who will deceive; who will respond to torture and who will endure it as a religious discipline.

What if there is only a 50 percent chance the suspect has the information we seek? Is torture justified then? What if it is only a 10 percent chance? The fact is that many people suspected of being terrorists turn out not to be [. . .] as our experience with the 1,100 some detainees taken into custody after September 11 has proved so well.[21] What if those innocent people had been manhandled even more than they were? What more surefire way could we imagine to foster resentment in the communities from which they came—the very communities whose citizens are potentially the source of exactly the kind of inside information about terrorist operatives that we need to stop terrorism in the first place?

Many experts on interrogation believe that torture is one of the *least* effective ways to gain accurate information from suspects. A 1963 C.I.A. training manual observed that "interrogatees who have withstood pain are more difficult to handle by other methods. The effect has not been to repress the subject but to restore his confidence and maturity." On the other hand, if the torture victim "cracks," he is likely to say anything to make the pain stop. Insists Eric Haney, former interrogator for the United States Army, "Torture just makes the person tell you what they think that you want to know so you'll stop hurting them." The French were unabashed in their employment of torture in Algeria, even though the names of the terrorists yielded up by its victims were, as they themselves later admitted, "not always necessarily the right name." Abdul Hakim Murad, the terrorist who talked in the Philippines, provided information about the airliners, but he also claimed to be responsible for the bombing of the Federal building in Oklahoma City. Many of the false code orange terrorist alerts the United States has experienced in the past two years have been prompted by bad information passed on by detainees under harsh questioning.

Other approaches are generally more effective. Art Hulnick, a former CIA officer, who interviewed North Korean prisoners after the Korean War, reported that prisoners taken into custody by American troops and treated humanely were much more forthcoming, over time, than those held by the South Koreans and tortured. The FBI teaches thirty techniques to make suspects talk without crossing the line into mistreatment—from inducing boasts to making false promises. Even Abdul Hakim Murad "spilled the beans" not as a result of torture itself but after Philippine intelligence officials pretended they were agents from Israel's Mossad[22] to which, they said, Hakim was being turned over.

The secret for "human intelligence collectors," as the questioners are now called, is to establish "positive control." Retired Army Maj. Gen. Bill Nash describes that as "imposing on [prisoners] a psychological sense of isolation, domination, and futility, and trying to establish the conditions by which you can then reward them for information, as opposed to punish them." In fact, one of the reasons the U.S. government objected to allowing American citizen Jose Padilla, the so-called dirty bomber, to see a lawyer was because it was afraid a lawyer's intrusion would harm "the military's efforts to develop a relationship of trust and dependency that is essential to effective interrogation." As Christopher Whitcomb, a former FBI interrogation instructor, put it:

Interrogation is an art form, not a street fight. It is built on guile, perseverance, and a keen understanding of how people respond to need. People will tell you anything if you present the questions in the proper context. You simply have to find the right way to ask.

"Everybody talks eventually," says former FBI agent Rick Smith. "It's just a matter of time."

But time is what ticking bomb advocates claim not to have. And yet the truth is that the stereotypical ticking bomb scenario—ten minutes to extract information needed to save lives—is almost entirely a fiction. Would torture be justified if the bomb were to go off in ten hours? How about ten days? Or ten months? The Al Qaeda suspects being mistreated by the United States and its allies today do not apparently possess information about events that are about to happen in ten minutes, for, if they did, even larger numbers of Americans would by now be dead. The United

States is clearly not limiting its torture to ticking bombers. But then, as the Israeli High Court found to its chagrin, "moderate physical pressure" to obtain intelligence not only tended to morph into unqualified torture but was gradually applied to more and more people—not just the ticking bomb terrorists.[23]

And then there is another slippery slope. For if it is legitimate to torture a terrorist to obtain crucial information to save hundreds of lives, is it also morally defensible to torture the terrorist's wife or children? How about his aged mother? How about his whole family? Where do we stop? At what point do we truly give up our souls?

Given all these drawbacks to torture, is there any way to salvage its "respectability" in the face of a ticking bomb? Alan Dershowitz thinks there is.[24] Dershowitz contends that, whether we like it or not, officials confronted with a ticking bomb would inevitably resort to torture and, what's more, the vast majority of us would want them to. But because any officer who did so might be subject to prosecution, despite the availability of the common law defense that the commission of a crime may be justified if it is necessary to prevent a greater evil, the onus of responsibility should not be left on the individual official. Instead, the authorities should apply to a court for a "torture warrant," similar to a search warrant, so that the courts must bear the burden of authorizing torture or the consequences of failing to do so. This is also the best way, he suggests, to limit its application. Dershowitz has assured us that "the suspect [in such cases] would be given immunity from prosecution based on information elicited by torture" and that "the warrant would limit the torture to nonlethal means, such as sterile needles being inserted beneath the nails to cause excruciating pain without endangering life." But will a warrant make torture right?

To see the shoals upon which the "torture warrant" flounders, consider this. There is no doubt that, despite official efforts to eradicate it, police brutality is practiced in many U.S. jurisdictions and probably always will be. Some police officers will claim, in their more candid moments, that the use of excessive force is often the only way to protect the lives of officers and the general public. Why ought the police not be able, therefore, to apply for "brutality warrants" in specialized cases? Why ought police officers who believe that a little shaving of the truth on the witness stand is worth sending a bunch of drug pushers to prison, thus protecting hundreds of youngsters from a life of drugs and crime, not be able to seek "testi-lying warrants"? Why ought correctional officers who argue that allowing dominant male prisoners to rape other prisoners helps preserve order among thugs and thus protects the lives of guards—why ought such officers not be allowed to seek "warrants to tolerate prisoner rape" in particularly dangerous situations? The answer in all cases is the same:

because the act itself (brutalizing citizens, committing perjury, facilitating rape) is itself abhorrent and illegal. Dershowitz's analogy to search warrants fails because, while a particular search may itself be illegal, the act of searching is not *ipso facto* unethical or a crime. For a society to start providing its imprimatur to criminal acts because they are common or may appear to provide a shortcut to admirable ends is an invitation to chaos.

Moreover, Dershowitz's hypothetical application of the torture warrant proposal to the events of September 11 shows exactly what is wrong with it. "Had law enforcement officials arrested terrorists boarding one of the [September 11] airplanes and learned that other planes, then airborne, were headed toward unknown occupied buildings," Dershowitz proposes, "there would have been an understandable incentive to torture those terrorists in order to learn the identity of the buildings and evacuate them." But this assumes that those law enforcement officials would have had time in the hour and a half or so between the boarding of the planes and the impact on their targets to (1) take the suspects into custody; (2) ascertain with enough certainty to warrant torture that the suspects were (a) terrorists who (b) had the needed information in their possession; (3) apply to a judge for a torture warrant and make the case for one; (4) inflict torture sufficient to retrieve the necessary facts; (5) evaluate the validity of those facts in order to be assured that no innocent plane would be identified and blown out of the sky; and (6) take the steps required to stop or mitigate the terrorist act. [. . .]

Trying to legitimize torture through the issuing of warrants will hardly make the practice scarcer, as Dershowitz would like, but institutionalize it as a respectable option. Of course some authorities may utilize torture under some circumstances just as others choose to take bribes. The question is, "What is the best way to eradicate these practices?" By regulating them or outlawing them and enforcing the law? That an evil seems pervasive or even (at the moment) inevitable is no reason to grant it official approval. We tried that when it came to slavery and the result was the Civil War. Had we adopted Professor Dershowitz's approach to child labor, American ten-year-olds would still be sweating in shops.

Dershowitz's idea of torture warrants is a nonstarter though it *is* comforting to know that, if the professor's plan is ever implemented, the needles will be sterile.

# Chapter VI, Readings 9 and 10

# The Debate in Israel

Perhaps no society has agonized over the question of torture and the "ticking time bomb" defense of it more than Israel, subject as it has long been to attacks against its civilian population.

In formal terms that debate was expressed in two telling documents. The first (Reading 9) was the report of a Commission of Inquiry headed by former Israeli Supreme Court Justice Moshe Landau (and hence known as the "Landau Commission Report") that was set up by the Israeli government in 1987 to review the interrogation practices of Israel's General Security Service (GSS), commonly called Shin Bet. The Commission concluded that in a "ticking time bomb" situation, the use of "moderate physical pressure" was justified as the lesser of two evils and that interrogators who employed it could cite the "necessity" defense—the notion that they had taken one harmful action to prevent a greater harm—to exonerate themselves from legal liability. What constituted "moderate physical pressure" was described in a secret annex to the report.

Twelve years after the Landau Commission had been established, the Supreme Court of Israel ruled on whether the techniques employed by the GSS were in fact permissible (Reading 10). (Not all the techniques had necessarily been endorsed by the Landau Commission; years after his Commission issued its report, Justice Landau said publicly that he felt betrayed by the GSS for exceeding the constraints the Commission had sought to put in place.[25]) The Court outlawed most of them and it went on to rule that the necessity defense, while it might be cited ex post facto, did not provide prior authorization for the use of impermissible force.

Reading 9

# Landau Commission Report

## Description of General Security Service (GSS) Activity

2.18 Basic differences exist between the essence of a police interrogation of an ordinary criminal, on the one hand, and an interrogation carried out by the GSS or persons suspected of hostile terrorist activity (HTA) or subversive political activity, on the other. The police investigation is aimed at collecting evidence against individuals within the society, suspected of criminal offences, and its purposes are to have the accused convicted so that he will change his ways, to deter him and others from committing future crimes, and to give him the punishment he deserves. Whereas the direct goal of the GSS interrogation is to protect the very existence of society and the State against terrorist acts directed against citizens, to collect information about terrorists and their modes of organization and to thwart and prevent the perpetration of terrorist acts whilst they are still at a state of incubation, by apprehending those who carried out such acts in the past—and they will surely continue to do so in the future—and those who are plotting such acts, as well as seeking out those who guide them.

Another difference between a police investigation and one by the GSS is that when the police are trying to uncover a criminal offense, they seek to collect evidence (testimonies from witnesses, real evidence, clues left at the scene of the crime, etc.) which will further the process of finding the culprit; whilst in a GSS interrogation, the investigator does not usually possess evidence of this kind: eye-witnesses to acts of terrorism, such as the murder of a Jew in an Arab area, are unwilling to assist the investigators and generally even provide cover for the perpetrators because of the local population's sympathy for and fear of the terrorists. Only rarely is the perpetrator of a terrorist act caught red-handed.

GSS interrogations in terrorist cases are hampered by the determination of those interrogated not to reveal information known to them, as the result of ideological indoctrination which includes a thorough briefing on how to cope with an interrogation, with this coping as such being considered an act of bravery by the terrorist's organization. On the other hand, there is the fear of the person under interrogation that he will be attacked while still inside the prison if he reveals information known to him, and his unwillingness to cooperate with the interrogators which is fed by the hope that he will at all events be freed from prison early in a prisoner exchange, as has happened in the past. Under these circumstances, the interrogation of an HTA suspect by the GSS turns into a difficult confrontation between the vital need to discover what he knows, based on a well-founded assumption, usually from classified sources, and the will of the person interrogated to keep silent and conceal what he knows or to mislead the interrogators by providing false information. [. . .]

2.20 [. . .] In the second and secret part of this Report [we have included a survey of] the interrogation methods applied by the GSS to HTA suspects from 1967 onwards, and of the permission given to interrogators from time to time to employ means of pressure, including physical pressure. Summing up the description of the development throughout the years of the grant of permission to use pressure, the Commission notes that among almost all those engaged in this subject the prevailing view is that recourse to some measure of physical pressure in the interrogation of HTA suspects is unavoidable. [. . .]

## Pleas in the Investigator's Defense

[. . .] 3.11 As far as we are concerned, the determining factor is, of course, the statutory provision in Sec. 22 of the Penal Law [. . .] which reads:

A person may be exempted from criminal responsibility for an act or omission if he can show that it was done or made in order to avoid consequences which could not otherwise be avoided and which would have inflicted grievous harm or injury on his person, honor or property or on the person or honor of others whom he was bound to protect or on property placed in his charge: Provided that he did no more than was reasonably necessary for that purpose and that the harm caused by him was not disproportionate to the harm avoided.

[. . .] Of interest to us here is the protection of others, which the section exempts from criminal responsibility, provided three cumulative conditions have been fulfilled:
1. That the accused acted in order to prevent grievous harm to his person or honor or to the person of others whom he was bound to protect or to property placed in his charge.
2. That this harm could not otherwise have been avoided.
3. That he did no more than was reasonably necessary for that purpose and that the harm caused thereby was not disproportionate in the circumstances of the case. [. . .]

3.12 We shall now consider the above-mentioned three conditions for the defense of necessity, as they are reflected in the interrogation of a suspect by a GSS investigator, during which the investigator performs an act or makes an omission, such as an injury to the person or well-being of the suspect, or a threat to him, which contain elements of a criminal offence. [. . .] But before this, we should discuss a fourth condition, which is not stated in Sec. 22, but which learned authors [. . .] suggest in order to qualify the defense of necessity: that the harm which the defendant acted to prevent must be imminent harm. Similarly, it was also stated in an opinion which the Military Advocate General wrote in 1986 concerning the interpretation of Sec. 22, that the section will apply only if obtaining immediate information from the suspect is vital for preventing injury to human life, and as an illustration he mentions the case of a bomb which has just been planted in a crowded supermarket, and which is about to explode at any moment.

It bears noting here that the requirement of imminence of the danger is sometimes intermixed by authors with the requirement of immediately obtaining information from the suspect.

According to this version, then, the defense of necessity is not applicable except when, because of the time factor, the danger is liable to be realized immediately, and THEREFORE it is essential to get the information immediately from the suspect. This is not our opinion. The section itself makes no mention of such a qualification; rather it is built entirely upon the idea of "the concept of the lesser evil." [. . .]

As regards the question under discussion: the harm done by violating a provision of the law during an interrogation must be weighed against the harm to the life or person of others which could occur sooner or LATER. This is the idea underlying the three conditions of Sec. 22. Prof. Paul H. Robinson of Rutgers University illustrates this choice in his monograph on *Criminal Law Defenses*, which contains the most complete discussion known to us on this topic. Under the heading "Lesser Evil Defence (Choice of Evils, Necessity)" he gives the following example:

Suppose a ship's crew discovers a slow leak soon after leaving port. The captain unreasonably refuses to return to shore. The crew must mutiny in order to save themselves and the passengers. If the leak would not pose an actual danger of capsizing the vessel for two days, should its crew be forced to wait until the danger is IMMINENT, even though the disabled ship will be too far out at sea to reach shore when it is? Or should they be able to act before it is too late, even though it may be several days before the danger of capsizing is present?

And as an additional example, closer in its facts to our subject:

Consider the case of the bombmaker, X, whose construction plans require a 10-day period for building the weapon. Suppose further that the actor, D, knows that X is going to set off the bombing at a school. He also knows that X's construction plans require 10 days to build the weapon, and that police and other authorities are unavailable to intervene. Under the simple requirement that the conduct be "necessary," the actor could trespass on X's property and abort the plan by disabling the bomb at any time, including the first day, as long as such an action was the least drastic means of preventing the project's completion. Under the "immediately necessary" restriction, the actor would be obliged to wait until the last day, presumably until the last moment that intervention would still be effective.

Here, the learned author comments that the second alternative is justified only to enable A to abandon his scheme in the meantime; however, many legislators would prefer to protect society at the cost of earlier intervention against one plotting such a scheme.

We are in accord with these remarks. They are consistent with the wording of our statutory provision in Sec. 22, which, as stated, makes no mention of any particular requirement for the imminence of the danger, but posits instead the flexible test of "the concept of the lesser evil." [. . .]

3.13 Regarding the first condition, the information which an interrogator can obtain from the suspect, about caches of explosive materials in the possession or knowledge of the suspect, about acts of terrorism which are about to be perpetrated, about the members of a terrorist group to which he belongs, about the headquarters of terrorist organizations inside the country or abroad, and about terrorist training camps—any such information can prevent mass killing and individual terrorist acts which are about to be carried out. GSS investigators are charged with the task of protecting the citizenry against this as part of their official tasks, as stated in Sec. 22. [. . .]

3.14 The second condition embodied in Sec. 22 is that it was impossible to prevent the anticipated harm in any other way. It has already been explained above, in regard to GSS interrogations, that the information possessed by a member of a terrorist organization (or a member of a group of local persons which has organized at its own initiative to perpetrate acts of terrorism) cannot be uncovered except through the interrogation of persons concerning whom the GSS has previous information about their affiliation with such an organization or group; we also saw that without some such previous information the GSS does not commence the interrogation of a suspect. Without such an interrogation there is no way to get to the arms caches and explosive materials stores, the location of which is a secret known only to the suspect and the members of his group—and only he can reveal information about fellow members of his group to his interrogators.

3.15 The third condition is that, for the purpose of obtaining this information, the interrogator did not do more than was reasonably necessary and did not thereby cause disproportionate harm under the circumstances. This condition should be discussed in light of "the concept of the lesser evil," with which we have dealt above. We will again begin with an extreme example, from an article by Adrian A. S. Zuckerman of Oxford University, entitled "The Right Against Self-Incrimination: An Obstacle to the Supervision of Interrogation." He discusses the inadmissibility of a confession obtained by beating a person interrogated, and adds:

This is not to say that it is impossible to envisage situations where the organs of the State may excusably resort to torture. Where it is known that a bomb has been planted in a crowded building, it is perhaps justifiable to torture the suspect so that lives may be saved by discovering its location.

This is an extreme example of actual torture, the use of which would perhaps be justified in order to uncover a bomb about to explode in a building full of people. Under such circumstances, the danger is indeed imminent. However, we cited above additional examples from Prof. Robinson's monograph, in which vigorous action to prevent the danger of loss of life is also justified, even though the danger will only be realized in course of time. And indeed, when the clock wired to the explosive charge is already ticking, what difference does it make, in terms of the necessity to act, whether the charge is certain to be detonated in five minutes or in five days? The deciding factor is not the element of time, but the comparison between the gravity of the two evils—the evil of contravening the law as opposed to the evil which will occur sooner or later; and as was already stated above, weighing these two evils, one against the other, must be performed according to the concepts of morality implanted in the heart of every decent and honest person. To put it bluntly, the alternative is: are we to accept the offense of assault entailed in slapping a suspect's face, or threatening him, in order to induce him to talk and reveal a cache of explosive materials meant for use in carrying out an act of mass terror against a civilian population, and thereby prevent the greater evil which is about to occur? The answer is self-evident.

3.16 Everything depends on weighing the two evils against each other. The correct test for this is what the doer of the deed reasonably believed, and not what the situation actually was.

The determinant is in terms of belief and not actuality. It is not whether the harm avoided was in fact greater than the harm caused, but whether the defendant reasonably believed it to be so. If it were necessary to bring in extrinsic evidence to determine the actual degree of the unrelated harms, the result might be in some case, although human life was in no way involved, that defendant would be convicted for doing what any ordinary person would have done under the circumstances—and that is not acceptable.

It is true that strict care must be taken, lest a breach of the structure of prohibitions of the criminal law bring about a loosening of the reins, with each interrogator taking matters into his own hands through the unbridled, arbitrary use of coercion against a suspect. In this way the image of the State as a law-abiding polity which preserves the rights of the citizen, is liable to be irreparably perverted, with it coming to resemble those regimes which grant their security organs unbridled power. In order to meet this danger, several measures must be taken: first, disproportionate exertion of pressure on the suspect is inadmissible; the pressure must never reach the level of physical torture or maltreatment of the suspect or grievous harm to his honor which deprives him of his human dignity. Second, the possible use of less serious measures must be weighed against the degree of anticipated danger, according to the information in the possession of the interrogator. Third, the physical and psychological means of pressure permitted for use by an interrogator must be defined and limited in advance, by issuing binding directives. Fourth, there must be strict supervision of the implementation in practice of the directives given to GSS interrogators. Fifth, the interrogator's superiors must react firmly and without hesitation to every deviation from the permissible, imposing disciplinary punishment, and in serious cases by causing criminal proceedings to be instituted against the offending interrogator. (In the second, secret, part of this Report, these means are defined more precisely.) [. . .]

## International Conventions

3.21 [. . .] [T]he European Convention of Human Rights, which was entered into by the member-states of the Council of Europe and took effect in 1950, states in Art. 3 that:

No one shall be subjected to torture or to inhuman or degrading treatment or punishment.

3.22 Under Art. 19, complaints about Convention violations are brought before the European Commission of Human Rights, and its decisions may be appealed in the European Court of Human Rights. A matter of special interest for us is the Judgment of the European Court of 18.1.78 on Ireland's complaint against the United Kingdom. Discussed there were certain methods used by the Northern Ireland police force in its "interrogation in depth" of persons suspected of terrorism. This is how the Court describes these five methods, which were termed "techniques" of "disorientation" or "sensory deprivation".

(1) Being made to stand against a wall for several hours "in a stress position," with fingers above the head, legs spread apart and standing on the toes, so that body weight is chiefly on the fingers and toes. Persons under interrogation were made to stand in this position for periods of between 6 and 15 hours.

(2) Covering the head with a bag continually, except during interrogation.

(3) Keeping persons under interrogation in a room full of a constant, loud hissing noise.

(4) Deprivation of sleep between interrogation sessions.

(5) Reducing diet and drink during interrogations.

These methods were given "high level" approval. Northern Ireland Police were briefed on their use at the Centre for British Intelligence, in a seminar held in April 1971. The European Commission on Human Rights emphasized that ill-treatment must reach a certain severe level, in order to be included in the ban contained in Art. 3 of the Convention. The Commission found that the above-mentioned methods could be construed as torture, in the sense of Art. 3. However, the Court disagreed with the Commission. It ruled that the term "torture" meant "deliberate inhuman treatment causing very serious and cruel suffering," which should be branded with "a special stigma." Although the aim of the above-mentioned "techniques" was to extract confessions from those interrogated—in order to discover the names of others and to obtain information—and although they were used systematically, they did not occasion suffering of the particular intensity and cruelty implied by the term "torture," as so understood. However, these same techniques, "as applied in combination," amounted to inhuman and degrading treatment. [. . .] In other words, it remains to be considered whether each of these acts separately constituted a deviation from what is permissible.

3.23 In the opinion of the European Commission of Human Rights, on complaints by a number of States against Greece, pertaining to violations of Art. 3 of the European Convention in the interrogation of political prisoners (The Greek Case), published in the 1969 Yearbook of the European Convention on Human Rights, it is stated that the Greek security forces violated the Article's provisions by their methods of interrogation. In discussing these cases, the Commission notes:

It appears from the testimony of a number of witnesses that a certain roughness of treatment of detainees by both police and military authorities is tolerated by most detainees and even taken for granted. Such roughness may take the form of slaps or blows of the hand on the head or face.

In this context the Commission remarks that the amount of physical violence which detainees are ready to accept, as being neither cruel nor inordinate, varies between different societies, and even between different sections of them. Such distinctions between individuals seem questionable to us. At all events, the implied conclusion is that the Commission itself held that a moderate measure of physical violence of this kind does not violate the prohibition in Art. 3, relating to torture and inhuman or degrading treatment. [. . .]

## Conclusions and Recommendations

[. . .] 4.6 We are convinced that effective activity by the GSS to thwart terrorist acts is impossible without use of the tool of the interrogation of suspects, in order to extract from them vital information known only to them and unobtainable by other methods.

The effective interrogation of terrorist suspects is impossible without the use of means of pressure, in order to overcome an obdurate will not to disclose information and to overcome the fear of the person under interrogation that harm will befall him from his own organization, if he does reveal information.

Interrogation of this kind is permissible under the law, as we interpreted it above, and we think that a confession thus obtained is admissible in a criminal trial, under the existing rulings of the Supreme Court.

4.7 The means of pressure should principally take the form of non-violent psychological pressure through a vigorous and extensive interrogation, with the use of stratagems, including acts of deception. However, when these do not attain their purpose, the exertion of a moderate measure of physical pressure cannot be avoided. GSS interrogators should be guided by setting clear boundaries in this matter, in order to prevent the use of inordinate physical pressure arbitrarily administered by the interrogator. As is set out in detail in the Second Part of this Report, guidelines concerning such boundaries have existed in the Service ever since the scope of investigation of HTA was expanded, as required by the new situation following the Six Days War. These guidelines underwent occasional changes, generally in the direction of restrictions on the use of physical force, which were imposed from time to time at the initiative of the political echelon, until today the authorization of physical contact with the person under interrogation is extremely limited.

4.8 These instructions are at present scattered among various internal GSS instructions. They should be collected in one document. In a chapter of this report, which for understandable reasons will be included in the second, secret part, we have therefore formulated a code of guidelines for GSS interrogators which define, on the basis of past experience, and with as much precision as possible, the boundaries of what is permitted to the interrogator and mainly what is prohibited to him. We are convinced that if these boundaries are maintained exactly in letter and in spirit, the effectiveness of the interrogation will be assured, while at the same time it will be far from the use of physical or mental torture, maltreatment of the person being interrogated, or the degradation of his human dignity.

# Supreme Court of Israel Judgment

## The Means Employed for Interrogation Purposes

22. An interrogation, by its very nature, places the suspect in a difficult position. "The criminal's interrogation;" wrote Justice Vitkon over twenty years ago, "is not a negotiation process between two open and fair vendors, conducting their business on the basis of maximum mutual trust" (Cr. A 216/74 *Cohen v The State of Israel*) 29(1) P.D. 340 at 352). An interrogation is a "competition of minds"; in which the investigator attempts to penetrate the suspect's thoughts and elicit from him the information the investigator seeks to obtain. [. . .]

In crystallizing the interrogation rules, two values or interests clash. *On the one hand,* lies the desire to uncover the truth, thereby fulfilling the public interest in exposing crime and preventing it. *On the other hand,* is the wish to protect the dignity and liberty of the individual being interrogated. This having been said, these interests and values are not absolute. A democratic, freedom-loving society does not accept that investigators use any means for the purpose of uncovering the truth. [. . .] At times, the price of truth is so high that a democratic society is not prepared to pay it. To the same extent however, a democratic society, desirous of liberty seeks to fight crime and to that end is prepared to accept that an interrogation may infringe upon the human dignity and liberty of a suspect provided it is done for a proper purpose and that the harm does not exceed that which is necessary. [. . .]

23. [. . .] The "law of interrogation" by its very nature, is intrinsically linked to the circumstances of each case. This having been said, a number of general principles are nonetheless worth noting:

*First,* a reasonable investigation is necessarily one free of torture, free of cruel, inhuman treatment of the subject and free of any degrading handling whatsoever. There is a prohibition on the use of "brutal or inhuman means" in the course of an investigation. Human dignity also includes the dignity of the suspect being interrogated. This conclusion is in perfect accord with (various) International Law treaties—to which Israel is a signatory—which prohibit the use of torture, "cruel, inhuman treatment" and "degrading treatment." These prohibitions are "absolute." There are no exceptions to them and there is no room for balancing. Indeed, violence directed at a suspect's body or spirit does not constitute a reasonable investigation practice. The use of violence during investigations can potentially lead to the investigator being held criminally liable.

*Second,* a reasonable investigation is likely to cause discomfort; it may result in insufficient sleep; the conditions under which it is conducted risk being unpleasant. Indeed, it is possible to conduct an effective investigation without resorting to violence. Within the confines of the law, it is permitted to resort to various machinations and specific sophisticated activities which serve investigators today (both for Police and GSS); similar investigations—accepted in the most progressive of societies—can be effective in achieving their goals. In the end result, the legality of an investigation is deduced from the propriety of its purpose and from its methods. Thus, for instance, sleep deprivation for a prolonged period, or sleep deprivation at night when this is not necessary to the investigation time wise may be deemed a use of an investigation method which surpasses the least restrictive means.

## From the General to the Particular

24. We shall now turn from the general to the particular. Plainly put, shaking is a prohibited investigation method. It harms the suspect's body. It violates his dignity. It is a violent method which does not form part of a legal investigation. It surpasses that which is necessary. Even the State did not argue that shaking is an "ordinary" investigation method which every investigator (in the GSS or police) is permitted to employ. The submission before us was that the justification for shaking is found in the "necessity" defense. That argument shall be dealt with below. . . .

25. It was argued before the Court that one of the investigation methods employed consists of the suspect crouching on the tips of his toes for five-minute intervals. The State did not deny this practice. This is a prohibited investigation method. It does not serve any purpose inherent to an investigation. It is degrading and infringes upon an individual's human dignity.

26. The "Shabach" method is composed of a number of cumulative components: the cuffing of the suspect, seating him on a low chair, covering his head with an opaque sack (head covering) and playing powerfully loud music in the area. Are any of the above acts encompassed by the general power to investigate? Our point of departure is that there are actions which are inherent to the investigation power. Therefore, we accept that the suspect's cuffing, for the purpose of preserving the investigators' safety, is an action included in the general power to investigate. Provided the suspect is cuffed for this purpose, it is within the investigator's authority to cuff him. The State's position is that the suspects are indeed cuffed with the intention of ensuring the investigators' safety or to prevent fleeing from legal custody. Even the applicants agree that it is permissible to cuff a suspect in similar circumstances and that cuffing constitutes an integral part of an interrogation. Notwithstanding, the

cuffing associated with the "Shabach" position is unlike routine cuffing. The suspect is cuffed with his hands tied behind his back. One hand is placed inside the gap between the chair's seat and back support, while the other is tied behind him, against the chair's back support. This is a distorted and unnatural position. The investigators' safety does not require it. Therefore, there is no relevant justification for handcuffing the suspect's hands with particularly small handcuffs, if this is in fact the practice. The use of these methods is prohibited. As was noted, "Cuffing causing pain is prohibited." Moreover, there are other ways of preventing the suspect from fleeing from legal custody which do not involve causing the suspect pain and suffering.

27. This is the law with respect to the method involving seating the suspect in question in the "Shabach" position. We accept that seating a man is inherent to the investigation. This is not the case when the chair which he is seated is a very low one, tilted forward facing the ground, and when he is sitting in this position for long hours. This sort of seating is not encompassed by the general power to interrogate. Even if we suppose that the seating of the suspect on a chair lower than that of his investigator can potentially serve a legitimate investigation objective (for instance, to establish the "rules of the game" in the contest of wills between the parties, or to emphasize the investigator's superiority over the suspect), there is no inherent investigative need for seating the suspect on a chair so low and tilted forward towards the ground, in a manner that causes him real pain and suffering. Clearly, the general power to conduct interrogations does not authorize seating a suspect on a forward tilting chair, in a manner that applies pressure and causes pain to his back, all the more so when his hands are tied behind the chair, in the manner described. All these methods do not fall within the sphere of a "fair" interrogation. They are not reasonable. They impinge upon the suspect's dignity, his bodily integrity and his basic rights in an excessive manner (or beyond what is necessary). They are not to be deemed as included within the general power to conduct interrogations.

28. We accept that there are interrogation related considerations concerned with preventing contact between the suspect under interrogation and other suspects and his investigators, which require means capable of preventing the said contact. The need to prevent contact may, for instance, flow from the need to safeguard the investigators' security, or that of the suspects and witnesses. It can also be part of the "mind game" which pins the information possessed by the suspect, against that found in the hands of his investigators. For this purpose, the power to interrogate—in principle and according to the circumstances of each particular case—includes preventing eye contact with a given person or place. In the case at bar, this was the explanation provided by the State for covering the

suspect's head with an opaque sack, while he is seated in the "Shabach" position. From what was stated in the declarations before us, the suspect's head is covered with an opaque sack throughout his "wait" in the "Shabach" position. It was argued that the sack (head covering) is entirely opaque, causing the suspect to suffocate. The edges of the sack are long, reaching the suspect's shoulders. All these methods are not inherent to an interrogation. They do not confirm the State's position, arguing that they are meant to prevent eye contact between the suspect being interrogated and other suspects. Indeed, even if such contact should be prevented, what is the purpose of causing the suspect to suffocate? Employing this method is not connected to the purpose of preventing the said contact and is consequently forbidden. Moreover, the statements clearly reveal that the suspect's head remains covered for several hours, throughout his wait. For these purposes, less harmful means must be employed, such as letting the suspect wait in a detention cell. Doing so will eliminate any need to cover the suspect's eyes. In the alternative, the suspect's eyes may be covered in a manner that does not cause him physical suffering. For it appears that at present, the suspect's head covering— which covers his entire head, rather than eyes alone—for a prolonged period of time, with no essential link to the goal of preventing contact between the suspects under investigation, is not part of a fair interrogation. It harms the suspect and his (human) image. It degrades him. It causes him to lose sight of time and place. It suffocates him. All these things are not included in the general authority to investigate. In the cases before us, the State declared that it will make an effort to find a "ventilated" sack. This is not sufficient. The covering of the head in the circumstances described, as distinguished from the covering of the eyes, is outside the scope of authority and is prohibited.

29. Cutting off the suspect from his surroundings can also include preventing him from listening to what is going on around him. We are prepared to assume that the authority to investigate an individual equally encompasses precluding him from hearing other suspects under investigation or voices and sounds that, if heard by the suspect, risk impeding the interrogation's success. Whether the means employed fall within the scope of a fair and reasonable interrogation warrant[s] examination at this time. In the case at bar, the detainee is found in the "Shabach" position while listening to the consecutive playing of powerfully loud music. Do these methods fall within the scope or the general authority to conduct interrogations? Here too, the answer is in the negative. Being exposed to powerfully loud music for a long period of time causes the suspect suffering. Furthermore, the suspect is tied (in place) in an uncomfortable position with his head covered (all the while). The use of the "Shabach" method is prohibited. It does not fall within the scope of the authority to

conduct a fair and effective interrogation. Powerfully loud music is a prohibited method for use in the context described before us.

30. To the above, we must add that the "Shabach" position includes all the outlined methods employed simultaneously. Their combination, in and of itself gives rise to particular pain and suffering. This is a harmful method, particularly when it is employed for a prolonged period of time. For these reasons, this method does not form part of the powers of interrogation. It is an unacceptable method. [. . .]

A similar—though not identical—combination of interrogation methods were discussed in the case of *Ireland v. United Kingdom* (1978) 2 EH 25. In that case, the Court probed five interrogation methods used by England for the purpose of investigating detainees suspected of terrorist activities in Northern Ireland. The methods were as follows: protracted standing against the wall on the tip of one's toes; covering of the suspect's head throughout the detention (except during the actual interrogation); exposing the suspect to powerfully loud noise for a prolonged period and deprivation of sleep, food and drink. The Court held that these methods did not constitute "torture." However, since they treated the suspect in an "inhuman and degrading" manner, they were nonetheless prohibited.

31. The interrogation of a person is likely to be lengthy, due to the suspect's failure to cooperate or due to the information's complexity or in light of the imperative need to obtain information urgently and immediately. Indeed, a person undergoing interrogation cannot sleep as does one who is not being interrogated. The suspect, subject to the investigators' questions for a prolonged period of time, is at times exhausted. This is often the inevitable result of an interrogation, or one of its side effects. This is part of the "discomfort" inherent to an interrogation. This being the case, depriving the suspect of sleep is, in our opinion, included in the general authority of the investigator. [. . .]

The above described situation is different from those in which sleep deprivation shifts from being a "side effect" inherent to the interrogation, to an end in itself. If the suspect is intentionally deprived of sleep for a prolonged period of time, for the purpose of tiring him out or "breaking" him—it shall not fall within the scope of a fair and reasonable investigation. Such means harm the rights and dignity of the suspect in a manner surpassing that which is required. [. . .]

## Physical Means and the "Necessity" Defense

33. [. . .] As noted, an explicit authorization permitting GSS to employ physical means is not to be found in our law. An authorization of this nature can, in the State's opinion, be obtained in specific cases by virtue

of the criminal law defense of "necessity," prescribed in the Penal Law. The language of the statute is as follows: (Article 34 (1)):

A person will not bear criminal liability for committing any act immediately necessary for the purpose of saving the life, liberty, body or property, of either himself or his fellow person, from substantial danger of serious harm, imminent from the particular state of things [circumstances], at the requisite timing, and absent alternative means for avoiding the harm.

The State's position is that by virtue of this "defense" to criminal liability, GSS investigators are also authorized to apply physical means, such as shaking, in the appropriate circumstances, in order to prevent serious harm to human life or body, in the absence of other alternatives. The State maintains that an act committed under conditions of "necessity" does not constitute a crime. Instead, it is deemed an act worth committing in such circumstances in order to prevent serious harm to a human life or body. [. . .] Not only is it legitimately permitted to engage in the fighting of terrorism, it is our moral duty to employ the necessary means for this purpose. This duty is particularly incumbent on the state authorities— and for our purposes, on the GSS investigators—who carry the burden of safeguarding the public peace. [. . .] From this flows the legality of the directives with respect to the use of physical means in GSS interrogations. In the course of their argument, the State's attorneys submitted the "ticking time bomb" argument . . .

34. We are prepared to assume that—although this matter is open to debate—[. . .]—the "necessity" defense is open to all, particularly an investigator, acting in an organizational capacity of the State in interrogations of that nature. Likewise, we are prepared to accept—although this matter is equally contentious—[. . .] that the "necessity" exception is likely to arise in instances of "ticking time bombs," and that the immediate need ("necessary in an immediate manner" for the preservation of human life) refers to the imminent nature of the act rather than that of the danger. Hence, the imminence criteria is satisfied even if the bomb is in a few days, or perhaps even after a few weeks, provided the danger is certain to materialize and there is no alternative means of preventing its materialization. In other words, there exists a concrete level of imminent danger of the explosion's occurrence.

Consequently we are prepared to presume, as was held by the *Inquiry Commission's Report*, that if a GSS investigator—who applied interrogation methods for the purpose of saving human life—is criminally indicted, the "necessity" defense is likely to be open to him in the appropriate circumstances Israel's Penal Law recognizes the "necessity" defense.

35. Indeed, we are prepared to accept that in the appropriate circumstances, GSS investigators may avail themselves of the "necessity" defense,

if criminally indicted. This however, is not the issue before this Court. [. . .] We are dealing with a different question. The question before us is whether it is possible to infer the authority to, in advance, establish permanent directives setting out the physical interrogation means that may be used under conditions of "necessity." [. . .]

36. In the Court's opinion, a general authority to establish directives respecting the use of physical means during the course of a GSS interrogation cannot be implied from the "necessity" defense. The "necessity" defense does not constitute a source of authority, allowing GSS investigators to make use [of] physical means during the course of interrogations. The reasoning underlying our position is anchored in the nature of the "necessity" defense. This defense deals with deciding those cases involving an individual reacting to a given set of facts; it is an ad hoc Endeavour, in reaction to an event. It is the result of an improvisation given the unpredictable character of the events. Thus, the very nature of the defense does not allow it to serve as the source of a general administrative power. The administrative power is based on establishing general, forward-looking criteria, as noted by Professor Enker:

Necessity is an after-the-fact judgment based on a narrow set of considerations in which we are concerned with the immediate consequences, not far-reaching and long-range consequences, on the basis of a clearly established order of priorities of both means and ultimate values. . . . The defense of Necessity does not define a code of primary normative behavior. Necessity is certainly not a basis for establishing a broad detailed code of behavior such as how one should go about conducting intelligence interrogations in security matters, when one may or may not use force, how much force may be used and the like. [. . .]

Moreover, the "necessity" defense has the effect of allowing one who acts under the circumstances of "necessity" to escape criminal liability. The "necessity" defense does not possess any additional normative value. In addition, it does not authorize the use of physical means for the purposes of allowing investigators to execute their duties in circumstances of necessity. . . . The lifting of criminal responsibility does not imply authorization to infringe upon a human right. . . .

37[. . .] If the State wishes to enable GSS investigators to utilize physical means in interrogations, they must seek the enactment of legislation for this purpose. This authorization would also free the investigator applying the physical means from criminal liability. This release would flow not from the "necessity" defense but from the "justification" defense which states:

A person shall not bear criminal liability for an act committed in one of the following cases:
(1) He was obliged or authorized by Law to commit it (Article 34(13) of the Penal Law. . . .

Endowing GSS investigators with the authority to apply physical force during the interrogation of suspects suspected of involvement in hostile terrorist activities, thereby harming the latter's dignity and liberty, raise[s] basic questions of law and society, of ethics and policy, and of the Rule of Law and security. These questions and the corresponding answers must be determined by the Legislative branch [and not implied from the presence of "necessity" as a defense to certain criminal charges]. This is required by the principle of the Separation of Powers and the Rule of Law, under our very understanding of democracy.

38. Our conclusion is therefore the following: According to the existing state of the law, neither the government nor the heads of security services possess the authority to establish directives and bestow authorization regarding the use of liberty infringing physical means during the interrogation of suspects suspected of hostile terrorist activities, beyond the general directives which can be inferred from the very concept of an interrogation. Similarly, the individual GSS investigator—like any police officer—does not possess the authority to employ physical means which infringe upon suspect's liberty during the interrogation, unless these means are inherently accessory to the very essence of an interrogation and are both fair and reasonable.

## Chapter VII

# Healing the Victims, Stopping the Torture

By now, having read much of what this book has offered, you may well be feeling pretty discouraged. Not only is it painful to face what human beings do to one another; it is just as difficult to imagine that they will soon stop doing it. And yet the truth is that since the end of the Second World War, enormous progress has been made in the struggle to curtail human viciousness—or at least the officially sanctioned versions of it. One organization alone—Amnesty International—estimates conservatively that since it was founded in 1961, it has helped free at least 40,000 Prisoners of Conscience (people imprisoned for their nonviolent political or religious beliefs, their identities, or their exercise of fundamental freedoms), many of whom would otherwise have been tortured or even killed.

The establishment of treatment centers for victims of torture; the ratification of the Convention against Torture and Other Cruel, Inhuman or Degrading Treatment or Punishment by dozens of nations; the creation of the International Criminal Court; the growing acceptance of the legal doctrine of "universal jurisdiction;" the decision in the Pinochet Case regarding the limits of sovereign immunity; the recognition of rape as a form of torture; and perhaps most importantly the spreading awareness among people in every corner of the globe that "rights" reflect not only ideals but opportunities to lodge claims against authorities with increasing odds that those claims will bear consequences—all these are indicative of a world in transition, not perhaps to a state in which torture is unheard of but at least to a place in which it is far less common than today.

We know very well how to put torturers out of business: by making their trade as notorious as piracy or slaveholding and by holding them to account for their crimes. The readings in this chapter point the way to that new world.

# Treating Torture Victims

It seems like a simple enough idea, really. Almost obvious. If victims of torture survive their ordeals, they do so with manifold scars, both physical and psychological, and, if they are to be healed, they need help. But it was not until 1982 that such help took institutional form in one of the earliest torture treatment centers—perhaps the first—the Rehabilitation and Research Centre for Torture Victims (RCT) in Copenhagen, Denmark. Today there are more than 150 of them. In the first reading, from "Treatment of Victims of Torture," Lone Jacobsen and Edith Montgomery give a straightforward account of the effects of torture on the victims and their families and how the Copenhagen center helps victims to heal.

The after-effects of torture are mental, physical, and social. [. . .] The whole family, not only the torture victim, is severely affected when one or more members have been tortured. [. . .]

## Mental Reactions

The victims describe the mental reactions after torture as the most disabling by giving them a feeling of having changed their personality. Before the torture, many of the victims were extrovert and active persons, but afterwards they prefer to isolate themselves from their surroundings. They have lost their self-respect and confidence in other people, and they avoid contact. *The feeling of having a changed identity* is one of the most characteristic effects of torture.

Other serious symptoms include *anxiety, sleep disturbances, and nightmares,* often combined. The anxiety is often chronic, and may be present even during sleep. Torture victims try to suppress their anxiety, but they are seldom successful; it is easily aroused and increased by associations with torture. People who have been isolated in small rooms during torture become very anxious and afraid when they are enclosed in small spaces, such as hospital examination rooms, lifts, and so on. The same anxiety is provoked when they have to meet authorities, especially uniformed ones, to the extent that they fail to come for appointments because of fear. Their very low self-respect and their suspicion, coupled with fear, make it almost impossible for them to explain themselves vis-à-vis the authorities. In particularly stressful situations, their fear may lead to panic so that they suddenly have to leave the room.

Torture victims usually only sleep for a few hours at a time. They wake up because of nightmares about torture that make them relive their extreme anxiety, and several hours may pass before they dare to go back to sleep. Their sleep is thus superficial, adding to the tiredness and irritability. When awake, victims may relate how memories of the torture can overwhelm them in the form of flashbacks,[1] and that they can do nothing to prevent them. A flashback is often provoked by everyday events that produce associations with their torture experiences (the sight of medical equipment, personnel in uniforms, etc.). [. . .] Torture victims do not share their painful memories with others. They are alone with them and afraid of becoming insane. Nightmares and flashbacks, however, are normal reactions to what they have gone through.

Torture victims almost always suffer from a severe feeling of *guilt*, such as the so-called survivor- or death-guilt, in which they blame themselves for having survived while others died. Torture victims have often been forced to witness the execution of comrades, friends and family members. In this meeting with death, they were not capable even of feeling appropriate emotions (overwhelming rage against the torturers, profound compassion for victims). Their feeling of guilt may also have been provoked by situations in which the torturers have forced them to perform unacceptable acts or express opinions contrary to their own convictions and ideals—possibly even in public (on television). Family members of victims are often at great risk of being harassed and arrested—even tortured or killed—because of the torture victims' ideological views. This is, of course, a great burden on the victim and gives him a feeling of guilt, which can be increased if family members are forced into exile against their will.

Many torture victims have a *negative self-image*, characterized by shame, feelings of guilt and loss of dignity. This self-image often stems from deep humiliation, for example during sexual torture, which is very common, but often not mentioned by the victims. On top of that, there is decreased memory and lack of concentration. All this makes the victims afraid that their brains have been destroyed by the torturers, as they were told during the torture. However, these symptoms can be ascribed to the long-lasting mental pressure to which they have been exposed.

Finally, torture victims may find it difficult to manage their feelings of aggression. They become easily excited and angry in stressful or noisy situations, and later feel depressed and guilty because of their loss of control. Depressive conditions, together with a feeling of guilt for having survived their murdered friends, increase the risk of suicide. Other factors associated with suicide include social isolation and loneliness. Torture survivors in exile without their families are especially at risk.

## Physical Reactions

Immediately after the torture, victims naturally have many serious physical pains—from nails that have been torn off, broken teeth, ruptured ear drums. They have wounds, haemorrhages, fractures, and so forth. No treatment was given in prison, or it was wrong or insufficient. In addition, the physical conditions were extremely bad. The cell was either very cold or very hot, and too small for a prisoner to stand upright or to sleep in a normal position. Access to toilets was very limited, or nonexistent, and in any case controlled by the guards. The nutrition was insufficient, lacking in proteins and vitamins—and perhaps even polluted. The level of noise prevented sleep. These conditions together, combined with the torture, greatly decreased the natural resistance to infections, often causing death. [. . .]

The severe beatings cause chronic muscle pain. If the victims have been suspended by their arms they have shoulder pain, radiating to the arms and accompanied by sensitivity disturbances including tiredness. [. . .]

[. . .] [U]p to 85 per cent of the torture victims had symptoms from the central and peripheral nervous systems, and about half of these had corresponding physical findings. The victims complained of headache, poor concentration, inadequate memory, dizziness and fatigue, which may have been caused by the many direct blows to the head. Consequently, some survivors suffer chronic pain in the face and head, and also on their bodies because of nerve injury from beating. The pains are severe, shooting or burning, but this chronic state of pain may improve in time. [. . .]

There may also be visible scars and marks from torture on the skin (cigarette burns, etc.). These marks are a constant reminder to the victim of his ordeal and thus further the mental pain. The scars may also cause itching.

## Children in Families That Have Survived Torture

Children in families that have suffered torture are affected by experiences from three qualitatively different sources: the children's own *direct experiences* of violence (such as assaults, beatings, witnessing violent events), *the loss of and separation from* important family members (e.g. during parental imprisonment or hiding), and the impact of torture and other traumatic experiences on *parental responsiveness and role function.*

Children depend on their parents' ability to project a sense of stability, permanence and competence, and several studies have focused on the buffering role of parents in situations in which children are confronted with violence. A direct impact of traumatic experiences on family functioning may, however, include parental loss and subsequent impaired care and/ or separation of children from family members. Post-trauma disturbances of parental responsiveness and impairment in parental role function are major sources of secondary stress in children. In chronically violent environments, child-rearing practices may become more authoritarian and restrictive, thus altering parent-child interactions, decreasing opportunities for play, and disturbing family communication. It may compromise the parental roles of discipliner, affection-giver, and role model, which may influence long-term moral development in children.

Studies of children of torture survivors seem to indicate that they suffer from various mental symptoms of an emotional, psychosomatic and behavioural nature. Anxiety, sleeping problems, including nightmares, and psychosomatic symptoms such as stomach pain or headache are frequent symptoms among these children. [. . .]

Factual information seems to help children to cope with a stressful situation. Lack of information makes the child a victim of his own imagination. Many torture survivors are not able to tell their wives and children what happened to them, and the torture experience can become a barrier between the survivor and his family. In some families, however, the torture-surviving parents tend to overburden the children with descriptions of traumatic experience in order to relieve themselves of the pressure. Too-detailed information of torture, however, can have negative consequences for the child, if the parents do not manage to take care of the child's anxiety, but rather overwhelm it with their own. [. . .]

## Living in Exile

People who have been tortured and later sought asylum in a country of exile have been forced to flee because of circumstances. This fact will influence their integration in the new country. A hasty flight has meant that the torture survivors were often unable to say goodbye to family members, dear friends, or even spouses. They often continue to be emotionally involved in the situation and problems of their home country, such as the political struggle they took part in, and they may be haunted by fantasies about the fate of those they left behind. Are they persecuted, imprisoned, or even tortured? Is an ill father left behind still alive? Does the family have money to cover the most basic needs of food, clothing, and so on? On the one hand the tortured refugee experiences a feeling of liberation from persecution and torture, but on the other a need, perhaps almost an inner demand, to return to the home country. This conflict can cause great suffering.

Countries of exile sometimes show a negative, perhaps even hostile, attitude to refugees and may thus consider the torture survivors as immigrants who are trying to obtain economic advantages—to take jobs away from Danes, for example—and as the cause of unemployment, and so on. As a consequence, torture survivors may isolate themselves vis-à-vis the people of the country of exile. It is the experience of the authors that survivors genuinely want to make contact with their new fellow citizens, but that they are hesitant because they feel themselves misunderstood for the above-mentioned reasons. Because of poor memory and reduced ability to concentrate, it is difficult for them to learn a new language, which is often very different from their own. This makes it even more difficult to make contact with their new countrymen.

Torture victims in exile have suffered many and massive losses: friends and family who were left behind, or died during the flight, loss of homeland, language, job, property and status, and other physical conditions, including the home landscape and climate. [. . .]

## Special Considerations

[. . .] It is important to stress that torture survivors are reluctant to tell others that they have been tortured. There is a silence about the trauma: not even family or close friends know what happened. The survivors are often convinced that nobody will believe them if they say they have been tortured, just as they were told by their torturers. The professionals may hesitate to ask because they feel uncertain about the client's reactions, or for other reasons. A *conspiracy of silence* may ensue in which both client and professional are silent about the trauma. [. . .]

Torture survivors' suspicion of other people is also directed at doctors, since prison doctors often help the torturers rather than the prisoners. The health personnel must therefore pay special attention to gaining further confidence, for instance by spending a lot of time in listening to the client's own version of his problems, and what he is wanting help for. The professional should explain all available options for help. [. . .]

## Preliminary Examinations

Most torture survivors who are treated at RCT today (1997) are referred by their own general practitioner or by the social services. [. . .] The treatment, paid for by the Danish state, is free for the client and the referring institution.

Before the start of treatment, the client is invited to a preliminary talk with the aim of assessing the mental and physical problems, the social situation, and the motivation for and expectations of the treatment. The situation of family members is also discussed.

Due to the torture victim's preoccupation with his physical condition, the rehabilitation begins with a thorough *physical examination*. Since the torture, which often took place many years previously, the victim has suffered physical pains and other symptoms that have taken away any joy with respect to his own body. The daily pains have made him fear that his torturers have destroyed his organs and caused chronic disease.

The examination must take place in surroundings in which the survivor is not exposed to situations that can be associated with previous torture experiences. At the Rehabilitation Centre, the doctors and nurses avoid wearing uniforms, and it is possible to avoid periods of waiting, which might remind the client of the time he was waiting for his own torture.

Many victims have been tortured naked, and the mere act of undressing in connection with an examination may provoke fear and unease. Otoscopy, examination of the ear, may recall electrical torture to the ear, and so on. This does not mean, however, that such examinations cannot be performed. The victim wants to go through them to get an explanation of his pains. The most important thing is to explain how the examinations take place, and what their aim is. But of course, if the client does not want to be examined, this must be respected. However, some examinations are so distressing that general anaesthetic may have to be used (for example, in the cases of gastroscopy, rectoscopy, and cystoscopy[2]).

When precautions as described above are taken, the victims are reassured that other people respect their bodies, without aiming to cause pain and injury. Such care also helps to create confidence between client and doctor, confidence that can be transferred to the other members of the professional team. [. . .]

## Somatic Treatment

Somatic treatment of torture victims, medical and surgical, does not differ fundamentally from treatment of other patients. *Drug treatment* is used particularly in connection with chronic pain affecting the musculoskeletal system. Mild analgesics such as paracetamol or NSAID preparations (for arthritis) may be tried. Morphine is used only exceptionally because of the risk of addiction. Sleeping tablets are rarely used, partly because of side-effects, partly because, in our experience, they are ineffective against the serious sleeping disturbances of torture victims.

The mental after-effects of torture are usually not treated with drugs. However, antidepressants may be used during depressive phases, and neuroleptics[3] and antidepressants in small doses may be used during anxiety-dominated crisis situations.

In some cases it may be obvious that disfiguring scars on the skin should be removed by *plastic surgery*. In surgical interventions it is necessary to admit the client to hospital. In such cases it is important to inform the staff of the department about the victim's possible reactions.

Finally, *dental treatment* is important. Muscular tension in the chewing muscles may produce headache, and the dentist may help by adapting occlusal splints[4] and re-establishing the biting and chewing function. It should be remembered that many victims have suffered electric torture to the gums and teeth, and have therefore resisted consulting a dentist because of associations with this violent form of torture.

It has gradually been realized that torture victims have a low *compliance*: that is, they often do not adhere to medically prescribed treatment, guidance, prophylactic activity, or examination. It may be that side effects from drugs produce associations with previous torture trauma—for example, palpitations in connection with sham executions, and dryness of the mouth from enforced thirst. [. . .]

Finally, it should not be forgotten that torture survivors in general mistrust the authorities. The mistrust may be directed particularly towards doctors if the clients have experienced doctor-torturers in the prisons.

In order to obtain good compliance it is therefore very important to spend a long time on introduction and instruction concerning the prescribed drug, especially with respect to effects and side-effects, and when an effect is expected to occur.

## Physiotherapy

The rheumatological examination is the basis for the examination and treatment of the client by a physiotherapist. The musculoskeletal pains of torture victims are often associated with daily routine; they may be present both at rest and during movement, and may be severe enough to disturb sleep. Physical torture, depending on its form, leaves tissue injury in muscles, joints and nerves.

The physiotherapist tries to map out the pain, by marking it on a drawing of the human body, and the degree of pain is evaluated. The victim's body carriage is influenced by fear and restrained feelings. The carriage may be characterized by slight collapse of the back and by a pulling forward of the shoulders—a pattern that may be fixed—leading to muscular tension and painful movement. Most of the victims at RCT have been exposed to *falanga* (systematic beating of the soles of the feet). This gives pain when walking, even a short distance. At the same time, damage to the nerve supply of the feet gives impaired balance while walking and standing. Almost all the victims have been beaten on the chest and restrained in awkward positions, which may lead to impaired and painful respiration. At the same time, the situation of continuous anxiety and stress leads to fast, superficial breathing. Physiotherapy includes massage and careful muscle extension to relieve tissue pain. Training in warm water makes muscles and joints move more easily and gives rise to a feeling of bodily well-being. It should be remembered that training in water must be done with great care, or perhaps completely omitted, if the client has been exposed to *submarino*—that is, has had his head submerged in water almost to the point of suffocation. It may be necessary to supply the client with various aids. After *falanga* torture, he should be provided with special footwear with shock-absorbing, flexible soles, often with additional orthopaedic support. Woolen underwear helps to keep muscles and joints warm, and a back support may relieve back pain.

With respect to physiotherapy, confidence and safety are essential preconditions, which also means that the suggested treatment cannot begin until the client accepts it.

## Nursing Care

At an early stage, the nurse will discuss the examinations with the client and arrange appointments. As mentioned, some of the examinations may be so stressful that they will have to be carried out under general anaesthetic at a hospital. In this case it is important for a nurse to accompany the client and advise the hospital staff about special precautions, in particular in the department of anaesthetics. At the start of the anaesthetic, for instance, the client should never be constrained or have his nose and mouth covered by the mask before he is fully asleep, since this can cause panic from associations with previous torture while lying constrained and defenceless. It is our experience that torture victims often relive part of their torture while falling asleep, and therefore become afraid. To hear a well-known voice or see the familiar face of his nurse will reduce fear and pain. [. . .]

[T]orture victims often experience physical symptoms for which there is no obvious organic basis. This is possibly due to somatization, a reaction against the massive and violent attack of the torture. These symptoms should not be ignored; on the other hand, endless investigations may not further the therapy. When examination results are normal, this should be stressed as something very positive by the nurse, doctor and psychotherapist. [. . .]

A large number of torture victims have suffered sexual torture, including violation of their sexual organs, and they have been told that they would never have a normal sex life again, or normal children. If they are worried about this, it may help to tell them that there is no evidence that torture has such after-effects. This fear is probably much stronger than they admit, and it is therefore important that the need for such discussions is considered at an early stage of the treatment. [. . .]

## Psychotherapy

The aim of the psychotherapy is to help the torture victim deal with the mental effects of traumatic experiences and so reduce his distress and help him to regain mastery of his own life. He feels incompetent and unable to cope with the challenges in his life situation, a state of mind that has been termed "demoralization." Feelings of guilt and shame, alienation, isolation from and resentment towards the surroundings are part of this state of mind, restricting the way the individual perceives himself and his possibilities in life. Symptoms of anxiety and depression are direct expressions of this state of mind.

Psychotherapy takes place within a professional context. It is conducted by trained professionals, and the activity is systematically guided by an articulated theory that explains the sources of the clients' suffering and prescribes methods for alleviating them. [. . .]

The establishment of a confiding relationship with a helping person is a first step towards healing and a prerequisite for psychotherapy. With torture victims the establishment of this therapeutic relationship may take a long time. The psychotherapist can facilitate the process by maintaining a listening and respectful attitude towards the client. The client's sense of isolation is gradually reduced through this attitude.

Many torture victims find it difficult to understand how talking about personal problems with an unknown person can be helpful. They often present their problems to the expert, and expect the correct cure to be prescribed. The psychotherapist must introduce the thinking behind psychotherapy, and its procedures, in an understandable and convincing way. The actual therapeutic school of the therapist has proved to be of less importance for healing than the personal skills of the individual psychotherapist and his/her ability to create an atmosphere of confidence and trustworthiness. When this is established, the client's ability and willingness to trust others is strengthened.

At an early stage, therapist and client agree on a therapeutic collaboration, a contract. The therapist commits him/herself to making available his/her knowledge and professional skills, the client to contributing with his history, thoughts and reflections. The therapist outlines the frequency and length of the sessions, and a "setting" is agreed on, usually individual talks on an out-patient basis once or twice a week.

When the client regards the therapy sessions as a safe place, he gradually dares to express thoughts and feelings that have previously been avoided. When strong emotions are expressed, the therapist provides a sense of security by his/her ability to listen calmly and by directly expressing his/her understanding and reassurance. This reawakens the client's hope for a better life in the future.

Often the client has had a narrow understanding of his problems, leaving little possibility for change. He might have lost faith in the values he once treasured and completely lost all meaning in his life. When client and therapist together explore the client's life, relationships and worldview, attention is drawn to new ways of understanding and dealing with his problems, and room for change is created. This can result in a growing sense of mastery and control over his own life and eventually in improved self-confidence.

During imprisonment and torture, most torture victims are told by the torturers that no one will believe them, should they later speak about their experiences. Talking about the traumatic events proves the torturers wrong, and strengthens the client's faith in himself. This reconstruction of the past must be done with great sensitivity and at a time and a pace that respect the client's need to feel safe. By exploring together his ideals and dreams, fights and conflicts before and after imprisonment, a connection between past and present is established, helping the client to re-create a meaning in life. Dealing with massive loss is another important theme in psychotherapy. Loss of family and friends, of home country, social position and material possessions, loss of health and abilities, loss of self-confidence and of confidence in others, and loss of personal identity—all are important subjects that must be discussed within the context of psychotherapy, with particular attention paid to the meaning of the losses in the present life of the torture victim.

Most torture victims feel that they will never become what they were before. They will continue to be vulnerable in future stress situations, and major changes in life such as childbirth, death of relatives, disease and ageing can reactivate the traumatic memories and cause symptoms of anxiety and depression to recur. With sufficient support, however, many torture victims will be able to regain mastery of their life and to create a meaningful future life with their family.

## Family-Oriented Rehabilitation

As mentioned, children in torture-surviving families are stressed by their own traumatic experiences, loss of and separation from important family members, and changes in parental responsiveness and role function. Such experiences may have long-lasting consequences for their development. Any rehabilitation programme for torture victims must therefore also attend to the needs of the family, particularly the children.

Three levels of intervention must take place simultaneously: preventive community intervention, adequate parent and family support, and specialized medical and psychological treatment of children with severe, prolonged traumatic reactions. Important features of any *preventive community intervention programme* are summarized in the STOP model:

*S = Structure.* A child who is experiencing inner chaos needs an outer structure in order to avoid becoming overwhelmed. School and kindergarten activities are very valuable: the school becomes an oasis in the middle of war or war-like conditions.

*T = Talking and Time.* All children who have had traumatic experiences need to be able to talk about them, supported by a grown-up who is able to listen and give them enough time. By talking, the child structures what has happened. Small children often express themselves better in drawings or play. The grown-up should listen and show an empathic and accepting attitude without interpreting.

*O = Organized play.* Children learn through play, but many traumatized children are not able to play by themselves; they have to be taught. During play the child can forget his terrors for a while. Also during play his hope for a better future is strengthened. A grown-up must be present to help the children organize their play in a healthy and meaningful way.

*P = Parent support.* Any programme for children should include support for parents in their role as caretakers. Parents must be informed of children's reactions to traumatic experiences and supported in their attempts to cope both with their own problems and with those of their children.

Parent support at RCT is often given in sessions, with the parents alone or the whole family together. The sessions are based on the family system's own strength and capacity for healing. The family's own attempts at solving its problems are pointed out to them, very often to their great surprise, because they are usually preoccupied with their defeats. The therapist draws the family's attention to the dilemmas they are experiencing, without suggesting concrete solutions.

Since a general feature in families that have survived torture is silence about the torture and imprisonment, an important issue during the family sessions is the re-establishment of open and accepting communication between the family members. Just how much torture is mentioned depends on the composition of the individual family, but some explanation is necessary, even for small children. At times the children's imaginings can be worse than reality, and some children feel that they carry the responsibility for the difficult family situation.

Another important issue is the shift in roles within the family before, during and after imprisonment. The oldest children have often had to assume the role of caregiver for their younger brothers and sisters during their father's absence; return to their earlier roles as children is complicated by their parents' poor emotional states. Questions to the family members about differences in role expectations and behaviour now and previously make them aware of the effects of these role shifts, and they help to make future changes possible. Questions concerning the family's ideas and thoughts about the future help them to realize the possibility for change.

Children who are severely affected by their experiences need *specialised treatment*, often in the form of individual psychotherapy. Psychotherapy is a long journey and demands trained professionals; otherwise damage instead of cure can result. A prerequisite for psychotherapy is a stable and accepting environment. To conduct psychotherapy during war-like conditions is not appropriate. In such environments the child should instead be supported and helped to build up defences in order to cope.

# Exposure

One of the key ingredients in improving human rights in a country is exposing the abuses to the light of day. Shame alone may not always be sufficient to force a regime to mend its ways, but it's a sure bet that keeping violations under wraps will guarantee their perpetuation.

A free press, for one thing, is an invaluable resource for holding governments to account for their crimes.

The United Nations maintains a Special Rapporteur on Torture who investigates human rights problems and reports back to the world body. Though special rapporteurs cannot conduct their in-country investigations without the cooperation of the host government, few governments wish to be seen as unwilling to cooperate entirely. After all, if they are committing no crimes, they have nothing to hide.

Despite the good work of many special rapporteurs, however, to say nothing of that of many UN High Commissioners for Human Rights, the United Nations is notorious for being hamstrung when it comes to holding its member countries to account. That is one reason independent non-governmental human rights organizations are so important. This reading is a classic case of the work of the oldest and largest such international NGO, Amnesty International. It concerns a detainee in Russia, Aleksei Mikheev, on whose behalf Amnesty had campaigned by generating thousands of communications to Russian authorities from around the world protesting Mikheev's torture by Russian police officers. The reading includes a press release issued in 2005 by Amnesty following the conviction of two officers for torturing the prisoner and a letter from a Russian human rights organization which had also worked on the case thanking Amnesty for its efforts.

Two Russian police officers have been convicted of crimes relating to the torture of Aleksei Mikheev in detention in September 1998. A court in Nizhnii Novgorod found that Igor Somov and Nikolai Kosterin had driven Aleksei Mikheev to suicide, due to their participation in torture that included electric shock and beatings, to make him confess to a crime that he did not commit.

Aleksei Mikheev threw himself out of the second floor window of the police station where he was being held, to escape the torture. The court sentenced the two police officers to four years' imprisonment. However, according to the Committee Against Torture, a Nizhnii Novgorod-based non-governmental organization, Igor Somov and Nikolai Kosterin were

not the only officers responsible for the torture and other police and pro-
curacy officials who were responsible have yet to be prosecuted.

Aleksei Mikheev suffered serious injuries including a broken spine and
is still wheelchair-bound. He continues his fight for justice and is seeking
compensation for material and moral injury and is pursuing his claim
through the European Court of Human Rights. The Committee Against
Torture in Nizhnii Novgorod will continue to support Aleksei Mikheev
with legal assistance.

Welcoming the conviction of the two police officers, Amnesty International calls for full redress for Aleksei Mikheev, including for all those
responsible for his torture to be brought to justice in accordance with
international standards.

Dear Sir or Madam:

Nizhniy Novogorod Committee Against Torture would like to share
our victory on national court on Mr. Mikheev's case with Amnesty
international. The representatives of AI were helping us all these years
since Mr. Mikheev was tortured by police officers. We would like to
thank you for the assistance and support and for public campaigns
devoted to this case. Thank to your activities Alexai Mikheev felt great
encourage from other people who knew about his tragedy. We believe
that your concern in this case has influenced national investigational
procedure that eventually resulted in punishment of two tortures.
Unfortunately, not all people were punished for this awful crime.
Nizhniy Novgorod Committee Against Torture continues working
this Mr. Mikheev's case. The victim has not received any redress yet
and no one was recognized guilty for uneffective and extremely long
investigation of his claim (7 years). In state bodies. So, we still have a
lot of work to do but the main and the most important step was already
made. Through you we would like to thank all these people who were
sending letters to Alexei in order to support him and all these police
officers who collected money for his treatment in Oslo hospital. [. . .]

Faithfully yours,

Kalyapin Igor

# Turkey's Turning Point

But how exactly can exposure of human rights crimes transform the human rights situation in a repressive state? In this brief reading from "Torture Spoken Here: Ending Global Torture," Minky Worden, media director for Human Rights Watch, takes the case of Turkey, a country that has had a long record of human rights abuses, and describes how a combination of publicity and internal political pressure, supplemented eventually by international pressure, led to significant reforms.

To those who say that torture is the natural state of mankind and that once entrenched, it is nearly impossible to roll back, Turkey is an important recent counterexample. Turkey was once nearly synonymous with torture. Human Rights Watch did a grim series of reports on torture in Turkey starting in 1983 that documented chilling stories of students, intellectuals, and government critics who were brutally tortured. The movie *Midnight Express* brought Turkey's torture into the popular imagination. But today, torture, once endemic in police stations and gendarmeries across Turkey, has been greatly reduced. The past five years have seen more human rights progress in Turkey than occurred in the previous five decades. Even the notorious Sultanahmet Prison, which until the 1970s held poets, writers, and political dissidents, has been put to use as the unlikely venue for one of Istanbul's poshest hotels, the Four Seasons (where leg irons and torture implements greet guests on a wall in the main reception area).

So Turkey may be starting to come to terms with its torturing past. What was the catalyst for Turkey's torture turning point and how can those lessons be applied around the world? Key factors included international and domestic pressure, state withdrawal of support for torture, and very basic legal reforms. Conventional wisdom holds that the European Union accession process was the key catalyst, and indeed it was an important factor. But in reality, the momentum for torture reform was homegrown, and began in Turkey long before the EU process in the late 1990s.

Common from Ottoman days onward, the worst modern outbreak of torture in Turkey dates from the 1980 military coup, when a group of generals seized power, extended martial law throughout the country, and detained enormous numbers of people, including opposition politicians, students, writers, and artists, holding them in incommunicado detention for up to ninety days. Between 1980 and 1994, 450 people died in police custody, many with gruesome evidence of torture.

In 1984, civilian rule was restored. But by the 1990s, police and the gendarmerie were struggling to cope with illegal armed organizations, particularly the Kurdistan Workers' Party, or PKK, which was then posing a considerable threat in Turkey's southeast. Government security forces tried to crush the armed groups by any means necessary, making it dangerous to be a young man in Kurdish villages at that time. "Security forces' standard response to any PKK activity was to round up all the males of the nearest villages and torture them," said Jonathan Sugden, a Human Rights Watch researcher who has documented human rights conditions in Turkey for nearly two decades. Deaths in custody went up again markedly, with at least forty-five detainees dying in 1994. "Hosing with cold water under pressure, electric shocks, and rape with truncheons were commonplace methods, but what actually killed people was the beatings: brain injuries when heads hit walls, or chest injuries with broken ribs," said Sugden.

## Reversing Turkey's Trend

With hindsight, the first concrete sign of progress toward ending torture came when Turkey ratified the European Torture Convention in 1988, apparently under pressure from a state complaint against Turkey in the Council of Europe for abuses committed since the military coup. Acceding to the European Torture Convention meant Turkey had to grant the European Committee for the Prevention of Torture (CPT) access to police stations for unscheduled visits, beginning in 1990. "It was to maintain diplomatic respectability, I think, that Turkey let the Committee in to monitor," said Sugden. "The authorities must have been certain they could manage the process, but in the event, they couldn't."

The reports of the earliest visits have not yet been published, but the deterrent effect of having possible outside monitors marching in at any moment was significant. Although the government technically had the right to veto publication of CPT reports, in December 1992, citing the gravity of their findings, the CPT stated without the government's approval that torture in Turkey was "widespread . . . a deeply-rooted problem." In response, the Turkish government shortened detention times and increased access to legal counsel, though police constantly subverted the safeguards. As the conflict in the southeast raged, deaths in custody peaked in 1994, and two years later the CPT made a further statement confirming that torture continued.

It was about this time that dogged domestic champions in the fight against torture began to have an impact. In January 1996, Sabri Ergul, a member of parliament, was alerted that the children of several constituents were being held in incommunicado detention. Ergul entered Manisa Police Headquarters unannounced: "I heard a cry and opened the door of the next room to find out what was going on. The young people were there. They were blindfolded and some of them were naked." Ergul contacted the media, and several TV channels showed footage of him hanging handwritten notices outside the police station saying THERE IS TORTURE HERE. Blindfolded, stripped naked, raped with batons, given electric shocks, hosed with pressurized water, and beaten, the teenagers who had confessed to their crimes under torture were found guilty and were sentenced to terms of up to twelve years in prison. Some were taken to the hospital with internal bleeding and psychological problems.

Until this moment, ordinary Turkish citizens had been able to tell themselves that the accounts of torture were just anti-Turkish propaganda spread by foreign meddlers. Here was credible confirmation that the allegations had been true all along. Ergul's revelations caused widespread consternation and public outrage. In early 1997 the government substantially reduced detention periods, abolished incommunicado detention in law for criminal detainees, and reduced incommunicado detention to four days for people detained for political offenses.

Another Turkish politician who was determined to rid her country of the taint of torture was Parliamentary Human Rights Commission chairwoman Sema Piskinsut. A medical doctor and parliamentary deputy, she formed a team that visited prisons and, by interviewing prisoners there, discovered the locations of secret interrogation rooms and torture equipment. A member of her team reported, "We have seen people who carry the marks of torture on their bodies. Doctors in our delegation proved with documents that a number of these people had been subjected to torture. Some of them still had bruises all over their faces, their eyes, etc. Since Serna Piskinsut was a doctor herself, she personally examined some forty female prisoners. We asked a prisoner who said he was harshly tortured in Urfa to speak about the place and the way in which he was tortured. The prisoner had difficulty in describing the interrogation room of the Urfa police department since he was blindfolded. Then we asked him to cover his eyes and to try to recall what happened. After some difficulty, he took us to the scene of torture. There, we saw the torture devices. The ground was wet, we saw mechanisms that made the prisoners subject to cold water shock, electric cables and wheels used for hanging people. We recorded and documented what we saw."

Sema Piskinsut turned out to be a tenacious foe of torture. She alerted the media, made a stink, and the public grew angry. She published a series of extremely detailed reports as official parliamentary documents. Other embarrassing revelations about the police and state followed, as did national public demonstrations against torture and corruption. "Serna Piskinsut was really offended that torturers were staining the reputation of her homeland," said Sugden. "With torture so thoroughly documented by a patriotic Turk of the political mainstream, the findings couldn't be written off or ignored." The press covered the grisly revelations, and the state had to respond with more reforms, including, in 1999, the institution of a system of police-station monitoring by local governors and prosecutors.

These incremental reforms began to add up to a significant system of safeguards. With greater scrutiny of police stations and a greater readiness to prosecute torturers (though still not to convict), eventually the result was a measurable reduction in the number and severity of torture cases.

In 1999, Turkey was rewarded for its modest progress by becoming a candidate for EU accession. It was the beginning of a virtuous circle as the EU accession process pushed reforms further forward. In 1999, the European Commission set a number of reform benchmarks for Turkey to be allowed into the EU, including combating torture. Movement was slow at first, but in 2002, an unlikely alliance of the media, the business community, trade unions, and human rights organizations sharply demanded more convincing reforms to keep the candidacy process alive. The government gave way, and the pace of reforms began to pick up under the current moderate Muslim government headed by Prime Minister Recep Tayyip Erdogan. Since 2002, Turkey has bolstered press and speech freedoms for civil society, and improved basic rights for women and Kurds. In July 2003, Turkey finally abolished incommunicado detention officially.

The gap between law and practice remains, but progress is striking. Today, most detainees get to see a lawyer, and most are brought before a judge within a matter of hours. Since 2000, there have been no deaths in police stations that appeared to be from torture. "Even lawyers who are highly skeptical of the present government and its reform program readily concede that torture is down, and that their clients are treated significantly better than they were a few years ago," said Sugden. Of course, problems remain, and backsliding is a possibility. Police sometimes take detainees to vacant lots or outside the city limits, provoking fears that they may shift to the *L.A. Confidential* system—after the film of the same name—of torturing detainees in a "safe house" or unregistered detention center.

"For decades, documenting torture in Turkey was extremely discouraging work. But the fact that Turkey has turned the corner on torture means that it can happen elsewhere," said Jeri Laber.[5]

Given the distinct improvement, it is worth examining how Turkey managed to curb torture: First, simply spotlighting a country's torture practices can help create domestic and diplomatic pressure to stop torture. Second, access to prisons and police stations by independent investigators is vital. Not knowing when an inspection may happen keeps police who might otherwise be tempted to get a confession the "easy" way off balance, and they may give a second thought before torturing. Third, shortening detention periods, and finally, abolishing incommunicado detention and ensuring immediate access to legal counsel in police stations can make a big difference. Turkey now has excellent protections against torture in law, but supervision of police stations is poor, which is why ill-treatment is still being reported.

The "struggle against terror" has been used routinely by the Turkish authorities to excuse torture. Turkey has had a long-standing problem with political violence and armed opposition groups, on a much larger scale than in other European countries. Turkey still has armed and violent insurgents. Despite this, now that the technical steps have been taken to open up the closed world of the interrogation center, torture is on the wane.

Where torture is currently the worst in the world today is where it is most cost-free for the perpetrators. If Turkey can turn the corner on torture, then progress should be possible in the rest of the world. In fact, with some alterations for local situations, the model of how the tide is being turned in Turkey could work in Uzbekistan, China, Egypt, Uganda, and Brazil as well.

"I hear talk about attacking the culture of torture through education, but I don't believe there is a cultural propensity to torture in Turkey or anywhere else. This is a question of political will to apply technical measures," said Sugden. "Even in a country where there are still illegal armed groups and violent clashes, as soon as the Turkish authorities applied the standard measures against torture, it began to fade away."

# Rape Is Torture

Political pressure, both domestic and international, is a critical component of human rights change. But if new standards are to be put in place and expected to last, they must ultimately be codified in law. Interestingly enough, once new legal understandings are arrived at, they tend in turn to influence cultural norms. (Contrary to the famous slogan of the segregationist movement in the United States, you really *can* legislate morality.)

One of the most significant changes in international human rights law was signaled by the 1997 decision of the European Court of Human Rights in *Aydin v. Turkey,* in which the Court found that rape of a female detainee was a violation of Article 3 of the European Convention for the Protection of Human Rights and Fundamental Freedoms, the article that prohibits torture. No longer could such an act be considered merely a private or social crime. Here is an excerpt from the Court's historic ruling.

European Court of Human Rights, Judgment of 25 September 1997

## As to the Facts

1. *The Applicant*
13. The applicant, Mrs. Şükran Aydın, is a Turkish citizen of Kurdish origin. [. . .] At the time of the events at issue she was 17 years old and living with her parents in the village of Tasit, which is about ten kilometres from the town of Derik where the district gendarmerie headquarters are located. The applicant had never traveled beyond her village before the events which led to her application to the Commission.
2. *The Situation in the South-East of Turkey*
14. Since approximately 1985, serious disturbances have raged in the South-East of Turkey between the security forces and the members of the PKK (Workers' Party of Kurdistan). This confrontation has so far, according to the Government, claimed the lives of 4,036 civilians and 3,884 members of the security forces.

At the time of the Court's consideration of the case, ten of the eleven provinces of south-eastern Turkey had since 1987 been subjected to emergency rule.

# I. Particular Circumstances of the Case

[. . .]

## F. The Commission's evaluation of the evidence
### and findings of fact

[. . .] 40. The Commission's findings can be summarised as follows: [. . .]
4. Having regard to her evidence and her demeanour before the delegates, and having given due consideration in particular to the medical reports drawn up by Dr Akkuş, Dr Çetin and the doctor from the Diyarbakır Maternity Hospital, the Commission found it established that during her custody at Derik gendarmerie headquarters

the applicant was blindfolded, beaten, stripped, placed inside a tyre and sprayed with high pressure water, and raped. It would appear probable that the applicant was subjected to such treatment on the basis of suspicion of collaboration by herself or members of her family with members of the PKK, the purpose being to gain information and/or to deter her family and other villagers from becoming implicated in terrorist activities.

# As to the Law

[. . .]

# II. Alleged Violation of Article 3 of the Convention

[. . .]

## C. The Court's assessment of the evidence and the
## facts established by the Commission

[. . .] 73. The Court considers that it should accept the facts as established by the Commission
[. . .] 2. *The Court's Assessment* [. . .]
81. As it has observed on many occasions, Article 3 of the Convention enshrines one of the fundamental values of democratic societies and as such it prohibits in absolute terms torture or inhuman or degrading treatment or punishment.[. . .].
82. In order to determine whether any particular form of ill-treatment should be qualified as torture, regard must be had to the distinction drawn in Article 3 between this notion and that of inhuman treatment or degrading treatment. This distinction would appear to have been embodied in the Convention to allow the special stigma of "torture" to attach only

to deliberate inhuman treatment causing very serious and cruel suffering [. . .].

83. While being held in detention the applicant was raped by a person whose identity has still to be determined. Rape of a detainee by an official of the State must be considered to be an especially grave and abhorrent form of ill-treatment given the ease with which the offender can exploit the vulnerability and weakened resistance of his victim. Furthermore, rape leaves deep psychological scars on the victim which do not respond to the passage of time as quickly as other forms of physical and mental violence. The applicant also experienced the acute physical pain of forced penetration, which must have left her feeling debased and violated both physically and emotionally.

84. The applicant was also subjected to a series of particularly terrifying and humiliating experiences while in custody at the hands of the security forces at Derik gendarmerie headquarters having regard to her sex and youth and the circumstances under which she was held. She was detained over a period of three days during which she must have been bewildered and disoriented by being kept blindfolded, and in a constant state of physical pain and mental anguish brought on by the beatings administered to her during questioning and by the apprehension of what would happen to her next. She was also paraded naked in humiliating circumstances thus adding to her overall sense of vulnerability and on one occasion she was pummeled with high pressure water while being spun around in a tyre.

85. The applicant and her family must have been taken from their village and brought to Derik gendarmerie headquarters for a purpose, which can only be explained on account of the security situation in the region [. . .] and the need of the security forces to elicit information. The suffering inflicted on the applicant during the period of her detention must also be seen as calculated to serve the same or related purposes.

86. Against this background the Court is satisfied that the accumulation of acts of physical and mental violence inflicted on the applicant and the especially cruel act of rape to which she was subjected amounted to torture in breach of Article 3 of the Convention. Indeed the Court would have reached this conclusion on either of these grounds taken separately.

87. In conclusion, there has been a violation of Article 3 of the Convention.

# Legal Challenges to Impunity

Changes in law are important, but if there is no mechanism through which to prosecute offenders, the law is little more than human aspiration set to paper. Over the last decade three significant developments have occurred in human rights jurisprudence that, collectively, hint at how impunity may eventually be ended for perpetrators of human rights crimes, including torture. The first of these developments, described briefly in a 2004 Question & Answer sheet published by Amnesty International and reproduced in Reading 5, was the creation of the International Criminal Court (ICC). Beginning with the Nuremburg Tribunal following World War II, the international community has occasionally established ad hoc bodies to try those accused of the most serious crimes. Most recently, the United Nations created courts to address genocide and other crimes against humanity committed in Rwanda and the former Yugoslavia. But until the ICC, no permanent or standing court had been authorized to undertake such prosecutions. Though as of this writing the ICC has not yet tried a case, it constitutes one of the best hopes for systematizing the effort to hold torturers accountable for their crimes.

But the ICC has its limits, as the reading makes clear. Under the Convention against Torture and other international human rights instruments, all states parties to the Convention are obligated either to prosecute those credibly accused of torture whom they find on their territories or to extradite them to a country that will. This is known as the principle of "universal jurisdiction," and the second important development is that it is being followed more and more readily by nations that take torture seriously. Reading 6 from *Crimes Against Humanity: The Struggle for Global Justice*, by prominent British barrister Geoffrey Robertson, explains the concept.

Perhaps the most significant individual case in human rights law over the last ten years (and the third critical development) was the 1999 ruling by the British Law Lords (the United Kingdom's highest court) that General Augusto Pinochet of Chile could not claim "sovereign immunity" from prosecution, as former heads of state always had, for crimes committed during his tenure as president of Chile, and could be extradited to Spain to stand trial for them. Though Pinochet eventually escaped his day in Spanish Court (on the grounds of ill health), a new precedent had been established. As to Pinochet himself, he returned to Chile, where he expected to be safe from the consequences of his atrocities, but a few years later was stripped of immunity and indicted on both tax evasion and murder charges. He died in December 2006, before the charges were resolved. Reading 7, again from Robertson, outlines the 1999 case.

# The International Criminal Court

The establishment of the Court is still a gift of hope to future generations, and a giant step forward in the march towards universal human rights and the rule of law. (Kofi Annan, UN Secretary-General, July 18, 1998, at the signing of the Rome Statute of the International Criminal Court in Rome)

## 1. What is the International Criminal Court?

The International Criminal Court (ICC) is a permanent independent judicial body created by the international community of states to prosecute the gravest possible crimes under international law: genocide, other crimes against humanity[6] and war crimes.

## 2. When was the ICC established?

In July 1998 a diplomatic conference adopted the Rome Statute of the ICC (Rome Statute) by an overwhelming vote of 120 in favor and only seven against[7] (21 abstained). The Rome Statute defines the crimes, how the court will work and what states must do to cooperate with it. The 60th ratification necessary to establish the ICC was deposited on 11 April 2002 and the Statute entered into force starting its jurisdiction on 1 July 2002.

In February 2003, the first 18 judges of the ICC were elected and the first Prosecutor[8] was elected in April 2003.

## 3. Why is the Court necessary?

Although the international community has over the past half century created international and regional systems of human rights protection, millions of people have continued to be the victims of genocide, crimes against humanity and war crimes.

Shamefully, only a handful of those responsible for these crimes have ever been brought to justice by national courts—most perpetrators have therefore committed these crimes in the knowledge that it was extremely unlikely they would be brought to justice for their actions.

The ICC serves the following purposes:

- It acts as a deterrent to people planning to commit grave crimes under international law;

- It prompts national prosecutors—who have the primary responsibility to bring those responsible for these crimes to justice—to do so;
- Victims and their families will have the chance to obtain justice and truth, and begin the process of reconciliation;
- It is a major step towards ending impunity.

## 4. What effect will the ICC have on national courts?

National courts will always have jurisdiction over such crimes. Under the principle of "complementarity,"[9] the ICC will only act when national courts are unable or unwilling to do so. For example, a government may be unwilling to prosecute its own citizens, especially if they are high ranking, or where the criminal justice system has collapsed as a result of an internal conflict, there may be no court capable of dealing with these types of crimes.

## 5. When can the court prosecute individuals suspected of committing grave crimes under international law?

The court has jurisdiction to prosecute individuals when:

- Crimes have been committed in the territory of a state which has ratified the Rome Statute;
- Crimes have been committed by a citizen of a state which has ratified the Rome Statute or a state which has not ratified the Rome Statute has made a declaration accepting the court's jurisdiction over the crime;
- Crimes have been committed in a situation which threatens or breaches international peace and security and the UN Security Council has referred the situation to the Court pursuant to Chapter 7 of the UN Charter.[10]

## 6. Will the Court be able to prosecute individuals for crimes committed before the Court's establishment?

No. The Court will only have jurisdiction over crimes committed after 1 July 2002, when the Rome Statute entered into force.

## Who will decide which cases the Court will prosecute?

The Rome Statute provides that cases can originate in the Court three different ways:

(1) The Court's Prosecutor can initiate an investigation into a situation where one or more of the crimes has been committed, based on

information from any source, including the victim or the victim's family, but only if the Court has jurisdiction over the crime and individual [. . .].

(2) States which have ratified the Rome Statute may ask the Prosecutor to investigate a situation where one or more of the crimes has been committed, but only if the Court has jurisdiction.

(3) The UN Security Council can ask the Prosecutor to investigate a situation where one or more of the crimes have been committed. Unlike methods 1 and 2, the ICC will have jurisdiction when the UN Security Council refers the situation to the Prosecutor, even if the crimes occurred in the territory of a state which has not ratified the Rome Statute or was committed by the national of such a state.

In each of these situations, however, it is up to the Prosecutor, not the states or the Security Council, to decide whether to open an investigation and, based on that investigation, whether to prosecute, subject to judicial approval.

## 8. Why is it essential that as many countries as possible ratify the Rome Statute?

The Prosecutor can only initiate an investigation where the crime has been committed in the territory of a state party to the Statute or the accused person is a citizen of a state party to the Statute, unless the Security Council refers a situation to the Court. The reluctance of the Security Council to establish *ad hoc* international criminal tribunals for situations other than the former Yugoslavia and Rwanda suggests that it is not likely to refer many situations to the Court. Therefore, to a great extent, the court's effectiveness will be measured by how many states ratify the Statute.

# Universal Jurisdiction

Crimes against humanity will only be deterred when their would-be per-petrators—be they political leaders, field commanders or soldiers and policemen—are given pause by the prospect that they will henceforth have no hiding place: that legal nemesis may someday, somewhere, overtake them. The prospect is only realistic if there exists an international crim-inal court cognizant of their offence, or, in its absence, a rule permit-ting their punishment by courts of countries into whose jurisdiction they may come or perchance be brought. It is this practical consideration which makes universal jurisdiction the most important attribute of a crime against humanity: it is an offence so serious that any court anywhere is empowered by international law to try it and to punish it, irrespective of its place of commission or the nationality of the offender or the victims. Jurisdiction arises, in other words, wherever an offender is found, and it arises because he is alleged to have offended in a particularly outra-geous way.

There is no doubt that universal jurisdiction is recognized in customary international law as the basis for proceedings in domestic courts against pirates and slave traders. Equally, universal jurisdiction over aircraft hi-jackers, hostage-takers and other types of international terrorists has been partially achieved through the modern machinery of an interna-tional treaty requiring signatories to punish offenders found within their borders or else to extradite them to countries which will put them on trial. But these are all crimes which occur across borders, or on the open seas, or in air space of questionable ownership: universal jurisdiction arises not because they are crimes against humanity, but because they are crimes *simpliciter*,[11] under any domestic law, which might otherwise go unpunished. As the Permanent Court of International Justice explained universal jurisdiction against pirates in the *Lotus Case*:

It is an offence against the law of nations; and as the scene of the pirate's opera-tions is the high seas, which it is not the right or duty of any nation to police, he is denied the protection of the flag which he may carry and is treated as an out-law—as the enemy of mankind—*hostis humanis generis*—whom any nation may in the interest of all capture and punish.

In fact, pirates—and the modern criminals such as hostage-takers, ter-rorists and international drug-traffickers, against whom universal juris-diction is developing through treaties—are not usually implicated in crimes against humanity. The terrorist under one treaty may be a freedom fighter under another; the drug dealer is a common criminal, heedless of the harm he puts in others' way, but it is an exaggeration to regard his offence as the equivalent of politically motivated mass murder. It follows that those courts and writers who have argued that universal jurisdiction for crimes against humanity arises on the same basis as universal juris- diction over piracy are advancing a fundamentally flawed argument. Piracy occurs in a place, the high seas, which requires universal jurisdiction, as the alternative to there being no jurisdiction at all. The crime against humanity normally occurs in a country where there is jurisdiction, albeit one which (because of the power of the state-backed perpetrator) will not be exercised, and the issue arises years, perhaps decades, later, when the perpetrator is found (or brought) within the jurisdiction of a nation with the exceptional resolve to bring a prosecution. [. . .]

Article 6(c) of the [Nuremburg] Charter[12] defined a class of crime of which sixteen Nazi leaders were convicted, which is so peculiarly horrific that the very fact that educated, rational and otherwise respected rulers of men were capable of conceiving and committing it must diminish what- ever value there is in being human. The judgement at Nuremberg and the Conventions which followed gave this particular crime a special sta- tus in international law, as imposing an *erga omnes*[13] obligation on every state to assist in its trial and punishment. This power to bring alleged perpetrators to justice is described by the phrase "universal jurisdiction": states have the power, individually or collectively, to conduct a trial even if they have no link with the place where the crime was committed, or with its perpetrator or its victims. Jurisdiction over ordinary crime depends on a link, usually territorial, between the state of trial and the crime itself, but in the case of crimes against humanity that link may be found in the simple fact that we are all human beings. So an international tribunal, a court without a country, may be empowered to punish, as may (if no such tribunal exists) the courts of any other country which gets its hands on any accused. Of course, universal jurisdiction in any state will normally proceed under a local statute empowering a court to exercise it and any international tribunal will require a charter or a statute subscribed to by the states which bring it into existence, either collectively through the UN (as a subsidiary organ of the Security Council) or individually through a treaty like the Nuremberg Charter or the Rome Statute of the Inter- national Criminal Court. The concept of universal jurisdiction for crimes against humanity is the solution that international law offers to the spec- tacle of impunity for tyrants and torturers who cover themselves with domestic immunities and amnesties and pardons. They can still hide, but in a world where jurisdiction over their crimes is universal, they cannot run. [. . .]

The reason why crimes against humanity, unlike ordinary crimes, in the absence of treaties attract universal jurisdiction is not found in the seriousness of the actual offence—the psychopathic serial killer may do more harm than the casual police torturer. Nor is it found by any literal analogy with the pirate or slave trader—unnattractive criminals certainly, but ones who are rarely acting on government service. What sets crimes against humanity apart, both in wickedness and in the need for special measures of deterrance, is the simple fact that it is a crime of unforgivable brutality ordained by a government—or at least by an organization exercising political power. It is not the mind of the individual torturer, but the fact that this individual is part of the apparatus of a state, which makes the crime so horrific and locates it in a different dimension from ordinary criminality. This factor also explains why individual responsibility and universal jurisdiction are necessary responses if any deterrance is to be achieved. There is a reasonable chance that torture and murder will not be committed by secret police, or ordered by generals or ministers, if they believe they may one day, under a different regime, or in another country, be called to account for their participation in criminal acts of state. Crimes against humanity are committed confidently, by officials who believe that the regime will continue in power—that, after all, is often the purpose of committing the crime. In the unlikely event of its collapse, a negotiated withdrawal is possible: at best, you keep the Swiss bank account; at worst, you appear before a truth commission. The doctrine of universal jurisdiction over crimes against humanity is justified because it may make some torturer pause at the prospect that sometime somewhere some prosecutor may feel strongly enough about his crime to put him on trial.

# The Case of Pinochet

That you between the 1st August 1973 and the 1st January 1990 agreed with others that a course of conduct would be pursued, namely:

a) that persons, whether living in Chile or other countries, that you knew or suspected would be disposed to pose a threat to the lives, safety, occupations, political positions, comforts and beliefs of yourself and other members of the conspiracy, and persons in respected social positions who might be considered by members of the public to pose to such a threat, would be abducted, would undergo the infliction of severe pain and suffering, causing grievous bodily harm, whether over a brief period or a period of several months or years;

b) that some of those victims would thereafter be killed;

c) that instruments for the purpose of inflicting such pain and suffering would be obtained and distributed in advance to military and other premises where such infliction of pain, suffering, harm and murder would be carried out;

d) that such pain, suffering, harm and murder would be inflicted by public officials who would take instructions from and report to you;

e) that such pain, suffering and harm would include rape, buggery and other sexual assault and humiliation;

f) that such pain, suffering, harm and murder would be inflicted in Chile and in other countries;

g) that the pain and suffering to be inflicted was not to be limited to such pain and suffering as would bring forward information useful to you from the victims, but would extend to such pain and suffering as would, through the medium of the accounts of survivors and rumor, terrify and subdue persons, both in Chile and in other countries, who might be disposed to criticize or oppose you or your fellow conspirators;

h) that the victims of the torture would include children and minors;

i) that such activities would be carried out in secret places and disavowed in public and international forums;

which course of conduct would necessarily involve the commission of the offence of torture, whether in Chile or elsewhere, by one or more public officials in the performance or purported performance of his or their duties, and pursuant to which conspiracy hundreds of thousands of persons were tortured.

Thirty other charges made specific and grisly allegations in respect of particular victims. To take some typical examples:

That you on or about 29th October 1976 being a public official, namely Commander in Chief of the Chilean Army, jointly with others intentionally inflicted severe pain or suffering on José Marcelino González Malpu, by applying electric current to his genital organs, shoulders and ankles and pretending to shoot his captive naked mother in front of him, in purported performance of official duties.

That you jointly with others intentionally inflicted severe pain or suffering on Pedro Hugo Arellano Carvajal by

a) tying him to a metal bed and forcing his hands against an electrified metal plate, throwing him across the room from the shock;

b) electrocuting him with electric wires attached to his chest, his penis and his toes:

c) tying him to a tree and whipping him;

d) placing him on board a helicopter, pushing him out with ropes tied to his trousers, and dragging him through thorns;

e) tying him to a rope and lowering him into a well, until he was nearly drowned, pulling him out, and lowering him back into the well when he failed to answer questions;

f) subjecting him to "Russian roulette";

g) forcing him take all his clothes off in the presence of the captive Rodríguez family who had been arrested with their sons, forcing him to witness torture of that family as the father was made to bugger his son, as, simultaneously, that son was made to bugger his younger brother;

h) forcing him to bugger one of those sons himself; in purported performance of official duties.

That you jointly with others intentionally inflicted severe pain or suffering on Irma del Carmen Parada González by:

a) stripping her of her clothes;

b) applying electric current to her mouth, vagina and breasts;

c) subjecting her to rape by two men;

d) putting her hands into chemicals and introducing them into a machine causing her to lose consciousness;

e) forcing her to eat putrid food and the human remains of her dead fellow captives;

in purported performance of official duties. [. . .]

That you in 1974 being a public official, namely Commander in Chief of the Chilean Army, jointly with others intentionally inflicted severe pain or suffering on others by employment of "Papi," a man who had visible open syphilitic sores on his body, to rape female captives and to use on them a dog trained in sexual practices with human beings, in purported performance of official duties. (prosecutor's charges against General Pinochet)

In 1978, Augusto Pinochet granted an amnesty to "all persons who as authors, accomplices, or accessories committed . . . criminal offences during the period of the State of Siege between 11 September 1973 and 10 March 1978," excluding only (at the insistence of the Carter administration) the Letelier car bombing. This self-amnesty was upheld in every case by the country's pro-Pinochet judiciary despite two rulings by the Inter-American Commission that it violated the American Convention's guarantee of an effective remedy for human rights violations. After seventeen years, Pinochet made Hastings Banda's[14] mistake of holding a referendum in the belief the people loved him or else feared him too much to vote against him: they voted instead for democracy, which he had to grant, although on terms which allowed him to appoint some senators and remain as commander-in-chief of the armed forces. On retirement from that position in 1998 Pinochet was made senator-for-life, which carries under Chilean law yet further immunity from prosecution. [. . .] It was from this impregnable position in "the Fatherland" that he sallied forth

in October 1998, to have his bad back attended to by doctors in Harley
Street, London W1.

## An Arrest in Harley Street

That Augusto Pinochet felt free to travel the world in 1998 was a measure of the impunity that had to this point been enjoyed in practice by
tyrants, notwithstanding the accumulation of treaties under which their
crimes were declared contrary to international law. Never before had a
former head of state, visiting another friendly country, been held legally
amenable to its criminal process. Little attention was being paid when
the Association of Progressive Prosecutors of Spain began a private action
in 1996 against Pinochet and members of the Argentinean junta, or when
their action was taken over by a Madrid investigating magistrate Bal-
thasar Garzón. [. . .] Garzón was in Spain, the evidence was in Chile, and
Pinochet was careful to travel only to Britain, where he was a frequent and
frequently honored visitor. He had always received red-carpet treatment:
as commander-in-chief of the Chilean army he was fêted by the Ministry of
Defense in the hope he would purchase British arms. These previous visits had been open and uneventful, even when he dined at the gastronomic
hub of London's liberal intelligentsia, the River Café: its proprietress,
Ms. Ruthie Rogers (wife of the architect who designed the European Court
of Human Rights), was so stomach-churned at the sight of his name on
the gold card print-out that she donated the cost of his meal to Amnesty
International. In October 1998 he did not even bother to take the elementary precaution of obtaining a diplomatic visa: he was, so he thought,
clad in the impregnable armor of state sovereignty, which had for centuries shielded every tyrant against legal attack. On arrival at Heathrow
Airport, Senator and Mrs. Pinochet were duly met by representatives of
the UK's ethical Foreign Office, who ushered them to the Hounslow
Suite, a VIP room hired for their comfort while FO lackeys went to collect their bags and have their passports stamped. The aging mass murderer later took tea with his good friend Lady Thatcher[15] and then went
into the private clinic.

It was then that the *Guardian* reported Pinochet's presence in London.
Under the headline "A Murderer Among Us," the paper's Latin American veteran Hugh O'Shaughnessy reported, "There is a foreign terrorist
in our midst who is hiding somewhere in London . . . If you are a patient
in the London Clinic, be particularly alert. Some people say General
Augusto Pinochet Ugarte is holed up there for treatment." This tipped off
magistrate Garzón, who through the Spanish Embassy made a request
for Pinochet's arrest under the European Convention on Extradition by
which almost all Continental countries agree to surrender persons wanted

for serious criminal offenses. The post-operative Pinochet became nervous and prepared to flee on the next plane, scheduled to depart at 7 a.m. on Saturday, 17 October. On 16 October, Garzón obtained a warrant in Spain for Pinochet's arrest: it was rushed to London where late that evening Scotland Yard anti-terrorist officers moved in to surround the clinic and its recumbent torturer, just a few hours before his flight. This arrest, one of Scotland Yard's finest operations, was greeted at first with astonishment and even outrage: Lady Thatcher condemned the inhumanity of the police, disturbing the rest of a "sick and frail old man." The Chief Justice refused the Spanish government (represented by the Crown Prosecution Service) an adjournment to prepare its case, and after a two-day hearing pronounced it plain that an ex-head of state had sovereign immunity for every crime he committed in exercising the functions of office, no matter how heinous. The argument that this immunity did not cover torture and other crimes which are contrary to international law had "some attraction," said the Chief Justice, but "where is one to draw the line?" Crimes against humanity were committed by heads of state pursuant to their official functions, said another judge, because "history shows that it has indeed on occasion been state policy to exterminate or oppress particular groups." General Pinochet was granted *habeas corpus*, but was ordered to stay in the clinic to recuperate from his operation and his law suit pending a prosecution appeal.

The *Pinochet* case proceeded directly to Britain's highest court, the House of Lords. Amnesty International and Human Rights Watch, concerned that developments in international law had not been appreciated in the lower court, were given leave to intervene in the action in support of the prosecution. After hearing argument for six days and deliberating for two weeks, the panel split 3–2 in favour of extradition, on the basis that sovereign immunity applied only to sovereigns who were exercising *legitimate* state functions and by no stretch of the imagination could widespread torture be regarded as legitimate conduct by anyone, let alone a head of state. It followed that the doctrine of sovereign immunity did not bar Pinochet's extradition to stand trial in Spain, if the Home Secretary decided in the exercise of his discretion that to do so would be neither unjust nor oppressive. The spotlight swung from the legal to the political arena as Home Secretary Jack Straw was showered with demands that he should show "compassion" for an old man and respect for the state sovereignty of Chile by sending its former ruler back where he belonged, where his impunity was said to be part of the deal for "national reconciliation." The Chilean government made loud diplomatic noises that refusal to return the Senator would be to insult its sovereign dignity. In the end Jack Straw played a scrupulously straight bat, finding no reason not to let the law take its course. So it came to pass that on 11 December

1998, fifty years almost to the day after the Universal Declaration, a man who had done so much to destroy its promises finally stood in the dock of a top security court in London.

A few days later, however, another panel of law lords was persuaded that one of their bretheren, Lord Hoffman, who had joined in the 3–2 majority decision, should not have sat because he had helped to fund-raise for Amnesty International. On the grounds, therefore, that justice had not been seen to be done, Pinochet was entitled to a fresh hearing before a court comprising seven judges who had never manifested support for human rights by connections with Amnesty. Their 6–1 judgment on 24 March 1999 proved historic: they held that an international law prohibition which had achieved *jus cogens*[16] status, such as the rule against torture committed systematically for policy reasons (i.e., a crime against humanity), dissolved the sovereign immunity which customary law granted to former officials and heads of state. However, a quirk of statutory extra-dition law—the "double criminality" principle that Britain could not extradite for a crime it could not itself punish at the time it was com-mitted—meant that Pinochet could be sent to Spain only for crimes com-mitted since 1988, when Britain introduced extra-territorial torture as an offense in its own law. Since his conspiracy to use torture to maintain power lasted until 1990, Pinochet could not hide behind the shield of Chile's immunity in respect of his last two years as dictator. In due course, the indefatigable Garzón uncovered thirty more cases of torture in 1988–9 for which Pinochet could be held responsible, and on 8 October 1999 the Bow Street magistrate ordered his extradition to Spain. Terrified of facing trial, Pinochet launched an appeal, but shortly before it was due to be heard, medical experts pronounced him unfit for trial due to brain damage caused by a stroke, whereupon the Home Secretary extended to Pinochet a compassion notably denied to victims of his own secret police, and he fled back to Chile. [. . .]

Pinochet's crimes in this class were no more Chile's business than they were Britain's business or Spain's business: they were committed against humanity in general because the very fact that a person can order them diminishes the human race. That such crimes override sovereignty was a doctrine first propounded by Robert Jackson[17] at the Nuremberg trial, and remained for decades a talking point in university common rooms and post-graduate theses; however, until the Serb and Croat bloodfeuding it had no practical application other than as a legal lasso for old Nazis like Eichmann[18] and Barbie.[19] Convicting war criminals in Yugoslavia and Rwanda was no great jump: these were states in the process of disso-lution, their armour of sovereignty cracked in the course of their disin-tegration. Apparently helpful precedents forged in the United States in respect to General Noriega[20] and the ex-Philippines president, Ferdinand

Marcos, were not true exceptions to the sovereignty rule, because the Philippines government waived its immunity over Marcos, while Noriega, never formally Panama's head of state, was prosecuted not for abusing state power but for his private criminal enterprise in running drugs. So the *Pinochet Case* became the first and paradigm test of international human rights law. [. . .]

## The Law Takes Its Course

[. . .] [T]he British government did something which could not have been expected, and which deserves a considerable measure of praise: it let the law take its course. The course that it took could not have been predicted, but in the course of the ride international human rights had acquired the quality of law: it had become, in some small degree, enforceable in the courts of the world. The judges who thought it had no impact against the sovereign state dwindled, from 3–0 at the initial hearing to 2–3, and then lost the last set, 1–6. Four judges held that the allegation of a crime against humanity set up an overriding imperative for trial, while five (the final majority) allowed the Torture Convention to override claims to immunity *rationae materiae*.[21] Thanks to the refusal of Britain's Home Secretary Jack Straw to intervene in the legal process, the *Pinochet Case* became the most important test for international law since Nuremberg itself. [. . .] [T]he question of principle was whether [Pinochet] could claim immunity from legal process on the basis that his crimes were committed while he was head of a sovereign state.

A pellucidly clear answer was given by the three-judge majority in the first House of Lords hearing, *Pinochet (No. 1)*.[22] The dictator enjoyed absolute immunity (*rationae personae*)[23] at the time the crimes were committed, by virtue of his position as head of the state of Chile. Once removed from this sovereign position, his immunity metamorphosed: it no longer attached to his person, but only to his acts—and only to those acts which had been properly performed in the course of his duties as head of state. The court said, quite simply, that the Vienna Convention read with the 1978 State Immunity Act is apt to confer immunity in respect of acts performed in the exercise of functions which international law recognizes as functions of a head of state. And it hardly needs saying that torture of his own subjects, or of aliens, would not be regarded by international law as a function of a head of state. All states disavow the use of torture as abhorrent, although from time to time some still resort to it . . . International law recognizes, of course, that the functions of a head of state may include activities which are wrongful, even illegal, by the law of his own state or by the laws of other states.

But international law has made plain that certain types of conduct, including torture and hostage-taking, are not acceptable conduct on the part of anyone. This applies as much to heads of state, or even more so, as it does to everyone else: the contrary conclusion would make a mockery of international law.

The court was fully satisfied that this was the law in 1973 when Pinochet seized power. The Nuremberg judgment, that those who commit crimes against humanity cannot invoke state immunity if that state, by authorizing their action, has moved outside its competence in international law, had been unanimoly approved as a statement of international law principles in 1946 by the [United Nations] General Assembly. Although the U.S. Supreme Court had said in *Nelson*[24] that acts of torture by police, army and security services are quintessentially "official" acts, this required further analysis. They are acts by officials, certainly, but they are not legitimate actions for officials to take. Because sovereign immunity is an international law rule, the functions of the sovereign cannot sensibly include behavior which is contrary to *jus cogens*, and which therefore every sovereign has an *erga omnes*[25] obligation to the international community to forswear. Hitler was acting "officially" when ordering the Final Solution, but his personal immunity could not subsequently avail him against prosecution for a crime against humanity. A head of state who kills his gardener in a fit of rage, or tortures for the pleasure of watching the death agonies of his victims (Montaigne's[26] definition of the furthest point in cruelty) could always have been prosecuted after his overthrow for these "private" crimes, because they are outside his retirement immunity, which is restricted to acts related to his official function. So too said the *Pinochet (No. 1)* majority: because the commission of international crimes is outside any official function, it is outside sovereign immunity.

This simple approach was eschewed by most of the seven judges in *Pinochet (No. 3)* after *Pinochet (No. 2)* had set aside the first decision because of one judge's connections with Amnesty International. Their long and laborious reasoning is a measure of the complexity and confusion of international law, but there was at least clear agreement that a head of state's personal and absolute immunity ceased, like the diplomat's, on relinquishing that position, and was replaced by a restrictive immunity that attached only to actions that had been performed as an official duty. Thus, there could be no immunity for ex-King Farouk's[27] private shopping sprees, or for murdering gardeners in fits of rage or for enjoying Montaigne's ultimate in torture as a means of personal gratification. (Emperor Bokassa,[28] accused of eating children, could not therefore have immunity in retirement from charges of cannibalism.) Where the law lords parted intellectual company was over whether crimes against humanity were outside the restrictive immunity because they could never be a legitimate function of a head of state, as *Pinochet (No. 1)* had held, or whether they were indeed, as the Supreme Court held in *Nelson*, paradigm official acts. If the latter, however, surprise, surprise: nobody in *Pinochet (No. 1)* had noticed that the Torture Convention, by defining "torture" as a crime which could be committed only by a person acting in an official capacity, had (for cases of torture) abolished sovereign immunity altogether! Since the Convention defined the offence of torture as an action done by a public official, it logically excluded the possibility of a plea for immunity being based on the fact that the defendant *was* a public official, because "no rational system of criminal justice can allow an immunity which is co-extensive with the offence." Otherwise, there would be the self-defeating syllogism:

Only public officials can commit torture.
Public officials are immune from prosecution.
Nobody can ever be prosecuted for torture.

The judges were simply not prepared to credit the diplomatic community with the breathtaking hypocrisy of producing a Torture Convention with this result.

There was general agreement with the analysis of Sir Arthur Watts, a distinguished jurist who had argued that individuals became subjects of international law when they committed crimes which "offend against the public order of the international community":

States are artificial legal persons: they can only act through the institutions and agencies of the State, which means ultimately through its officials and other individuals acting on behalf of the State. For international conduct which is so serious as to be tainted with criminality to be regarded as attributable only to the impersonal state and not to the individuals who ordered or perpetrated it is both unrealistic and offensive to common notions of justice.

Where the judges in *Pinochet (No. 3)* differed was over the way to effectuate this insight: most of them thought that lifting the veil of sovereignty required not only an allegation of criminality so serious that it breached *jus cogens*, but in addition the availability of universal jurisdiction, in the sense of a machinery that would permit prosecution in any national court. The better view (that of Lord Millet) is that this follows automatically from the *jus cogens* quality of the rule, but others more cautiously required a convention which imposed a duty on state parties to "prosecute or extradite." This practical machinery had been supplied by the Torture Convention, to which Britain, Spain and Chile were parties, which expressly required them to prosecute suspects found within their borders or else extradite them to a jurisdiction which was prepared to put them on trial. The Convention requires all states to outlaw torture, defined as the infliction of severe pain "by or with the acquiescence of a public official or other person acting in an official capacity." It follows that the most official person of all, the head of state, could not possibly escape an accountability which fell on the apparatchiks who carried out his orders.

For simplicity and conceptual neatness, the reasoning in *Pinochet (No. 1)*, that immunity is lost in respect of crimes against humanity because these are not state functions, is to be preferred. It was vaguely supported by Lord Hutton and given an interesting twist by Lord Millet, who suggested that any immunity should be confined to acts performed in the "representative" capacity of the head of state, and not to killings and torture ordered in the capacity of a head of government or army commander or party leader. Warning of the danger of raising the concept of sovereignty to the "status of some holy fetish," this judge displayed the most accurate understanding of the post-Nuremberg development of universal jurisdiction over crimes against humanity, for which state officers of any rank have no immunity.

The trend was clear. War crimes had been replaced by crimes against humanity. The way in which a state treated its own citizens within its own borders had become a matter of legitimate concern to the international community . . . crimes attract universal jurisdiction if two criteria are satisfied: first they must be contrary to a peremptory norm of international law so as to infringe a *jus cogens*. Secondly, they must be so serious and on such a scale that they can justly be regarded as an attack on the international legal order.

*Pinochet (No. 3)* confirmed the trend. Nuremberg had established liability for crimes against humanity committed in wartime, and later developments had removed the requirement for any connection with hostilities. In the case of torture, the judges confirmed that, as with genocide, the prohibition has been elevated in the hierarchy of international rules to *jus cogens*, signalling "to all members of the international community and the individuals over whom they wield authority that the prohibition of torture is an absolute value from which nobody must deviate." The Torture Convention established a regime under which there could be no safe haven—the duty it imposed on all states which found a torturer in their midst was either to try him or to extradite him. Pinochet had been arrested in Britain, which in December 1988 ratified the Convention by passing a local law which made it a crime for anyone to torture anyone else anywhere in the world. It followed that the General could be put on trial at the Old Bailey for tortures committed after that date, or else extradited to Spain to stand trial there.

This conclusion was a striking example of a court taking a treaty not just at its word but (in the absence of express words) at its spirit. The Torture Convention has no reference to any waiver by the parties of sovereign immunity, and there is not a single mention in the *travaux préparatoires*[29] or the literature that any state indicated duiring the years of drafting that it was prepared to give up this attribute of sovereignty. Indeed, many of the signatories to the Convention are among the seventy-three states which regularly use torture, and their leaders would never have signed it if they had thought it might impact on their retirement plans. None of the lawyers on the anti-Pinochet teams (a number of them QCs[30] or professors of international law, or both) even advanced the argument that the Torture Convention was intended to abolish sovereign immunity, because it wasn't. It was ratified as another exercise in cynical diplomacy, without any belief that it would be enforced. But what nobody could have anticipated is that the English judges would approach this treaty as if it were a contract or a parliamentary statute, without a trace of of the scepticism that affects anyone who knows with what hypocrisy these conventions are drafted and ratified, by diplomats who never intend them to have any effect beyond inducing a feel-good factor and a good human rights rating to wave in front of aid donors. The Torture Convention was signed by dozens of states which still torture, by Chile while Pinochet himself was still head of state and could never have intended to provide for his own arrest, and by the government of Mrs. Thatcher, the General's most effusive supporter. The General's tactics of objecting to judges who might know about human rights produced an apolitical bench who, with an almost touching naivety, took the Torture Convention to mean what it said. With uncanny, uncynical decency, they proceeded to hoist the old torturer by his own petard.

There was one anxious dissent, from a judge with some international law experience, who feared that an RUC[31] officer on holiday in Florida might suddenly be accused of torture in Northern Ireland. This is a bad example, because a "suggestion of immunity" would immediately issue from the State Department, just as it had for Prince Charles. But it is not difficult to think of more likely cases, and the objection must be addressed. Some of the majority judges did so, by arguing that immunity is only extinguished by an allegation of torture "when committed as part of a widespread or systematic attack against any civilian population," i.e. when what is being alleged fits the Rome Statute definition of a crime against humanity. This solution is reasonable, because no doubt there will be politically motivated accusations against former leaders whose conduct is more debatable than Pinochet's (his role as torturer of our time is a matter of historical record). The answer is surely to confine prosecutions to crimes against humanity, and to rely upon domestic legal systems to eliminate charges based on insufficient evidence. The logical response to anxiety about malicious prosecution is not to abandon the pursuit of torture suspects, but rather to hasten the establishment of an international criminal court to try them with every guarantee of fairness.

The case of General Pinochet assumes its historic dimension because he was the first to be held potentially liable to prosecution for a crime against humanity committed in peacetime, notwithstanding a cloak of sovereign immunity which the state he headed was determined not to waive. It was symbolic that the ruling in *Pinochet (No. 3)* came on 24 March 1999, the very day that NATO countries began to bomb the sovereign state of Serbia in an effort to stop the atrocities its forces were committing against its own nationals in Kosovo. It was as if the world community had finally decided to obliterate its memory of appeasing Hitler by evolving international law to a position where it could no longer accept that the way in which a state treats its own citizens is purely an internal matter. The point at which interference with sovereignty was justified was when the repression reached such a level of severity that it disturbed world peace. No longer is this a messy and overly subjective test, because it can now be satisfied by evidence that the State, through officials of its government, is committing crimes against humanity as a matter of policy. [. . .]

But on 3 March 2000, seventeen months after his arrest, Augusto Pinochet arrived back in Chile. [. . .] Medical experts had diagnosed irreversible brain damage from his recent strokes, causing such loss of memory and understanding as would render him incapable of being fairly tried under the European Convention guarantees. His last contribution to human rights came when the UK government was ordered by the Court of Appeal to disclose the confidential medical reports, because *any* claim to avoid charges of crimes against humanity must be decided by "the highest standards of transparency". Pinochet's victims were angry at his escape, believing that he had gulled the doctors, but it was richly ironic that a dictator who denied human rights to thousands he killed and tortured should end his life as the pathetic beneficiary of human rights standards. The real lesson, however, is about the need to round up the other torturers while they are still in sound mind. [. . .] Augusto Pinochet had at least served one noble purpose in his life: that of helping the world to work out how to put tyrants on trial.

# Filartiga v. Pena-Irala

Imagine learning many years after you had been tortured that your torturer was at large and living a quiet life in the same neighborhood as you. Imagine running into your torturer on the subway or in a restaurant. And imagine not being able to do anything about it.

Such have been the experiences of some immigrants in the United States who came to this country to try to build a new life and realized that the person who had been responsible for destroying their old lives was also resident here. Despite the obligation of the U.S. government as a state party to the Convention against Torture to prosecute such people or extradite them to stand trial in another country, very few torturers who live in the United States have been brought to justice by government action alone.

But in 1980 victims of torture gained a powerful new tool to hold their torturers to account. Basing its judgment upon a law passed in 1789, the Alien Tort Claims Act, a U.S. court ruled that a torturer in residence in the U.S. could be sued by his victims or their families. Since that ruling dozens of cases have been brought, many of them by the Center for Justice and Accountability, a legal resource center established by Amnesty International USA and others in 1998. On September 3, 2004, for example, Judge Oliver Wanger of the Eastern District of California in Fresno issued a historic decision holding Modesto, California, resident Alvaro Saravia responsible for the assassination of revered Archbishop Oscar Romero of El Salvador. In the case, *Doe v. Saravia*, Judge Wanger ordered Saravia to pay $10 million, $2.5 million in compensatory damages and $7.5 million in punitive damages, to the plaintiff, a relative of the archbishop's. In December, 2005 a federal jury found a former El Salvador military colonel, Nicolas Carranza, who had served as vice minister for defense from 1979 to 1981, responsible for crimes against humanity and ordered him to pay $6 million in damages to four people who had been tortured or had relatives killed by Carranza's security forces.

And it all started with *Filartiga v. Pena-Irala*, a dramatic story that is told in Richard Pierre Claude's 1983 article from *Human Rights Quarterly*.

"My clinic is called the 'Clinic of Hope,' and our praxis is hope," Dr. Joel Filártiga stated in 1982. He was referring to El Sanatorio la Esperanza, which he founded and operates. It is the largest private health clinic for the poor in Paraguay. This clinic serves between 32,000 and 37,000 *campesinos* (peasants) in the central great valley and surrounding mountains around Ybycui. From a tobacco-producing family, Joel Holden Filártiga Ferreira chose to work in the rural area centered at Ybycui because, in his words, "there was no doctor there to serve the people." In Paraguay there is an overall shortage of health manpower, mainly at the technical and auxiliary levels. Though the capital city of Asunción contains only 16.5 percent of the population, more than 75 percent of all health professionals are concentrated there. Whether in the city or countryside, there are few health facilities for the poor. [. . .]

La Esperanza receives no government aid. It operates on the basis of Dr. Filártiga's volunteer work, with the assistance of his wife, Nidia, acting as nurse and with the part-time help of their three daughters. Until his death in 1976, Joel, Jr. acted as a driver and chauffeur at the clinic. Patients often pay for medical services by stacking wood or by giving such goods as vegetables and chickens. Since the tragic day when the Filártigas' son was murdered, no charges have been levied on Thursdays as a way of honoring Joelito's memory. As this income is not sufficient to meet the expenses of the clinic, fundraising is done internationally by the sale of Dr. Filártiga's artwork—which primarily consists of pen and ink drawings designed to symbolize human anguish connected with political irresponsibility.

While Dr. Filártiga was away [. . .] in early 1976, a group of Paraguayan guerrillas initially organized in Argentina, the Organización Politico-Militar (OPM), surprised authorities by successfully infiltrating the border town of Posadas, Argentina. In March and April confrontations between OPM guerrillas and the Paraguayan police involved several shootouts with loss of life on both sides. A wave of ferocious repression resulted in hundreds of people being detained for their supposed involvement with the OPM. [. . .]

## The Killing of Joelito

Late during the night of 29 March 1976, Américo Peña and three other police officials kidnapped Joel Filártiga from the Filártiga home in Asunción and took him to the police station (*comisaria*). There they tortured him brutally for one and one-half hours as they questioned him about his father's activities. The entire torture and interrogation session was tape recorded. However, no evidence against Dr. Filártiga was obtained; instead the recording carried Joelito's voice pleading, "I do not know anything. Why are you doing this to me?"

Peña and the three other police beat and whipped the youth severely over his entire body. They also resorted to the use of high voltage electric shocks administered to Joelito through his fingertips and through a wire inserted in his penis. The electric shocks were ultimately increased to such a frequency and intensity that Joelito died of cardiac arrest. In the face of his unexpected death, Peña and the other officers panicked and attempted to disguise their deed by severing Joelito's major arteries so that the body could not be embalmed and thus would require quick burial.

Paraguayan law excuses from punishment a "crime of passion" by a husband who kills another caught in adultery with his wife. To bring the killing of Joelito under this shield, the four policemen took the body to Peña's own house (which was only two doors down the street from the Filártiga residence in Asunción). The police inspector supervised the placing of the corpse into the bed of the seventeen-year-old daughter— Rosario Villalba—of Peña's mistress, Juana B. Villalba. Peña then contacted Rosario's husband, Hugo Duarte, and told him to come to the Peña residence immediately. Pleading a toothache, Duarte left his work as a night clerk and arrived home only to be beaten by Peña and the other police. He was forced to agree to a fabricated story to the effect that he had found Joelito in bed with his wife and killed him in a fit of passion. Duarte was then arrested, and Dr. Hernan Molines, the coroner, made out a false medical report supportive of the "crime of passion" theory. Judge Diogenes Martinez, who was later assigned to try the case, arrived at the house to legalize the falsified death certificate.

Dr. Joel Filártiga requested and obtained an independent autopsy from three prominent Paraguayan physicians. They concluded that Joelito was whipped and beaten in the commonly known execution style used by police and that he died of cardiac arrest caused by electric shocks. "I thought the most important thing was to document the facts," Dr. Filártiga said. As part of the documentation, he took many photographs of the corpse.

Paraguayan law allows a private party, on leave of the court, to proceed with a criminal suit in conjunction with the state, but with his/her own lawyer and witnesses. The Filártigas brought such a suit to challenge the government's version of Joelito's death—the "crime of passion" theory. When Dr. Filártiga's attorney, Horacio Galeano Peronne, asked that key police officers be summoned, the lawyer was arrested. He was taken to the central police headquarters where he was caged and shackled to a wall. Inspector Peña arrived on the occasion, 30 September 1976, and threatened to kill Galeano Perrone as well as members of the Filártiga family and friends if they continued to press the lawsuit against him. Harassment tactics were used further to reinforce the threat. Dr. Filártiga was threatened with a loss of his medical license. Anonymous phone calls were frequent and frightening. Mrs. Filártiga and her daughter were detained in jail for one day. Attorney Galeano Perrone was disbarred. Finally, a Paraguayan court denied the Filártiga request to file the suit.

Even though the Paraguayan legal process failed, the process of affecting public opinion did not. Before Joelito's funeral, the family decided upon the unusual step of displaying the nude, wrecked body of the deceased for public viewing. The outpouring of local sympathy for the Filártigas was substantial, with two thousand people attending the funeral. Five thousand color duplicates of a photo of Joelito's tortured corpse were circulated in Paraguay and abroad. Pictures and documentation of the crime were sent to Amnesty International in London. Human rights groups worldwide took an interest in the case. The U.S. Embassy sponsored a widely publicized exhibition of Dr. Filártiga's art at the Paraguayan-American Cultural Center. Asunción newspapers carried a photograph of the September 1976 affair, portraying [U.S.] Ambassador George Landau shaking hands with Dr. Filártiga. The exhibit was dedicated to Joelito's memory.

## The Filártigas' Search for Justice

By late 1977, the case of the politically motivated torture-murder of Joelito Filártiga had become a major international human rights issue. Under a barrage of criticism for human rights violations in Paraguay, reinforced by suspension of international loans to the country and protests by U.S. Ambassador Robert White, General Stroessner[32] "retired" Inspector Peña from the police. Shortly thereafter, on 21 July 1978, Américo Peña, his mistress Juana B. Villalba, their son, and her niece, using their real names, entered the United States. They claimed to be tourists en route to visit Disney World, but instead they went to Brooklyn, New York. There they lived until exiled Paraguayans and human rights groups, primarily the Council of Hemispheric Affairs, discovered Peña's whereabouts. As a result, the U.S. Immigration and Naturalization Service arrested Peña and those with him, and charged him with overstaying their three-month visa.

Upon arraignment the day after their arrest, Peña, his mistress, son, and niece requested immediate voluntary deportation, and they were ordered deported within five days. But the Immigration and Naturalization Service obtained an order from U.S. District Court Judge Eugene H. Nickerson staying the deportation order to allow further investigation of Peña's activities while in the United States. Dolly Filártiga, living in Washington, D.C., at the time and seeking political asylum in the United States, was joined by her father—then in New York—in an effort to use U.S. legal process to question Peña. As a result of the request to hold Peña, Judge Nickerson issued a temporary stay of the deportation order to allow the defendants to secure an attorney, to permit questioning by the Filártigas, and to give the Immigration and Naturalization Service an opportunity to review the circumstances surrounding Peña's entry to the United States.

The Filártigas sought legal representation from Michael Maggio—an immigration attorney in Washington, working in conjunction with the Center for Constitutional Rights in New York. The legal strategy was the creation of Center lawyers Peter Weiss, Rhonda Copelon, and Jose Antonio Lugo. They intervened in the deportation proceeding to file a $10 million civil suit against Americo Peña under the antique terms of a little-used provision of the Judiciary Act of 1789. That law, the Alien Tort Statute, now codified as Title 28 of the United States Code, Section 1350, provides: "The district courts shall have original jurisdiction of any civil action by an alien for a tort only, committed in violation of the law of nations or a treaty of the United States."

Peña's lawyers filed a motion to dismiss the Filártigas' alien tort action, denying that torture is a tort (personal wrong) in violation of the law of nations (international law). Peña claimed that the proper forum for such a hearing was Paraguay (invoking the doctrine of *forum non conveniens*[33]), describing as "mind-boggling" the notion that in the name of human rights a United States court could hold a man in custody on a civil matter. Américo Peña's attorney, Murray D. Brochin, said that there were no grounds to detain his client further and that the suit was simply an attempt to "propagandize against conditions in Paraguay." Peña's defense of *forum non conveniens* became more persuasive when, just before Judge Nickerson was to rule on the motion, the Paraguayan Supreme Court suddenly and unexpectedly reversed the lower court's ruling denying the Filártigas standing to bring their criminal action. The timing of the court action in Asunción, the circumstances surrounding it, and the ruling itself led to charges that it was politically inspired. In fact, the Filártiga suit was later dismissed in Paraguay. [. . .]

Judge Nickerson finally ruled in Peña's favor. He held that precedent constrained him to interpret the jurisdiction provisions of the Alien Tort Statute so as to preclude consideration of a foreign country's treatment of its own citizens. The ruling rested on recent cases dealing, not with human rights, but with unrelated claims. Nevertheless, the district court postponed Peña's deportation while the Filártigas unsuccessfully petitioned the United States Supreme Court for a stay of the deportation order. When the high court did not oblige, Judge Nickerson granted the motion to dismiss the case on 14 May 1979, acknowledging the strength of Peña's argument but leaving the door open for appeal.

The Filártigas filed notice that they would seek a review of Judge Nickerson's decision in the Second Circuit Court of Appeals. [. . .] Argument in *Filártiga v. Pena-Irala* took place before Chief Justice Feinberg and Circuit Judges Kaufman and Kearse. Their historic decision came down on 30 June 1980. They unanimously held that officially sanctioned torture is a violation of international law. They therefore found that the Alien Tort Statute provided a basis for the exercise of federal jurisdiction in the wrongful death action brought by the Paraguayan plaintiffs against the Paraguayan defendant.

Because Judge Nickerson in the trial court had dismissed the Filártiga suit for lack of subject-matter jurisdiction, the threshold question for the court of appeals was whether the conduct alleged by the appellants violated the law of nations. In his skillfully composed opinion, Judge Kaufman acknowledged the relevance to that question of the views of leading jurists and scholars. He noted that torture has been consistently condemned by numerous international treaties, including the American Convention of Human Rights, the International Covenant on Civil and Political Rights, and the Universal Declaration of Human Rights. Torture is also renounced as an inhuman act in the Declaration on the Protection of All Persons from Being Subject to Torture. In that resolution of the United Nations General Assembly, torture is defined as "any act by which severe pain and suffering, whether physical or mental, is intentionally inflicted by or at the instigation of a public official on a person for such purposes as intimidating him or other persons." It also calls for redress and compensation for torture victims "in accordance with national law." Judge Kaufman approvingly noted that these declarations are supposed to specify the obligations of member nations under the Charter of the United Nations.

The United Nations Charter is a treaty to which both the United States and Paraguay adhere. Nevertheless, the court did not rely on the Charter to bring the Filártiga complaint within the treaty provision of the Alien Tort Statute. Rather, the court relied on the Charter and clarifying declarations as evidence of an expression of the evolving law of nations. The court acknowledged that "there is no universal agreement as to the precise extent of the 'human rights and fundamental freedoms' guaranteed to all by the Charter," but "there is at present no dissent from the view that the guarantees include, at a bare minimum, the right to be free from torture." The court ruled further: "This prohibition has become part of customary international law, as evidenced and defined by the Universal Declaration of Human Rights."

Having found human rights in customary international law, the court was positioned to broaden the reading previously given to the Alien Tort Statute in cases concerning a state's treatment of its own citizens. These cases, which had inhibited Judge Nickerson, involved commercial matters, not human rights. Such cases involving theft and fraud, while lamentable, did not satisfy the jurisdiction requirements of the Alien Tort Statute, but torture has been elevated to an offense against all humanity and a violation of customary international law which is a changing and evolving facet of the law of nations.

In the final paragraph of his opinion, Judge Kaufman employed memorable language which sensitively characterized the impetus behind the modern evolution of customary international law:

From the ashes of the Second World War arose the United Nations Organization, amid hopes that an era of peace and cooperation had at last begun. Though many of these aspirations have remained elusive goals, that circumstance cannot diminish the true progress that has been made. In the modern age, humanitarian and practical considerations have combined to lead the nations of the world to recognize that respect for fundamental human rights is in their individual and collective interest. Among the rights universally proclaimed by all nations, as we have noted, is the right to be free of physical torture. Indeed, for purposes of civil liability, the torturer has become—like the pirate and slave trader before him— *hostis humani generis*, an enemy of all mankind.

The Filártiga episode in Paraguay and later litigation in the United States are important for many reasons. First, the heroic example of the Filártiga family in undertaking humanitarian efforts on behalf of the public health needs of the poor involves a consciousness-raising process. It has had a salutary effect upon the Ybycui peasantry. They and the residents of Asunción have been educated by Dr. Filártiga's example, and that of his family, to their human rights and to the prospects for their solidarity. Dr. Filártiga said: "After Joelito died, a peasant told me, 'You may not understand, Doctor, what is happening to you because you are too close to it. But we do understand. Your son was killed, not because he was the son of Filártiga, but because he was the son of one serving us, the poor people. The punishment is not just for you but it is also for us the poor.'"

Second, the example of the Filártiga family in "telling the world" of their human rights complaint demonstrates the efficacy of international public opinion. The painful and hazardous process of building international contact and cooperation with human rights groups helped the Filártigas in their task of "making the world understand." The work of diverse groups was effective in explaining events in Paraguay. Such groups as Amnesty International, the International Commission of Jurists, the Council for Hemispheric Affairs, the Paraguayan Commission for the Defense of Human Rights, the International League for Human Rights, and the Inter-American Commission for Human Rights all helped in the mobilization of shame. In the light of the reports of such groups, Dr. Filártiga said that the family was consoled by the lesson that "the dead count when they leave a testimony." He said that reports of such organizations have impressed upon Paraguayans the lesson that "the torturers are seen as criminals publicly judged."

Third, the court of appeals decision represents a victory, not only for the Filártiga family but also for the many governmental and nongovernmental organizations which lent their fact-finding skills to scrutinize the problem of institutionalized torture in Paraguay and elsewhere. Such groups are sustained by an occasional moral victory. Several of them joined efforts in the multiple friends of the court briefs presenting research and analysis that discernibly influenced the judgment of the court of appeals.

Fourth, the ruling in *Filartiga v. Pena* "that deliberate torture perpetrated under color of official authority violates universally accepted norms of the international law of human rights regardless of the nationality of the parties" is a significant contribution to the growing weight of authority focusing on international standards of basic human rights. In this, the United States is by no means alone. In the period 1948 to 1973, the constitutions or other important laws of over 75 states either expressly referred to or clearly borrowed from the Universal Declaration of Human Rights. The Declaration has also been relied upon in a number of cases in domestic courts of various nations. In *Filartiga v. Pena*, the United States joined a growing number of countries whose courts have recognized that international law transcends sovereign boundaries to protect individuals from their own government officials.

Finally, *Filartiga v. Pena* should have an important impact on the prospects for international human rights enforcement. International law and its implementation is based upon a horizontal power structure with no central enforcing authority. Compliance is the result of any given state's internal motivation, desire for accommodation, need for reciprocity with other states, and—in the words of Thomas Jefferson—its "decent respect for the opinion of mankind." Where the United States is concerned, the *Filartiga* ruling means that those who flagrantly disregard accepted norms of the international law of human rights should not expect refuge from justice in the United States and that, in appropriate cases, the doors of United States courts are open to the persecuted who find themselves shut out of their homeland. As if welcoming the opportunity to place the United States on the right side of social justice, Judge Kaufman concluded the *Filartiga v. Pena* opinion thus: "Our holding today giving effect to a jurisdictional provision enacted by our First Congress, is a small but important step in the fulfillment of the ageless dream to free all people from brutal violence." The unanimous Court of Appeals for the Second Circuit found that torture is a violation of international law, and the district court applied this rule to the allegations made by the Filártigas. Thus the issue was crystallized as one of the progressive application of international law in general and of the application of international law by national courts in particular. This development cannot help but encourage those such as Dr. Filártiga who courageously reject establishment-serving myths and frauds and those human rights groups which seek to widen the scope of protection for the individual against the abuse of power.

# Truth Commissions

Sometimes it is not possible for one reason or another to take legal action against an alleged torturer. The individual may be beyond reach of the law (either geographically or because he is no longer living); a government may be reluctant to press a case for political reasons or there may be no extant court with jurisdiction to hear the matter.

An alternative that has found much favor in the last few years is the truth commission—a body designed to provide victims with a forum in which to tell their stories and to force the society to hear them. This reading is from the chapter entitled "The Contribution of Truth Commissions," by Priscilla B. Hayner, in the book *An End To Torture.*

At the point of transition following a brutal and repressive regime, a state and its people are left with a legacy of violence, bitterness and pain—and often many hundreds or thousands of perpetrators who deserve prosecution and punishment for their crimes. Yet the experience of successful prosecutions after a period of massive atrocities has been limited, as under-resourced and sometimes politically compromised judicial systems struggle to confront such widespread and politically contentious crimes. Struggling with the limited options for confronting past atrocities, and with an eye towards the challenge of building a human rights culture for the future, many new governments have turned to mechanisms outside the judicial system to both confront and learn from the horrific crimes of the past. There has been increasing interest, especially, in mechanisms of official truth-seeking, through the creation of temporary commissions to dig up, investigate and analyse the pattern of politically motivated rights crimes of the past.

Such transitional truth-seeking bodies have become much more common in the 1990s, and have taken on the generic name of "truth commissions." Officially sanctioned by the government (and sometimes with the agreement of the former armed opposition), these bodies focus on documenting and investigating a pattern of abuses in the past, and set down recommendations of how to prevent the recurrence of such practices in the future. Each of these truth-seeking bodies to date has been unique, different in form, structure and mandate from those that have gone before. Not all, in fact, are formally called truth commissions: in Guatemala, for example, there was a "Historical Clarification Commission" created out of the United Nations-negotiated peace accords; in

Argentina, a "Commission on the Disappearance of Persons," and in some countries they are simply called commissions of inquiry. Nevertheless, these bodies all share certain common elements and are created for similar purposes. By "truth commission," a fairly specific kind of investigatory commission is implied. I point to four identifying characteristics: first, a truth commission is focused on the past. Second, it investigates not a singular event, but the record of abuses over a period of time (often highlighting a few cases to demonstrate and describe patterns or large numbers of abuses). Third, a truth commission is a temporary body, generally concluding with the submission of a report. And finally, a truth commission is somehow officially sanctioned by the government (and/or by the opposition, where relevant) to investigate the past. This official sanction allows the commission more power, access to information and protection to undertake investigations, and a greater likelihood that its conclusions and recommendations will be given serious consideration.

We should expect differences between commissions, as each country must shape a process from its own historical, political and cultural context. Unlike courts, which generally stand as permanent bodies, and about which there are many international norms regarding their appropriate structure, components, powers, and the minimal standards under which their proceedings should be undertaken, there are many aspects of truth commissions which will differ from country to country. Some are given subpoena powers, or even strong search-and-seizure powers, and hold public hearings in front of television cameras. Others hold all investigations and interviews of victims and witnesses behind closed doors, may not have the power to compel witnesses to testify, and release information to the public only through a final report. Also, commissions' mandates will differ on the types of abuses to be investigated, perhaps including acts by the armed opposition as well as government forces, for example, or perhaps limited to certain specific practices such as disappearances. Such variations are a natural reflection of the differences in countries' politics, political culture, history and needs.

Truth commissions can play a critical role in a country struggling to come to terms with a history of massive human rights crimes. A number of past commissions have been notable successes: their investigations welcomed by survivors of the violence and by human rights advocates alike, their reports widely read, their summary of facts considered conclusive and fair. Such commissions are often referred to as having a "cathartic" effect in society, as fulfilling the important step of formally acknowledging a long-silenced past. But not all truth commissions have been so successful. Some have been significantly limited from a full and fair accounting of the past—limited by mandate, by political constraints or restricted access to information, or by a basic lack of resources, for example—and have reported only a narrow slice of the "truth." Some commission reports have been kept confidential after being submitted to the government.

A truth commission should be distinguished from a government human rights office set up to watch over current human rights abuses, and also from nongovernmental projects documenting past abuses. There are also important distinctions between these truth commissions and criminal prosecutions, with important strengths and weaknesses in either approach. A truth commission is not a court of law; it does not determine individual criminal liability or order criminal sanctions. On the other hand, a truth commission can do many things that courts can't or generally don't do. Trials focus on the actions of specific individuals; truth commissions focus on the large pattern of overall events. It is true that some trials help shed light on overall patterns of rights violations, but this is generally not their focus or intent. Also, courts do not typically investigate the various social or political factors which led to the violence, or the internal structure of abusive forces, such as death squads or the intelligence branch of the armed forces, all of which might be the focus of a truth commission. Courts do not submit policy recommendations or suggestions for political, military or judicial reforms. And finally, while court records may be public, court opinions are generally not widely distributed and widely read, as is typical of truth commission reports. In brief, a truth commission's strengths are in those very areas which fall outside the parameters or capabilities of a court.

Similarly, these truth-seeking bodies should be distinguished from international tribunals, such as the International Criminal Tribunal for the Former Yugoslavia and the International Criminal Tribunal for Rwanda, both created by the United Nations, or the permanent International Criminal Court [. . .]. These international tribunals have been established in response to massive state violence, but they function with the purpose and powers of a court, very different from a commission of investigation, which typically has fewer powers but a much broader scope of inquiry. [. . .]

## Understanding and Preventing Torture: What Contribution from Truth Commissions?

Although the specific mandate and form may differ between commissions, all aim to contribute to learning about the past, offer official acknowledgement to victims, suggest political, military, police or judicial reforms necessary to keep such abuses from being repeated, and often to recommend reparations for victims. Understanding and preventing torture is a prominent aspect of this work.

A WINDOW INTO THE PRACTICE OF TORTURE

The first task is to establish exactly what did happen, remove the silence surrounding often still painful and controversial events, and make the information publicly accessible so that it cannot be further denied. Towards this end, many commission reports have included horrifying accounts of torture, sometimes presented in the victims' own powerful voices.

The Argentine commission report is perhaps the strongest in this aspect. Although its mandate was to focus on those disappeared under the seven-year military dictatorship in Argentina, the commission relied on survivors of the military detention centres to understand the practices of disappearance, which often included months of torture before being killed. Many of the 450 pages of the commission's report include passages like this one, excerpted from the testimony of Dr. Norberto Liwsky—which the commission calls "typical" of all the cases it heard. Liwsky testifies:

One day they put me face-down on the torture table, tied me up (as always), and calmly began to strip the skin from the soles of my feet. I imagine, though I didn't see because I was blindfolded, that they were doing it with a razor blade or a scalpel. I could feel them pulling as if they were trying to separate the skin at the edge of the wound with a pair of pincers. I passed out. From then on, strangely enough, I was able to faint very easily. . . .

In between torture sessions they left me hanging by my arms from hooks fixed in the wall of the cell where they had thrown me . . . sometimes they put me onto the torture table and stretched me out, tying my hands and feet to a machine that I can't describe since I never saw it, but which gave me the feeling that they were going to tear part of my body off . . . .

The most vivid and terrifying memory I have of all that time was of always living with death. I felt it was impossible to think. I desperately tried to summon up a thought in order to convince myself I wasn't dead. That I wasn't mad. At the same time, I wished with all my heart that they would kill me as soon as possible.

Or this passage of Teresa Celia Meschiati, who testified, after describing intense torture with electric prods,

I tried to kill myself by drinking foul water in the tub which was meant for another kind of torture called *submarine*, but I did not succeed.

The gradually increasing intensity of the electric prod was matched by the sadism of my torturers. There were five of them, whose names were: Guillermo Barreiro, Luis Manzanelli, José López, Jorge Romero, and Fermín de los Santos.

When the commission excerpted testimony which happened to include the names of accused perpetrators, they chose to reprint the names as cited. The commission made no conclusions about culpability, however, and did not publish a final and complete list of those found to be responsible for abuses.

In addition to testimony of survivors, the Argentine commission was able to reconstruct the location and even the floor plans of over three hundred secret detention centres, visiting each one, with survivors, to confirm them. This list is included in the commission report. It is not known how many people survived these detention centres, as the commission only kept track of the disappeared, those who were abducted and never seen again. The annex to the commission report lists by name each of the close to nine thousand disappeared that it was able to document.

In El Salvador, the UN Commission on the Truth took direct testimony from over 2,000 people, accounting for 7,000 victims. Of these, 20 per cent reported acts of torture (another 15 per cent concerned enforced disappearances, many of whom were likely also tortured). A statistical analysis of the testimony collected by the commission (as well as testimony handed into the commission from the files of non-governmental organizations, United Nations bodies and the government) is included in the appendix to the report, an extremely useful window into understanding the pattern of abusive practices over time and across the different regions of the country, how it affected different population groups, and what groups the accused perpetrators were from—including the military, police, death squads and the armed opposition. The text of the report itself, however, includes little detail on the practice of torture, as the approximately thirty cases chosen for in-depth investigation are all disappearances, judicial executions, assassinations by death squads, or large-scale massacres. Thus a first-hand narrative, such as in the Argentine report, or even a descriptive overview of common practices, summarizing testimony received, is not included.

Not many truth commissions have held public hearings, due to serious concerns for security and fear of witnesses. In Latin America, public hearings were considered virtually unthinkable, for just these reasons (some survivors were even too fearful to appear for a private, confidential hearing). In Africa, however, a number of commissions have held public hearings, allowing victims a public stage to receive recognition for the pains suffered, and allowing the process of the truth commission to be shared nationally. The Truth and Reconciliation Commission in South Africa, tasked to uncover "as complete a picture as possible" about "killings, abduction, torture, and severe ill-treatment," has gone the furthest in this regard. In addition to receiving testimony *in camera*, the commission held public hearings all around the country, in poor black townships and in major cities, in large churches and dusty town halls, where over two thousand victims, survivors or witnesses were heard. Each of these hearings was videotaped by a special camera crew from the South African Broadcasting Corporation, and clips of the hearings were shown on the nightly news. Five hours or more of live coverage of the hearings were broadcast on the radio each day. Torture survivors described details of their torture; mothers described how sons were killed; fathers recounted land mines that had killed infant children. Over a period of more than a year, the country was washed over with story upon story of abuse and killings, to the point where it was no longer possible for anyone reasonably to deny the extent of abuse that had taken place. It was widely understood, however, that even the approximately twenty thousand victims documented by the commission were but a small portion of the true total.

In addition to hearing from victims, the South African commission also received public testimony directly from perpetrators, who admitted to the gruesome details of their own past crimes. In the first example ever of public admission from so many perpetrators (and occasionally what seemed to be genuine apology), hearing upon hearing presented torturers and killers sitting on stage, under oath, answering days of questions from lawyers, commissioners, and even directly from their former victims. These amazing scenes were possible only because the commission offered something in return: amnesty for those who disclosed the full truth and proved their crimes to be politically motivated and proportional to the political end pursued. Over 7,000 perpetrators applied for amnesty, some 1,600 of them for gross violations of human rights (other applications were for politically motivated property crimes, illegally transporting weapons, or similar acts which did not constitute a gross violation of human rights).

In many circumstances it is impossible to count the total number of victims of a previous regime. Often, where there have been years of abusive practices, it is simply impossible for a commission to document every case—for lack of time and resources, and in the interest of focusing the commission's energies on investigation as well as collecting information. In addition, some of those who lost a loved one or witnessed disappearances or massacres may not want to give testimony: some are still traumatized, or fearful of the consequences of speaking out; others, such as some former anti-apartheid activists in South Africa, simply don't consider themselves to be victims. "I knew the consequences, the sacrifices, of fighting against the government," they say, and they don't want to ask for sympathy now. While it is thus difficult for a commission to tabulate an accurate number of torture survivors, even preliminary numbers can help to signal what the total might be. This can be important not only for historical purposes but also can assist in designing support services that would be appropriate for the needs of this population.

But some truth commissions have explicitly excluded torture survivors in their count of victims, such as the commissions in Chile, Argentina and Uruguay. The focus of a truth commission's investigations is determined by the terms of reference handed to it upon creation, which in the case of Chile and Argentina was through a presidential decree, and in Uruguay from parliament. The mandates of these commissions were focused on the investigation of the disappeared (and, in the case of Chile, also killings), and they therefore did not even try to keep track of or calculate the number of people who suffered from torture and survived.

The Uruguayan commission missed the majority of the human rights violations that had taken place during the military regime because of this limited mandate: illegal detention and torture, which affected a huge proportion of the population, were ignored. As the Chilean rights advocate José Zalaquett noted, "A systematic practice of 'disappearances' as in Argentina, or, on a lesser scale, as in Chile, was not part of the Uruguayan military's repressive methodology." Writing in 1989, Zalaquett continued,

Although it is public knowledge in Uruguay and abroad that torture was systematically practiced during the military rule, there is no officially sanctioned record documenting this practice. The military does not publicly admit to it. In private it attempts to justify torture as a last resort and a lesser evil.

The Argentine commission was also tasked to investigate only disappearances, and the Chilean commission was given the slightly broader (but still limited) mandate to cover disappearances, executions, kidnappings, attempts on life by private citizens for political purposes, and torture that resulted in death. In both countries, the commissions took testimony from surviving victims of torture better to understand the experience of those killed or disappeared, but the survivors themselves were not counted in the total calculation of victims, nor were their names printed in the commissions' published list of victims.

In stark contrast to the Argentine commission report, the Chilean report includes almost no direct testimony or first-person accounts of torture or other abuse. Instead, it describes, in relatively few pages and in general terms, the kinds of torture used and the effect that it had on prisoners. Yet it is clear from these descriptions how uncompromisingly brutal the torture was, such as this description of the period between September and December 1973 (the most violent period of the Chilean dictatorship, immediately following the coup):

During these months mistreatment and torture were an almost universal feature of detention. . . . Torture methods were extremely varied. An almost universal technique was violent and continued beating until blood flowed and bones were broken. Another form was to make detention conditions so harsh that they themselves constituted torture. . . . It was also common to hang prisoners up by their arms with their feet off the ground for very long periods of time. They might be held under water, foul smelling substances, or excrement to the brink of suffocation. There are many accusations of sexual degradation and rape. A common practice was simulated firing squad.

In a number of cases, the report describes prisoners being "tortured to the point of madness." And it makes clear how widespread torture was:

It would be impossible to present a comprehensive list of all the torture sites— there were so many—in our country during the period we are considering. During these months torture was not practiced in every single detention site, but certainly most of them.

Yet, despite these horrifying descriptions, the Chilean report defines those who survived such treatment not to be victims—only those who died from torture: "the Commission has defined as victims of human rights violations those who were subjected to: . . . torture resulting in death," the report makes clear. Ironically, the reason for this narrow definition was because the universe of torture survivors was so large. Gisela von Muhlenbrock, as assistant to the president of Chile who helped to draft the executive decree which established the commission, says that they limited the universe of victims according to how much they would be able to afford to pay in reparations. When I asked her why torture victims were not counted as victims, she said, "We asked ourselves, 'How much can we afford?' We couldn't afford to extend compensation to everyone; so we limited the universe in terms of things we could finance." A number of commissioners and the executive secretary of the follow-up reparations body described this limited definition as both logical and necessary. "It would have been impossible to cover torture; there were far too many cases to investigate them all," they said.

This narrow definition of "victim" by this well-known commission in Chile contributed to a skewing of the popular understanding of who counts as a victim of the military regime: just as the commission defined it, the popular understanding is that those who survived the torture camps are not "victims," only those who died. In an interview in Chile in 1996, for example, one journalist, who herself was twice arrested and tortured under the military regime, told me, "Those who survived torture are not victims in Chile. They are not considered victims. When we say 'victim,' we mean only those who were killed or disappeared." Many others told me the same.

This narrow definition of victim has had a number of significant consequences. First, because the focus was on those who died, no one has a clear sense of how many people survived detention and torture in Chile. Human rights activists and other close observers of the human rights situation in Chile cite numbers ranging from 10,000 to 200,000. Some human rights professionals, when asked how many torture survivors there were, wouldn't even hazard a guess. The correct figure is probably somewhere between 50,000 and 100,000.

The second important consequence of this narrow definition of victim is in restricting who has access to reparations: virtually all reparations in

Chile are targeted to the families of those who died or disappeared. There is an extensive reparations programme for these families, including monthly cash payments, educational and medical benefits, and exemption from military service. Victims of torture, however, receive neither official recognition nor reparation (with the exception of access to a special mental health programme, although this programme is not well known and very few have taken advantage of it). The executive secretary of the Corporation for Reparation and Reconciliation, the follow-up body to the Chilean truth commission, told me how he sometimes saw first hand the lack of fairness in this policy: "One woman came into my office and sat down to say, 'The tragedy of my family is that they didn't kill my father. He's destroyed, but they allowed him to live. It would have been better if they had killed him.' Her family gets no reparations, but her father is completely destroyed as a person."

### Reparations to Victims

Many truth commissions have recommended that financial or other reparations be awarded to surviving victims or to families of those killed or disappeared. In Chile and Argentina, individual reparations programmes were targeted to the families of those victims listed in the commissions' reports (and also those who later reported a case that should have been included). A similar programme is expected in South Africa, where a central aspect of the commission's mandate is to study and propose a reparations policy. Commissions elsewhere have also recommended financial reparations programmes, such as in El Salvador, Haiti and Uganda, but these recommendations have not been implemented, largely due to limited resources and competing financial priorities.

The Haitian commission, for example, recommended that a special reparations commission be created as a follow-up body, to determine the "legal, moral, and material obligations" due to victims of violence. Listed first in its long chapter on recommendations, the commission outlines this proposal in some detail, suggesting that funds should come from the state, from national and international private donations, and from voluntary contributions via the United Nations.

The El Salvador report called for a special fund, "an autonomous body with the necessary legal and administrative powers to award appropriate material compensation to the victims of violence in the shortest time possible." It further recommended that not less than 1 per cent of all international assistance that reaches El Salvador be set aside for this fund. But neither the Salvadoran government nor the international community was enthusiastic about this proposal, and the recommended fund was never established.

The likelihood that a reparations programme will be implemented in any country will be determined by the level of political interest and political will, the resources available to the state, and the number of victims that require compensation. Where resources are very limited, symbolic, community, or development-oriented reparations might be considered, such as memorials, days of remembrance, or schools or community centres built in the name of victims. Many commissions have left detailed recommendations in support of such initiatives.

### PREVENTING ABUSES IN THE FUTURE

Ultimately, a commission of inquiry into past abuses aims not only to describe what happened, but to put forward measures that will prevent such abuses from happening again. Although these commissions themselves do not have the power to implement policies or reform, they are often asked to make substantial recommendations for changes necessary in political, military, police or judicial structures, in the legal framework to protect rights, or in the social or educational sphere to promote a wider understanding of basic human rights.

The commissions in El Salvador and Chile put forward the most significant and detailed recommendations, and both of these reports were given considerable attention over the ensuing years as policy-makers used these recommendations as a guide in designing reform packages. But the reforms suggested were not always easily or quickly implemented. In El Salvador, for example, there was considerable resistance in parliament to the proposal that extrajudicial confessions be prohibited from being submitted as evidence in court, which would remove a primary motivation for torturing suspects, as well as to the recommendation that the right to an attorney be guaranteed from the moment of arrest, and other recommendations to protect the rights of detainees. As common crime rose and popular demands for hard-line measures against criminals increased, politicians balked at such restrictions on what they considered to be tools in their crime-fighting strategy. But the recommendations from the Salvadoran truth commission were considered to be obligatory, by prior agreement between the parties to the peace accords, and the United Nations therefore continued to push for their implementation. After considerable delay, it was only with the intervention of a senior United Nations envoy from New York, Alvaro de Soto, that some of these reforms were passed, although some in slightly compromised form.

Yet the challenge of halting years or decades of abusive practices goes far beyond writing new laws and passing new regulations. Many states which have all the right laws in place, as well as other layers of safeguards or protections, still continue to battle ongoing abuses by security forces.

[. . .] Therefore, while truth commissions have certainly contributed to necessary reforms, they have not necessarily put a stop to torture.

For example, fourteen years after the end of military rule in Argentina (and thirteen years after its truth commission report was released), torture by the police and prison guards continued. In late 1997, a UN Human Rights Committee criticized Argentina for "tolerating the continued practice of torture," despite the fact that the country is a signatory to the International Convention against Torture. "Many Argentines die after being tortured by the police, and the Argentine authorities have done little to stop the practice," the *New York Times* reported, citing comments of Gonzales Poblete, vice president of the UN Committee. These practices of torture do not appear to be politically motivated, but are certainly reminiscent of the common practice under military rule.

Serious problems also continue in Brazil. Jim Cavallaro, Human Rights Watch representative in Brazil, told me in late 1996 that "Torture in Brazil neither began nor ended with the military dictatorship." They have been torturing people for years, with clear evidence of death squads back into the 1950s, he said.

The end of the military dictatorship was by no means an end to the practice of torture, although it did end the legitimacy of torturing people from an upper-middle-class background. But torture against poor, darker-skinned people is routinely practiced in Brazil.

Cavallaro continued

Some say there is more torture now than during the military dictatorship. Or that it's easier to torture people now than during the military dictatorship. Before, it was possible to torture the wrong person—the cousin of a general, for example—but no one living in *favela* [a city slum], selling drugs, with a second grade education, is the cousin of a general.

No one is keeping track of the how much torture goes on, he says; no one reports it.

Even as the South African Truth and Reconciliation Commission was under way, with daily hearings airing accounts of torture and killings, there were new charges that torture was still practiced by the police. It is estimated by human rights observers, such as Peter Jordi of the Witswatersrand University Law Clinic, that 1 to 2 per cent of all detainees suffered some form of torture in 1997; the primary methods employed were suffocation and electrocution. In one three-month period in 1997, the Independent Complaints Directorate of South Africa, the police oversight body, reported that 255 people died in police custody or due to police action, many from shootings. These charges of ongoing abuses received far less attention than the truth commission hearings about the past, although there were some serious proposals on the table to address the problem, as well as attention from the truth commission regarding what police reforms or police-training initiatives should be recommended in their report.

## Special Considerations

### WOMEN'S EXPERIENCES UNDERREPORTED

In many cultures, rape carries great social stigma, embarrassment and shame for the victim. Many women are thus understandably uncomfortable providing testimony about sexual abuse in public hearings, or even in private hearings if their testimony would then be published in a public report—with their name, and perhaps the name of the accused, printed for all to see. As a result, the full truth about women's experiences in periods of widespread conflict and repression has not been effectively recorded or reported by most truth commissions.

A number of truth commissions have been aware of the underreporting of the experiences of women victims, especially in the area of sexual crimes. In South Africa, for example, the commission found that although women made up about half of the deponents giving testimony, much of their testimony reported violence against men—their husbands, brothers or sons, for example. Women's own experiences seemed to be overshadowed or silenced. This underreporting was especially severe on the subject of sexual violence, where an extremely small number of cases were reported compared to the known widespread occurrence of rape by the police and in the inter-communal violence of the KwaZulu-Natal region.

Clearly, without special attention to facilitate or encourage the reporting of women's experiences, the true picture of these violations will remain largely shrouded in silence and hidden from the history books. There are a few examples of special attention towards this issue, although none entirely successful. In South Africa, the commission held three special women's hearings, with female commissioners on the panel and, in one case, allowing women to give testimony about sexual abuse from behind a screen, out of the view of the public and television cameras. Only in Haiti, however, has a truth commission been specifically directed in its founding mandate to pay special attention to sexual abuses against women. This resulted in considerable attention being given to the issue in the commission's investigations, and a whole chapter of its report dedicated to the subject.

## The Challenge of Healing and Reconciliation

If someone had asked me when I was set free: did they torture you a lot? I would have replied: Yes, for the whole of the three months . . . If I were asked that same question today, I would say that I've now lived through seven years of torture. (Miguel D'Agostino, file No. 3901, Argentine National Commission on the Disappeared)

Healing from torture is a painful and long-term process, as the expanding literature on this subject makes clear. Many survivors of torture must struggle daily to live with their memories. As should be expected, the idea of forgiving one's torturer and reconciling with one's former opponents or repressors is an idea that not all are willing to embrace. These two tasks—healing and reconciliation—together form the backbone of perhaps the most difficult side of any transition out of a repressive past. While negotiated transitions or constitutional agreements can settle the political differences between former opponents and lead to formal peace, many victims and former fighters of the resolved conflict may be left both traumatized and unwilling to forgive their former opponents. When victims and perpetrators run into the many tens of thousands, or when the country is deeply polarized down ideological, race, class or geographic lines, some sort of national process may be necessary to confront and try to counter these differences. It is partly out of this felt need to give greater attention and support to victims, as well as consciously to promote national reconciliation, that truth commissions have become such an attractive transitional mechanism.

Truth commissions claim many purposes and goals, and promoting healing for victims and reconciliation for the nation are prominent among them. The names of some commissions make their aim clear: the National Commission on Truth and Reconciliation in Chile and the Truth and Reconciliation Commission in South Africa, for example, set the tone for these commissions and the debate and discussion around them. Posters around South Africa, and large banners hung behind the stage of every public hearing, announced the truth commission with the bold motto "Truth, The Road to Reconciliation."

Yet it should not be assumed that truth always leads to healing and reconciliation, or at least not for every person. For some, it helps enormously to have the opportunity to tell one's story to an official state body. But for others, healing will require access to longer-term structures for psychological and emotional support. Likewise, it has yet to be proven that reconciliation will always be advanced from confronting the pains of past conflict. Healing and reconciliation are both long-term processes that go far beyond the capacity of any one short-term commission. Yet, given the scarcity of transitional mechanisms and the limited resources to pour into peacemaking projects, many national leaders pin high hopes on the ability of truth commissions to carry a country down the path of reconciliation, healing and peace, and many couch their support for such a commission in those terms.

Clearly, some scepticism about the inherent healing qualities of truth commissions is deserved. Many questions remain that demand greater study and exploration. But this scepticism should be tempered by indications of quite positive contributions from national truth-seeking in some circumstances. For example, I have spoken with many victims who say that only by learning the full truth about their past horror can they ever begin to heal. Only by remembering, telling their story, and learning the full details about what happened and who was responsible are they able to put the past behind them. Similarly, in South Africa, many survivors told me that they could only forgive their perpetrators if they were told the full truth; almost incomprehensibly, hearing even the most gruesome details of the torture and murder of a loved one somehow brought them some peace.

In South Africa, as elsewhere, the future will be shaped by the past. And a past that carries silenced pain, resentment and unaddressed latent conflict will not be soon forgotten nor easily shaped into a peaceful future. A truth commission can help to unsilence this past, pay respect to victims, and outline needed reforms. Yet it cannot work alone. Real change in the future will depend on the political will of national and local leaders, a commitment to institute far-reaching reforms, and a long-term view towards developing a culture of respect for basic human rights.

# Training and Education

It may seem like a fruitless exercise to expect that anyone who is inclined to be a torturer could be trained or educated out of that predilection but recall from Chapter IV that it is possible to "make" or train a torturer who under other circumstances might never opt for that path at all. Is it likewise possible to "inoculate" military, security, or police authorities against becoming human rights violators? The field of human rights education is in its infancy but in "Human Rights Education for the Police" Marc DuBois, an attorney from New Orleans, describes training and education offered to the police that may hold a clue to what ought to become a far more widespread practice, namely, trying to prevent abuse before it occurs.

[T]he battle against human rights violations has focused almost exclusively on two targets, the political elite and the masses, while ignoring the actors, the men and women comprising the police, army, or security forces of a country. These are the performers in this tragic political drama, the ones who execute suspected insurgency sympathizers, beat the soles of detainees' feet, break into houses to seize activists' files, or simply impose "tolls" upon peasants carrying their produce to the market. Government officials must share final responsibility, but the policeman's baton and warrantless search are the points where inequitable power relations intersect victims of abuse. [. . .]

## Two Examples of Human Rights Training Programs for the Police

When compared to most governments, the expertise of NGOs in the area of human rights (and, perhaps, education) makes their participation a vital component of effective training. It is with that in mind that I turn to a brief examination of two existing programs. The first is a course called "Human Dignity and the Police," developed by the John Jay College of Criminal Justice (New York). The second is a program of LEA [law enforcement agents] education seminars given by the Legal Resources Foundation of Zimbabwe. These two programs were selected because the contrast in approaches and content illustrates the broad range of options and highlights many of the important issues. [. . .]

## A Course in Human Dignity

Commenced in 1992, the John Jay course has been given to more than 330 police officers in Latin America, South America, and the Caribbean basin as part of the U.S. government's International Criminal Investigations Training Assistance Program (ICI- TAP). [. . .]

The foundation of the course is a belief that human dignity precedes human rights; that after learning to respect human dignity, LEAs will (re)conceptualize human rights as possessing innate value rather than as impeding the rule of law and order. The course involves a variety of exercises and discussions intended to: (1) establish participants' intellectual understanding of human dignity; (2) have participants recall a violation of their dignity by authority figures both in the past and by the police organization; (3) increase participant awareness of the vulnerability of marginalized sectors of society; (4) increase their understanding of the effects of peer pressure and personal responsibility; and (5) generate potential solutions and codes of conduct from the participants themselves. The course employs a "nontraditional" method of teaching which draws upon the participants' own experiences with loss of dignity: "Teaching police to understand how it feels to have their dignity taken away is the exact nature of this course."

There are several features that distinguish "Human Dignity" from other courses. First, the course seeks to impact directly on human rights through a change in attitudes, but without confronting the trainees as if they were all potential or actual abusers. Avoiding antagonism is crucial to the success of the course. [. . .] To begin with, the participants, rather than the outside world, develop the working definition of the word *dignity* to be used in the course. This precludes them from later denying its validity in their reality. Ensuing exercises ask participants to present a historical figure who championed human dignity, to reexperience an incident in their childhood when an authority figure violated their dignity, and to do the same for a recent occasion when the police organization violated it. Participants realize that violations of dignity cause permanent scars, and instructors lead the analysis so as to nullify rationalizations (e.g., being abused is good for a person because it toughens him or her). These early exercises aim to break down the "we-they" mentality that permeates security forces by situating LEAs in the position of victim and establishing a kinship with those injured by abusive authority. These exercises also ease suspicions about the course and demonstrate that the instructors care about the participants.

A second virtue of the course is the way in which it strikes at the group processes and normative systems underpinning violations of human dignity by LEAs. In the opening exercise, participants complete a brief survey that asks, for instance, whether they have witnessed an abusive use of force by the police or whether such violations can have profound, lifelong impact. The subsequent discussion of responses establishes the diversity of opinion and validity of a range of perceptions within a group of respected peers. In this way, individuals realize that their understanding of what is necessary and true (e.g., justifications for abusive behavior) is not the only "true" understanding. [. . .]

Several exercises are designed to develop a sense of personal responsibility for one's actions. Participants are asked to: (1) help a close friend understand his son, once a thoughtful and caring person, who, after joining the police force, is becoming cynical, distrustful, and judgmental; (2) in a variation of no. 1, to help the friend understand the son who is cynical and depressed (suicidal) as a result of receiving dangerous assignments and being shunned by other officers following his testimony against fellow officers; and (3) to develop a plan of action in response to a letter from a mother whose twelve-year-old son suffered brain damage from a beating (in a case of mistaken identity) by the police. All three of these exercises demand that participants examine the various forces influencing police behavior (such as peer groups and authority) and reflect upon what can be done to combat their negative effects. The final exercises of the course direct earlier learning to practical problems, such as designing a workable police code of conduct and a plan for improving police relations with the public.

## EDUCATIONAL SEMINARS FOR LAW ENFORCEMENT AGENTS

A network of paralegals and volunteers created by the Legal Resources Foundation (LRF) disseminates legal advice and offers legal rights education throughout Zimbabwe. In conjunction with this work, the LRF has conducted week-long seminars for police officers, community relations liaison officers (CRLO, a branch of the police), and, most surprisingly, Central Intelligence Office (CIO) agents. There is also an attempt to train police instructors so that they are then able to incorporate relevant information in regular police training programs.

The LRF's law enforcement agent education program does not focus directly on human rights but on legal competence. The program is based on the perception that, after years of emergency regulations, LEA personnel do not know or understand current law. The assumption underlying the approach of the program, then, is that by teaching the relevant law in areas where abuses occur—arrest; detention; entry, search, and seizure; confessions, statements, and admissions; bail—violations of rights will be decreased. The course also aims to sensitize LEA personnel as to the role of LEAs, lawyers, judges, and the public. Lessons are comprised mainly of lecture and discussion, and the subject matter is predominantly legal: relevant legislation and definitions, powers conferred on the police, and the nature of infringements on rights as delineated by court decisions or human rights articles. Furthermore, there is an effort to strike a balance between a theoretical and practical understanding of the laws. In the end, recommendations are made and suggested police procedure is outlined. [. . .]

## Understanding the Objectives of Human Rights Education for the Police

[. . .] The first step in planning a training program for LEAs is to identify the major institutional and individual factors that contribute to abuse. Once identified, diminishing the impact of these factors becomes the educational objective that determines the content of the course. Note, however, that within one country, these factors may vary according to rank, service, or geographic region. The second step is to design a course that takes into account the fact that human rights education (HRE) for security personnel differs from other education because the subject itself antagonizes the students, creating a formidable barrier to learning.

In and of itself, human rights education for LEAs will be unsuccessful without a certain level of structural support, meaning that watchdog activities must continue. However, the remedial capacity of structural change is also limited. The luster of its desirability regularly outshines its effectiveness in transforming or even ameliorating the lives of the oppressed. This is partly because police forces both inherit and develop their own standards, operating procedures, and autonomy. Eliminating legal and political structures that allow human rights violations to take place is of crucial importance, but such efforts must be accompanied by an attack upon the *normative systems* within security forces which evolved along with those structures.

New governments and laws do not automatically lead to an improvement in the human rights climate of a given country because of hangover effects—the ways of the past flourish in the present via individual policemen. Their experience from an era of violation—their ignorance, rationalizations, and power relationships—survives. In the context of human rights there are several hangovers that mitigate the positive effects of structural changes, each of which might be addressed in training: colonial, state-of-emergency, and impunity hangovers.

The legacy of colonization is that foreigners introduced police forces not to preserve law and order for the benefit of the citizenry but to perpetuate inequity and injustice for their benefit. This original structure has not disappeared; it continues to shape organizational patterns and perceptions long after decolonization. To counteract this effect, both police and the public need to reconceptualize their relationship. An effective exercise might explore the negative connotations associated with colonialism and then ask trainees to compare the present police force with its predecessor. A state-of-emergency hangover stems from the sheer number of internal security forces (ISF) personnel who were trained or who served while the nation was under a state of emergency (or other similar phenomena such as martial law). The problem is that emergency restrictions tend "to become perpetual or to effect far-reaching authoritarian changes in the *ordinary legal norms.*" Even where there is no absence of de jure protection, some security forces operate in an atmosphere of impunity, able to violate the law with no fear of retribution. As a consequence of these three phenomena, LEAs incorporate abuse into modes of operation and create values capable of enduring new legislation or elections.

As the preceding discussion makes apparent, the treatment for these hangovers must include both a dose of new structure and a regimen of perceptual modification. This is because abuses such as the use of torture or arbitrary detention do not evolve in a vacuum—policemen have been taught that their actions are justified. In short, LEAs do not measure the ethical component of their actions against the backdrop of international human rights law. Instead, normative subsystems within the force, unit, or peer group justify many violations.

To a large extent, justifying abusive behavior involves discrediting human rights law. Security forces conceptualize human rights as contradicting their primary objective—preserving law and order. Research by the Centre for the Victims of Torture (Nepal) indicates that torturers are "trained to believe that what they are doing is right . . . and [those concerned] have to understand that they think that torture is the right thing to do." This conceptualization of human rights galvanizes the "we-they" mentality pervading security forces: "we" need to arrest criminals, "they" speak to us of procedural rights; "we" understand what is reality, "they" speak of utopian aspirations; "we" risk our lives in the line of duty, "they" endanger the country; "we" need to stick together against "them." Moreover, this "we-they" dichotomy is fueled by the "inequity" of human rights law itself, insofar as it applies to actions by LEAs but not to actions of criminals or (sometimes) rebels.

There are two processes common to virtually any law enforcement agency which should be dealt with in HRE for the police because they interplay with all of the above factors. The first is the way in which chain of command structure dislocates the individual officer, extinguishing his sense of responsibility for his actions. The excuse that one is following orders enables the individual officer to ignore both the law and his own sense of right and wrong. The second is the way in which being part of a group, in this case a peer group composed of other LEAs, affects behavior. The group dynamics in which much of police work takes place or is judged pressures LEAs to maintain a certain image (e.g., one cannot afford to appear to others as being soft) and allows a policeman to justify behavior by the fact that it comports with the behavior of others (each of whom is performing the same externally focused justification).

There are other reasons for abuse which can be addressed by HRE and which do not involve such complex psychological phenomena. In some countries, the elements of a law or the boundaries it places on the exercise of police discretion are incomprehensible. In particular, this ambiguity characterizes new decrees, the terms of which have not yet been defined by the courts or senior officials (as in the case of a return to constitutional rule following a state of emergency). A typical law might state that in order to make an arrest "The (detaining authority) *must first* be *satisfied* that a person: a) is *concerned* in *acts* prejudicial to *public* order, or b) has been recently *concerned* in *acts* prejudicial to public order." There is nothing in this law which delineates permissible actions or guides a decision regarding the arrest or questioning of a person. What is an act "prejudicial to public order?" What does "satisfied" mean? Changes in written law restoring constitutional protections to the people do not by themselves alter, say, the policeman's sense of how much suspicion (if any) is needed to arrest and question an individual. The Legal Resources Foundation's LEA education project articulates the need for its training program as follows: "A majority, if not all, of Zimbabwe's law enforcement agents were trained during the existence of the state of emergency in terms of which extraordinarily wide and extensive powers were given to them. With the removal of the state of emergency, these powers have been drastically curtailed, the result being that a vacuum has been left because law enforcement agents have never had to operate and effectively perform their duties under what may be regarded as peace-time conditions." In other cases, ignorance rather than ambiguity is the problem. In discussing UN human rights training courses for more than three thousand administrators of justice, government officials, LEAs, and others, Jan Martenson (former UN under-secretary-general for human rights) stated: "The result was invariably the same, the people said: We didn't know, we didn't know that these standards existed, that our country had ratified them, and particularly we didn't know that we had to apply them also in our daily activities."

In the end, a host of tangled factors cause violations of human rights. Since it is neither politically nor financially possible to replace the rank-and-file personnel of these forces in most countries, retraining and re-education are imperative. [. . .]

## Pedagogical Issues in Human Rights Education for the Police

[. . .] Generally speaking, perhaps the most important factor in human rights education for LEAs is to create an atmosphere that is nonthreatening. For instance, research by the Washington Office on Latin America (WOLA) shows that the mere mention of the term human rights "makes Latin American officers bristle; it's accompanied in their minds by the word 'violation,' and so . . . is perceived as accusatory." Furthermore, demonstrating a sensitivity to human rights or dignity issues invites the label of "soft" and jeopardizes the standing of a policeman in his professional peer group. Finally, as has been pointed out by Dean James T. Curran of John Jay College, for police officers in many parts of the world the only alternative to being an LEA is abject poverty, meaning that they fear disturbing the status quo because it places their livelihoods at risk.

In addition to the examples of programs discussed above, successful programs must combine two approaches to overcome the antagonism or skepticism of participants. First, they should not focus expressly on human rights but upon human dignity, professionalism, or other "disguised" subjects [. . .]. As one academic has stated along these lines, "Human rights is something wimps do, and 'human rights training' is perceived as an oxymoron. You've got to find an expanded vocabulary." Second, whether using role-play, group projects, or questions based on hypothetical situations, it is important to remain practical, to build upon the experiences and assignments of the participants. A survey of actual or potential trainees would be one way to develop a course grounded in their reality. Another way would be to involve police officers or experts capable of speaking to the police culture in the planning and implementation stages of the course. With regard to this problem, an official in the Philippines, where government human rights training for police and military is part of a nationwide, constitutionally mandated HRE campaign, proposes ten ways to increase acceptance of human rights education by Philippine military and police.

1. Arrange for clear command structure endorsements, meaning that commanding officers should be physically present at the education in order to send a clear signal of its importance.
2. Avoid legalese and emphasize the Filipino context so as to ensure understanding.
3. Use some trainers who are members of LEAs in addition to outside specialists.
4. Appeal to professional ethics and codes of conduct.
5. Standards must be fair, meaning that violations shall include abuse by criminals or insurgents.

6.  Underscore the point that respecting human rights is in each officer's best interests.
7.  Emphasize basic human needs by using carrots (promotions) rather than sticks (threats of investigations and sanctions) in such a way that the satisfaction of the trainee's human needs (e.g., food for the family, education for the children) is tied to respecting the human needs of others.
8.  Establish a reward system for trainees.
9.  Establish a reward system for trainers.
10.  Make use of external and internal assistance and resources.

Once these initial obstacles have been cleared (or minimized), it is the interplay between course format, instructor identity, and course content that will determine the effectiveness of the course. [. . .]

### CONTENT: A WEALTH OF UNTESTED OPTIONS

[. . .] Aside from what has been discussed above, there are other potentially fruitful curricula. For instance, teachings from religion might be used to help convince LEAs of the need to respect the rights or dignity of others. Similarly, specialized content could deal with issues such as sensitizing LEAs to the rights of women or the needs of female sexual assault victims. To reiterate, for programs to be effective, they must change attitudes in both individuals and forces (dismantle normative frameworks that justify abuse) and eliminate deficiencies of knowledge or skill that give rise to abuse. They must also relate to the participants, meaning that HRE should focus on those laws (from that country's constitution or UN documents) that directly define the behavior of LEAs, rather than model documents that are not operative locally (in other words, there is probably little value in teaching Latin American LEAs about the U.S. Constitution). [. . .]

One approach to human rights training has been a focus on professional conduct. [. . .] The basic idea is to encourage respect for human rights as a matter of honor and institutional dignity rather than to focus directly on human rights. The strength of this approach is that by building on these existing values it is not necessary to deconstruct the normative system. Such training would work well with an emphasis on potential situations, using hypotheticals to develop participants' sense of correct behavior (e.g., a suspect surrenders after fighting with officers or an unarmed person accidentally approaches a roadblock in a high-security zone). The major drawback to professionalism training is that following orders or refusing to testify against a fellow officer are also matters of honor, ones that push policemen to act contrary to human rights law.

Therefore, if professionalism training is to work, it must be accompanied by training directed toward changing LEA perception of honor and duty where they conflict with human rights. [. . .]

Finally, in one of the final exercises of "Human Dignity," the participants are asked to design their own code of police conduct and develop a strategy to implement it. This exercise should prove extremely fertile for human rights activists. It is difficult for outsiders to understand the inner dynamics of a particular police unit or force. Given the great perceptual gap between LEAs and activists, a key to effective structural changes and developing appropriate (and therefore successful) training curricula could lie in these expert suggestions. The fox knows best how to protect the hens. It is simply that we would not entrust it to do so.

# Appendix: Excerpts from Documents

United Nations Convention against Torture and Other Cruel, Inhuman or Degrading Treatment or Punishment

The States Parties to this Convention,

Considering that, in accordance with the principles proclaimed in the Charter of the United Nations, recognition of the equal and inalienable rights of all members of the human family is the foundation of freedom, justice and peace in the world,

Recognizing that those rights derive from the inherent dignity of the human person,

Considering the obligation of States under the Charter, in particular Article 55, to promote universal respect for, and observance of, human rights and fundamental freedoms [. . .]

Have agreed as follows:

Article 1

1. For the purposes of this Convention, torture means any act by which severe pain or suffering, whether physical or mental, is intentionally inflicted on a person for such purposes as obtaining from him or a third person information or a confession, punishing him for an act he or a third person has committed or is suspected of having committed, or intimidating or coercing him or a third person, or for any reason based on discrimination of any kind, when such pain or suffering is inflicted by or at the instigation of or with the consent or acquiescence of a public official or other person acting in an official capacity. It does not include pain or suffering arising only from, inherent in or incidental to lawful sanctions.

## Article 2

1. Each State Party shall take effective legislative, administrative, judicial or other measures to prevent acts of torture in any territory under its jurisdiction.

2. No exceptional circumstances whatsoever, whether a state of war or a threat of war, internal political instability or any other public emergency, may be invoked as a justification of torture.

3. An order from a superior officer or a public authority may not be invoked as a justification of torture.

## Article 3

1. No State Party shall expel, return ("refouler") or extradite a person to another State where there are substantial grounds for believing that he would be in danger of being subjected to torture.

## Article 4

1. Each State Party shall ensure that all acts of torture are offences under its criminal law. The same shall apply to an attempt to commit torture and to an act by any person which constitutes complicity or participation in torture.

2. Each State Party shall make these offences punishable by appropriate penalties which take into account their grave nature.

## Article 6

1. Upon being satisfied, after an examination of information available to it, that the circumstances so warrant, any State Party in whose territory a person alleged to have committed any offence referred to in article 4 is present, shall take him into custody or take other legal measures to ensure his presence. The custody and other legal measures shall be as provided in the law of that State but may be continued only for such time as is necessary to enable any criminal or extradition proceedings to be instituted.

3. Any person in custody pursuant to paragraph 1 of this article shall be assisted in communicating immediately with the nearest appropriate representative of the State of which he is a national, or, if he is a stateless person, to the representative of the State where he usually resides.

## Article 8

1. The offences referred to in article 4 shall be deemed to be included as extraditable offences in any extradition treaty existing between States

Parties. States Parties undertake to include such offences as extraditable offences in every extradition treaty to be concluded between them.

## Article 10

1. Each State Party shall ensure that education and information regarding the prohibition against torture are fully included in the training of law enforcement personnel, civil or military, medical personnel, public officials and other persons who may be involved in the custody, interrogation or treatment of any individual subjected to any form of arrest, detention or imprisonment.

2. Each State Party shall include this prohibition in the rules or instructions issued in regard to the duties and functions of any such persons.

## Article 11

Each State Party shall keep under systematic review interrogation rules, instructions, methods and practices as well as arrangements for the custody and treatment of persons subjected to any form of arrest, detention or imprisonment in any territory under its jurisdiction, with a view to preventing any cases of torture.

## Article 12

Each State Party shall ensure that its competent authorities proceed to a prompt and impartial investigation, wherever there is reasonable ground to believe that an act of torture has been committed in any territory under its jurisdiction.

## Article 13

Each State Party shall ensure that any individual who alleges he has been subjected to torture in any territory under its jurisdiction has the right to complain to and to have his case promptly and impartially examined by its competent authorities. Steps shall be taken to ensure that the complainant and witnesses are protected against all ill-treatment or intimidation as a consequence of his complaint or any evidence given.

## Article 14

1. Each State Party shall ensure in its legal system that the victim of an act of torture obtains redress and has an enforceable right to fair and adequate compensation including the means for as full rehabilitation as possible. In the event of the death of the victim as a result of an act of torture, his dependents shall be entitled to compensation.

Article 15

Each State Party shall ensure that any statement which is established to have been made as a result of torture shall not be invoked as evidence in any proceedings, except against a person accused of torture as evidence that the statement was made.

Article 16

1. Each State Party shall undertake to prevent in any territory under its jurisdiction other acts of cruel, inhuman or degrading treatment or punishment which do not amount to torture as defined in article 1, when such acts are committed by or at the instigation of or with the consent or acquiescence of a public official or other person acting in an official capacity. In particular, the obligations contained in articles 10, 11, 12 and 13 shall apply with the substitution for references to torture or references to other forms of cruel, inhuman or degrading treatment or punishment.

## International Standards Against Torture

### Universal Declaration of Human Rights
No one shall be subjected to torture or to cruel, inhuman or degrading treatment or punishment. (Article 5)

### International Covenant on Civil and Political Rights
No one shall be subjected to torture or to cruel, inhuman or degrading treatment or punishment. In particular, no one shall be subjected without his free consent to medical or scientific experimentation. (Article 7)

All persons deprived of their liberty shall be treated with humanity and with respect for the inherent dignity of the human person. (Article 10)

### European Convention for the Protection of Human Rights and Fundamental Freedoms
No one shall be subjected to torture or to inhuman or degrading treatment or punishment. (Article 3)

### American Convention on Human Rights
No one shall be subjected to torture or to cruel, inhuman, or degrading punishment or treatment. All persons deprived of their liberty shall be treated with respect for the inherent dignity of the human person. (Article 5)

### African Charter on Human and Peoples' Rights

Every individual shall have the right to the respect of the dignity inherent in a human being and to the recognition of his legal status. All forms of exploitation and degradation of man, particularly slavery, slave trade, torture, cruel, inhuman or degrading punishment and treatment, shall be prohibited. (Article 5)

### UN Declaration on the Protection of All Persons from Being Subjected to Torture and Other Cruel, Inhuman or Degrading Treatment or Punishment

No State may permit or tolerate torture or other cruel, inhuman or degrading treatment or punishment. (Article 3)

### UN Convention against Torture and Other Cruel, Inhuman or Degrading Treatment or Punishment

Each State Party shall take effective legislative, administrative, judicial or other measures to prevent acts of torture in any territory under its jurisdiction. (Article 2)

### Inter-American Convention to Prevent and Punish Torture

The States Parties shall ensure that all acts of torture and attempts to commit torture are offenses under their criminal law and shall make such acts punishable by severe penalties that take into account their serious nature. (Article 6)

### UN Body of Principles for the Protection of All Persons under Any Form of Detention or Imprisonment

No person under any form of detention or imprisonment shall be subjected to torture or to cruel, inhuman or degrading treatment or punishment. (Principle 6)

### UN Standard Minimum Rules for the Treatment of Prisoners

Corporal punishment, punishment by placing in a dark cell, and all cruel, inhuman or degrading punishments shall be completely prohibited as punishments for disciplinary offences. (Rule 31)

### Convention on the Rights of the Child

No child shall be subjected to torture or other cruel, inhuman or degrading treatment or punishment. (Article 37)

### United Nations Rules for the Protection of Juveniles Deprived of their Liberty

All disciplinary measures constituting cruel, inhuman or degrading treatment shall be strictly prohibited, including corporal punishment, placement in a dark cell, closed or solitary confinement or any other punishment that may compromise the physical or mental health of the juvenile concerned. (Article 67)

### United Nations Rules for the Protection of Juveniles Deprived of Their Liberty

No member of the detention facility or institutional personnel may inflict, instigate or tolerate any act of torture or any form of harsh, cruel, inhuman or degrading treatment, punishment, correction or discipline under any pretext or circumstance whatsoever. (Article 87)

### International Convention on the Elimination of All Forms of Racial Discrimination

In compliance with the fundamental obligations laid down in article 2 of this Convention, States Parties undertake . . . to guarantee the right of everyone, without distinction as to race, colour, or national or ethnic origin, to equality before the law, notably in the enjoyment of the following rights:

(b) The right to security of person and protection by the State against violence or bodily harm, whether inflicted by government officials or by any individual group or institution. (Article 5)

### International Convention on the Protection of the Rights of All Migrant Workers and Members of Their Families

No migrant worker or member of his or her family shall be subjected to torture or to cruel, inhuman or degrading treatment or punishment. (Article 10)

Migrant workers and members of their families shall be entitled to effective protection by the State against violence, physical injury, threats and intimidation, whether by public officials or by private individuals, groups or institutions. (Article 16.2)

### UN Declaration on the Elimination of Violence against Women

Women are entitled to the equal enjoyment and protection of all human rights and fundamental freedoms in the political, economic, social, cultural, civil or any other field, These rights include, *inter alia*:

(h) The right not to be subjected to torture, or other cruel, inhuman or degrading treatment or punishment. (Article 3)

**UN Code of Conduct for Law Enforcement Officials**
No law enforcement official may inflict, instigate or tolerate any act of torture or other cruel, inhuman or degrading treatment or punishment. (Article 5)

**UN Principles of Medical Ethics relevant to the Role of Health Personnel, particularly Physicians, in the Protection of Prisoners and Detainees against Torture and Other Cruel, Inhuman or Degrading Treatment or Punishment**
It is a gross contravention of medical ethics, as well as an offence under applicable international instruments, for health personnel, particularly physicians, to engage, actively or passively, in acts which constitute participation in, complicity in, incitement to or attempts to commit torture or other cruel, inhuman or degrading treatment or punishment. (Principle 2)

**Geneva Conventions of August 12, 1949 (common Article 3)**
. . . the following acts are and shall remain prohibited at any time and in any place whatsoever with respect to the above-mentioned persons:
(a) violence to life and person, in particular, mutilation, cruel treatment and torture;
(c) outrages upon personal dignity, in particular humiliating and degrading treatment.

## U.S. Army Field Manual FM34–52, Intelligence, Interrogation, May 8, 1987

Chapter 1
[. . .] Prohibition Against Use of Force
The use of force, mental torture, threats, insults, or exposure to unpleasant and inhumane treatment of any kind is prohibited by law and is neither authorized nor condoned by the U.S. Government. Experience indicates that the use of force is not necessary to gain the cooperation of sources for interrogation. Therefore, the use of force is a poor technique, as it yields unreliable results, may damage subsequent collection efforts, and can induce the source to say whatever he thinks the interrogator wants to hear. However, the use of force is not to be confused with psychological ploys, verbal trickery, or other nonviolent and noncoercive ruses used by the interrogator in questioning hesitant or uncooperative sources.

The psychological techniques and principles outlined should neither be confused with, nor construed to be synonymous with, unauthorized techniques such as brainwashing, mental torture, or any other form of mental coercion to include drugs. These techniques and principles are intended to serve as guides in obtaining the willing cooperation of a source. The absence of threats in interrogation is intentional, as their enforcement and use normally constitute violations of international law and may result in prosecution under the UCMJ.

Additionally, the inability to carry out a threat of violence or force renders an interrogator ineffective should the source challenge the threat. Consequently, from both legal and moral viewpoints, the restrictions established by international law, agreements, and customs render threats of force, violence, and deprivation useless as interrogation techniques.

# How to Get Involved

If you would like to get involved in efforts to stop torture, the following organizations may be of interest to you.

Amnesty International USA
www.amnestyusa.org

Center for Justice and Accountability
www.cja.org

Human Rights First
www.humanrightsfirst.org

Human Rights Watch
www.hrw.org

The Center for Victims of Torture
wws.cvt.org

Physicians for Human Rights
www.phrusa.org

Torture Abolition and Survivors Support Coalition International
www.tassc.org

Unitarian Universalist Service Committee
www.uusc.org

# Notes

*Introduction*

1. Adam Hochschild, *King Leopold's Ghost: A Story of Greed, Terror, and Heroism in Colonial Africa* (New York: Houghton Mifflin, 1998), 120–23.

2. Geoffrey Robertson, *Crimes Against Humanity: The Struggle for Global Justice* (New York: New Press, 2000), 390–91.

3. Archdiocese of São Paulo, *Torture in Brazil: A Report by the Archdiocese of São Paulo,* trans Jaime Wright, ed. Joan Dassin (New York: Vintage, 1986), 16–17.

4. William F. Schulz, *Tainted Legacy: 9/11 and the Ruin of Human Rights* (New York: Thunder's Mouth Press/Nation Books, 2003), 155.

5. Jean Paul Sartre, *Being and Nothingness* (New York: Washington Square Press, 1966).

6. And the stories can be hard to read. Far more than one Amnesty International supporter has told me that, when they receive a direct mail appeal for funds from us in their mailbox, they can't stand to read the letter, though we try hard to avoid anything too gruesome. Then, too, it is easy to become numb to atrocity.

7. David Buss, "The Evolution of Evil," http://www.edge.org (accessed January 8, 2006).

8. Pew Research Center for the People and the Press, "America's Place in the World," November 17, 2005: 15 percent say it is "often" justified, 31 percent "sometimes," and 17 percent "rarely."

9. Executive Order Outlining Treatment of al-Qaida and Taliban Detainees, February 7, 2002.

10. *Meet the Press,* September 16, 2001.

11. Memo from Jay Bybee, Office of Legal Counsel in the Justice Department, to Alberto Gonzalez, White House legal counsel, August 1, 2002.

12. Moreover, the U.S. has invoked certain "reservations" to its own ratification of CAT, including restricting the definition of crimes under the Convention to those which would be considered crimes under the U.S. Constitution.

13. And, indeed, in a landmark case referenced in John Conroy's book *Unspeakable Acts, Ordinary People* (Chapter V, Reading 6) the European Court of Human Rights ruled that, while five punishments inflicted on IRA prisoners by British forces in 1971 "did not constitute a practice of torture within the meaning of Article 3" of the European Convention on Human Rights, they *did* constitute a

violation of the provision prohibiting "inhuman and degrading treatment" in that same article, and therefore were in violation of the Convention.

14. Anna Akhmatova, "Instead of a Preface," in Carolyn Forche, ed., *Against Forgetting: Twentieth Century Poetry of Witness* (New York: W.W. Norton, 1993), 101–2.

*Chapter I. Torture in Western History*

1. Greek city-state.

2. The ancient Greek word for torture denoting a test or trial to determine whether something or someone is real or genuine, hence, an inquiry after truth by use of "the question."

3. Athenian orator and teacher of Demosthenes (d. 350 B.C.E.).

4. Athenian orator and statesman (384–322 B.C.E.).

5. Roman ecclesiastical law compiled from the opinions of the ancient Church fathers, decrees of general Church councils, and epistles and bulls issued by the Holy See. [At the request of the author of this piece, Professor J. H. Langbein, we are reiterating here that, unless otherwise specified, all notes in this book are the annotations of the editor and were not written by the authors of the respective excerpts—Ed.]

6. Within the context of what was considered torture in that era.

7. The part of the accusation that weighs most heavily against the accused; the gist of the case.

8. Lateran Councils, named after the Lateran Palace in Rome, were meetings of the Church hierarchy called to act on various decrees.

9. Roman law as interpreted by medieval jurists.

10. Christian Thomasius (1655–1728) was a German educator and jurist who wrote extensively on the relationship between law and morality.

11. See Readings 6 and 7 in this chapter.

12. The medieval interpreters of Roman-canon law.

13. The authority and power of the Roman Catholic Church to teach religious truth.

14. Disobedience of authority.

15. A Christian sect founded by Peter Valdes of Lyon, France, that rejected the authority of the Roman Catholic Church, relying on that of the Bible instead.

16. A heretical sect that denied the reality of Christ's incarnation.

17. To be exterminated.

18. Place of employment.

19. Everything short of death; see also Reading 4 in this chapter.

20. Edward Peters, *Torture* (Philadelphia: University of Pennsylvania Press, 1985), 82–84.

21. Michel Foucault, *Discipline and Punish: The Birth of the Prison* (New York: Pantheon, 1977), 9; see also Reading 5 in this chapter.

22. A branch of the Franciscan order of monks that observes vows of poverty and austerity.

23. Hyppolite Clarion was a leading French actress (Comédie-Française) who appeared in many of the plays of Voltaire.

24. Catherine II (Catherine the Great), Tsarina of Russia (1729–96).

25. Minos was a character in Greek mythology, son of Europa and Zeus and a

famous lawgiver, who was consigned to Hades to judge human souls. Numa (Numa Pompilius), purportedly second king of Rome (c. 715–673 B.C.E.), was known for his reforms. Solon (c. 640–559 B.C.E.), an Athenian poet and statesman, granted rights, including habeas corpus, to citizens and freed some of the slaves.

26. A reference to Viscount Horatio Nelson (1758–1805), blinded in his right eye in the war with France.

27. The Landau Commission, headed by retired Israeli Supreme Court Justice Moshe Landau, reviewed Israeli interrogation and detention policies in 1987 and made recommendations for what was and was not permissible. The Commission sanctioned the use of what of what it called "moderate physical pressure," which many human rights organizations regarded as tantamount to torture. See Chapter VI, Reading 9.

*Chapter II. Being Tortured*

1. Noncommissioned officers.

2. "Therre" is Pheto's rendering of English as pronounced by white South Africans.

3. Earlier in the book Pheto describes van Niekerk as "the first policeman to assault me . . . a 300 pound bully with an equally heavy voice" (49).

4. The Music Drama Arts and Literature Institute was formed in 1972 and sought to "promote self determination, self realisation and self support in theatre arts."

5. The interrogator is speaking Afrikaans, a language derived from Dutch.

6. Soweto, an acronym for "southwest townships," is an urban area ten miles southwest of Johannesburg and the scene in 1976 of a massive uprising against apartheid.

7. Police headquarters in Johannesburg.

8. A pejorative Afrikaner word for blacks.

9. Seven tiers of cells where the inmates considered the most dangerous were housed.

10. With his hands high above his head.

11. A phosphorescent light stick.

12. A Soviet prison complex in downtown Moscow that had been the headquarters of the KGB (secret police) and where Solzhenitsyn had been held.

13. Another prison and investigation complex, also used by the KGB, in the Lefortovo neighborhood of old Moscow.

14. The Soviet secret police station of the city of Khabrovsk in the Russian Far East.

15. Uruguayan prison for political prisoners.

16. An acclaimed Argentine pianist who denounced Argentina's military government and was subsequently banned from performing. He moved to Uruguay in 1977 where he was abducted by the secret police, tortured, and imprisoned for "subversive association" and "offences against the constitution."

17. Boulanger (1887–1979) was a world-renowned composer, music teacher, and the first woman conductor of a major American orchestra.

18. The coup d'état of April 21, 1967, which the Greek military junta referred to as a "revolution."

19. The building that housed the junta's security police.

20. One of the major resistance organizations.

21. *Free World*, a right-wing newspaper established a year before the coup that would have supported the military regime.

22. A Greek word for "informer" or "snitch."

23. The room used for torture at the Asphalia was a penthouse on the flat roof, originally a laundry.

24. Beating on the soles of the feet.

25. An island concentration camp used during and after the Greek Civil War (1946–49) for political internees and the indoctrination of left-wing conscripts.

26. Dislocation.

27. The first woman prime minister of India, she served from 1966–77 and then again from 1980 until her assassination in 1984.

28. Rahman (1920–75) was one of the cofounders and the first prime minister of Bangladesh.

29. A town 75 miles northeast of Calcutta.

30. The paramilitary force organized by the Pakistan army during the 1971 war.

31. The Bangladesh Liberation Army, the guerilla forces that fought against the Pakistan army.

32. The capital of Bangladesh, formerly East Pakistan.

33. Those native to the Bengal region in eastern India and western Bangladesh (formerly East Pakistan).

34. The practice of preventing women from being exposed to the view of men or strangers through the use of veils, curtains, seclusion, and so on.

35. Those native to the northern Indian state of Punjab.

36. Those native to the northeastern Indian state of Bihar.

37. A classical language of India and liturgical language of Hinduism, Buddhism, and Jainism.

38. Indian poet and dramatist who lived sometime between 170 B.C.E. and 634 C.E.

39. A district just outside Dacca.

40. A reference to the occupation of the Chinese city of Nanking during the Sino-Japanese War, an occupation often referred to as "The Rape of Nanking" because of the extensive number of sexual assaults committed by Japanese soldiers.

41. Amnesty International, *Crimes of Hate, Conspiracy of Silence: Torture and Ill-Treatment Based on Sexual Orientation*, AI Index: ACT 40/016.2001.

*Chapter III. Who Are the Torturers?*

1. See Victor Nell, "Cruelty's Rewards: The Gratifications of Perpetrators and Spectators," *Behavioral and Brain Sciences* 29, 3(2006): 211–24; http://www.bbsonline.org.

2. King of Belgium, 1865–1909.

3. A place in the country; a farm.

4. The thirty-five-year-old graduate student, teacher, and leader of a socialist national student union who was abducted on September 12, 1982, from a street in downtown Tegucigalpa and later tortured and murdered by the Honduran military.

5. Canadian Broadcasting Corporation.

6. The Toronto subway.

7. The Fat One.

8. "Balls," testicles, i.e., manliness.

9. Left-wing guerillas in Nicaragua.

10. Anastasio Somoza (1925–80), president of Nicaragua from 1967 to 1972 and again from 1974 to 1979 when he was overthrown.

11. Brigadier general who assumed the position of commander of the Honduran armed forces in January 1982.

12. Controversial as much for its effect upon the participants in the experiment, who were in many cases forced to reevaluate their self-images as good, decent human beings, as for anything else.

13. The center for military police training.

14. The Greek military police. EAT-ESA was the Special Interrogation School of those police.

15. A name given to psychological and physical abuse, particularly of military and police recruits.

16. Personal correspondence, September 28, 2005.

17. Disruption in the normal processes of consciousness, perception, memory, and identity.

18. Schutzstaffel Totenkopf, literally the "SS Death's Head." This was the unit that produced concentration camp guards and an elite armored military division responsible for multiple war crimes.

19. The third largest city in Brazil.

20. An American employee of the Office of Public Safety (a division of the Agency for International Development), which provided foreign police with equipment and training to make them more effective in suppressing dissent. Mitrione was alleged to have conducted training in torture techniques in Brazil and Uruguay. In 1970 in Uruguay he was abducted and later executed by the urban guerillas known as the Tupamaros. His story was portrayed in the 1972 film *State of Siege* by Costa-Gravas.

21. A torture technique in which the victim's wrists are tied to an iron bar or wooden stick wedged behind his knees. The bar is then suspended in the air, causing the victim to hang helplessly upside down. The victim is usually then subjected to further torture.

22. A device used for electric torture when other forms of electricity are not available. Wires from a field telephone are attached to sensitive parts of a victim's body and then the phone is hand-cranked to generate an electric charge.

23. Towering concrete statue of Christ, a landmark in Rio de Janeiro.

24. Cities in southern Vietnam. Tay Ninh is approximately sixty miles northwest of Saigon (now Ho Chi Minh City). The city of Phu Cuong is now known as Thu Dat Mot and sits on the Saigon River, fifteen miles north of Saigon.

25. A native hut.

26. Noncommissioned officers.

27. The Army of the Republic of Vietnam (South Vietnam), with which the Americans were allied.

28. Executive officer; second in command.

29. French essayist and novelist (1897–1962).

30. An allusion to the philosopher Jean Paul Sartre's famous line from the play *No Exit* (1944) that "Hell is other people" ("L'enfer, c'est les autres").

31. The title of the major work of the nineteenth-century philosopher Arthur Schopenhauer (1788–1860).

32. The prison camp in Belgium where Améry was held and tortured.

33. A reference to political philosopher Hannah Arendt's famous observations

about the "banality of evil" in her book *Eichmann on Trial* (1963), prompted by her observation of the trial of the former Nazi SS officer Adolf Eichmann.

34. Front de Libération Nationale, the ruling party in Algeria during the French-Algerian war.

35. A kind of water torture, such as being submerged in a bathtub until one almost drowns.

36. Urban guerrilla organization and political party in Uruguay, formed in the 1960s.

37. The Contras (from the Spanish term La Contra, short for movement of the *contrarrevolucionarios*, counterrevolutionaries) were the armed opponents of Nicaragua's Sandinista government following the July 1979 overthrow of Anastasio Somoza.

38. Fusil Automatique Leger, a light automatic rifle.

39. Kalashnikov assault rifle (AK-47) and a U.S. semiautomatic rifle (M14).

40. See Reading 3 in this chapter.

41. See Chapter II, Reading 5, 67–68.

42. Dirección Nacional de Inteligencia, the Chilean secret police.

43. Movimiento de la Izquierda Revolucionaria, a leftist organization founded in the 1960s.

*Chapter IV. The Dynamics of Torture*

1. The main character of Solzhenitsyn's *The First Circle.* A functionary in the ministry of foreign affairs, he is arrested and tortured for warning a friend that he has been labeled an enemy of the state.

2. A form of torture in which the prisoner is put into a very small prison cell with a bright light that is never turned off.

3. An opening or glass pane in a door or wall that allows for observation.

4. Greek philosopher (341–270 B.C.E.)

5. Timerman was publisher and editor of the prominent newspaper *La Opinión* from 1971 until his arrest in 1977.

6. The name of the clandestine prison in the village of Martínez, twenty kilometers north of Buenos Aires, in which Timerman was held.

7. Theodor Herzl (1860–1904) was the founder of political Zionism who worked to establish a Jewish national state in Palestine.

8. Will; capacity to act.

9. A pfennig was to the German mark as the penny is to the dollar.

10. Undermine or vitiate.

11. An allusion to the German philosopher Immanuel Kant, who wrote that we should "so act as to treat humanity, whether in your own person or that of any other, always at the same time as an end, and never merely as a means."

12. Subject to external control or imposition.

13. This story is excerpted by Copelon from Angela Browne, *When Battered Women Kill* (New York: Free Press, 1987), 56–58, 90–93. Molly eventually killed Jim (131–33).

14. UN Center for Social Development and Humanitarian Affairs, *Violence Against Women in the Family* (New York: United Nations, 1989), 33.

15. "Binding instruments" refers to all those international declarations, covenants, conventions, and treaties that address and define the nature of torture (see Appendix).

*Chapter V*

1. The Nazi Schutzstaffel (Guard Detachment), which encompassed everyone from civilian diplomats to the Totenkopfverbande (Death's Head) units of concentration and death camp guards.

2. The Nazi Sturmabteilung (Storm Detachment), which was made up of the storm troopers, often called "Brownshirts."

3. Rousset reports an SS man haranguing a professor as follows: "You used to be a professor. Well, you're no professor now. You're no big shot anymore. You're nothing but a little runt now. Just as little as you can be. I'm the big fellow now" (author's note).

4. Seventeen alleged "spies," including thirteen Jews, were hanged in Baghdad's Liberation Square.

5. The Ba'ath Party was an Arab nationalist party that came to power in Iraq in 1963 and stayed in power until the toppling of Saddam Hussein in 2003.

6. Chief of Internal Security who was himself executed in 1973 after reportedly being involved in a coup plot.

7. Former Iraqi prime minister tortured and sentenced to fifteen years in prison in 1966 on charges of being a "Zionist agent."

8. Professor of law at Harvard Law School who has advocated that courts be empowered to issue "torture warrants" to legalize torture under certain circumstances. See Chapter VI, Reading 4.

9. Where many foreign nationals rounded up in the hours and days immediately following September 11, 2001, were held and in some cases mistreated.

10. Served as prime minister of Northern Ireland from 1971 to 1972.

11. A 1972 report to the British Government on interrogation procedures of prisoners taken into custody by the British in Northern Ireland. It followed upon the 1971 Compton Report, which investigated allegations of physical brutality by UK security forces in Northern Ireland.

12. Joe Clarke was among the dozen Republican men arrested and tortured in 1971 by British government forces, news of whose torture prompted the British prime minister to request the investigation that resulted in the Compton Report.

13. A member of the British House of Lords who served, among other posts, as secretary of state for defense and secretary of state for foreign and commonwealth affairs.

14. Hooding, noise bombardment, food deprivation, sleep deprivation, and forced standing at a wall.

15. Irish Republican Army, a paramilitary organization in Northern Ireland.

16. A paramilitary group that split from the Official IRA in 1969.

17. Served as British prime minister from 1970 to 1974.

18. One of the twelve men referred to in note 12 above.

*Chapter VI. The Ethics of Torture*

1. In the City of London an Officer called the Chamberlain has cognizance of disputes between Masters and their Apprentices. If the Apprentice is deemed to be in the wrong, and after being admonished continues refactory [persists in doing wrong], he is put into a place of confinement called Little-ease, till he professes repentance and promises good behavior. Little-ease is a small dark closet where the patient is kept with his body bent in a painful posture. [. . .] This process, it is evident is as much a process of torture as anything can be. Upon enquiry I could not learn of any Apprentice who was actually shut up; but they

are frequently threatened with it, and I heard of one who was actually brought to the door with very good effect (author's footnote).

2. Disapproved of; censured; held in disrepute.

3. Duration.

4. Painful.

5. Liable to.

6. Reduction.

7. Pressing or urgent situation.

8. Reinhard Heydrich (1904–42) was the Nazi deputy-protector of Bohemia and Moravia. He was assassinated by Czech patriots in Prague. Though Levin doesn't mention it, the village of Lidice was razed to the ground by the Nazis in retaliation for the assassination and all of its citizens murdered or deported.

9. See Reading 1 in this chapter.

10. W. L. Twining and P. E. Twining, "Bentham on Torture," *Northern Ireland Legal Quarterly* 24, 314 (1973); see also reading 1 in this chapter

11. See Reading 9 in this chapter.

12. Augusto Pinochet was head of the military government that ruled Chile from 1973 to 1990.

13. Idi Amin was president of Uganda from 1971 to 1979.

14. Stephen Budiansky, "Truth Extraction," *Atlantic Monthly* (June 2005).

15. Spittoon.

16. "A Nasty Business," *Atlantic Monthly* (January 2002): 49–52. The author refused us permission to reprint his essay in this book.

17. A reference to the eight-year war in Indochina that resulted in a French defeat in 1954 at the hands of Ho Chi Minh's forces.

18. *The Battle of Algiers* (1966).

19. U.S. forces occupying the Philippines at the turn of the twentieth century were notorious for their use of the "water cure" in which a bamboo stick was stuck down the subject's throat and enormous quantities of water—the filthier the better—poured in.

20. In a Gallup/CNN/USA Today poll.

21. A reference to hundreds of foreign nationals, virtually all of them Muslim, who were detained by U.S. authorities in sweeps of immigrant communities in the days following the 9/11 attacks. Many of them were badly mistreated in the course of their detention and denied access to lawyers and families; most were eventually deported. Few, if any, had any connections to terrorism.

22. Israeli intelligence.

23. See Reading 10 in this chapter.

24. See Reading 4 in this chapter.

25. Eitan Felner, "Torture and Terrorism; Painful Lessons from Israel," in Kenneth Roth and Minky Worden, eds., *Torture: Does It Make Us Safer? Is It Ever OK?* (New York: New Press/Human Rights Watch, 2005), 39.

*Chapter VII. Healing the Victims, Stopping the Torture*

1. A memory of a traumatic event that may be so severe as to cause a person to lose contact for a period of time with present reality.

2. Examinations of the stomach, rectum, colon, urinary tract, and bladder, all of which may involve the use of intrusive instruments.

3. Antipsychotic medications.

4. Devices designed to improve the fit of the upper and lower jaws.

5. Executive Director of Helsinki Watch from 1979 to 1995.

6. Including torture.

7. Including the United States.

8. Luis Moreno-Ocampo, a widely-respected Argentine who prosecuted large-scale mass killings by the military in that country, was appointed in 2003.

9. The U.S. has opposed the ICC because, among other reasons, it fears capricious prosecutions but the principle of "complementarity" makes such prosecutions highly unlikely for if an American were charged with a crime by the Court, he or she could be tried in a U.S. court and the decision of that court would dispose of the case.

10. Under Chapter 7 of the UN Charter the Security Council shall "decide what measures shall be taken . . . to maintain or restore international peace and security" when it "shall determine the existence of any threat to the peace, breach of the peace or act of aggression."

11. Absolutely and without qualification.

12. The Charter establishing the Nuremburg Tribunal to try Nazi war criminals after World War II.

13. Universal; extending to everyone.

14. President of Malawi from 1966 to 1994.

15. Margaret Thatcher was prime minister of Great Britain from 1979 to 1990.

16. A peremptory norm of general international law accepted and recognized by the international community from which no derogation is possible.

17. U.S. Supreme Court Justice (1941–54) and Chief U.S. Prosecutor at the International War Crimes Tribunal in Nuremberg following World War II.

18. Adolf Eichmann was Chief of the Jewish Office of the Nazi Gestapo. He was taken into custody in Argentina in May 1960 and tried and convicted in Israel of crimes against humanity and the Jewish people. Eichmann was executed in 1962.

19. Klaus Barbie was an SS officer so renowned for his brutality that he became known as the "Butcher of Lyon." He was finally arrested in 1987 in France, and tried and sentenced to life in prison, where he died from cancer in 1991.

20. The military leader of Panama from 1983 to 1989 who was captured by the U.S. and tried for drug trafficking. He resides today in a U.S. federal prison.

21. Functional immunity available to any state official for his official acts.

22. "(No. 1)" refers to the first decision of the British House of Lords in favor of extradition; "(No. 2)" to the decision to set the first verdict aside due to a possible conflict of interest; and "(No. 3)" to the final decision of the Law Lords dissolving Pinochet's sovereign immunity.

23. Personal immunity available to some officials but ceasing upon the end of official functions.

24. *Saudi Arabia v. Nelson* (1993), 113 S Ct 1471, in which the U.S. Supreme Court held that Scott Nelson, a U.S. engineer working in Saudi Arabia who was imprisoned and tortured as reprisal for publicizing safety, could not sue that country because "a foreign State's exercise of the power of its police has long been understood . . . as peculiarly sovereign in nature."

25. Legal obligation to the international community as a whole; literally, "in relation to everyone" in Latin.

26. French essayist (1533–92).

27. King of Egypt from 1936 to 1952 who was known as the "Thief of Cairo" for his notorious habit of pilfering objects when on state visits.

28. Jean-Bedel Bokassa was emperor of the Central African Republic from 1966 to 1974.

29. Official records of negotiations over a treaty or convention.

30. Queen's Counsel are barristers appointed by the British Crown to be "Her Majesty's learned counsel in the law."

31. The Royal Ulster Constabulary was the largely Protestant police force in Northern Ireland often accused of brutality toward the Catholic population there.

32. Alfredo Stroessner was president of Paraguay from 1954 to 1989.

33. A forum that is not convenient. This doctrine is employed when the court chosen by the plaintiff (the party suing) is inconvenient for witnesses or poses an undue hardship on the defendants, who must petition the court for an order transferring the case to a more convenient venue.

# Bibliography

Améry, Jean. *At the Mind's Limits: Contemplations by a Survivor on Auschwitz and Its Realities.* Bloomington: Indiana University Press, 1980.

Amnesty International. "Russian Federation: Police Officers Convicted of Torturing Man in Detention." Press Release, 2005.

———. "Uzbekistan: Support Human Rights Defender Ruslan Sharipov/Fear of Safety/Fear of Torture and Ill-Treatment." Urgent Action, 2003.

Amnesty International USA. Q & A on the International Criminal Court, 2004.

Arendt, Hannah. *The Origins of Totalitarianism.* New York: Harcourt Brace, 1951.

Atkinson, Keith. "The Torturer's Tale." *Toronto Life,* March 1989, 39–41, 55–56.

Aussaresses, Paul. *The Battle of the Casbah: Terrorism and Counter-Terrorism in Algeria, 1955–1957.* Trans. Robert L. Miller. New York: Enigma Books, 2002.

Beccaria, Cesare. "An Essay on Crimes and Punishments." In Isaac Kramnick, ed., *The Portable Enlightenment Reader,* 525–32. London: Penguin, 1995.

Bentham, Jeremy. "Of Torture." In W. L. Twining and P. E. Twining, "Bentham on Torture." *Northern Ireland Legal Quarterly* 24, 314 (1973): 345–56.

Bernstein, Richard. "Kidnapping Has Germans Debating Police Torture." *New York Times,* April 10, 2003.

Brownmiller, Susan. *Against Our Will: Men, Women, and Rape.* New York: Simon and Schuster, 1975.

Central Intelligence Agency. *Human Resource Exploitation Training Manual: Coercive Techniques.* 1983. http://www.gwu.edu/~nsarchiv/NSAEBB/NSAEBB122/CIA

Claude, Richard Pierre. "The Case of Joelito Filártiga and the Clinic of Hope." *Human Rights Quarterly* 5 (1983): 275–95.

Conroy, John. *Unspeakable Acts, Ordinary People: The Dynamics of Torture: An Examination of the Practice of Torture in Three Democracies.* New York: Knopf, 2000.

Copelon, Rhonda. "Intimate Terror: Understanding Domestic Violence as Torture." In Rebecca J. Cook, ed., *Human Rights of Women: National and International Perspectives,* 116–52. Philadelphia: University of Pennsylvania Press, 1994.

Crelinsten, Ronald. "How to Make a Torturer." *Index on Censorship* 34, 1 (February 2005): 72–77.

———. "In Their Own Words: The World of the Torturer." In Crelinsten and Alex P. Schmid, eds., *The Politics of Pain: Torturers and Their Masters,* 35–64. Boulder, Colo.: Westview Press, 1995.

Cuevas, Tomasa. *Prison of Women: Testimonies of War and Resistance in Spain, 1939–1975.* Ed. and trans. Mary E. Giles. Albany: State University of New York Press, 1998.

Danner, Mark. *Torture and Truth: America, Abu Ghraib, and the War on Terror.* London: Granta, 2005.

Dershowitz, Alan. *Why Terrorism Works: Understanding the Threat, Responding to the Challenge.* New Haven, Conn.: Yale University Press, 2002.

DuBois, Marc. "Human Rights Education for the Police." In George J. Andreopoulos and Richard Pierre Claude, eds., *Human Rights Education for the Twenty-First Century*, 310–33. Philadelphia: University of Pennsylvania Press, 1997.

DuBois, Page. *Torture and Truth.* London: Routledge, 1991.

Edwards, William, Wesley J. Gabel, and Floyd E. Hosmer. "On the Physical Death of Jesus Christ." *Journal of the American Medical Association* 255 (March 1986): 1455–63.

European Court of Human Rights. *Aydın v. Turkey.* Judgment of September 25, 1997. Reports of Judgments and Decisions 1997-VI.

Evans, Malcolm D. and Rod Morgan. *Preventing Torture: A Study of the European Convention for the Prevention of Torture and Inhuman or Degrading Treatment or Punishment.* Oxford: Clarendon Press, 1998.

Fanon, Frantz. *The Wretched of the Earth.* Trans. Richard Philcox. New York: Grove Press, 2004.

Foucault, Michel. *Discipline and Punish: The Birth of the Prison.* Trans. Alan Sheridan. New York: Pantheon, 1977.

Golston, Joan C. "Ritual Abuse: Raising Hell in Psychotherapy. The Political Military and Multigenerational Training of Torturers: Violent Initiation and the Role of Traumatic Dissociation." *Treating Abuse Today* 3, 6 (1993): 12–19.

Haritos-Fatouros, Mika. "The Official Torturer: A Learning Model for Obedience to the Authority of Violence." *Journal of Applied Social Psychology* 18, 13 (1988): 1107–20.

Hayner, Priscilla B. "The Contribution of Truth Commissions." In Bertil Dunér, ed., *An End to Torture: Strategies for Its Eradication.* London: Zed Books, 1998.

Hochschild, Adam. *King Leopold's Ghost: A Story of Greed, Terror, and Heroism in Colonial Africa.* New York: Houghton Mifflin, 1998.

———. "The Torturers' Notebooks." *New York Times,* May 24, 1999.

Jacobsen, Lone and Edith Montgomery. "Treatment of Victims of Torture." In Bertil Dunér, ed., *An End to Torture: Strategies for Its Eradication,* 134–49. London: Zed Books, 1998.

Korovessis, Pericles. *The Method: A Personal Account of the Tortures in Greece.* Trans. Les Nightingale and Catherine Patrarkis. London: Allison and Busby, 1970.

Landau Commission Report. *Israel Law Review* 23, 2–3 (1989): 154–85.

Langbein, John H. *Torture and the Law of Proof: Europe and England in the Ancien Régime.* Chicago: University of Chicago Press, 1977.

Langguth, A. J. *Hidden Terrors: The Truth About U.S. Police Operations in Latin America.* New York: Pantheon, 1978.

Levin, Michael. "The Case for Torture." *Newsweek,* June 7, 1982.

Lomax, Eric. *The Railway Man: A POW's Searing Account of War, Brutality, and Forgiveness.* New York: Norton, 1995.

Makiya, Kanan. *Republic of Fear: The Politics of Modern Iraq.* Updated ed. Berkeley: University of California Press, 1998.

Milgram, Stanley. "The Perils of Obedience." *Harper's,* December 6, 1973.

Millett, Kate. *The Politics of Cruelty: An Essay on the Literature of Political Imprisonment.* New York: Norton, 1994.

Moran, Sherwood F. "Suggestions for Japanese Interpreters Based on Work in the Field." Letter dated July 17, 1943 to Division Intelligence Section, Headquarters, First Marine Division, Fleet Marine Force. UNMC Doc. 168/292 of May 27, 1944.

*The New English Bible with the Apocrypha.* New York: Cambridge University Press, 1971.

Peters, Edward. *Torture.* Expanded ed. Philadelphia: University of Pennsylvania Press, 1999.

Pheto, Molefe. *And Night Fell: Memoirs of a Political Prisoner in South Africa.* London: Allison and Busby, 1983.

Rejali, Darius M. *Torture and Democracy.* Princeton, N.J.: Princeton University Press, 2007. From "Does Torture Work?" Salon.com, June 21, 2004.

Robertson, Geoffrey. *Crimes Against Humanity: The Struggle for Global Justice.* New York: New Press, 2000.

Scarry, Elaine. *The Body in Pain: The Making and Unmaking of the World.* New York: Oxford University Press, 1985.

Schulz, William. "The Ticklish Case of a Ticking Bomb: Is Torture Ever Justified?" In Schulz, *Tainted Legacy: 9/11 and the Ruin of Human Rights,* 155–70. New York: Thunder Mouth Press/Nation Books, 2003.

Shue, Henry. "Torture." *Philosophy and Public Affairs* 7, 2 (Winter 1978): 124–43.

Solzhenitsyn, Aleksandr. *The Gulag Archipelago, 1918–1956: An Experiment in Literary Investigation.* New York: Harper and Row, 1973.

Staub, Ervin. "The Psychology and Culture of Torture and Torturers." In Peter Suedfeld, ed., *Psychology and Torture,* 49–68. New York: Hemisphere, 1990.

Supreme Court of Israel. Judgment Concerning the Legality of the General Security Service's Interrogation Methods. 38 ILM 1471, 1488 (1999).

Sussman, David. "What's Wrong with Torture." *Philosophy and Public Affairs* 33, 1 (Winter 2005): 1–33.

Timerman, Jacobo. *Prisoner Without a Name, Cell Without a Number.* New York: Knopf, 1981.

Translation of Sworn Statement Provided by [name blacked out], Detainee # [number blacked out], 1430/21 Jan 04. Translated by Mr. Johnson Isho. Verified by Mr. Abdelilah Alazadi. Reprinted in Mark Danner, *Torture and Truth: America, Abu Ghraib, and the War on Terror.* New York: New York Review of Books, 2004.

Vidal-Naquet, Pierre. *Torture: Cancer of Democracy.* New York: Penguin, 1963.

Vietnam Veterans Against the War. *The Winter Soldier Investigation: An Inquiry into American War Crimes.* Boston: Beacon Press, 1972.

Voltaire. "On Torture and Capital Punishment." In Isaac Kramnick, ed., *The Portable Enlightenment Reader,* 532–35. London: Penguin, 1995.

Weschler, Lawrence. *A Miracle, a Universe: Settling Accounts with Torturers.* New York: Pantheon, 1990.

Worden, Minky. "Torture Spoken Here: Ending Global Torture." In Kenneth Roth and Worden, eds., *Torture: A Human Rights Perspective,* 99–105. New York: New Press/Human Rights Watch, 2005.

# Acknowledgments

This book was first conceptualized more than five years ago. I thought it would be a relatively easy undertaking: just pull together the most important and insightful texts on torture and excerpt the gist of each one. Interns would gather the books and articles and I would do the reading on those incessant plane rides required of me as Executive Director of Amnesty International USA and the editing on a few free weekends.

What a fool I was! Interns did indeed gather lots of books and articles but one year turned into the next and what we were calling "The Torture Reader" never seemed to progress much beyond the gathering . . . of dust. Until the intrepid Peter Agree, social sciences editor at Penn Press, gently suggested that perhaps what we needed was a "developmental editor," that is, someone to do all the things that I hadn't done.

Enter Mary Murrell. Editor, scholar, and currently pursuing her Ph.D. in anthropology, Mary immersed herself in the literature of torture and within three months had pulled together a proposed table of contents, including suggested excerpts for virtually all eight chapters. It was a tour de force and it saved the book and my reputation. I would say that *The Phenomenon of Torture* is more Mary's book than mine except that I take full responsibility for the end product. But you wouldn't have it in your hands if it had not been for her.

Or for Mary Anne Feeney, my beloved assistant at Amnesty who toiled at my side for years to see the book to completion—supervising interns, researching readings, overseeing the permissions process, and doing dozens of other tasks she never bothered to tell me about. For this book and for everything else Mary Anne did to make my life at Amnesty a pleasure, I owe her my eternal gratitude.

And those interns I keep mentioning—Alex Acree, Joshua Cantor, Samantha Ettari, Nora Feeney, Darrel Frost, Carol Gallo, Alexandra Glendis, Ian Stern Millican, Jeannie Rangel, Valeria Scorza, Nicholas Sheehan, Erin Smith, and Zach Tucker—along with AIUSA research staffers Rachel Ward and Trine Christensen, spent hours on the Internet (and even occasionally—can you believe it?—at a real library) tracking down sources, reproducing readings, scanning and editing. I thank them all but especially Carol Gallo who took the lion's share of responsibility for the permissions and who, during the final weeks of the process, when Mary Anne had the audacity to be out of the office in order to get married, filled in for her expertly and helped me pull the final editing together in a highly professional manner.

Finally, let me not for a moment forget to thank those who provided financial assistance to the project, including two extraordinarily generous donors to Amnesty, Cynthia and Peter Hibbard, whose gift to support our antitorture work included support for this book, and Professor Bert Lockwood, Series Editor of the Penn Presss Studies in Human Rights, a former board member of Amnesty USA, and a good friend, who located additional resources at a critical time in the book's production.

My wife Beth Graham gets the last words, though actually they were among the first. "I have an idea for a new book," I told her years ago. She listened carefully and then, wise as always, she asked me, "Are you sure it will be all that easy?" Damn.

# Credits and Permissions

Reading 7. Voltaire, "On Torture and Capital Punishment," in Isaac Kramnick, ed., *The Portable Enlightenment Reader*, 532–35 (London: Penguin, 1995).

Reading 8. Malcolm D. Evans and Rod Morgan, *Preventing Torture: A Study of the European Convention for the Prevention of Torture and Inhuman or Degrading Treatment or Punishment* (Oxford: Clarendon Press, 1998).

## Chapter II

Reading 1. Eric Lomax, *The Railway Man: A POW's Searing Account of War, Brutality, and Forgiveness* (New York: W.W. Norton; London: Jonathan Cape, 1995), copyright © 1995 Eric Lomax. Reprinted by permission of W.W. Norton & Company, Inc. (United States) and The Random House Group Ltd. (world).

Reading 2. Molefe Pheto, *And Night Fell: Memoirs of a Political Prisoner in South Africa* (London: Allison and Busby, 1983).

Reading 3. Translation of Sworn Statement Provided by [name blacked out], Detainee # [number blacked out], 1430/21 Jan 04, translated by Mr. Johnson Isho, verified by Mr. Abdelilah Alazadi, reprinted in Mark Danner, *Torture and Truth: America, Abu Ghraib, and the War on Terror* (New York: New York Review of Books, 2004).

Reading 4. Aleksandr I. Solzhenitsyn, *The Gulag Archipelago 1918–1956: An Experiment in Literary Investigation*, copyright © 1973 Aleksandr I. Solzhenitsyn; English translation (New York: Harper and Row; London: Collins Harvill, 1974), 103–9, copyright © 1973, 1974 Harper & Row Publishers, Inc. Reprinted by permission of HarperCollins Publishers and Random House Group Ltd.

Reading 5. Lawrence Weschler, *A Miracle, a Universe: Settling Accounts with Torturers* (New York: Pantheon, 1990), copyright 1990 Lawrence Weschler. Used by permission of Pantheon Books, a division of Random House, Inc.

Reading 6. Pericles Korovessis, *The Method: A Personal Account of the Tortures in Greece*, trans. Les Nightingale and Catherine Patrarkis (London: Allison and Busby, 1970).

Reading 7. Jean Améry, *At the Mind's Limits: Contemplations by a Survivor on Auschwitz and Its Realities* (Bloomington: Indiana University Press, 1980), copyright 1980 Indiana University Press. Reprinted by permission.

Reading 8. Susan Brownmiller, *Against Our Will: Men, Women, and Rape* (New York: Simon and Schuster, 1975), 78–86, copyright © 1975, 2003 Susan Brownmiller.

Reading 9. Amnesty International, "Uzbekistan: Support Human Rights Defender Ruslan Sharipov/Fear of Safety/Fear of Torture and Ill-Treatment," Urgent Action, 2003.

Reading 10. Tomasa Cuevas, *Prison of Women: Testimonies of War and Resistance in Spain, 1939–1975*, ed. and trans. Mary E. Giles (Albany: State University of New York Press, 1998), © 1998 State University of New York. All rights reserved.

## Chapter III

Reading 1. Adam Hochschild, *King Leopold's Ghost: A Story of Greed, Terror, and Heroism in Colonial Africa* (New York: Houghton Mifflin, 1998; London: Macmillan, 1999), copyright © 1998 Adam Hochschild. Reprinted by permission of Houghton Mifflin Company and Macmillan Publishers Ltd. All rights reserved.

Reading 2. Keith Atkinson, "The Torturer's Tale," *Toronto Life*, March 1989, 39–41, 55–56.

Reading 3. Stanley Milgram, "The Perils of Obedience," *Harper's*, December 6, 1973, 62–66, 75–77, copyright © renewed 2001 Alexandra Milgram. Permission granted by Alexandra Milgram.

Reading 4. Mika Haritos-Fatouros, "The Official Torturer: A Learning Model for Obedience to the Authority of Violence," *Journal of Applied Social Psychology* 18, 13 (1988): 1107–20, copyright © V.H. Winston & Son, Inc. Used with permission; all rights reserved.

Reading 5. Joan C. Golston, "Ritual Abuse: Raising Hell in Psychotherapy; The Political Military and Multigenerational Training of Torturers: Violent Initiation and the Role of Traumatic Dissociation," *Treating Abuse Today* 3, 6 (1993): 12–19.

Reading 6. A. J. Langguth, *Hidden Terrors* (New York: Pantheon, 1978), copyright © 1978 A. J. Langguth. Used by permission of Pantheon Books, a division of Random House, Inc.; reprinted by permission of International Creative Management, Inc. (UK).

Reading 7. Vietnam Veterans Against the War, *The Winter Soldier Investigation: An Inquiry into American War Crimes* (Boston: Beacon Press, 1972), copyright © 1972 Vietnam Veterans Against the War. Reprinted by permission of Beacon Press, Boston.

Reading 8. Jean Améry, *At the Mind's Limits: Contemplations by a Survivor on Auschwitz and Its Realities* (Bloomington: Indiana University Press, 1980), copyright 1980 Indiana University Press. Reprinted by permission.

Chapter IV

*National and International Perspectives* (Philadelphia: University of Pennsylvania Press, 1994), 116–39, copyright © 1994 University of Pennsylvania Press. Reproduced by permission of University of Pennsylvania Press.

## Chapter V

Reading 1. Pierre Vidal-Naquet, *Torture: Cancer of Democracy, France and Algeria, 1954–62,* trans. Barry Richard (New York: Penguin, 1963), copyright © 1972 Les Éditions de Minuit, *La torture dans la République: essai d'histoire et de politique contemporaines (1954–1962)* (Paris: Les Éditions de Minuit, 1972). Reprinted by permission of Georges Borchardt, Inc., for Les Éditions de Minuit.

Reading 2. Hannah Arendt, *The Origins of Totalitarianism* (New York: Harcourt Brace, 1951), copyright 1948, 1976 Hannah Arendt. Edited and reprinted by permission of Harcourt, Inc.

Reading 3. Kanan Makiya, *Republic of Fear: The Politics of Modern Iraq* (Berkeley: University of California Press, 1998), copyright © 1998 University of California Press (original edition 1989 under pseudonym Samir al-Khalil). Reprinted by permission of University of California Press.

Reading 4. Ervin Staub, "The Psychology and Culture of Torture and Torturers," in Peter Suedfeld, ed., *Psychology and Torture,* 49–68 (New York: Hemisphere, 1990). Reproduced by permission of Routledge/Taylor & Francis Group, LLC.

Reading 5. Ronald Crelinsten, "How to Make a Torturer," *Index on Censorship* 34, 1 (February 2005): 72–77. Reprinted by permission of Ronald Crelinsten.

Reading 6. John Conroy, *Unspeakable Acts, Ordinary People: The Dynamics of Torture: An Examination of the Practice of Torture in Three Democracies* (New York: Alfred A. Knopf, 2000), copyright © 2000 John Conroy. Used by permission of Alfred A. Knopf, a division of Random House, Inc.

## Chapter VI

Reading 1. Jeremy Bentham, "Of Torture," in W. L. Twining and P. E. Twining, "Bentham on Torture," *Northern Ireland Legal Quarterly* 24, 314 (1973): 345–56.

Reading 2. Michael Levin, "The Case for Torture," *Newsweek,* June 7, 1982. Reprinted by permission of Michael Levin.

## Chapter VII